PATENT
COPYRIGHT
& TRADEMARK

INTELLECTUAL PROPERTY LAW
DICTIONARY

√HA

by Attorney Stephen R. Elias

Printing History

Nolo Press is committed to keeping its books up-to-date. Each new printing, whether or not it is called a new edition, has been completely revised to reflect the latest law changes. This book was printed and updated on the last date indicated below. To check whether a later printing or edition has been issued, call (415) 549-1976.

PLEASE READ THIS: Please be aware that laws and procedures are constantly changing and are subject to differing interpretations. You have the responsibility to check all material you read here before relying on it. Of necessity, neither Nolo Press nor the authors make any guarantees concerning the information in this book or the use to which it is put.

First Edition: June 1985
Second Printing: January 1989

Copy Editor: Sarah Stewart
Book Design: Glenn Voloshin
Production: Toni Ihara, Keija Kimura, and Stephanie Harolde
Illustrations: Linda Allison, Mari Stein, Rubin Elias & Backburner Graphics
                 Antique lamp courtesy of Crescent Electric Co., Oakland, CA.
Typesetting: Adapt, San Francisco, CA.
Printing: Delta Lithograph

ISBN 0-917316-97-5
Library of Congress Card Catalog No.: 85-71562
Copyright © 1985 by Stephen R. Elias

Acknowledgements

To paraphrase the inquisitor in Orwell's *1984*, "no one ever really writes a book by himself". This is certainly true in the case of this dictionary, which contains enormous contributions from many wonderful people. Equally important are the people who have supported the idea of this dictionary over the past couple of years. Because this dictionary is truly something different, I have had serious self-doubts, many of which might have meant the end of this project without such encouragement.

It's now time to name names, in alphabetical order. In doing so, I give grateful thanks for their contributions. The flaws (alas) are my own doing.

This dictionary owes much to Catherine Elias-Jermany, who from the first moment unswervingly supported the odd idea that I might actually write a dictonary.

Mary Jane Foran contributed heavily to the trade secret and contract portions while Ellen Lyons gave yeoman service to the trademark chapter.

Bruce E. Methven, a knowledgeable lawyer working for Guttierrez & Neal, a San Francisco law firm specializing in business advice, trial work, and the law of franchising copyrights, trade secrets, and trademarks, provided invaluable comments and insight for the trade secret and copyright portions of the dictionary.

David Pressman, the author of *Patent it Yourself*, McGraw-Hill (soon to be published by Nolo Press) reviewed the patent and trademark parts of the dictionary, at great personal expense, and unstintingly provided his enormous expertise and insight so that these sections would be both accurate and understandable.

Glenn Voloshin and Toni Ihara, both of whom demonstrated an unbelievable patience (with me as well as the book), an innovative spirit, and the highest level of skill in transforming hundreds of pages of raw and picky text into a useful and attractive dictionary.

Because everyone at Nolo is ultimately vital to the success of every project, including this one, my eternal thanks to Jack Devaney, Stephanie Harolde, Barbara Hodovan, Amy Ihara, Keija Kimura, Kate Miller, John O'Donnell, Carol Pladsen, and Staci Smith for their various contributions and for just being such wonderful people.

Thanks to Jake Warner for his ideas, support, editing, wit, wisdom, friendship and.....even though I have now authored a dictionary, words fail me.

Dedication

To my mother Edna, and to the memory of my father Julian, both of whom initiated this entire project.

Contents

Introduction to Dictionary

Here is a legal dictionary which defines and discusses words and phrases having to do with the law of intellectual property. It is different than standard legal dictionaries in several important ways.

First, we focus on the legal terminology in common use throughout the world wherever commerce meets creativity.

Second, we explain the entries in straightforward language as part of a determined effort to bridge the gap between the arcane and often needlessly complicated terminology of lawyers, and the everyday need of the scientist, business person, educator, and artist to understand these concepts. Put another way, we have done our best to make this book a sort of Rosetta stone, through which people who are members of one of a number of creative cultures can learn to understand, if not speak, the language of the law.

Third, this book is designed not only to provide you with definitions of intellectual property terms, but also to give you the context in which these terms arise and the circumstances under which their meanings change. It is our strong belief that only when you understand the myriad of ways in which many of these terms are used will you feel fully at home with them.

And now for a brief but important warning. Although many of the definitions appear as definitive statements of "the law" (lawyers would say "black letter law"), we urge you not to accept them as the final word. Intellectual property law changes almost as rapidly as the new technologies it seeks to define and regulate. And, the context in which a term is used can be as important to its meaning as any dictionary definition. This is especially true in an area where the lawyers who have created the "jargon" often don't understand the artistic, scientific and literary disciplines they are attempting to deal with. So, while this book should be of great assistance to all readers who desire to understand the terminology associated with intellectual property law, we urge you to accept our contribution as an invitation to further exploration rather than as the "ultimate truth".

How to Use This Dictionary: This book is easy to use. It is divided into five parts, one for each major substantive area of "intellectual property law". Part 1 *Trade Secret*, Part 2 *Copyright*, Part 3 *Trademark*, Part 4 *Patent*, and, Part 5 *Contract and Warranty* (as they relate to these other areas).

At the beginning of each part we provide a brief overview of the principal legal issues having to do with that subject area. This is followed by an alphabetical listing of all relevant words and phrases. If you know the broad legal area of classification for a word or phrase you are interested in, (e.g., that the **Berne Convention** has to do with copyright law) simply turn to the appropriate part (in this example, Part 2) and find the relevant entry.

If you are not sure which part a word or phrase is in (say, you want to learn about how to protect a marketing idea), you have two alternative additional ways to access the information. You can skim the overview page at the beginning of each part to obtain a summary of the concepts covered. Or, you can refer to the index. If you still cannot find what you're looking for, consider just browsing. Although we have undoubtedly left out some terms, we have gone to considerable effort to be comprehensive. So please don't give up if you fail on your first try.

Now let's take a moment to understand how each entry is organized. The main entry (the word and phrase to be defined) is in **bold** lettering. Throughout the definition you will see a number of terms or phrases that are in **bold italics**. This means that they are independent entries elsewhere in the dictionary.

If there is an outlined number after the term (e.g., **Trade secret** 1) it means that entry is defined in the part represented by the number. Thus, a 1 stands for *Trade Secret*, a 2 for *Copyright*, a 3 for *Trademark*, a 4 for *Patent*, and a 5 for *Contract and Warranty*. If there is no number after the term (the usual situation) the term is defined in the same part. For references within the same part, simply turn to the appropriate entry. For references belonging to another part, simply locate the appropriate entry in that other part.

At the end of most entries where a definition has been provided, there is one or more 'Related terms'. These are intended to provide you with clues for further reading if you have not quite found what you're looking for in that entry. The following is an example of how a specific entry in the trade secret part is organized:

contract requirements for
non-disclosure agreement An
agreement in which a person promises not to disclose **trade secrets**
may only be enforced if it meets the
requirements for the formation of a

valid contract. A **non-disclosure agreement** can exist either in explicit written form or may be implied by the law to exist if the position maintained by the employee in the company qualifies as a **confidential employment relationship**. An essential ingredient of **non-disclosure** or **confidentiality agreements** (whether express or implied) is that the employee, contractor or other party must receive something of value (called **consideration** 5 in contract law) in exchange for the express or implied promise not to disclose. Consideration is generally interpreted fairly loosely to include money, property, professional advancement, employment, etc. Related terms: **consideration** 5 and **non-disclosure agreement**.

Some readers may wonder why most of the entries use jargon to define other jargon. This was intentional. A primary purpose of this dictionary is to provide a vocabulary bridge for the reader who starts with little or no information about these subjects, and wants to pursue any given topic through more intensive research. Introducing legal jargon in context will help the reader use whatever legal indexes or source materials he or she picks up next.

Because we anticipate that many readers will in fact want to explore intellectual property law terminology in more detail, the last several pages of each part contain a guide for doing further research, including suggestions for research techniques specially suited to the particular subject, and a listing of the legal resources for further reading that we feel will best assist you in gaining a deeper understanding of the concepts covered.

Enjoy.

1

Introduction

This section defines the legal words and phrases commonly used when discussing how people and businesses can protect their valuable and confidential ideas from improper use by others. Information that is not generally known in the community, and that can provide its owner with a **competitive advantage** in the market place, is commonly referred to as a **trade secret** or **proprietary business information**.

A trade secret is generally considered to be "property" that can be owned, and protected under the law against **wrongful acquisition** by others if, and only if, the owner takes the necessary steps to preserve its secrecy. If proper steps are not taken to keep valuable information secret, courts will generally rule that anyone who innocently learns of the information is entitled to use it.

Assuming that a trade secret owner makes all reasonable attempts to keep the secret under wraps, the courts will offer the owner protection against such wrongful acts as 1) disclosures by employees (current and former) in violation of their **duty of trust** toward their employer, 2) disclosures by employees (current and former) in violation of a **confidentiality agreement** entered into with their employer, 3) disclosures by persons who have signed agreements with the owner promising not to disclose the information **(non-disclosure agreements)**, 4) **industrial espionage**, 5) the use of wrongfully acquired trade secrets by competitors, and 6) disclosures by any person owing an implied duty to the employer not to make such disclosure.

If a trade secret owner is able to convince a court that the secret is deserving of protection, and that the defendant has wrongfully disclosed (or is about to disclose) the secret, or has wrongfully acquired it in some way, the court may issue **temporary restraining orders, preliminary and permanent injunctions**, and whatever other orders may be necessary to prevent further disclosure or use of the secret. The court may also award the plaintiff **actual damages** resulting from the defendant's wrongful acts. Further, in cases involving willful or deliberate theft of trade secrets, the courts in most states are authorized to award **punitive damages**. In extreme cases, criminal laws may even be invoked and the trade secret thief subjected to criminal prosecution.

Definitions

accidental disclosure of trade secrets Inadvertently allowing valuable business information to be disclosed to the public with a resulting loss of trade secret protection.

Example: Independent Robotics conducts a guided tour of their plant. One of their engineers accidently leaves a top secret diagram of a new robot in full view where it is seen by an inquiring competitor on the tour. Although this trade secret was disclosed accidently, rather than on purpose, it has still lost its trade secret status due to the fact that the secret was blown without any wrongful conduct by the competitor. Related terms: *loss of trade secret*.

actual or apparent authority to make trade secret agreement The situation in which an employee or agent of a business entity (e.g., sole proprietorship, partnership, corporation, or joint venture) may make binding agreements on behalf of the entity. In the course of developing and promoting products or services that utilize trade secrets, it is often necessary to disclose the secrets to other business entities (e.g., publishers, distributors, manufacturers, etc). As part of doing this, the representative of the business gaining access to the secret is commonly asked to sign a *non-disclosure agreement* (an agreement to maintain the information as a trade secret and not disclose it to others).

However, what happens to the trade secret if the representative is not autho-

rized by the company to sign such an agreement? Unless a person has actual authority to sign, or occupies a position or office in the business that would reasonably give rise to the belief that proper authority exists (this is called apparent authority), the non-disclosure agreement will probably not be binding. In other words, disclosure to a person who lacks the actual or apparent authority to bind the business might result in the loss of trade secret status.

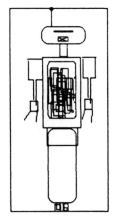

Example: Your burning desire to bring your brilliant variable-speed motor to the attention of Universal Motors leads you to deliver a full description of your design to the receptionist at a local Universal Motors Plant. Before handing over the envelope, however, you ask the receptionist to sign a non-disclosure agreement on behalf of the company. She complies. If the receptionist actually has authority from the company to sign such agreements, then her signature will be binding. If she has no authority, however, her signature will probably not bind the company, since normally a receptionist for a large corporation has the "apparent authority" to do little more than answer the phone and greet visitors. If the person signing the agreement occupies a managerial position however (say, "Technical Acquisitions Officer"), apparent authority might be held to exist even if actual authority did not. Related terms: *non-disclosure agreements*.

advantage over competitors See *competitive advantage*.

algorithm Any procedure or series of steps that can be used to solve a specific type of problem. Generally, algorithms are found in mathematical form. But, the term is also commonly used to describe the sequential steps found in any given computer program routine. An example is the code in a computer game program that tells the computer to end the game when a specific key is pressed. Especially in computer law circles, the concept of ''algorithm'' and ''routine'' have become virtually synonymous. Any algorithm that is innovative in some degree and is treated as confidential can qualify as a *trade secret* . Related terms: *software and trade secrets*.

anti-competition agreements See *covenants not to compete*.

anti-misappropriation injunctions See *injunctions against trade secret misappropriation*.

anti-trust law The body of law consisting of treaties, federal and state statutes, and court opinions that 1) restrict businesses from engaging in practices with the intent to create a dominant or monopolistic market position, and 2) prohibit businesses from making agreements with other businesses or individuals that impose significant restrictions or restraints on trade, such as price fixing, *territorial restriction agreements*, bid rigging, and *tying arrangements*. Related terms: *anti-trust law and trade secrets*.

anti-trust law and trade secrets The primary purpose of *anti-trust law* is to preserve a free, competitive marketplace by preventing companies from engaging in behavior that unduly dominates the marketplace or restricts free trade. Most commercial activity is too economically insignificant to violate the anti-trust laws. However, in some circumstances the commercial exploitation of trade secrets can cause a business to risk such violations. This can occur, for example, if the owner of a trade secret allows (*licenses*) others to use it in a way that unfairly discriminates against some businesses, or helps one company to attain a monopolistic position in the market. Whether any

particular activity violates the anti-trust laws depends on the amount of trade restricted, whether (in the U.S.) the trade is interstate (and thus falls under the federal anti-trust statutes), and whether the trade is governed by treaty or by foreign laws. Realistically, it also depends on how lenient or strict the court with jurisdiction over the cases is, at the time the suit is brought. Related terms: *licensing of trade secrets* and *anti-trust law and patents* 4.

authorization to sign trade secret agreements See *actual and apparent authority to make trade secret agreements*.

beta-testing Testing a product on site and under actual conditions of expected use is called ''beta-testing''. When computer software is first developed, it is necessary to use it exhaustively under real-life conditions to make sure that the program code will work properly. To accomplish this goal, it is common for the software developer to allow a number of people free use of the software on site in exchange for keeping track of any problems they might encounter. In order to preserve the software as a trade secret during the beta-test phase, it is customary to require the beta-testers to sign *non-disclosure agreements*. Related terms: *non-disclosure agreements* and *software and trade secrets*.

business information as trade secret Information about the operation of a specific business can qualify as a trade secret if disclosure would affect the competitive relationship between the business owning the information and the business acquiring it. Examples of such information are:

- information concerning the characteristics of customers
- information relevant to the cost and pricing of goods
- sources of supply (especially if disclosure would divulge the nature of a secret ingredient)
- books and records of the business
- mailing lists and other sales information
- customer lists
- information regarding new business opportunities (such as the price and phys-

ical characteristics of real estate)

● information regarding the effectiveness and performance of personnel, distributors, suppliers, etc.

On the other hand, business information is not protectible as a trade secret if it can be **independently developed** with little difficulty. Information that might not generally qualify as a trade secret, for example, would be general employee handbooks, or personnel policies that discuss the rights and responsibilities of workers. Related terms: *competitive advantage* and *know-how as trade secrets*.

business opportunity See *business information as trade secret*.

business sales, covenant not to compete See *covenant not to compete, business sales*.

commercial piracy See *piracy*.

commercial secret In Japan, a secret of a business nature, such as a confidential *customer list*, price list, source of supply, accounting technique, or the like. In Japan, a distinction is sometimes made between a "commercial secret" and an *industrial secret* for the purpose of deciding what kind of legal protection to provide. However, there, as elsewhere, both types of secrets are commonly lumped together under the *trade secret* label. Related terms: *business information as trade secret*.

competition by former employees See *confidential employment relations* and *covenant not to compete*.

competitive advantage Any confidential information, idea, item, or state of events that can potentially be exploited to enhance the income or assets of a business. Whether or not information qualifies as a *trade secret* depends in large part on the degree to which it offers its owner the opportunity to obtain a competitive advantage in the business world. If the owner of information cannot derive an economic benefit from it, there is no trade secret. Conversely, if keeping the information secret will give its owner a competitive advantage, the item will qualify as a trade secret.

Example: Universal Programming, Inc. develops and distributes business software. One of their employees creates an innovative software routine permitting screens to be quickly and efficiently edited while programming is in process. If other software companies have developed equally quick and efficient screen editors, Universal's program does not provide them with any particular advantage. Although the program uses an innovative approach, it probably will not qualify as a protectable trade secret.

On the other hand, suppose that the new screen editor works faster than others in general use throughout the industry, or offers one or more unique features. This would give Universal a competitive advantage, since it could then produce software faster than its competitors. In this situation, the screen editor program would qualify for trade secret status as long as Universal treats the program as confidential. Related terms: *trade secret defined*.

compilation of information as a trade secret A genuinely innovative structuring or re-organization of otherwise public information, which provides its possessor with a *competitive advantage* and which is treated as confidential, qualifies as a trade secret. Trade secrets are often thought to involve a new approach, formula, device or method for accomplishing a given end. However, the law of trade secrets also recognizes that information that is not itself new or secret can be manipulated and stored in innovative ways, providing a business with a competitive advantage.

Example: A hearing aid manufacturer designs an innovative way to construct a specialized mailing list of deaf Americans from available census data. Although the census data is certainly not a "trade secret", the mailing list would qualify as a trade secret in that it is not available to anyone else, and would provide the manufacturer with a competitive edge.

Much existing information is now being re-organized so that it can be more easily stored in and retrieved from computer *databases*. These new formats themselves often qualify as innovative compilations, which deserve treatment as *trade secrets* if they are treated as confidential, since they often allow a business to analyze old information in new ways that can lead to

a competitive edge. Related terms: *business information as trade secrets* and *databases and trade secrets* .

computer programs and trade secrets See *software and trade secrets*.

confidential employment relationship
The type of relationship between an employer and an employee that by law precludes the employee from disclosing or making commercial use of *trade secrets* learned in the course of the relationship. Anyone who works in a firm engaged in highly technical pursuits is sure to encounter information that the firm considers to be a trade secret. Much of trade secret law is, accordingly, concerned with rules that define the employees' rights and duties vis-a-vis the employer's secrets, during the time of the employment and afterwards.

In many businesses an employee who routinely comes in contact with trade secrets during the course of his work is viewed by the law as having a "confidential employment relationship". The higher the level of employment, the more willing a court usually is, to say that this type of relationship exists. The lower the level of an employee's responsibility, on the other hand, the less willing the court usually is to find that such relationship exists. Thus, an engineer, scientist, or corporate executive will have a harder time using trade secrets for the benefit of himself or a competitor than will a receptionist, office clerk, or janitor. However, any employee may be found liable for *theft of trade secrets* if he or she is proved to have intentionally set out to steal them.

It is common practice for firms possessing trade secrets to require employees with access to sensitive material to sign *confidentiality agreements*, promising not to utilize any of the firm's trade secrets during future employment. Whether or not such an agreement is signed, however, if an employee or former employee uses information obtained in the course of a confidential employment relationship, to benefit either himself or a competitor, courts will usually impose a damage award against the employee. Related terms: *confidentiality agreements* and *duty of trust*.

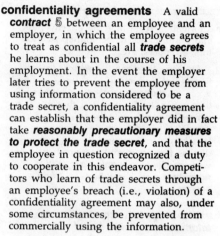

confidentiality agreements A valid *contract* 5 between an employee and an employer, in which the employee agrees to treat as confidential all *trade secrets* he learns about in the course of his employment. In the event the employer later tries to prevent the employee from using information considered to be a trade secret, a confidentiality agreement can establish that the employer did in fact take *reasonably precautionary measures to protect the trade secret*, and that the employee in question recognized a duty to cooperate in this endeavor. Competitors who learn of trade secrets through an employee's breach (i.e., violation) of a confidentiality agreement may also, under some circumstances, be prevented from commercially using the information.

Proving the existence of a confidentiality agreement is often necessary to establish that the information in question is a trade secret, subject to legal protection. Put differently, an employer's failure to require such an agreement may preclude him from later claiming the disclosed information as a trade secret. If, however, the court determines that a *confidential employment relationship* or *duty of trust* existed between the employer and employee, it is usually not necessary to show the existence of a written confidentiality agreement.

The term *non-disclosure agreement* is commonly used in place of "confidentiality agreement". However, "non-disclosure agreement" more properly describes agreements between trade secret owners and others in a non-employment setting. Related terms: *maintaining as a trade secret* and *non-disclosure agreement*.

contract requirements for non-disclosure agreement To be fully enforceable, an agreement in which a person promises not to disclose specific *trade secrets* must meet the requirements for the formation of a valid *contract* 5. Such agreements may be put in explicit written form, or be oral, or may be implied by law to exist.

An essential ingredient of *non-disclosure agreements* and *confidentiality agreements* (whether written, oral or implied) is that both parties must either receive something of value (called *consideration* 5 in contract law) in exchange for their agreement, or, at least one party must act in reliance on a promise made by the other party (**promissory estoppel** 5).

Consideration is generally interpreted quite loosely. In the trade secret context, it can mean money, property, professional advancement, employment, opportunity to use software for free, information learned from a **beta-tester**, and any other tangible or intangible advantage. But, if a business or person is sued because a non-disclosure or confidentiality agreement was breached, such defendant potentially has a defense if the signer of the non-disclosure agreement clearly received no consideration.

It should be remembered that in many types of relationships, such as a **confidential employment relationship**, an agreement not to disclose is implied either from the facts or by operation of law. For instance, an agreement by a venture capitalist to review a product may carry with it the implicit agreement to keep the information confidential, even if words to this effect were never spoken. And, the director of a corporation (for example), is considered by the law to have implicitly agreed to not disclose trade secret information belonging to the corporation. In these types of situations, the "consideration" may either be implied from the relationship itself, or, the legal need for consideration may be dispensed with altogether because the trade secret owner justifiably relied on the other party's explicit or implicit agreement to not disclose the information. Simply put, when faced with a written, oral, or implied agreement that appears to lack consideration, the court will usually find some way of upholding the agreement anyway.

Example: MND software company asks Donna Katz to **beta-test** a new computer program. Donna is not an employee of MND, and is not paid or given anything of value, such as free merchandise or use of the equipment, to conduct the test. However, MND still requires that Donna sign a general **non-disclosure agreement**. Since Donna receives no advantage for signing the agreement, it may be unenforceable under normal contract law principles, due to the absence of consideration on Donna's side. However, if Donna 1) was an employee and the agreement had been required as an initial condition of employement, or 2) received free use of the program over a period of

time in exchange for her efforts (usually the case), or 3) was provided with the temporary use of a computer, or 4) received some other tangible or intangible advantage, the consideration requirement would be deemed satisfied. And, even if no such consideration could be found, the court might enforce the agreement anyway, on the ground MND justifiably relied on Donna's promise not to disclose.

Because of the "consideration" requirement, most agreements expressly recite that "good and valuable consideration" has been provided. However, on rare occasion, a court will look behind this wording to see whether such consideration was really provided. If it wasn't, words alone will not form the basis of a contract (or a binding non-disclosure agreement). Either some actual consideration will have to be shown, or some of the other ways to get around this requirement will have to be argued.

Related terms: **contract** 5 and **consideration** 5.

contributions of trade secrets by Japanese companies Japanese corporations forming joint ventures with foreign partners may not contribute **trade secrets** or **know-how** which have been or are about to be used in an already existing Japanese enterprise. Likewise, any joint venture involving non-Japanese interests may not purchase certain types of technology from an existing Japanese corporation. This is often called the "in kind" rule.

copyright and trade secret law compatibility Here are the salient points of how **trade secret** and **copyright** 2 legal protections work together under the **Copyright Act of 1976** 2.

- A trade secret is any information that provides a business with a **competitive advantage** and is **treated confidentially.**

- A copyright is the exclusive right to reproduce, display, perform, distribute, and make alterations in an **original work of authorship** 2. Simply put, copyright law protects the original expressions of ideas, but not the ideas themselves.

- Trade secret and copyright protection are both available for **unpublished works** 2, as long as the idea or ideas in the work qualify as a trade secret, and the requisite measures, such as keeping the informa-

tion confidential, are taken to preserve trade secret status.

- Trade secret and copyright protection may both be available for works that are distributed under a *copyright* 2 licensing arrangement requiring the licensee (user) to recognize and maintain the trade secret aspects of the work. This dual protection is especially pertinent for the computer software business, and is applicable in England as well as in the U.S.

- Works that are widely distributed without specific licensing agreements, or works that are considered *published* 2 under the Copyright Act of 1976, may be entitled to copyright protection (if certain formalities are observed) but will generally lose their trade secret status.

- The *deposit* 2 that accompanies a copyright *registration* 2 with the the *U.S. Copyright Office* operates to disclose any trade secrets in the work unless it is made in a way that prevents someone examining the deposit from figuring out the secret. Trade secret status for a registered work may depend on what is actually deposited.

- There are several methods for simultaneously registering a computer program and maintaining trade secrets. One common way is to withhold the *source code* 2 and deposit *object code*.

- Trade secret protection is generally not available for software if the source code is made available to the public on an unrestricted basis through such means as a copyright deposit, listing in a computer magazine, or on a medium of distribution (e.g., floppy disk).

Related terms: *software and trade secrets* and *trade secret protection compared with other intellectual property protections*.

copyright notice, effect of on trade secret status An *original work of authorship* 2 (e.g., book, record, artwork, software, flowchart, film) may continue to be a *trade secret*, even though it contains a *copyright notice* 2 as long as the work is distributed on a restricted basis and is continually *maintained as a trade secret*. Only when a work is *published* 2 (i.e., distributed without restriction) will it necessarily lose its trade secret status. Related terms: *copyright and trade secret law compatibility*.

covenant not to compete by employee A written promise by an employee not to compete with his or her employer, or take employment with a competing business, for a specified length of time after the employer-employee relationship has been terminated.

Employers often must expose employees to important *trade secrets* that, if used by the employees or discovered by other companies, could ruin the employer's *competitive advantage*. In such cases, covenants not to compete are often seen as the only practical way to prevent such employees from improperly utilizing the secrets in their new business or employment.

Agreements restricting the right of employees to compete have often proved difficult to enforce in court, since by nature they tend to deprive employees of their right to earn a living. Whether or not a covenant not to compete will be enforced can depend on the position the employee occupied with the company. Employees with higher levels of responsibility may be held to their promise whereas those with less important responsibilities may be able to escape from the restriction, since 1) they presumably would not be in as great a position to harm the employer's interest, and 2) their ability to support themselves may be more severely affected.

These agreements are totally banned in some countries, and in some states such as California. Most states, however, will uphold covenants not to compete (i.e., enforce them in court), if they are seen as necessary to protect trade secrets and are very narrowly drafted so as to restrict the employee's general right to work and/or engage in commerce as little as possible.

Example: Peter Erickson is hired as a laser specialist by a company engaged in making holographs for amusement parks. As a condition of employment, Peter is required to sign a covenant not to engage in any holography or related laser work for a five year period after leaving the company. Because the agreement is much broader in scope and longer in duration than it needs to be, most courts will refuse to enforce it and Peter is free to take up employment where he wishes upon leaving the company. Assume now that the "covenant not to compete" is limited to work specifically involving amusement park holographs for a two year period. This narrower covenant might be enforceable (at least in most states).

Simply put, covenants not to compete will only be enforced to the degree necessary to maintain the competitive position of the former employer. And, they won't be enforced at all in some states.

covenant not to compete by the owners of a sold business When an existing business is sold, the owners, officers, or directors are commonly required, as a condition of the sale, to promise in writing not to compete with the purchased business for a specific period of time. These promises (or covenants) constitute recognition that part of the value of the purchased business consists of *trade secrets*. If the former owners or officers were permitted to utilize this information in competing businesses, the purchasers of the existing business would not be getting their money's worth. For this reason, these covenants are generally enforced.

customer lists A list of a business's customers may qualify as a *trade secret* when the list contributes to the business's *competitive advantage*, and is kept secret. In trade secret law, there are essentially three types of customer lists: retail customer lists, wholesale customer lists, and professional client lists.

The kind of list easiest to protect under trade secret law is the retail list compiled by the business itself. This is true for two primary reasons: 1) because the individual names on the list are obtained usually as the result of the business's effort to establish good will, and 2) a specific retail customer list gives its possessor a significant *competitive advantage* over other firms. *Professional client lists* are usually protectable as trade secrets for the same reason.

Wholesale customer lists (i.e., lists of retailers a wholesaler sells to) are often not protectible as trade secrets. This is because the potential retail customers of a particular category of wholesaler are usually easy to identify. Thus, lists of these customers often do not provide the wholesaler with a competitive advantage. However, there are exceptions to this. For example, a list of bookstores that order certain types of books and pay their bills promptly may be very valuable to a wholesale book distributor. Related terms: *business information as trade secrets*.

damages in trade secret infringement actions If a *trade secret owner* can establish in court that a *trade secret* was *improperly acquired* or disclosed, the court may issue an *injunction* requiring the present holder of the secret to restore it to the owner, and to refrain from any further use or mention of the secret for a specified period of time. In addition, if the trade secret has in fact been commercially exploited before the injunction is issued, the trade secret owner may be able to recover either 1) money damages measured by the profits earned by the competitor as a result of the use of the trade secret, or 2) money damages measured by the loss of profits by the trade secret owner, due to the improper trade secret leak.

Further, if the improper acquisition or disclosure was intentional, and the circumstances warrant, the court usually has authority to punish the defendants by imposing *punitive damages* 5 or treble damages (three times the amount of proven actual damages), depending on the state. This means, generally, that the court can award the plaintiff much more than the actual damages established in court. For example, in punitive damages states, even though the plaintiff only proves $10,000.00 worth of damages, the court has authority to award any amount (say $1,000,000.00) that it finds necessary to teach the wrongdoer (and potential wrongdoers) a lesson. In states where punitive damages are defined as treble damages, the court could obviously only impose a $30,000 judgment. Related terms: *trade secret infringement action* and *injunctions against misappropriation of trade secrets*.

databases and trade secret A database is information of any type organized in a manner to facilitate its retrieval in a meaningful form. An encyclopedia is a database because it is organized alphabetically and stores information that can be retrieved by subject. The term "database" is currently in common use in reference to computer databases. These usually consist of information organized in such a way that a specific item can be quickly retrieved, either separately or in combination with others, from a computer. Along with other *compilations of* information, databases may be protected as trade secrets under certain circumstances.

A database often contains component materials that are protected by **copyright** 2. Commonly this **copyrighted** 2 material is owned by someone other than the database owner. This type of database can still be a **trade secret**, even though some or all of its contents are owned by others.

Suppose that Windtronics Inc. creates a database consisting of all the articles ever published on wind power. The database structure allows retrieval by key word and/or by any one or more of two hundred key wind-power concepts. Windtronics then establishes a thriving consulting business, based on its ability to retrieve information quickly from its database.

Windtronics must obtain permission from the authors of the articles, since the creation of the database necessarily involves copying the articles into electronic form. But, the database itself can be a tradesecret if it is maintained as one.

Related terms: **compilations of information as trade secret**.

devices as trade secrets See **physical devices, ability to maintain as trade secrets**.

disclosure of confidential information See **confidentiality agreements** and **non-disclosure agreements**.

duty of trust The obligation of one party to take another party's best interests into account when engaging in commercial activity potentially affecting the other party. Over the years, the courts have recognized that certain relationships involve a higher than normal degree of trust, which everyone in the business relies on in the course of his or her related activities. These relationships are often referred to as ' 'fiduciary relationships''. For instance, an employer and a high level employee or provider of service (e.g., an executive, expert, lawyer, accountant) have a duty of trust, or fiduciary duty, to deal fairly with each other under all circumstances. This duty commonly extends to activities affecting **trade secrets**.

If a person breaches a duty of trust

(fiduciary duty), the courts in both the U.S. and England are usually willing to grant whatever remedy is necessary to undo the harm caused by the breach. So, if an employee breaches a duty owed to his employer by disclosing **trade secrets** to a competitor, the employer may go to court to prevent further such breaches, to receive an award of damages from the employee, and to prevent the competitor from using the disclosed trade secrets. Related terms: **confidential employment relationship** and **trade secret infringement actions**.

employees' covenant not to compete See **covenant not to compete by employees**.

employees, notice of trade secrets See **notice to employees of trade secrets**.

employees rights and duties towards trade secrets See **confidential employment relationship**.

employment contracts and trade secrets See **confidentiality agreements** and **covenants not to compete by employee** .

encryption to protect trade secrets See reasonably precautionary measures to protect trade secrets

European Economic Community (EEC) Known as the "Common Market", the EEC was established by the Treaty of Rome in 1957 for the purpose of promoting free movement of goods among its members. The member nations, which include most of the Western European and Scandinavian countries, as well as the United Kingdom, have ceded certain authority to the EEC, including the rights to 1) issue rules governing competition, 2) give effect to joint economic and social policies, and 3) create institutions for the implementation of its rules and policies. Accordingly, the EEC regulates technology transfers between Common Market members, and regulates commerce in intellectual and industrial properties.

exit interview An interview conducted by an employer with a departing employee, in which the employee is 1) reminded of the trade secrets that she has knowledge of, and 2) warned that her unauthorized disclosure of the trade secrets may result in her being held liable for damages. Related terms: *notice to employees of trade secrets*.

fiduciary duty and trade secrets See *duty of trust*.

field of use in trade secret licensing
A condition placed in a trade secret *license* 5 that restricts use of the trade secret to particular types or fields of commerce. Suppose Law Systems Associates develops an innovative *algorithm* as part of a new expert legal program, which it is developing for an independent software publisher. Law Systems recognizes that the algorithm gives them a *competitive advantage* and therefore qualifies as a trade secret as long as it is kept secret. However, Law Systems also believes that the algorithm might be useful to other programmers developing expert systems in other fields. Law Systems can license the algorithm as a trade secret to potential developers of non-legal expert systems, while continuing to use it to develop their own legal system. In such a case, the license would restrict the licensees' use of the algorithm to the specific field of use intended by the license. Related terms: *licensing of trade secrets*.

formulas as trade secrets Among the types of information protectable as a *trade secret* is any product formula that is treated as confidential and that will add to a business's *competitive advantage*. Examples of the many formulas that have been granted trade secret status are those for softdrinks, butter flavoring, industrial solvents, floor wax, and rat poison. A formula can be any combination of ingredients that results in a particular product. Related terms: *trade secret defined*.

Freedom of Information Act, exemption of trade secrets The Freedom of Information Act (FOIA), located in 5 United States Code, Section 552, provides the public with broad access to documents possessed by the executive branch of the federal government, with the exception of records that fall into ten exempt categories. The sixth of these categories applies to any record containing a trade secret. Because the federal

government often requires businesses to submit information containing trade secrets, a number of federal agencies routinely possess records which, if disclosed to the public, would give these trade secrets away.

Although trade secrets are exempt from disclosure under the FOIA, it is often difficult, if not impossible, for an agency official to tell whether a given piece of information is or is not a trade secret. So, when companies submit information containing what they consider to be trade secrets, they should clearly label the material as such to put the agency official on notice, should a request be made for disclosure. Then, if the agency receives a request for the information, the company can be contacted and given a chance to argue why it should not be disclosed. However, if the agency chooses to release the information in question against the company's wishes, there is little that can be done about it, as the courts have prohibited lawsuits against agencies to prevent them from disclosing information (called ''reverse FOIA suits''). Related terms: *government agency restrictions on disclosure of trade secrets*.

geographical licenses See *territorial restriction agreements* and *licensing of trade secrets*.

good will The estimated commercial value of a business's name or reputation in the marketplace.

government agency restrictions on disclosure of trade secrets Regulations establishing when a government agency may disclose a company's trade secrets to third parties. These rules are important because, in the course of their many regulatory roles, the federal and state governments routinely require businesses to submit information that is otherwise protectable as trade secrets. What if the government agency in question then discloses the information to a competitor under the federal *Freedom of Information Act*, a state public records act, or some other public record disclosure procedure? The information will lose its trade secret status (and thus its value), since the law only prohibits others from using a trade secret that has been obtained by wrongful means.

To prevent this from happening, most

agencies have policiesunder which they attempt to prevent trade secrets from being disclosed to the detriment of the business submitting them. Also, many agencies will inform the business in question when trade secret information has been requested, so that the business can take steps to oppose disclosure. Companies submitting trade secrets to a government agency are usually conversant with these agency restrictions, and monitor the agency to make sure the restrictions are observed. In addition, they attempt to submit information in a form that will meet government regulations without giving away the trade secret. Related terms: *Freedom of Information Act, exemption of trade secrets*.

head start rule   A type of judicial relief sometimes granted in *trade secret infringement actions* wherein the infringer is prevented from using a *trade secret* for as long a period of time as it would have taken him independently to develop the information that comprise the secret. In other words, the rightful trade secret owner is provided with a commercial "head start" in the information's use. This "head start" remedy shows recognition that the essential value of a trade secret is the *competitive advantage* it affords its owner. Related terms: *trade secret infringement action*.

hiring employees from competitors to obtain trade secrets   See *improper acquisition of trade secrets*.

ideas as trade secrets   Ideas alone can be protected as *trade secrets* if they are generally unknown in the business community, offer a *competitive advantage*, and are treated confidentially. The real value of any such idea will ultimately depend on its commercial success. However, an idea that offers the possibility of helping a business compete should be *maintained as a trade secret* until such time as it appears to lack feasibility or others independently think of it. Otherwise, a golden opportunity for a *head start* on potential competitors may be lost.

Trade secret protection for ideas should be contrasted with *copyright protection* 2, which only protects the actual expression of the idea and not the idea itself.

Because of this difference, trade secret law can protect the conception and development stages of a work before copyright protection takes over. Related terms: *trade secret compared with other intellectual property protections*.

illegal restraint of trade   Commercial activity by one business showing a strong tendency to restrict or curtail the free flow of commerce. Examples of illegal restraints are *tying arrangements* (requiring the purchase of one product as a prerequisite to buying another), price setting agreements (two or more businesses agree to set prices at a particular level), and *territorial restriction agreements* (private agreements to restrict the use of a trade secret to certain geographical areas). Related terms: *anti-trust laws and trade secrets* and *licensing of trade secrets*.

implied duty not to disclose trade secrets   The responsibility that the law automatically places on persons who occupy positions of responsibility and/or trust in a business to keep the business's secrets and not disclose them to others. Although this type of duty is often expressly spelled out in *confidentiality agreements* or *non-disclosure agreements*, the law infers this duty to exist in many higher-level employment relationships as well. Related terms: *confidential employment relationship* and *duty of trust*.

improper acquisition of trade secrets   When a trade secret is obtained by a business through means that the law considers wrongful. These include:

- obtaining *trade secrets* belonging to another through theft, misrepresentation, or *industrial espionage*

- knowingly obtaining or using trade secrets that have been improperly disclosed by a breach of a *non-disclosure agreement*, or a *confidentiality agreement*, or an *simplied duty not to disclose trade secrets*, or a *duty of trust*

- obtaining trade secrets by inducing one to breach an express or implied agreement not to disclose them

If a company knowingly obtains another company's trade secrets through any of these activities, the injured business can file a *trade secret infringement* action to stop the other company from using the information, and perhaps to recover money damages and punitive damages in court.

Example: The Bayside Graphics company develops a program that greatly improves the graphics capability of a popular business-forecasting package. Treating the program as a trade secret, Bayside requires its lower-level and middle-level employees, and all of its promotors, marketers, financiers, and developers to sign **confidentiality** and **non-disclosure agreements**. In addition, tight physical security is maintained at Bayside's development laboratory. However, no non-disclosure agreements have been required of certain Bayside top-management people.

If any one person who signed the non-disclosure agreement breaches the agreement by passing trade secrets to a competitor, and the competitor has reason to suspect a breach, the acquisition or use of the trade secret by the competitor would be improper. If the competitor hires a former member of Bayside's top management who has not signed a non-disclosure agreement, and gets her to disclose trade secrets belonging to Bayside, the acquisition is improper, due to the former manager's breach of her **duty of trust, confidential employment relationship**, or **implied duty not to disclose the trade secret**. Or, if the competitor discovers a five-minute period during the night when Bayside's trash cans are unprotected, steals the trash, and thereby discovers the trade secret, improper acquisition has also occurred.

In any of these situations, Bayside may obtain an injunction to stop the competitor from utilizing the trade secret, and, depending on the circumstances, may be able to recover from the competitor any profits that were made as a result of the improperly acquired trade secret.

improper disclosure of tradesecrets

When someone communicates a trade secret to others in violation of a **confidentiality agreement, non-disclosure agreement, duty of trust**, or **confidential employment relationship**. In the event such an improper disclosure is made, the discloser may be held liable for any resulting harm to the **trade secret owner**. Related terms: **improper acquisition of a trade secret**.

improperly acquired   See **improper acquisition of a trade secret**

Independent conception, defense to trade secret claim

In order for a **trade secret owner** to obtain relief in court against a competitor who is using a **trade secret** belonging to the owner, there must be a showing that the competitor **improperly acquired** the trade secret. A trade secret is not improperly acquired if it is independently conceived of, or discovered by a competitor through **parallel research**, without recourse to confidential information taken from any other source. Accordingly, when a business is sued because of an alleged trade secret theft, it can win if it proves that it had independently conceived of, or discovered, the secret in question. To preserve their ability to do this, most large companies do not examine any work developed by an outsider unless the outsider signs a written statement giving up her right to treat the work as a trade secret. Related terms: **unsolicited idea disclosures** and **improper acquisition of trade secret**.

independently developed   See **independent conception, defense to trade secret claim**.

industrial espionage

In the trade secret context, activity directed toward discovering a company's **trade secrets** by such illicit or illegal means as:

- electronic surveillance
- bribery of employees to disclose confidential information
- placing a spy among the company's employees
- tapping into a company's phones or computers
- theft of documents containing confidential information In the U.S., an owner of trade secrets that have been obtained through industrial espionage may recover large damages if the secrets are subsequently used by the guilty party. Also, many states and foreign countries (Germany for instance) are treating such activity as a serious crime.

On the other hand, some countries do not view trade secret theft quite so seriously. In Japan, for example, the practice has sometimes been condoned. For instance, the "Institute of Industrial

Protection" has been organized, in part, for the purpose of training industrial spies and counterspies to gather information for the use of their various corporations. Related terms: *improper acquisition of trade secrets*.

industrial innovations as trade secrets   See *trade secret defined* and *competitive advantage*.

industrial secret   Trade secrets of a technical, technological, scientific, or mechanical nature, such as (but not limited to) secret processes, formulae, unregistered industrial designs, manufacturing techniques and methods, secret machinery, devices, and the like. Although Japan distinguishes between "industrial secrets" and *commercial secrets* in certain respects, the various state courts in the U.S. treat all trade secrets alike, regardless of their type. In other words, whether or not a trade secret is *business information*, *know-how* or an "industrial secret" has no legal consequence in the U.S. Related terms: *trade secret defined*.

information and items that qualify as trade secrets   Virtually any type of information or device that adds to a business's *competitive advantage*, and is maintained as a secret will qualify for protection under the trade secret laws. For more information about specific types of trade secrets, see the following entries: *trade secret, defined, patterns and designs as trade secrets , physical devices, ability to maintain as trade secrets, business information as trade secrets, methods and techniques as trade secrets, processes as trade secrets, formulas as trade secrets, industrial secrets, commercial secrets, unique ideas as trade secrets, software and trade secrets* and *know how as trade secrets* .

in-house trade secrets   A trade secret may still legally exist (and thus be entitled to protection), despite the fact a large number of people know about it. For example, in large corporations, trade secrets that are limited to the workplace and to employees who "need to know" (i.e., who necessarily learn of the trade secret in the course of their work) may in fact be known by thousands of people. Yet, as long as the business takes adequate measures to prevent the secrets

from being disclosed to the public or to other businesses, the trade secret status of the information is maintained, and protection against *improper acquisition*, and *improper disclosure*, of the trade secret may be obtained in the courts. Related terms: *reasonably precautionary measures to protect trade secrets*.

infringement of trade secret   When a business makes commercial use of a *trade secret* that has been *improperly disclosed* or *improperly acquired* from another business. Related terms: *improper acquisition of trade secret* and *trade secret infringement action*.

injunctions in trade secret cases   A court order directed at persons or businesses who have either *improperly acquired* trade secrets, or who threaten to *improperly disclose* them. Typically, an injunction is sought,

as part of a *trade secret infringement action*, to prohibit a defendant from using a trade secret belonging to the plaintiff (the person bringing the action) or from disclosing it to others. This type of judicial relief is common in trade secret litigation, since one of the trade secret owner's primary goals is to stop any further erosion of the *competitive advantage* gained by the secret information.

Although courts are not authorized to issue final injunctions in *trade secret infringement actions* unless a trial has occurred (or a summary judgment has been granted, the parties have settled, or the case has been dismissed on some ground) the court does have authority to issue temporary, or provisional orders directed toward the defendant. These generally require the defendant to do, or desist from doing, certain things relating to the trade secret in question, pending further action by the court. Such "temporary" or "provisional" court orders are commonly called *temporary restraining orders* (an initial emergency order usually only good for two or three weeks, until the court can consider more long lasting relief) and *preliminary injunctions* (more long lasting provisional relief, only granted after the court has had a chance to hear both sides and consider their arguments). Together, these orders allow an injured business to obtain immediate and continuous protection pending a final court determination as to whether the infringement occurred, and if so, what final relief to grant.

To grant a temporary restraining order, the court need only conclude that irreparable injury will occur if the status quo isn't maintained. To issue a preliminary injunction, however, which will last throughout the pendency of the case, the court must find it probable both that 1) irreparable injury will occur in the absence of the preliminary injunction (in trade secret actions, such injury is often presumed) and 2) the plaintiff will probably win in the end (prevail on the merits). In other words, to award provisional relief in the form of a preliminary injunction, the court must decide preliminarily in favor of the injured business on the infringement issue, pending a final decision later in the case. Once this occurs, the parties will often settle rather than fight the case all the way through to trial and beyond.

Example: Space Age Robotics Inc.(SARI) is a small business with five employees. It has spent three years developing a computer security system that visually recognizes a small group of people, and respond only to their voice commands. Having solved most of the bugs in the system, SARI plans to make a product announcement in about a month. However, Fred Gregory, the chief engineer, decides his bread will be better buttered across the street at Universal Systems Inc., and suddenly joins that company. A week or two later, SARI learns from the grapevine that Fred is working around the clock to build a similar visual recognition system for Universal.

Claiming trade secret infringement, SARI immediately files an action against Fred and Universal, and asks the court to first grant a temporary restraining order, and then a preliminary injunction, preventing Fred from making any further disclosures to Universal, and Universal from disclosing to anyone else anything they have already learned from Fred. The basis for this request (motion) is that if it is not granted, SARI will suffer irreparable injury because its valuable trade secrets will be lost. The court issues a temporary restraining order (TRO) and schedules a hearing 14 days later, at which time SARI's motion for a preliminary injunction is considered. At this hearing, both SARI and Universal present both oral arguments regarding the appli-

cable law as well as written statements of their respective legal positions (called "points and authorities"). In support of their legal arguments, both sides also submit written statements under oath (affidavits or declarations) describing the facts in the case as they seem them. Although witnesses occasionally appear in preliminary injunction hearings, this is somewhat exceptional, and none appear in this case.

The judge determines that a preliminary injunction is necessary to preserve SARI's trade secrets and that, when the case is finally tried, SARI will probably win. Accordingly, a preliminary injunction to remain in effect pending the trial of the case is issued against Fred and Universal. Because the trial will not occur for at least a year, and because both SARI and Universal need to get on with their respective businesses, they decide to settle the dispute as follows: Universal agrees to scrap its budding vision project, Fred agrees to keep his knowledge to himself, and SARI agrees to drop its infringement action and request for damages.

in-kind rule   See *contributions of trade secrets by Japanese companies*.

Institute of Industrial Protection   A commercial institute in Japan that trains corporate security agents in the ins and outs of protecting against *theft of trade secrets*, and obtaining *trade secrets* from other companies. Related terms: *industrial espionage* and *improper acquisition of trade secrets*.

know-how as trade secrets   The International Chamber of Commerce defines industrial know-how to include applied technical knowledge, methods, and data necessary for realizing or carrying out techniques that serve industrial purposes. As long as this type of information is specialized, not generally known in the relevant business community, provides a company with a *competitive advantage*, and is *maintained as a trade secret*, it will qualify as such.

In France, Germany, Japan, the U.S., and many other countries, know-how can constitute a trade secret even when the general process or method to which it relates is *patented* ⊄ or otherwise known about publically. For example,

Trade Secret

swordmaking methods are widely known in Japan, but such factors as ceramic techniques, temperature of the fire, and temperature of the water often determine whether the sword is a masterpiece or a failure. Because the know-how associated with any or all of these factors can provide a competitive advantage, it accordingly qualifies as a trade secret. Related terms: *methods and techniques as trade secret* and *business information as trade secret*.

kuntsgriff German for ''know how''. Related terms: *know-how as trade secret*.

licensing of trade secrets When the owner of a *trade secret* gives another person or entity authorization to use the trade secret during a defined period, and for a specific purpose. Under a trade secret *license* 5, ownership remains with the original owner, while the licensee has the right to use the trade secret as long as the specific terms and time limits of the license are complied with.

Under one common type of license, the owner is paid a royalty based on a percentage of the retail or wholesale price of each item sold that takes advantage of the trade secret. Many other compensation arrangements are possible. For example, the license may provide for a flat fee for each use of the secret, a monthly or annual fee, the reciprocal use of information belonging to the licensee, or some combination of all of these arrangements.

The license agreement should always include a clause stating that the trade secret in question is confidential information and must properly be *maintained as a trade secret* by the licensee.

Trade secret licenses are subject to applicable anti-trust prohibitions against monopolistic or *restraint of trade* activities.

For the types of agreements commonly used in licensing trade secrets, see *exclusive licenses* 5, *non-exclusive licenses* 5, *geographical licenses* 5 and *field of use in trade secret licenses*.

loss of trade secrets Many conduct that releases trade secrets into the *public domain*, with a resulting loss in judicial protection.

Example: Acme Publishing Co. conceives of a new way to generate publication-quality graphics on a small computer. This new approach is cheaper, faster, and produces better quality work than anything else on the market. Initially Acme takes all the steps necessary to preserve the idea, as a *trade secret*. However, over a few drinks at a trade show, Acme's chief executive officer tells an employee from another publishing company about the idea without first asking for a *non-disclosure agreement*. Such behavior might result in the loss of the idea as a trade secret, especially if the other publisher proceeds to implement the idea and tell others about it. The behavior of the Acme CEO would definitely constitute a defense should Acme bring a lawsuit against the other publisher alleging infringement. Related terms: *reasonably precautionary measures to protect trade secrets*.

machine language and trade secrets See *software and trade secret*.

maintaining as a trade secret Taking all reasonable measures under the circumstances to preserve the secrecy of information considered to be a company trade secret. Information will not be afforded protection by the courts as a trade secret unless it has been maintained as one. Related terms: *reasonably precautionary measures to protect trade secrets*.

methods and techniques as trade secrets Specialized business knowledge about a particular subject (commonly known as business *know-how*) can qualify as a trade secret in many countries if treated as such. Examples of such know-how are 1) specialized barbeque methods of cooking, including the use of special cuts of meat and secret sauces, and 2) methods and techniques for running group sessions of a how-to-quit-smoking organization. Related terms: *know-how as trade secret*.

On the other hand, general business knowledge or expertise not related to a specific process or method is usually not *protectable as a trade secret*. Why not? As with other types of trade secrets, the courts will usually not protect information which is known to, or available to, the business community. Related terms: *business information as trade secrets*.

misappropriation of trade secrets
See *theft of trade secrets*.

money damages A common type of judicial relief in *trade secret infringement actions* (and most other types of lawsuits as well), where the court awards the plaintiff a sum of money (to be paid by the defendant) as compensation for specific and proven economic harm caused by the infringement. Related terms: *damages in trade secret infringement cases*.

non-competition clauses in employment contracts See *covenant not to compete by employee*.

non-disclosure agreement A legally binding *contract* 5 in which a party promises to treat specific information as a *trade secret* and not to disclose this information to others without proper authorization. If the trade secret is later disclosed in violation of the "non-disclosure agreement", the trade secret owner can file a *trade secret infringement action*, obtain an *injunction* to stop any further use of the trade secret, recover *money damages*, and possibly recover *punitive damages* 5 or *treble damages* in certain situations.

Trade secret non-disclosure agreements are used whenever it is necessary to disclose a trade secret to another person or business for such purposes as development, marketing, evaluation, or to gain fiscal backing. Through the conscientious use of non-disclosure agreements, trade secrets can be distributed to a large number of people without destroying their protectable status.

Although non-disclosure agreements are usually in the form of written contracts, they may also be implied if the context of a business relationship suggests that such agreement was intended by the parties. For example, in the United Kingdom, even if a non-disclosure clause is not included in a *license agreement* 5 involving a trade secret, an *obligation of confidentiality* is an implied part of the contract. Related terms: *contract requirements for non-disclosure and confidentiality agreements*.

notice to employees of trade secrets In order for industrial or *business information* to qualify as a *trade secret*, employers must insure that it is treated as confidential. This requires that all employees, and anyone else who may come in contact with the information, know in no uncertain terms that the information is confidential, and that they have an obligation not to disclose it. The best way to give this notice is to require all employees coming in contact with the secret to sign *confidentiality agreements*. However, an express written notice to employees regarding the status of the information and their *obligation of confidentiality* under their employment contract, backed up by adequate physical security measures, will also usually provide a basis for judicially protecting the information in the event of a later threatened or actual disclosure.

Commonly used devices to back up confidentiality agreements and notices to employees regarding the trade secret status of particular information, include: signs on walls, confidentiality labels on documents, initial employment interviews in which the nature of the business's trade secrets are discussed and the need to keep them confidential stressed, and *exit interviews*, in which departing employees are warned against disclosing the company's trade secrets in their new employment. Related terms: *reasonably precautionary measures to protect trade secrets*.

notice to new employer regarding former employees When an employee who knows about *trade secrets* takes a new job with a competing company, the trade secret owner will often send the new employer a letter emphasizing that the employee in question is legally bound not to disclose the trade secrets and that, even if he does, any such disclosure may not be used by the new employer. This serves to put the new employer on notice that the information is a protectable trade secret. In this circumstance, if the new employer makes use of the secrets, the use will be wrongful and the former employer may obtain greater damages and other enhanced judicial relief. Related terms: *improper disclosure of trade secrets* and *trade secret infringement actions*.

novelty and trade secrets For information to qualify as a *trade secret*, it must generally not be known or used in the relevant industry. Otherwise, it would not provide its possessor with a *competi-*

tive advantage and there would be no point in keeping it secret. Strictly speaking, however, information comprising a trade secret need not be novel in the sense of "new" or "innovative". Assume, for example, that a robot manufacturer re-discovers a principle of movement first pioneered by the nineteenth century European moving doll industry. If this particular principle has been lost to the world and is not, therefore, generally available to the robot manufacturing community, it can qualify as a trade secret, even though it is in no way novel. Also, as long as a trade secret provides its owner with a competitive advantage, it can be identical to trade secrets currently possessed by others if it was independently conceived, and not generally known to others in the business. For instance, if a new cola company inadvertently stumbles on the exact cola formula used by an existing company, both the new and old companies are entitled to protect their formulas as trade secrets, even though the second formula is not novel. Related terms: *competitive advantage* and *trade secrets defined*.

The role of "novelty" in the trade secret context should be compared with the meaning of the term as used in *patent* 4 law. There, an invention must be definitely novel to qualify for a patent. Related terms: *novelty* 4 and *non-obviousness* 4.

patterns and designs

object code and trade secrets See *software and trade secrets*.

obligation of confidentiality The legal *duty* 5 assumed by an employee or other person when they agree (either expressly or by implication) not to disclose a *trade secret*. Breach of this duty may result in liability for any economic harm suffered by the *trade secret owner*. Related terms: *implied duty not to disclose trade secret* and *confidential employment relationships*.

ownership of trade secret rights See *trade secret owner*.

parallel research When similar information or ideas are developed by two or more companies through their independent efforts. Related terms: *independent conception, defense to infringement action* and *unsolicited idea disclosures*.

patent application, effect on trade secrets Applying for a *patent* 4 does not affect the *trade secret* status of information. Why not? Because the *patent application* 4 is kept confidential by the *U.S. Patent and Trademark Office* 4 unless or until the patent is granted and the *issue fee* 4 paid. Once the patent is granted, however, the trade secret status of the information contained in the application is lost. This is because the grant of a seventeen-year monopoly under the patent is explicitly made in exchange for full public disclosure of the technology, ideas, and methodology connected with the patented *invention* 4.

Because many patent applications are ultimately denied on one ground or another, *inventors* 4 are well advised to hold on to the trade secret status of their invention as long as possible. Also, because patent applications often take several years to process, maintaining trade secret status of an invention will give the inventor a head start on development and sale of the product.

patterns and designs as trade secrets Patterns may qualify as *trade secrets* if they create a *competitive advantage* and are kept secret. Examples of patterns that have been protected as trade secrets are 1) advanced design plans for a new minicomputer 2) designs for electronic circuitry, and 3) schematic plans for an innovative metal door frame. Related terms: *trade secrets defined* and *industrial secrets*.

physical devices, ability to maintain as trade secrets Physical devices (e.g., tools, products, components, etc) can qualify as trade secrets if they provide their owner with a *competitive advantage* and are kept secret. Such devices can easily be protected when they are used solely in the trade secret developer's (or owner's) manufacturing or production process. However, a problem exists when an attempt is made to maintain trade secret status in products that are widely distributed. This is because anyone may examine these products and figure out how they work. This is referred to as *reverse engineering*. Once this is done, the trade secret has entered the *public domain*. This thinking has been extended to computer programs, although perhaps trade secret protection can be preserved if the purchaser or user has signed a license agreement that prohibits reverse engineering. Related terms: *reverse engineering*.

Example: Jason invents a device that allows people to use their microcomputers for the purpose of pre-programming videotape recorders to reject certain kinds of ads. He calls it AdOut. Physically, AdOut consists of an integrated circuit board inside a black box, and ports to interface it with a VCR and Computer. Jason has designed the box so that it can be opened to replace the board, if it fails. If Caryl Curious were to open the box, examine the board, figure out how AdOut works, and start manufacturing his own device called AdScreen, Jason would have no grounds for relief against Caryl under trade secret laws. Why not? Because Caryl lawfully obtained the necessary information through reverse engineering. If, however, Jason either owns a *patent* 4️⃣ or *copyright* 2️⃣ on some part of AdOut copied by Caryl, Jason can claim protection on that ground.

Suppose now that instead of allowing the box to be opened, Jason seals it after installing the circuit board, so that no one can get inside without destroying the entire product. In this situation, it is quite possible that Jason will be able to maintain AdOut as a trade secret. Related terms: *trade secret protection compared to other intellectual property protections* and *reverse engineering*.

piracy   A colloquial phrase, meaning any activity directed toward the *improper acquisition of trade secrets* or other forms of *intellectual property* 5️⃣ that belong to another. The word has no legal significance. Related terms: *theft of trade secrets*, *improper acquisition of trade secrets*, and *industrial espionage*.

post-employment restraints on employees   See *covenant not to compete by employee*.

pre-determination of rights in technical data   Contracts with the government for research and development projects that are likely to produce *trade secrets* routinely contain clauses pre-determining who will own the rights to the secrets in question.

Example: The federal government contracts with a biological engineering firm to "manufacture" a new life form that will survive on the Moon. Because such a project is likely to result in a number of extremely valuable discoveries, the contract between the biotech firm and the government should deal with who will own the rights to the new life forms. Although this can be a subject for negotiation, the government will typically demand ownership of the main product being developed, but will allow the private party to own the rights to any "side-products". Related terms: *proprietary interest in trade secrets*.

Predetermination of rights provisions may also be found in agreements between universities and corporations, and corporations and independent contractors.

preliminary injunctions in trade secret infringement actions   Court orders commonly issued in *trade secret infringement actions*, which prevent the defendant from taking certain actions, such as using or disclosing the trade secret in issue, pending a final decision in the case. Related terms: *injunctions in trade secret cases*.

premature disclosure   See *abandonment of trade secrets*.

processes as trade secrets   A process consists of a series of steps that lead to a particular result. Any process can qualify for *trade secret* status if it is generally not known in the industry, adds to a business's *competitive advantage*, and is *maintained as a trade secret*. Among the processes that have been afforded *protection as a trade secret* in the past are those involving photographic development, silk screening, and centrifugal processing for blood plasma fractionation, and the making of chocolate powder, cyclamates, and tobacco flavoring. Related terms: *trade secret defined*.

professional client lists   See *customer lists*.

proprietary interest in trade secrets   When *trade secret* information is developed by employees in the course of their employment, for purposes related to such employment, the employer is said to have a "proprietary interest" in the information. When courts were first asked to protect trade secrets, they had to come up with a rationale to justify such protec-

tion. Initially, the judicial response was to treat trade secrets as property belonging to the employer (i.e., the employer was said to have a proprietary interest in the secrets). This analysis, while adequate for some types of infringement, only allowed court-ordered relief in situations where trade secrets were stolen outright. Conversely, relief was not available when a trade secret was lost due to a negligent breach of a contractual *duty* 5 not to disclose.

Now, however, the courts focus primarily on the contractual relationship between the owner of the trade secret and persons who have come in contact with it, and are more willing to grant relief when they find a breach of express or implied contractual obligations to have occurred. Related terms: *trade secret owner* and *Trade secret, defined*.

protecting a trade secret Valuable business information is typically protected from discovery by others in a two step process. The first step is to take all *reasonably precautionary measures* to preserve the information as confidential. As long as this is done, the information will qualify as a "trade secret". Then, if the information is improperly acquired by others, it is possible to obtain a broad range of judicial relief. Related terms: *Reasonably precautionary measures to protect trade secrets* and *trade secret infringement action*

provisional relief in trade secret infringement action Orders by a court in a *trade secret infringement action* that are granted in advance of trial. Related terms: *injunctions in trade secret cases*.

public domain When something enters the public domain, it leaves the domain of protectable property. *Intellectual property* 5 enters the public domain when the public becomes entitled to use it without permission from its inventor, originator, author, or former owner. This generally occurs when 1) the property is not entitled to protection in the first place (e.g., works funded by the federal government) or 2) the owner of the property fails to take certain actions (e.g., publishing a book without a proper copyright notice), or 3) the owner of the property does something forbidden under the law (e.g.,

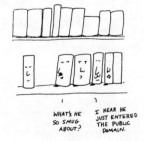

WHAT'S HE SO SMUG ABOUT?

I HEAR HE JUST ENTERED THE PUBLIC DOMAIN.

uses a patent in violation of the anti-trust laws). Related terms: *trade secret protection compared with other intellectual property protection*.

public knowledge and trade secrets Information cannot qualify as a *trade secret* if the public has obtained knowledge of it through proper means. Once this has occurred, the information has entered the *public domain* unless its expression is also protected under the *copyright* 2 or *patent* 4 laws. Even if the secret becomes public because of someone's improper actions (such as the breaking of a *non-disclosure agreement* or *industrial espionage*), it will still be in the public domain if dissemination of the information is widespread. In short, once the trade secret cat is out of the owner's bag, the trade secret is gone unless the cat stays very close to home and is quickly retrieved. Related terms: *trade secret defined*.

Example: Microwave Systems wants to raise some venture capital to fund the promotion of its new microwave satellite "dish" system, which it plans to sell to the average television owner for an affordable price. To accomplish this goal it prepares a magazine article describing in detail its revolutionary system. Manfred Manufacturer reads this article and learns enough details to start his own "dish" business. Microwave would not be able to claim an *infringement of tradesecret*, since its ideas became a matter of public knowledge through its own disclosure.

Suppose, now, that no article appeared, and Manfred learns of the details of Microwave System's dish through the breach of a *non-disclosure agreement* by one of Microwave's former employees. If only Manfred and a few of his associates know about the information, it may still qualify for trade secret status. If, on the other hand, the employee published the information in a major computer magazine, the trade secret is lost, regardless of the initial wrongfulness of the employee's action. Of course, Microwave would probably be able to recover damages from the offending employee for the loss.

public records and trade secrets Any information contained in a public record (a document, tape, disk, or other medium that is open to inspection by the public) cannot qualify as a trade secret, since by definition it is no longer confidential. However, because companies are often asked by state and federal governments to file documents that, of necessity, contain trade secrets, such information is usually specifically exempted from laws allowing disclosure of government information to the public, such as the *Freedom of Information Act*. Related terms: *Freedom of Information Act and trade secrets* and *government agencies restrictions on disclosure of trade secrets*.

read-only memories and trade secrets
Internal operating instructions and other programs that are a physical part of the computer (e.g., read-only memories or ROM) do not usually qualify for protection as a trade secret, once the computer is marketed. This is because it is usually possible to figure out the design and logic of the ROM through *reverse engineering*. Related terms: *software and trade secrets* and *reverse engineering*.

reasonably precautionary measures to protect trade secrets
All steps that a business can reasonably be expected to take in order to prevent its trade secrets from being disclosed to others. Information will only qualify as a trade secret if its owner takes appropriate measures to keep it secret. What constitutes an appropriate measure will vary from case to case. The question usually arises when a *trade secret infringement action* has been filed, and the defendant claims that the information should not be considered as a trade secret. In this situation, the court will determine whether the business claiming the infringement has taken the necessary ''reasonably precautionary measures'' under the circumstances to maintain the confidentiality of the information. If so, the information will be protected. If not, the information will be denied trade secret status, and judicial relief will be denied. Clearly, a certain amount of Monday morning quarterbacking is involved in these decisions.

Measures typically considered to be reasonable precautions are:

- requiring employees to sign *confidentiality agreements*
- requiring all outside persons with whom the information is shared to sign *non-disclosure agreements*

- restricting physical access to the area where the trade secrets are located
- enforcing company rules regarding confidentiality of the information and physical access to it
- using encryption (i.e., code) or other devices to make sure that trade secret information cannot easily be understood, even if read by an unauthorized person
- giving notice to all persons coming in contact with the information that it is considered a trade secret
- posting warnings on the wall
- conducting *exit interviews* with employees, specifically warning them against *improper disclosure of trade secrets*
- adequately protecting against unauthorized intrusion into computer databases that contain the information
- depending on the scope of the operation and the value of the secrets, taking such physical security measures as posting guards, maintaining tight control over keys (including keys to the photocopy machine) and requiring visitors to wear badges

restricted disclosure
See *non-disclosure agreement* and *confidentiality agreement*.

retail customer lists
See *Customer lists as trade secrets*.

reverse engineering
The act of examining a product or device and figuring out the ideas and methods involved in its creation and structure. Normally we think of engineering as the intellectual means by which something is built, or an idea is transformed into practice. In this context, ''reverse engineering'' consists of taking apart and reducing a product or device into its constituent parts and concepts. The idea of reverse engineering is of crucial importance to *trade secret* law. This is because of the rule that any information learned about an item through the process of legitimate reverse engineering is considered to be in the *public domain* and no longer *protectable as a trade secret*.

Example: Ivan creates a machine capable of producing holographic games (games consisting of pictures projected onto three-dimensional space so that the

images and characters appear realistic). Ivan treats the details of production as a trade secret. Once the machine is marketed, however, it will probably be possible to figure out through reverse engineering how it is constructed. If this is done, the machine can be freely manufactured and sold by the party doing the reverse engineering without Ivan being entitled to any court relief on trade secret grounds. Of course, Ivan might still be entitled to some protection under the *patent* 4 or *copyright* 2 laws. Related terms: *Physical devices, ability to maintain as trade secrets*.

reverse FOIA suits   See *Freedom of Information Act, exemption of trade secrets*.

screening incoming information for unsolicited disclosures   When a business establishes procedures to prevent outsiders from volunteering ideas or information to the company. This is done because many companies shun being placed in the position of being accused of stealing someone's ideas. One way to avoid this is to avoid receiving outside suggestions in the first place. Related terms: *unsolicited idea disclosures*.

secrecy, requirement of for trade secret   See *trade secret defined*.

software and trade secrets   A new computer program will almost always qualify for *trade secret* status at least during its development and testing stage. From the time the program is first conceived "information" and "ideas" exist which can give their owner a **competitive edge** so long as they are kept secret.

Once a program is put down on tape, disk or paper in tangible form (i.e., *fixed in a tangible medium of expression* 2), it can still remain a trade secret, but is also protected under the *copyright* 2 laws. When the program is later distributed, these dual protections can continue if certain precautions are taken. For instance, if all "purchasers" of the program are required to sign a *license* 5 forbidding disclosure of trade secrets, both trade secret and copyright protection can be available for distributed copies. Or, if the owner of the program only distributes *object code* (usually the case except for programs written in BASIC)

and keeps the *source code* locked in a secure place, it is similarly possible to maintain both trade secret and copyright protection for the program. If the software owner decides to *register* 2 the program with the *U.S. Copyright Office* 2, *depositing* 2 an object code printout when registering the program may allow the trade secret to be maintained, along with the registered copyright.

Putting a *notice of copyright* 2 on a program does not necessarily affect its trade secret status. Again, if all recipients of a program are required to sign *non-disclosure agreements*, it may be possible to retain the program's trade secret status. However, if the program is actually *published* 2 without restriction, trade secret status will be lost as to any code that a user can figure out through *reverse engineering*.

Example: Harry Hildebrand conceives of a computer program to facilitate copying of information from 8-inch diskettes onto 5-1/4 inch diskettes, regardless of format. Because such a device will probably have great commercial value, the basic ideas behind it will qualify as a trade secret as long as Harry treats them that way. Suppose that Harry decides to press ahead with his idea. First he draws a structured chart containing the main logic flow of the program. Then he writes the actual instructions (called source code if a higher level computer language such as BASIC or Pascal is used) which will enable the machine to take the steps necessary for successful diskette conversion.

Once the source code is written, Harry "loads" it into his computer. The computer processes the code through a "compiler" or "interpreter" both of which translate the source code into a form closer to what the machine can understand. This is called object code. The object code, in turn, is acted on by the computer (perhaps with the help of another program contained in read only memory (ROM) form) to produce the instructions that the computer can now work from. Each of these steps produces information which, separately and together, can properly qualify as a trade secret if it is treated as such.

Once the program is "up and running" on the computer, Harry has others *beta-test* the program to see if it actually works, and whether programming "bugs" need to be corrected. Because Harry still considers the program to be a trade secret, he has the beta-testers sign **non-disclosure agreements** in which they agree to keep the program confidential and preserve its trade-secret status. In addition, because the program is now fixed in tangible form, it is also protected under copyright law without losing trade secret status.

To preserve this copyright status after the program is distributed, Harry places a copyright notice on the program. To preserve its trade secret status, Harry only distributes the program to purchasers willing to sign a license in which they agree to preserve any trade secrets they discover. In addition Harry only distributes the program in object code and keeps his source code locked in his safe. When he registers the program with the copyright office, he deposits the object code. Related terms: **trade secret protection compared with other intellectual property protections**.

source code The specific instructions written by a programmer to tell a computer what to do. Source code is usually written in a computer language such as Fortran, Forth, Pascal, etc., which must then usually be translated by the computer (compiled or interpreted) into a different form known as **object code** or machine language, that can be understood by the computer.

Understanding the difference between source code and object code is crucial in knowing how best to legally protect software. This is because source code is easily understandable by anyone conversant with the programming language being used, while object code, (which in binary form consists of ones and zeros, and in Hexidecimal consists of countless combinations of letters and numbers) can only be understood after a lengthy and difficult **reverse engineering** process (generally termed "decompiling"). Therefore, when **registering** 2 software for copyright protection or distributing programs for use by the public, it is often advisable to use object code, and keep the source code locked up in the company safe. Related terms: **software and trade secrets** and **trade secret protection compared with other intellectual property protection**.

specific performance of covenant not to compete If a former employee, or former owner of a business threatens to violate a contract (covenant) not to compete with the business, a court order may sometimes be obtained that specifically requires the owner or employee to comply with the agreement. Whether or not a court will order **specific performance** of a **covenant not to compete** depends on a number of "fairness" or **equity** 5 factors, such as the length of time competition is prohibited, the effect of the agreement on the employee's ability to make a living, and whether the basic agreement was too broad to begin with. Related terms: **covenant not to compete by employee** and **covenant not to compete by a sold business**.

technological assistance contract A **trade secret** or **know-how** licensing agreement in Japan is usually termed a "technological assistance contract".

technology theft See **theft of trade secrets** and **industrial espionage**.

temporary restraining order An order that can be quickly obtained by the plaintiff in a **trade secret infringement action** (and many other types of cases), with little or sometimes no notice to the defendant. It is designed to place events in a holding pattern (called maintaining the status quo) until the court can more fully determine what kind of protection is required. Typically, temporary restraining orders only last for a few days, or at most, two to three weeks. Related terms: **injunctions in trade secret cases**.

territorial restriction agreements Trade secret **licenses** 5 are sometimes restricted in operation to a particular part of the U.S., and on the international market, are commonly granted separately to different countries or groups of countries. These restrictions allow a trade secret owner to distribute his information or product through a number of different publishing, marketing, or manufacturing enterprises that are regionally strong, rather than through just one national or international operation. For instance the owner of a secret ingredient for a fried chicken batter might issue fifty licenses, each one restricted to a particular state, and then might issue foreign licenses to individual nations or groups of nations,

such as the **European Economic Community** (EEC, or Common Market).

Territorial restrictions in trade secret licenses are also designed to allow the owner of a trade secret to restrict use of the information to areas other than those in which the owner's business is located. In this way the owner hopes to escape competition in his or her area of operation, but still receives the maximum benefit from the trade secret. For example, suppose a New York law book publisher develops a computerized "expert system" for helping people prepare their own divorce cases. If the publisher is only interested in marketing the system in New York state, it might well license the basic program, with its attendant trade secrets, for use in all other states. Related terms: **licensing of trade secrets**.

theft of trade secrets The unauthorized, intentional and **improper acquisition of a trade secret** belonging to another for the purpose of commercially exploiting it one's own interest. Because **trade secrets** are in fact a type of valuable property, the criminal law in an increasing number of states authorizes criminal prosecution for their theft. Although these laws differ from state to state, the typical law applies to anybody who, with a wrongful intent, 1) physically takes records or articles reflecting the trade secret, 2) copies or photographs such records or articles, 3) assists in either of these acts, or 4) discloses the trade secret to another after having received knowledge of the secret in the course of a **confidential employment relationship**. In other words, intentionally helping in any way to deprive a business of its trade secrets may be a criminal offense.

Example: Alice Engineer is hired by LaserDisk, Inc. to design a home laser disk unit. Necessarily, as part of her work, Alice is informed of certain Laserdisk trade secrets relevant to her design work. About a year later, Alice becomes unhappy with her employment and takes a much better job at a competing company. In exchange for this job, she discloses Laser Disk's trade secrets to the new company. Because Alice learned of the trade secrets in the course of a trust relationship at LaserDisk (a relationship usually considered to exist between highly skilled employees and their

employer), she may be criminally prosecuted if the state in question has a trade secret theft law. In every state, Alice could be sued civilly in a **trade secret infringement action**. Related terms: **trade secret infringement Action** and **confidential employment relationship**.

Japan takes a different attitude toward trade secret theft. At times seeming to view industrial espionage as a strong form of loyalty towards one's own company, the Japanese legal system does not engage in criminal prosecution for this activity. Related terms: **Institute of Industrial Protection**.

tools as trade secrets See **physical devices and trade secrets**.

tour de main A French term for know-how. See **know-how as trade secret**.

trade secret defined In most states, a trade secret may consist of any **formula**, **pattern**, **physical device**, **idea**, **process**, **compilation of information** or other information 1) that provides a business with a **competitive advantage** and 2) that is treated in a way that can reasonably be expected to prevent the public or competitors from learning about it, absent **improper acquisition** or **theft**.

When deciding whether information qualifies as a trade secret under this definition, courts will typically consider the following factors:

- the extent to which the information is known outside of the particular business entity

- the extent to which it is known by employees and others involved in the business

- the extent to which measures have been taken to guard the secrecy of the information

- the value of the information to the business

- the difficulty with which the information could be properly acquired or independently duplicated by others

As should now be evident, there is no crisp and definite meaning of trade secret. A trade secret is created and defined solely by reference to how information is handled, and to the value inherent in keeping it secret. Even if an item or piece of information otherwise qualifies as a trade secret, its moment-to- moment status will depend on how it is treated.

trade secret, exception to FOIA See *Freedom of Information Act and trade secrets*.

trade secret infringement action A lawsuit brought by the owner of a *trade secret* for the purpose of 1) preventing another person or business from using the trade secret without proper authorization, and 2) collecting damages for the economic injury suffered as a result of the trade secret's *improper acquisition* and use. All persons responsible for the improper acquisition, and all those who have benefited from such acquisition, are typically named as defendants in infringement actions.

Among the most common situations that give rise to infringement actions are:

- a *theft of trade secrets* occuring through *industrial espionage*, or
- an employee having knowledge of a trade secret changes employment and discloses the secret to her new employer in violation of an express or implied *confidentiality agreement* , or
- *improper disclosure of trade secrets* made in violation of a *non-disclosure agreement*

To prevail in an infringement suit, the plaintiff (person bringing the suit) must be able to show that the information alleged to be a trade secret:

- provides the plaintiff with a competitive advantage
- has been continually treated by the plaintiff as a trade secret, and
- was either *improperly acquired* by the defendant (if accused of making commercial use of the secret) or *improperly disclosed* by the defendant (if accused of leaking the information in the first place)

The defendants in trade secret infringement cases commonly attempt to rebut the plaintiff's case by proving that:

- the information claimed to be a trade secret was widely known in the industry, and thus not a trade secret, or
- the information was lawfully disclosed by a person having knowledge of it, or

- the information was lawfully acquired through *reverse engineering*, or
- the information was the result of an *independent conception*, or
- the trade secret was being used by its owner in violation of the *anti-trust laws*

If the plaintiff is able to establish that a trade secret was, in fact, improperly used, disclosed, or acquired by a defendant, the court can enjoin its further commercial use. Sometimes such *injunctions* are permanent (i.e., are final court orders in the case). More commonly, the courts will employ the *head start rule*. This operates to give the rightful owner of the trade secret a "head start" in commercially exploiting it, by prohibiting its use by the competitor for such period of time as it would have taken the competitor independently to develop the information.

Because court cases tend to drag on for years, courts are authorized to issue *preliminary injunctions* prohibiting the competitor from using the secret in question pending a final determination in the case. These preliminary orders are often viewed by the parties as harbingers of how the case will finally turn out, and accordingly lead to settlement in advance of trial in the majority of trade secret cases. Related terms: *injunctions in trade secret cases*.

In addition to injunctive relief (both provisional and final), a court may award *damages* suffered by the original *trade secret owner*. These can consist of lost profits resulting from sales by the trade secret infringer, profits realized by the infringer from the wrongfully acquired trade secret, and, occasionally, *punitive damages* or treble damages, depending on the state where the action is being tried. Related terms: *damages in trade secret infringement actions*.

trade secret owner Ownership of a trade secret is usually determined by the circumstances of its creation. For example, one common type of trade secret arises from research and development activities conducted by manufacturing concerns (e.g., Bell Laboratories). In this instance, the company sponsoring the research and development is the owner of any trade secrets produced by that activity. Another typical trade secret is a retail customer list, which would belong to the business or individual who compiled the list.

Generally speaking, any trade secret developed by an employee in the course of employment belongs to the employer rather than the employee. However, trade secrets developed by employees on their own time, and with their own equipment, can sometimes belong to the employees. For example, suppose a chef develops a special recipe and baking process for cheesecake in her off-work hours, and in her own kitchen. Even though she bakes the cheesecake for the restaurant, she would probably be entitled to preserve the recipe and process as her own trade secret.

If, on the other hand, the recipe and process were developed at work with the restaurant facilities, the restaurant would own the trade secret.

What does it mean to own a trade secret? Simply, that the owner has a right to seek relief in court in the event someone else *improperly acquires* or *improperly discloses* the trade secret. Also, the trade secret owner is entitled to grant others a *license* 5 to utilize the secret.

trade secret protection compared with other intellectual property protection

Trade secret law is only one of several legal ways to reap the full commercial benefit of *intellectual property* 5 by protecting it against unauthorized use and exploitation. The other principal protections are national and international *copyright* 2, *trademark* 3, and *patent* 4 laws.

In the United States, trade secret law consists mostly of a series of state court decisions that extend protection to trade secrets in a variety of contexts. United States copyright and patent laws, on the other hand, are required by the U.S. Constitution, and are embodied exclusively in federal statutes passed by Congress. Trademarks are protected under both federal and state laws that prohibit trademark infringement and *unfair competition* 3.

There are no broad international agreements or treaties protecting trade secrets. However, several major international treaties provide reciprocal copyright protection to the nationals and works of most countries. Related terms: *Universal Copyright Convention* 2, *Berne Convention* 2, and *Buenos Aires Convention* 2. Patent protection is broadly recognized under the *Paris Convention* 4 and the

Patent Cooperation Treaty 4. Trademarks are also given broad international protection under the *Paris Convention* 3.

Which form of intellectual property protection is best? This depends, of course, on the item to be protected and the context in which protection is needed. Also, in many instances, more than one of these protections is available for any one item. In other words, they overlap. Let's look at how to approach the problem of choosing the best, or best combination, of intellectual property protections.

First, any item or information susceptible to either copyright or patent protection is also potentially a trade secret. So, from the time the "lightbulb" first goes on in someone's head, the potential for a trade secret exists. Whether it exists in fact primarily depends on 1) whether the idea might afford its creator some *competitive advantage* and 2) whether it is treated as a secret. This principle does not work in reverse, however. An item may qualify as a trade secret, but not be patentable or entitled to copyright protection. Related terms: *statutory subject matter* 4 and *copyrightable materials* 2.

Example: John discovers that by making a simple modification in an existing copyrighted word-processing program belonging to someone else, he can speed up its operation by 50%. This idea by itself might qualify as a trade secret in that John may be able to utilize his version of the program to operate a word-processing business, or might sell the idea to the copyright owner of the pre-existing program. However, John can neither copyright his idea (since it's simply a minor modification of an existing copyrighted work) nor patent it (because as a stand-alone *algorithm* , and for other reasons, it probably won't qualify).

During the development stage of any idea, all expressions and manifestations of the idea can continue to enjoy trade secret status if the primary conditions for such status are maintained (i.e. confidentiality and some competitive advantage). It is only when the developer actually produces a finished product, whether it's a machine, a painting, a book, or a drawing and description of a new invention, that a decision must be made about further protection.

As a rule, the ultimate product will

either qualify as being patentable or copyrightable, but not both, although there is at least one point of intersection where this becomes confused. Thus, **design patents** 4 and copyright protection for graphic and pictorial representations may both apply to the same device. Also, some computer programs may be both patentable and protectable by copyright. Generally, however, expressions of ideas fixed in tangible media are subject to copyright protection, while things qualifying as inventions (e.g., devices, processes, compositions, products) will be protected by patent.

A work is protected by copyright the moment it becomes **fixed in a tangible medium of expression** 2. However, whether this copyright will endure depends on whether the copyright owner places a proper notice on his or her work when it is published. Also, in the United States, timely **registration** 2 with the **Copyright office** 2 affords considerable additional protection.

Because an item automatically acquires copyright status upon its creation, rather than when it's first published, there is usually a substantial period during which both trade secret and copyright protection apply (i.e., between creation and distribution). This is because a work is usually modified, edited, and polished for some time after it is first "fixed" but before it is ''distributed''. As long as it is maintained as a secret during this period, the work enjoys both trade secret and copyright protection.

Once distributed, however, a work will usually no longer qualify as a trade secret. There are a number of important exceptions to this rule, however. In the case of software, there are often two different forms of expression for each program — the **source code** and the **object code**. It is possible to distribute the object code of a particular program and even register it with the copyright office, and yet maintain the ideas in the program as a trade secret if each person receiving the work is required to sign a license restricting disclosure of the secrets, or the program is made secure against **reverse engineering**. This generally will not work if an item is offered for sale to the world at large, but may be possible if a program is distributed to end users under a restrictive license.

It is also possible to **prosecute a**

patent application 4 while maintaining the trade secret status of an **invention**. This is because **patent applications** 4 are kept secret unless or until a patent is granted. However, once a patent is granted and an **issue fee** paid, trade secret status is lost, dut to the full disclosure of the ideas underlying the invention in the patent application.

Even if a patent is granted, a subsequent challenge to the patent may cause it to be invalidated. In such a case, the item's trade secret status cannot be revived, and the owner will have lost all protection. For this reason, some inventors, especially in the rapidly changing computer field, prefer to protect their inventions as trade secrets, and forego patent protection altogether. (See chart next page.)

trade secrets and anti-trust laws See *anti-trust law and trade secrets*.

tying arrangements Requiring customers to purchase certain products as a condition to their obtaining other products, even though they would not, otherwise, purchase the additional goods from that seller. Tying arrangements usually occur when a seller has sufficient economic power, or a sufficiently unique and useful product, to enforce its conditions on the customers. This practice can be considered a violation of anti-trust law, as an impermissible "restraint on trade", except when a trade secret is involved and the "tying" is necessitated by an overriding business reason, and not designed to secure competitive advantage. For instance, when quality control requires that all related goods come from the same source (e.g., all Hot Dog Harry's franchises must purchase their supplies from the central company), no anti-trust law is violated. On the other hand, when a computer manufacturer of both hardware and software required customers to buy its hardware as a condition of purchasing its software, it was held to have engaged in an illegal "tying arrangement". Related terms: *anti-trust law and trade secrets*.

unique ideas as trade secrets See *ideas as trade secrets*.

Trade Secret

Trade Secret Compared With Other Intellectual Property Protections

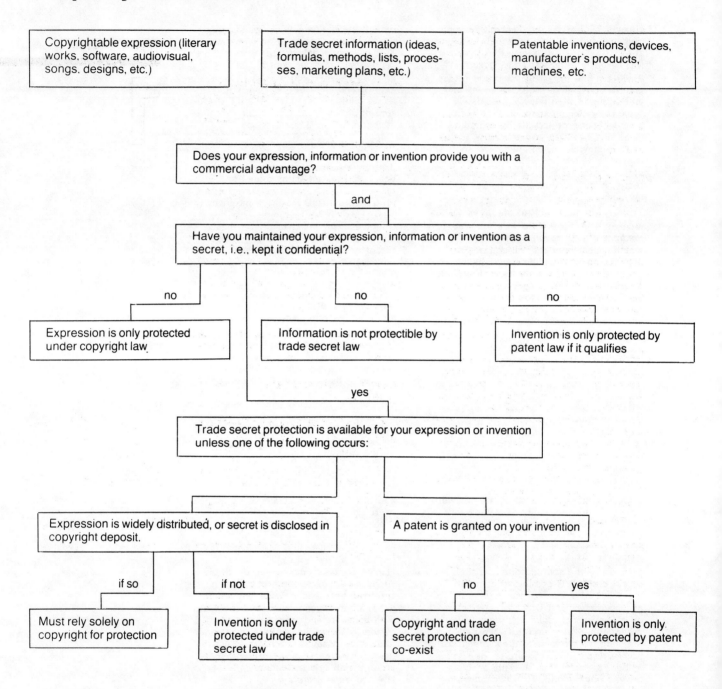

Uniform Trade Secret Protection Act

A model statute prepared for the ultimate purpose of creating the same trade secret laws in all fifty states. At present, only California and perhaps a few other states have adopted it. Overall, the provisions of this model legislation are consistent with the general principles of trade secret law adopted by the courts under the common law. Related terms: *trade secret defined*.

unjust enrichment and trade secrets

When faced with cases involving the *improper acquisition of a trade secret*, some courts have ordered the guilty party to pay the *trade secret owner* all profits earned from the trade secret in question. The legal theory underlying this type of relief is that, without it, the wrongful possessor would be unjustly enriched. The unjust enrichment theory has been used also as grounds for extending judicial protection to the trade secret in the first place. Related terms: *trade secret infringement action*.

unsolicited idea disclosure

The communication of an innovative idea to others without their requesting it, generally for the purpose of enlisting the aid of the other parties to commercially develop or promote the idea. Although a person may have many bright ideas, they usually must be discussed with others if they are ever to be put into practice. It is therefore common for an "idea" person to approach a well known company to see if it is "interested" in commercially exploiting the idea.

This can (and often does) present a problem for the company. For example, the idea may be close to an idea the company already has or is developing, and the company may not be interested in the version being presented. However, if the disclosure is made, and the company later markets a product that appears to incorporate the idea, the "idea" person can accuse the company of trade secret theft. Then, the company, even though innocent, can be forced into an expensive lawsuit. For this reason, companies routinely require people who present an "unsolicited idea" to sign agreements waiving all rights to sue for *infringement of trade secret*. If the idea person does not want to sign the agreement, the secret will not be examined. In fact, companies often go to great lengths to make sure the idea person does not get past the front door, absent the signing of an agreement.

utility model substitute for trade secret protection in Japan

In addition to standard *patent* 4 protection, Japanese law offers statutory protection for minor inventions in the form of a *utility model*. Minor inventions are those that may not meet the *novelty* 4 or *non-obviousness* 4 requirement for a regular patent, but that may consist of improvements in, or revisions of, existing technology or other developments considered deserving of some protection.

Because trade secret protection is not as well developed in Japan as it is in other countries, the utility model doctrine sometimes provides an attractive protective option for items that are not fully patentable, and that might not be protected as a trade secret in that country.

waiver agreement for unsolicited idea disclosures

See *unsolicited idea disclosures*.

wholesale customer lists

See *customer lists*.

World Intellectual Property Organization (WIPO)

This organization was formed to facilitate international agreements regulating intellectual property. WIPO's membership consists of representatives from countries (and groups of countries) including 1) most European countries, 2) UNESCO, 3) Japan and 4) the United States. WIPO is a policy-making body only, with no delegated authority to make binding decisions or impose sanctions.

One proposed treaty currently before WIPO would allow software to be accorded trade secret status, and would allow its creators to fix by contract the conditions for disclosure and use of the software. The treaty would specifically require its members' courts to entertain a cause of action (i.e., legal complaint) for infringement of a trade secret.

wrongfully acquiring trade secrets

See *improper acquisition of trade secrets*.

wrongfully disclosing trade secrets

See *improper disclosure of trade secrets*.

Research Notes

This note assumes that you wish to delve deeper into the topics defined in this part of the dictionary. Instead of just providing you with a bibliography, we want to suggest a general research strategy. First, find some simplified background resources (often published as ''self-help'' law books) to obtain a general overview of your subject. Some of these are listed in **Step #1** below. Then consult more intensive background materials (listed in **Step #2**). These will go into greater detail and will also usually provide you with references (citations) to the primary law itself (**Step #3**). Finally, use *Legal Research: How to Find and Understand the Law* by Stephen Elias, Nolo Press, or another basic legal research guide, to assist you in using the law library and understanding the law you find there.

Step #1: Basic Background Resources

Legal Protection for Software by Dan Remer, Nolo Press contains an excellent summary of basic trade secret concepts, especially in the computer software context. Other basic background resources are *Who Owns What is in your Head* by Stanley H. Lieberstein, Hawthorn Books and *Trade Secrets* by James Pooley, published by Osborn/McGraw Hill.

Step #2: Intensive Background Resources

There is no national trade secret law. Instead, trade secret law is determined by the legislature or courts of each state and trade secret protection is obtained primarily in the state courts. Although some states now have statutes governing what trade secrets are, and how they can be inforced, (Arkansas, California, Kansas, Louisiana, Minnesota, North Carolina, Utah, Ohio, and Washington, and perhaps a few other states) trade secret law in most states is governed by the court decisions applying ''common law' principles that have developed over the past hundred years or so. Accordingly, except in the states mentioned above, in order to find out what the law is, your ultimate research mission will primarily be to find one or more state court cases that fit your situation. The following intensive background resources can be used to this end.

Milgram on Trade Secrets , a comprehensive treatment of trade secret law published by Mathew Bender as volume 12 of its *Business Organizations* series, is probably the most complete resource regarding trade-secret related issues, especially if you have a specific and/or detailed question. This is an especially valuable resource if you desire to locate primary resource materials, especially court opinions.

Trade Secret Law Handbook by Melvin F. Jager, published by Clark Boardman, contains mini-discussions of most trade-secret related concepts, a number of sample agreements and licenses, and references to cases and statutes where appropriate. This publication also contains the text of the Uniform Trade Secrets Act, a piece of model legislation tailored by the National Conference of Commissioners on Uniform State Laws, which has been adopted in the states listed above and is pending approval in 9 other states. Also contained in this book are appendices on state laws governing covenants not to compete and who owns employee inventions.

Some discussion of trade secrets can be found in *American Jurisrpudence, Second Series (AmJur.2d)* under the index headings "Property", and "unfair trade practices".

Law review articles: Especially in regard to recent Trade secret developments regarding as computer software protection and protection of semi-conductor chips, often the best sources of information are articles appearing in scholarly journals called ' 'law reviews''. By looking under "Trade Secret" in the *Index to Legal Periodicals* or *Current Law Index*, you will find frequent references to articles on current topics of interest. These references refer you to law reviews. A key to the abbreviations used is located at the front of the index volume you are using. Law libraries always store law review publications alphabetically in one particular location. The reference librarian can help here.

Step #3: Access Primary Source Materials

For direct access to summaries of cases involving trade secret principles consult the West Publishing Company state or regional digests under "Trade Regulation", "Contracts", "Agency", and "Master-Servant".

For direct access to state statutes governing trade secrets, use the term "Trade Secret", "Proprietary information", or "Commercial Secret" in the index accompanying the statutes of the state in question.

Introduction

This section defines the words and phrases commonly used to describe when and how authors and owners of **original works of expression** can protect these works from being used or altered by others without permission. This subject is generally known as "copyright law". The U.S. Constitution requires that **original works of authorship** be protected by copyright. The exclusive source of this protection is found under the federal copyright statutes. For all works published prior to 1978, the controlling law is the Copyright Act of 1909. All works published after January 1, 1978 are subject to the Copyright Act of 1976.

The Copyright laws protect the form a particular expression takes, not the ideas being expressed. Thus, a copyright protects a particular song, novel or computer game about a romance in space, and not the idea of having a love affair among the stars.

Most types of expression qualify for copyright protection the moment they are created and **fixed in a tangible medium of expression**. This is true even though a work is unpublished. After **publication**, a proper **copyright notice** must be placed on the work for copyright protection to continue in the U.S. Other countries do not require any notice at all.

Additional copyright law protections, which become relevant in the event the courts are used to protect a copyright, can be gained in the U.S. by **registering** the work with the **U.S. Copyright Office**.

Most copyrights last for the life of an author plus fifty years. However, if the work belongs to an employer of the author, or has been commissioned under a **work made for hire** contract agreement, or the author publishes and registers under a pseudonym, or anonymously, the copyright will last between seventy-five to hundred years.

The author (or composer, artist, photographer, programmer, sculptor, etc.) is considered the **owner of the copyright** unless the work was created in the employment context or a work made for hire. In either of these situations the employer/commissioner of the work made for hire is considered the owner. All or part of a copyright may be **transferred** to others by the owner. When all rights are transferred unconditionally, it is generally termed an **assignment**. When only some of the rights associated with the copyright are transferred, it is termed a **license**.

Regardless of the type of copyright transfer, the author or other original copyright owner is entitled to **terminate** it after thirty five years from the date of the transfer. This means that an original copyright owner can recapture ownership of the copyright.

In the event a person infringes (violates) the **exclusive rights of a copyright owner**, the courts will issue temporary restraining orders, preliminary injunctions, and permanent injunctions to prevent further violations, award **money damages** if appropriate, and in some circumstances award **attorneys fees**.

Copyright protection rules are fairly similar worldwide, due to several international treaties, the most important of which are the **Universal Copyright Convention** and the **Berne Copyright Convention**. The U.S. is a member of the Universal Copyright Convention. Therefore, both U.S. authors (composers, artists, etc.) and works first published in the U.S. are entitled to full copyright protection in the other U.C.C. member countries (most nations).

Definitions

abridgment of works An alteration of a *work of authorship* that results in a significant portion being changed or left out. Related terms: *derivative works*.

actual damages for copyright infringement The actual dollars and cents loss suffered by a *copyright owner* as a result of his or her copyrighted work being distributed, copied, displayed, performed, or altered by someone else without proper authorization. Related terms: *damages for copyright infringement* and *copyright infringement*.

adaptations or alterations of original works See *derivative works*.

All Rights Reserved A phrase used to obtain copyright protection for works published in countries covered by the *Buenos Aires Convention*. Related terms: *Buenos Aires Convention*.

anthologies, copyrightability of See *compilations of unoriginal or original material*.

Apple v. Franklin case An influential 1983 United States Federal Court of Appeals decision in which the court ruled that computer *operating systems* consisting of *object code* embedded in *read-only memory chips (ROMs)* qualify for copyright protection. *Apple Computer, Inc. v. Franklin Computer Corporation*, (3rd Cir. 1983) 714 F.2d 1240. This case arose when Franklin Computer Co. mar-

keted a computer that was able to use software written for the Apple Computer (i.e., Apple compatible). This was accomplished by copying the ROM chip that Apple used as an operating system for its Apple II line of computers. Because the Franklin Computers had the same operating system as the Apple, they could also use the same software. In short, by copying the Apple operating system, Franklin was able to compete directly with Apple in the sale of computers.

Apple sued Franklin for copyright infringement on the ground that the operating system contained in the Apple ROM was protected by copyright. Franklin defended on the ground that neither object code nor operating systems could be protected by copyright, especially when embedded in a ROM. The court ruled in favor of Apple, deciding that an operating system consisting of object code qualifies as "software" under the Copyright Act, whether it is embedded in a chip or simply maintained as code on a disk or tape.

Since this case, there is substantial agreement among experts that object code in the United States is now considered a work of expression protectable under the *Copyright Act of 1976*. This same approach has been followed by courts in Australia and Japan. Related terms: *registration of copyright* and *software and copyright*.

archival copies A term used in the
U.S. *Software Protection Act of 1980* for
copies of software made by a software
owner strictly for back up purposes (i.e.,
in case something happens to the original
copy). Under this act, a software owner
(i.e., most retail purchasers of computer
software and anyone else who buys the
software outright) is entitled to make
archival copies as long as the copies are
either retained by the owner or sold to
the new owner, along with the original
software.

Example: Ned Applequist goes down to
his local computer software outlet and
pays $49.95 for WordScan, a spelling
checker. Ned is now considered the
owner of this one copy of WordScan, and
under the Software Protection Act, Ned
can now make archival copies. However,
if Ned transfers ownership of the original
disk to Karen Goodperson for $20.00 he
must either destroy any archival copies
that have been made,or give them to the
purchaser (Karen) as part of the sale.
Simply put, two or more people cannot
legally possess copies of a program that
has only been purchased once.

There is some dispute over whether a
software purchaser actually owns the
program when the software package has
been distributed under a license rather
than by outright sale. To the extent that a
program isn't owned, the archival copy
provision of the copyright act doesn't
apply. Related terms: *shrink-wrapped
licenses*.

arrangements, musical See *musical
arrangements, copyrightability of*.

assignment of copyright A type of
contract 5 under which ownership of one
or more of the *bundle of rights* making
up a *copyright* is transferred outright to a
new owner. For example, a book author
might assign her exclusive right to reproduce, distribute, and display her works to
her publisher, while retaining the exclusive right to prepare *derivative works* . In
this instance, the publisher will have a
free hand in marketing the book, while
the author will retain control over the
right to change or adapt the book for
other versions, translations, and media
(e.g., movies, video).

Generally, assignments of copyright
rights involve transfers of ownership
without any restrictions as to time, place,

or manner of use. This concept should be
compared with *licenses* 5, which typically impose one or more conditions on
the *licensee* 5. Related terms: *transfer of
copyright ownership* and *assignments* 5.

**attorneys fees in infringement
actions** See *infringement actions*.

audiovisual works To quote the U.S.
Copyright Act of 1976, "audio visual
works" are "works that consist of a series
of related images which are intrinsically
intended to be shown by the use of
machines or devices such as projectors,
viewers, or electronic equipment, together
with accompanying sounds, if any,
regardless of the nature of the material
objects, such as films or tapes, in which
the works are embodied" (17 U.S.C.A.
section 101). Movies, videotapes,
videodisks, training films, and computer
games are among the products considered
as audiovisual works under the Copyright
Act of 1976.

Audiovisual works are but one of several categories established by the Copyright Act for the purpose of classifying
original works of expression. Although it
is not necessary to place a work of
expression in any particular category for it
to be protected under the copyright laws,
such categorization is required if *registration* of the work with the *U.S. Copyright
Office* is desired. Related terms: *registration of copyright*.

author as owner of copyright When
a work is first created, its *author* is automatically considered the owner of the
copyright, with one major exception. This
is when an author assigns all of his or
her copyright ownership rights to another
party prior to the work being created.
Typically, this occurs when a publisher
agrees to publish a work as yet uncreat-
ed, in exchange for the pre-transfer of all
copyright rights. In this situation, the
publisher, rather than the author, is the
owner of the copyright upon creation of
the work.

Under the *Copyright Act of 1976*, the
"author" is defined as 1) the person
actually creating the work, or 2) the
employer, if the work is prepared by an
employee acting within the scope of his
or her employment, or 3) the party com-
missioning a *work made for hire*.

Ownership of a copyright means that

the "author" enjoys the sole right to reproduce (i.e., make copies of), display, distribute, and prepare **derivative works** from the **original work of authorship** and to prevent others from doing so without his or her permission.

This copyright ownership can in fact be divided among many parties, even though the author remains as the "copyright owner". When this occurs, the term "copyright owner" takes on two different meanings. It applies both to the author (or to any party that owns all of the rights associated with the copyright), and to owners of individual copyright rights. Transfer of copyright ownership must be accomplished through written documents termed **exclusive licenses** or **assignments** 5.

Example: Vixen Publications might purchase the entire copyright in Andrew Fox's book "RED" before it is written, in exchange for an advance against royalties of 12% of the retail price of each hard cover book sold and 8% of the cover price of paperbacks. Vixen would then be the copyright owner. Vixen might then transfer parts of its copyright ownership to a number of others. This might include licensing 1) foreign language rights to publishers in several European countries, 2) movie rights to a film producer and 3) video game rights to a video game maker. There would also be termed "copyright owner" if the transfer were in writing. Related terms: **transfers of copyright ownership** and **author defined** .

author defined   The term "author" refers to the originator of any original work of expression that is entitled to protection under the copyright laws. The "author" of a work is either:

● the person who creates it, or

● the person or business who pays another to create it in the employment context, or

● the person or business that commissions the work under a valid **work made for hire** contract

For copyright purposes, a songwriter authors the song, a movie producer authors the movie, a computer programmer authors the program and the toy designer authors the toy (unique toy designs unrelated to their function are protectable by copyright), unless the creator is not independent but has created the work in an employment relationship,

or under a "work made for hire" contract. If this is the situation the person paying for the work is the author. Related terms: **author as owner of copyright**.

back-up copies of program   See **archival copies**.

based on   When one **original work of authorship** has heavily relied upon an earlier one for its content and expression, it is said to be "based on" the earlier work. For example, a foreign language translation of a book is based on the book as it was originally written; a movie that borrows the main characters, the storyline, and some dialogue from a book is based on that book, and a song that has substantially the same melody as an earlier song is based on that song, even if the words are different.

For works covered by the **Copyright Act of 1909** , a **copyright owner** has an exclusive right to prepare works "based on " the original work. Under the **Copyright Act of 1976**, a work is considered to be a **derivative work** when it is based on another. Although the author initially owns the exclusive right to prepare derivative works, this right can be transferred to others. Related terms: **derivative work**.

Berne Convention   An international treaty that provides a means for reciprocal copyright protection in each of the countries signing it. Under this treaty, **original works of authorship** are automatically entitled to protection in all signatory countries, upon their initial **publication** in any one country. No **notice of copyright** is required for protection under this treaty. In addition, each member country has agreed to protect the **moral rights** of the author (generally, the right to proclaim or disclaim authorship and the right to protect the reputation of the work) and to extend copyright protection for at least the life of the author plus fifty years.

Each member country extends these protections to the nationals of all other member countries and to works first published in such countries. Thus, even though the U.S. is not a member of the Berne Convention, it is possible for a U.S. author to obtain Berne Convention protection by **simultaneous publication** in a Berne Convention country.

Many countries are members of both the Berne Convention and another more important major international copyright treaty called the *Universal Copyright Convention*. To the extent the provisions of these two treaties overlap, the author is entitled to the most liberal protection available. Related terms: *international copyright protection*.

best edition of a work If the author (or other copyright owner) chooses to *register* a work with the *U.S. Copyright Office*, the "best edition" must be included with the application as a *deposit*. Additionally, with some exceptions, if the work is not registered for copyright purposes, the best edition of a work must be deposited by its author (or other original owner) with the Library of Congress.

Congress has defined "best edition of a work" as "the edition, published in the United States at any time before the date of deposit, that the Library of Congress determines to be most suitable for its purposes" (17 U.S.C. section 101). The U.S. Copyright Office has regulations governing what it considers to be the best version of a work for different types of deposits. These are found in Title 37 of the Code of Federal Regulations (CFR). Related terms: *deposits with the U.S. Copyright Office*.

box-top licenses See *shrink-wrapped licenses*.

Buenos Aires Convention An international treaty between the United States and sixteen South and Central American Countries, which provides a means for reciprocal copyright protection in the signatory countries. Under this convention (treaty), each signatory country will afford copyright protection to any work produced by a citizen or permanent resident of any other signatory country, assuming that the work has a copyright notice on it in the following form:

All Rights Reserved

Because all but three of the countries signing the "Buenos Aires Convention" (Uruguay, Honduras and Bolivia) have also signed the *Universal Copyright Convention* (U.C.C.), the requirements of which have become the international standard, the Buenos Aires Convention is not of great importance. In other words, the U.C.C., which provides reciprocal

protection for any work with the following notice: © (Year of publication) (Author's Name) provides parallel copyright protection in 14 of the 17 Buenos Aires countries. To gain protection in Uruguay, Honduras and Bolivia as well, many copyright owners include both notices as follows:

© (year of publication) (author's name). All Rights Reserved.

For this book this would be:

© 1985 Stephen R. Elias. All Rights Reserved.

Related terms: *international copyright protection*.

bundle of rights The different rights belonging to an *author* of a work or expression which, taken together, are referred to as a *copyright*. Briefly, these are the exclusive rights to reproduce (copy), distribute, display, perform, and prepare *derivative works* from, the protected work. Related terms: *copyright*.

certificate of registration When the *U.S. Copyright Office* approves a copyright application for registration, they mail the author (or other owner) a "certificate" that consists simply of the copyright application stamped with a copyright registration number, the registration date, and the copyright office seal at the top. Registration is required before an owner can bring a copyright *infringement action*, and the certificate will serve as evidence in court that the copyright is valid, and that the statements in the certificate (e.g., the year the work was created, the fact of authorship, whether other works are incorporated in the work being copyrighted, etc.) are true. Related terms: *infringement action*.

charts, copyrightability of See *flow-charts*.

chips and chip masks See *Semiconductor Chip Protection Act of 1984*.

co-authors See *joint works*.

collective work In the words of the U.S. Copyright Act of 1976, " [a] collective work is a work such as a periodical issue, anthology, or encyclopedia, in which a number of contributions consti-

- A SLICE FOR JAPAN?

YES PLEASE, A BIT.

A GULP FOR ME.

YOUR RIGHT TO DIVIDE YOUR COPYRIGHT

tuting separate and independent works in themselves, are assembled into a collective whole" (17 U.S.C. section 101). Generally, to make a collective work, permission must be obtained from the owners of the copyrights on the constituent parts. But, assuming this is done, the overall collection of such independent works is itself subject to independent copyright protection by the person or entity creating the collection. Related terms: *compilation of original or unoriginal material*.

comment, fair use   See *fair use*.

common law copyright laws   A set of legal principles pertaining to copyright developed by the English courts over several hundred years. Until January 1978, these common law rules were still used by the American Courts (primarily for unpublished works), in addition to the rules set out in the *Copyright Act of 1909*, to determine whether a copyright existed, and the extent to which a *work of authorship* should receive legal protection. In other words, even if a copyright owner did not follow the rules set down in the U.S. *Copyright Act of 1909*, the work might still qualify for some copyright protection (especially for unpublished works) by invoking common-law copyright rights.

Effective January 1, 1978, however, the U.S. Congress prohibited any further use of these "common law" copyright principles. Instead, the *Copyright Act of 1976* is now the exclusive source of copyright law in the United States, at least in respect to any work of authorship first published after January 1, 1978. Related terms: *Copyright Act of 1976*.

compilations of original or unoriginal material   According to the U.S. Copyright Act, "[a] compilation is a work formed by the collection and assembling of preexisting materials or of data that are selected, coordinated, or arranged in such a way that the resulting work as a whole constitutes an *original work of authorship*. The term "compilation" includes collective works" (17 U.S.C. section 101). A compilation or collective work is entitled to copyright protection even if the individual parts are in the *public domain* (i.e., can be used by anyone) or are subject to another creator's copyright. How-

ever, in the latter case it would be necessary to obtain permission from these other *copyright owners* in order to use the copyrighted portions.

Example: Suppose Harry wants to make and market a record of five songs that were written and performed by local folk musicians. Assuming these individual songs are subject to copyright protection (i.e., their composers own the exclusive right to reproduce, perform, copy and distribute the songs), Harry would have to get the composers' permission to include the songs on the album. Otherwise Harry would be infringing the composers' copyright. This would traditionally be accomplished by means of a contract called a *license*, which would provide royalties to each composer for each record sold. Harry, however, would own the copyright in the overall record and would have full authority to authorize the copying and distribution of the record without regard to the wishes of the individual composers (unless their license contract reserved to them such authority). Other examples of compilations are *databases* (collections of information arranged in a unique way to facilitate updating and retrieval), *anthologies*, and *collective works*.

compulsory license   An arrangement under which the owner of an *exclusive copyright right* is required by the law to grant a person a *non-exclusive license* to exercise that right. Generally, compulsory licenses are not required in the U.S. That is, a copyright owner has the right to "sit on" her *work of authorship* and not let it see the light of day. However, there is one basic statutory exception to this rule. Under the *Copyright Act of 1976*, once a non-dramatic musical composition has been recorded and distributed to the public, any person or group is entitled to record the music for the purpose of distributing such recording to the general public for its private use. If the owner of the *copyright* in the music refuses to grant to such other person or group a *license* 5 on a voluntary basis, the *Copyright Act of 1976* provides that such license shall be granted involuntarily, for a fee set by statute.

Example: Suppose Fenona and the Ferraros, a punk rock group, obtains a license from composer Lou Riveter to record his song "Up the Stars". The record is released to the public and does quite well. If Barry and the Bushmen decide they also want to record "Up the Stars" for distribution to the public for private use (i.e., not just to Muzak or to a radio station, merely for public playing) Riveter must either voluntarily grant them a license, or he will be forced to grant a compulsory license under the terms of the Copyright Act of 1976.

Under the terms of a compulsory license, the *licensee* is permitted to make a new *arrangement* of the composition as long as the basic melody or fundamental character of the work is not altered. But the new arrangement is not entitled to separate *copyright protection* unless the original *copyright owner* gives permission.

Example: Sammy Silvertoes composes a tender country and western ballad, and licenses famous country singer Justine Carbo to record it. Later, Pauline and the Pukies, a neo-punk musical group, obtains a compulsory license to record the song. At least to Sammy's ear, they turn it into an unrecognizable mess. Sammy can revoke the license and prevent the recording from being further distributed or played. Of course, since musical tastes differ, a disagreement over this issue may result. In that event, the matter is either settled in court (as with any other contract dispute), or, increasingly, in arbitration.

Suppose, now, that instead of mangling the ballad, a new group performs an arrangement that preserves the ballad's basic melody and character, and that becomes a smash hit. Despite the creativity that went into the new arrangement, the group has no right to obtain a *copyright* on it unless permission is obtained from Sammy Silvertoes. In such a situation, however, it is likely that Sammy would agree to the arrangement's being copyrighted, in exchange for a portion of royalties earned on it.

The *Copyright Act of 1909* also provided for *compulsory licenses* (called a "compulsory mechanical license"), under somewhat different circumstances, in respect to songs first published prior to January 1, 1978.

Although not usually termed a "compulsory license", in some copyright *infringement actions* a court may order a *copyright owner* to grant a license to an

innocent infringer instead of ordering the infringement stopped.

Example: Suppose that Willie reasonably assumes a particular tune to be in the *public domain*, and uses it in his new song. After the song is recorded and selling well, Willie is sued by Carol, who claims copyright ownership in the tune. Even if the court finds that Carol does own a copyright in the tune, the court can require Carol to grant Willie a "compulsory" license to use the tune in exchange for reasonable royalties. Related terms: *innocent infringement of copyright*.

Finally, under a provision of the *Universal Copyright Convention*, to which the U.S. subscribes, an author may be required by a signatory country to grant a compulsory license for the purpose of having his or her work of expression translated into the language primarily utilized in the requesting country. This assumes that no translation has been published within six years of the work's original date of publication. In essence, this rule precludes authors in most countries from preventing the translation of their works into different languages.

computer databases, copyright of

Collections of information or resources placed in a computer and organized to allow for rapid updating and retrieval are known as "computer databases". Examples of computer databases are:

- a mailing list organized so that mailings can be made according to certain criteria such as area, income, or interest

- all the articles published on any particular subject, organized so that people can quickly retrieve and read the article dealing with their particular point of interest, and

- a listing of all items in a record store's inventory arranged to permit an inventory analysis by such variables as supplier, performer's nationality, record price, length of time in stock, etc.

Computer databases commonly consist either of information that is not protectable by copyright (e.g., because it's in the public domain), or information that is protected by a copyright owned by another. Nevertheless, the structure and organization of the database itself can qualify as an *original work of authorship* (termed a *compilation*), and thus be subject to

BDOS ERROR R/O
INSERT FLOPPY DISK
NOT FLOPPY EARS

copyright protection.

Example: Suppose Catherine Jermany gathers all articles written in ten leading education journals since 1980, and then indexes them, using several hundred subject-matter headings that she has developed. Next, Catherine enters the full text of each article into her computer. Finally, using a pre-existing database manager program, she relates the index to each article and paragraph, so that by choosing a particular index heading a user can produce on the screen any paragraph of any article relevant to that subject. This database would qualify as an original work of authorship, and thus would be subject to copyright protection. However, to the extent that the constituent articles were already subject to copyright protection by their authors (or the assignees or licensees of the authors), Catherine would still have to obtain the authors' permission to reproduce the articles' text for commercial purposes.

In order to register a computer database copyright with the U.S. Copyright Office, it is necessary to use *Form TX*. On this form, the parts of the database being treated as an original work of authorship must be specified and distinguished from the parts that are owned by someone else. Related terms: *compilations of original or unoriginal material*.

Computer Software Protection Act of 1980 A U.S. statute that amended the *Copyright Act of 1976* specifically to affirm that copyright protection is available for computer software. Furthermore, the 1980 Act specifies the situations in which computer programs can be copied and altered without permission of the copyright owner. Related terms: *computer software, copyright of* and *archival copies*.

computer software, copyright of The 1980 U.S. Computer Software Copyright Act expressly confirms that computer software is to be protected in the same manner as other *original works of authorship*. The Act defines a program as "a set of statements or instructions to be used directly or indirectly in a computer to bring about a certain result." Thus, any computer program, as defined by the Act, can be protected by copyright if it constitutes an original work of authorship.

In the early 1980s, there was a debate over which programs could meet this basic criterion for copyright protection. The debate grew especially heated when the programs were in *object code* form (binary or hexidecimal) or were mechanically reproduced in a silicon chip as part of an integrated circuit with such names as *read-only-memory (ROM), programmable read-only memory* (PROM) and *eraseable programmable read-only-memory* (EPROM). This dispute, which centered on whether such programs were "hardware" (and therefore not subject to copyright) or "software" (and thus deserving of such protection), resembled discussions about whether a human soul exists independent of the body.

Also in question was whether integrated circuits and the templates used in making them, could be protected under the Copyright Act.

Now, however, most of these questions are gradually being answered, at least in most industrialized countries. Recent court decisions in the U.S. and Australia have extended copyright protection to software regardless of its form (i.e., *source code* or object code), and regardless of whether it is embedded in a chip or exists as an independent work on a computer disk or diskette.

Also, the U.S. Congress passed the *Semiconductor Chip Protection Act of 1984* to extend a limited form of protection to semiconductor chips and *chip masks*. Related terms: *Apple v. Franklin case* and *Semiconductor Chip Protection Act of 1984*.

conflicts in copyright transfers See *overlapping transfers of copyright rights*.

conveyance of copyright Conveyance is an old-fashioned legal word meaning sale. See *transfers of copyright ownership* .

copies For purposes of the copyright law, a copy is the physical form in which an expression is retained over time. This includes such things as photocopies, tape recordings, photographs, carbons, manuscripts, printings, molds (e.g., for plastic toy designs), computer disks and diskettes, videotape, videodiskS, and ROMS. As defined by the U.S. Copyright Act, copies are "material objects, other

than phonorecords, in which a work is fixed by any method now known or later developed, and from which the work can be perceived, reproduced, or otherwise communicated, either directly or with the aid of a machine or device. The term 'copies' includes the material object, other than a phonorecord, in which the work is first fixed'' (17 U.S.C. section 101).

The right to prepare copies of an *original work of authorship* (i.e., put the work into some fixed form) is one of the primary rights protected by the overall copyright. Related terms: *copyright*.

copying, infringement of copyright

With some exceptions, permission must be obtained from the *copyright owner* to make even one *copy* of an *original work of authorship*. Therefore, except as we note below, making a copy without such permission is a violation (called an infringement) of the owner's copyright. If this occurs, the copyright owner is entitled to seek remedies from the court. Related terms: *infringement action*.

Example: Philbert writes an article criticizing the way computers are being marketed to the consumer. To make sure everyone knows that he claims copyright protection in the article, Philbert puts the required statutory notice on the article "© copyright 1985, Philbert Treblip." Deciding that he would like to see the article published, Philbert sends *copies* to a number of newspapers and periodicals, with letters indicating that he expects payment if the article is used. Because Philbert's copyright gives him the exclusive right to make copies, each copy is protected by the copyright act. If a newspaper copies the article for publication purposes without Philbert's permission, it would be infringing Philbert's copyright.

Other examples of infringement through copying are 1) copying a computer's operating system embedded in a chip (ROM) for the purpose of building a competing computer, 2) making multiple photocopies of a book for distribution to a club, and 3) using a copyrighted tune in a new song with different lyrics.

As mentioned, there are certain circumstances in which *copies* may be made without a copyright owner's permission. These circumstances are generally referred to under the heading of *fair use*, and usually involve situations where the copying is for a purpose other than commer-

cial gain. Also, there are special rules permitting copying of computer programs for backup or *archival copy* purposes. Related terms: *archival copies* and *fair use*.

copyright Literally, the exclusive right held by the author or developer of an *original work of authorship* to make *copies* of such work and utilize them for commercial purposes. In fact, under the *Copyright Act of 1976* (applicable to all works first published after January 1, 1978), a copyright consists of a *bundle of rights*. These are:

- the exclusive right to make copies
- the exclusive right to authorize others to make copies
- the exclusive right to make *derivative works* (i.e., similar works based on the original) such as translations or updated versions)
- the exclusive right to sell (market) the work
- the exclusive right to display the work
- the exclusive right to perform the work (in the case of plays, musical compositions, etc.), and
- the exclusive right to obtain court relief in the event others infringe (i.e., violate) these rights

Each of these exclusive rights can be further divided through *transfers of copyright ownership*. Through such transfers, for example, a party can become the owner of the exclusive right to make derivative works, or the owner of the right to prepare copies in a specific language, or the owner of one or more exlusive rights during a specific period of time, or the owner of the right to distribute copies for a specific purpose (e.g., software for a specific brand of computer), or the owner of the right to distribute in a specific geographical area. The term "copyright", accordingly, applies both to the entire bundle of rights and to any individual exclusive right that is a part of such a bundle.

The *Copyright Act of 1909*, which applies to all works first published prior to January 1, 1978, does not spell out the copyright rights in the same way that the 1976 act does. However, the basic rights granted by that statute are essentially the same as those listed above.

Under the laws of most countries, any *original work of authorship* is considered the property of its owner, and others are prevented from using this property without the owner's consent. Usually, the owner is the originator of the work (the actual author or somebody who has paid for the work under an employment or *work made for hire* contract). Sometimes, however, full ownership is *transferred* to somebody else before the work is finished. For instance, it is common for software programmers to *assign* 5 all of their copyright rights to the publisher before they begin programming, in exchange for advance royalties. Usually termed a *grant of rights* 5 this type of transfer shifts ownership of the copyright from the author to the publisher.

Among the categories of expressive works that receive copyright status in the U.S. and many other countries are:

- *literary works*
- *audiovisual works*
- *computer software*
- *graphic works*
- *musical arrangements*, and
- *sound recordings*

In short, virtually any type of expression that can be *fixed in a tangible medium of expression* may be eligible for a copyright.

It is important to understand, however, that copyright law protects only the expression itself, and not the underlying ideas and concepts. Thus, it is often possible to produce legitimately an expression very similar to one that is copyrighted, as long as the original expression itself is not copied or used as a basis for the later work.

Although a copyright owner's permission must be obtained to make *copies* for commercial purposes, it is sometimes possible to copy without permission in situations collectively labeled as *fair use*.

Under the Copyright Act of 1976, an *original work of authorship* is extended copyright protection the instant it becomes reduced to (fixed in)some tangible form. This means that such protection is available for both published and unpublished works. The protection lasts for a long period of time. This can be for:

- the life of the author plus 50 years, or
- 75 years from the date of publication or 100 years from the date of creation, whichever is shorter, when the author is an employer or commissioner of a *work made for hire*, or when the author uses a pseudonym, or remains anonymous.

However, this protection can be lost prematurely if the copyright owner allows the work to enter the *public domain* (i.e., it becomes usable by the public without restriction). This can happen, for example, if a work is *published* without having the proper *notice of copyright* attached (unless the number of distributed copies is relatively small, or the number is large but the copyright owner takes reasonable measures to correct the oversight).

Under the Copyright Act of 1909 (only applicable to works published prior to January 1, 1978) a copyright could originally last for a total of 56 years. Now, however, the copyright in works that were first published prior to January 1, 1978 may last for a total of 75 years, depending on whether *renewal* has occurred in a timely manner.

In addition to the automatic protection extended a *copyright owner* by the law, it is possible to gain additional protective benefits in the United States by registering the copyright with the *U.S. Copyright Office*. Such registration is mandatory before a copyright *infringement action* can be filed. If the registration occurs in a timely manner (either within 3 months of publication or before the infringing activity begins) it is much easier for the *copyright owner* to go to court and obtain relief against infringers. Related terms: *duration of copyright*.

Copyright Act of 1909   The copyright act in force from 1910 through December 31, 1977. Works that were first published prior to January 1, 1978 are still covered by the 1909 Act, unless the copyright has expired. Related Terms: *Copyright Act of 1976*.

Copyright Act of 1976   A comprehensive statute passed by Congress in 1976, which substantially changed the law in the United States in respect to *copyright protection* for *original works of authorship* first *published* after January 1, 1978. The 1976 Act also affected pre-1978 copyrights in certain ways. Located in Title 17,

United States Code, Section 100 and following, the 1976 Copyright Act is now the exclusive source of copyright law in the United States for new works. All state copyright laws are preempted by it.

Under the prior law (the **Copyright Act of 1909**) federal copyright protection applied only to published works. This protection could be permanently lost if even a single copy were distributed without the proper **notice of copyright**. Under the 1976 Act, however, an **original work of expression** is automatically protected from the time it first becomes **fixed in a tangible medium of expression** (i.e., typed on paper, programmed on a floppy disk, photographed, videotaped, etc.), and, accordingly, is protected whether published or not. Furthermore, under the 1976 Act a work can remain protected even if some **copies** are distributed without a proper notice being attached.

In addition to making these major changes, the 1976 Act has 1) broadened the scope of what can be protected by copyright, 2) altered the procedures for registering a copyright with the **U.S. Copyright Office**, 3) changed the rules relating to fair use by specifying the contexts where it is and is not permitted, 4) lengthened the period of protection, 5) specifically defined **works made for hire**, 6) changed the circumstances under which a **compulsory license** may be obtained, and 7) eliminated the need for a **renewal of a copyright**.

copyright and patents   As a general matter, the **copyright** and **patent** 4 laws cover entirely different types of items. Copyright law extends legal protection to all forms of expression **fixed in a tangible medium of expression** (but not to the underlying concepts), while patents protect ideas that are cast in the form of useful, **novel** 4 and **non-obvious** 4 inventions (e.g., devices, substances, and mechanical processes). However, both laws do intersect in the two areas of product design and computer software.

First, a product's design that has nothing to do with how the product functions is entitled to copyright protection as a **pictorial, graphic or sculptural work**, while the patent law provides for patent protection in respect to novel, non-obvious and ornamental designs (called **design patents** 4). A design patent is far more difficult to obtain than

a copyright, but offers a broader scope of protection. However, copyright protection lasts longer. One type of protection is not exclusive of the other. For instance, a truly innovative design for a computer that has no functional value would qualify for both copyright protection (as a pictorial, graphic or sculptural work) and a design patent.

Related terms: **pictorial, graphic, and sculptural works** and **design patents** 4.

Second, certain computer programs can be protected under both the patent and the copyright laws, as long as the software in question is **claimed** 4 as part of a physical process. Related terms: **algorithms** 4.

copyright as personal property   It is often useful to think of a **copyright** as a form of personal property that can be protected against theft. In the copyright world, "stealing" is usually called **infringement**, or **piracy**. As with other types of property, a copyright is considered to be an asset and can be bought and sold. In the case of bankruptcy, a copyright is treated the same as other personal property. It can be sold and the proceeds used to satisfy creditors. The generic term for the type of property created by the copyright, **patent** 4, **trademark** 3, and **trade secret** 1 laws is **intellectual property** 5. Related terms: **protection of intellectual property**.

copyright claimant   The party considered to be the basic owner of the copyright in a work as it is registered with the **U.S. Copyright Office**. The copyright claimant can be any of the following parties:

- the actual **author of the work**, or

- an employer whose employee created the work in the scope of his or her employment, or

- the party who has commissioned a **work made for hire** (as this term is defined in the **Copyright Act of 1976**), or

- a party to whom **all rights** 5 in a work have been assigned, or

- a party who has come to own all of the exclusive rights that make up the copyright

The name of the copyright claimant must be put in the **copyright registration** form filed with the U.S. Copyright Office as part of the registration process.

copyright infringement Any use of a *copyrighted work* that is inconsistent with the copyright owner's *exclusive rights* in the work. Common examples of infringement are:

- making unauthorized *copies* of the original work for commercial purposes
- using a composer's tune in a subsequent song with different words
- using important computer software subroutines authored by someone else
- adapting another's work in one medium (such as a book) for use in another medium (such as a movie), and
- outright plagarism of somebody else's prior *original work of authorship*

Whether or not a second work will be found to have infringed an earlier work usually depends on whether there is a substantial similarity between the two, and if so, whether the author of the second work had *access* to the earlier work. The greater the similarity, the greater the chance of a court finding that infringement has occurred. Conversely, the less the similarity, the less the liklihood of an infringement being found. Once infringement of a copyright is suspected, the owner may seek judicial relief as long as the copyright is registered with the *U.S. Copyright Office* first. Related terms: *derivative work* and *infringement actions*.

Example 1: Suppose Beverly uses the computer language BASIC to author a *copyrighted work* that gives legal advice on the divorce procedures of the state of California. Jeff, who lives in Colorado, decides that the program would be a big seller in that state. Accordingly, Jeff makes small alterations in the program so it will apply to Colorado law, and distributes it under his own name. Because the major part of Jeff's program is a copy of Beverly's program, Jeff has infringed on Beverly's exclusive right (as part of her copyright) to make *copies* of, and prepare *derivative works* from, the original work.

Suppose now that instead of copying Beverly's program, Jeff borrowed some of Beverly's ideas, but wrote his own new program in a different computer programming language. As long as Jeff's program is not *based* on Beverly's (e.g., a translation or a substantially similar rendition programmed primarily on the basis of the logic found in Beverly's program) but is instead an independent creation, Jeff will not have infringed Beverly's copyright. Whether or not one program is "based" on another is decided after an analysis of the particular facts of each situation.

Example 2: Joseph writes a book on media law which is used widely as a textbook in media classes. Peter, a media law teacher, wants to use the book as a textbook, but doesn't want each of his students to have to pay the $20.00 cover price. Accordingly, Peter makes 25 photocopies of the book and distributes a copy to each student for the cost of the copying. Peter has infringed Joseph's copyright. Although Peter did not make the *copies* for personal profit, Joseph has been deprived of income because of the unauthorized copying. While the *fair use* provisions of the *Copyright Act of 1976* allows some unauthorized copying for strictly educational purposes, copying an entire textbook or even a substantial part of one, exceeds what is allowed under the fair use doctrine. Related terms: *fair-use*.

copyright notice See *notice of copyright*.

copyright office See *U.S. Copyright Office*.

copyright owner Under the *Copyright Act of 1976*, the term "copyright owner" has two distinct meanings. First, it means the person or entity who is listed as the owner in the *U.S. Copyright Office* and on the *notice* attached to the *copyrighted* work. This is either the original author or developer, or a person or entity to whom all rights under the copyright have been transferred. Related terms: *author as owner of copyright*.

Second, "copyright owner" also means a person or entity who has an *exclusive right* to exercise any portion of one or more of the constituent rights that make up the whole *copyright*, and who therefore has a right to sue infringers of that right. These "consituent rights" consist of the following:

- the right to reproduce (copy) the work
- the right to prepare derivative works from

the work

- the right to distribute copies of the work
- the right to perform the work, and
- the right to display the work

So, under licenses granted by the basic **copyright owner**, one party can own the exclusive right to make **copies** of and distribute a particular work, while another party can own the exclusive right to prepare **derivative works** from the same work. Similarly, one party may have the exclusive right to distribute a work in a particular state or country, while this same exclusive right may reside in another party in respect to another state or country. As long as the right granted is an exclusive one, the party who has received it is also termed a "copyright owner".

Although different people can own different rights based on a copyright, there is only one actual "copyright", and, unless all of the copyright rights end up being solely owned by a different party, the original developer (whether it be the author, employer, commissioner of a work made for hire, or assignee of all rights) is still considered the owner of the basic copyright by the U.S. Copyright Office. Related terms: **author as owner of copyright** and **transfer of copyright ownership**.

copyright registration See **registration of copyright**.

copyright registration forms Special forms issued by the **U.S. Copyright Office** for the purpose of registering copyrights. These forms can be obtained directly from the copyright office. The most commonly used ones are **Form TX** for nondramatic **literary works**, including computer programs, **Form PA** for **audiovisual works**, **Form VA** for **graphic, art, and sculptural works**, **Form SR** for **sound recordings** and **Form SE** for serials and periodicals. Related terms: **registration of copyright**.

copyrighted work A work is said to be **copyrighted** when it is entitled to copyright protection. Although such protection is available as soon as the work becomes **fixed in a tangible medium of expression**, a **published work** may lose copyright protection in the U.S. unless an appropriate **notice of copyright** has been placed on each copy. However, such

notice is not required in countries that subscribe to the **Berne Convention**.

The term "copyrighted" is often used incorrectly to refer to the **registration** of the copyright with the **U.S. Copyright Office**. Registration affords a **copyright owner** additional protection, but it is not required for basic copyright protection. Because the U.S. is a member of the **Universal Copyright Convention**, it is also possible for a U.S. author to obtain full copyright protection in over a hundred other countries, without registering the work, by placing a proper notice of copyright on it. Related terms: **Registration of Copyright** and **international copyright protection**.

court remedies for copyright infringement See **remedies for copyright infringement**.

criminal copyright infringement
Infringement of a copyright can be a criminal act under the Copyright Act of 1976 (17 U.S.C. Section 506) if it is done intentionally and with full knowledge that an infringement is occurring. As a practical matter, the U.S. Department of Justice rarely brings criminal charges against copyright infringers, and only when a large amount of money is at stake, and the purpose of the infringement is commercial in nature.

creation of work Under the **Copyright Act of 1976**, the following rules are used to analyze when a work is first entitled to copyright protection (i.e., when it is first "created"):

- creation of a work occurs when it first becomes "physicalized" in some form
- intermediate forms of a work are created in the course of its development — each intermediate form is afforded copyright protection as a representative expression of the same underlying work, and
- each new version of an original work is a separate creation

Example: Todd is in the business of making complex charts showing the conceptual relationships involved in different scientific fields. Todd carries an idea for a particular chart around in his head for weeks before he takes pen (or typewriter or word processor) in hand and sets it down in physical form. Once his idea becomes physicalized, however, whether by being drawn on paper, programmed on a computer, or constructed out of plastic, a **work of authorship** has been created. Todd next makes changes and improvements in the physical representation of his idea. Each new manifestation of Todd's idea counts as the original work, as of that moment. In other words, as long as Todd is working on the same idea, he has created only one work despite a number of ncremental changes. If, however, Todd decides to produce the final chart in both a printed version and a version specially tailored for a computerized slide show, Todd would then have two different versions of the same work and could obtain separate copyright protection for each. Related terms: **derivative works**, and **fixed in a tangible medium of expression** .

credit line   A written acknowledgement of authorship. A credit line is commonly used when one person's **original work of authorship** is being used by somebody else in a different work. When an author gives her permission for somebody else to use her work, or a portion of it, it is common to condition the permission on a credit line appearing in the new work.

criticism, fair use   See **fair use**.

customs, preventing importation of infringing works   See **importation of infringing works**.

damages for copyright infringement
Damages in copyright **infringement actions** are commonly awarded under three legal theories: "actual damages" (also called "compensatory damages"), "profits" and "statutory damages".

Actual damages are the value in money of any demonstrable loss suffered as a result of the infringing activity.

Example: A book on resisting rape, authored by Susan Lopez, contains a practical chapter on how to purchase and care for a handgun. If Rachel Sanders also writes a book on resisting rape (or any other subject) and uses Susan's chapter on handguns without first obtaining her permission, Rachel has infringed Susan's copyright. In this situation, a court would commonly compute Susan's damages by estimating how many sales of

Susan's book were lost because people wanting the handgun information bought Rachel's book instead.

In addition to receiving a damage award based on her own lost income, Susan might also be awarded damages in the form of "profits" wrongfully earned by Rachel. This is because the law does not allow an infringer to profit from his or her illegal act.

In many copyright cases, both "actual damages" and "profits" are difficult to prove. For that reason, federal courts are authorized under the **Copyright Act** [17 USC Sec. 504(c)] to award **statutory damages** (i.e., damages provided for by statute) without regard as to whether actual damages have been proven. However, statutory damages may only be awarded if the person claiming copyright infringment **registered** his work with the **U.S. Copyright Office** either before the infringing activity began, or within 3 months of the work's **publication** date.

Assuming the regisration requirements have been met, statutory damages can range from $250.00 and $50,000.00 per each willful infringement. For example, suppose Paul **copies** an article on computers written by Anthony and published in Hawaii, and, without authorization, sells it as his own in Alaska. Even though Anthony might not be able to prove any actual injury as a result of Paul's infringement, the Court will very likely be willing to make an award of statutory damages, assuming Anthony registered his work in a timely fashion.

For non-willful (i.e., non-intentional) infringements, statutory damages may be from $250.00 to $10,000.00 per infringement. The amount of the award will depend on the circumstances. These include the seriousness of the infringing act and the financial worth of the infringer.

A plaintiff in an **infringement action** who has registered the copyright in a timely fashion, may opt for either "actual damages" or "statutory damages", but cannot receive both. Related terms: **infringement action** and **injunctions, infringement action**.

databases, copyright of   See **computer databases, copyright of**.

deceptive works, no copyright   Under the *Copyright Act of 1976*, any expressive work that is fraudulent or deceptive in its message is not entitled to copyright protection. This means that a person accused of *copyright infringement* can defend on the ground that the *original work of authorship* was deceptive, and that the allegedly infringing work made enough changes to correct this deception. So, even though the later work is *based on* the earlier work (i.e., constitutes a *derivative work*), it does not constitute an infringement, since the earlier work is not *copyrightable* subject matter.

defects in copyright notice, fixing of
Under the *Copyright Act of 1976*, a defective *notice of copyright* on works published in the United States can permanently nullify copyright protection, unless, only a small number of copies with the defective notice have been distributed, or reasonable efforts are made to correct the situation. These efforts include 1) attempting to track down the defectively-noticed copies and having a correct notice placed on them, and 2) registering the work within five years of its publication date. Under the *Copyright Act of 1909*, (which covers all works first published prior to January 1, 1978) a defect in the copyright notice almost always results in the *copyright* being lost, and the work entering the *public domain*.

In the countries that have signed the *Berne Convention*, no copyright notice is required, and full protection will be afforded regardless whether a *work of authorship* carries a defective notice, or no notice at all. The U.S. is not a member of the Berne Convention. Related terms: *notice of copyright* and *international copyright protection*.

de minimis   A term used by the U.S. Copyright Office to characterize changes in a work that are too small to warrant a separate registration. Under copyright office regulations, there is only one registration allowed per deposit. Yet, what happens if an author makes several minor changes in his book, calls it a new version, and tries for another registration? In this situation the copyright office will consider the changes "de minimis" and reject a new registration. Related terms: *single registration rule*.

deposit with U.S. Copyright Office
Actual copies, photographs, or other representations of an *original work of authorship* that are filed with the *U.S. Copyright Office* and the Library of Congress as part of the copyright *registration* process. For most categories of works, it is necessary to deposit two copies of the work's *best edition*. For some types of works, however, such as computer programs and motion pictures, only one copy is necessary. The form a deposit must take differs according to the media being used, but must generally be sufficient to identify the work being registered. Related terms: *registration of copyright* and *identifying material*.

derivative work   According to the *Copyright Act of 1976*, "a derivative work is a work based upon one or more pre-existing works, such as translations, musical arrangements, dramatizations, fictionalizations, films, recordings, abridgements, condensations, and any other form in which a work may be recast, transformed, or adapted. A work consisting of editorial revisions, annotations, elaborations, or other modifications which, as whole, represent an original work of authorship is a derivative work (17 U.S.C. section 101).

Examples of derivative works are: 1) an English translation of a book written in French; 2) an updated version of a computer program rewritten in a different programming language, 3) a movie "based" on a play, 4) condensed versions of articles such as those found in *Readers Digest*, 5) annotations to literary works (e.g., *Cliff Notes*), and 6) a jazz version of a popular tune.

The exclusive right to make derivative works is an important part of the *bundle of rights* that make up every *copyright*. Absent a *transfer* of this right by a written *license*, or by permission from the owner, no one else can exercise it except for their personal use.

Countries that have signed the Paris protocol portion of the *Universal Copyright Convention* call "derivative works" *adaptations of original works*. The legal treatment provided by this treaty is roughly the same as that afforded derivative works in the U.S. (i.e., they cannot be prepared without the original *copyright owner's* permission).

Example: Joe wants to adapt a popular

NEW MOON COPYRIGHT — CROISSANT AND ESPRESSO COPYRIGHT — HAVE A GOOD DAY COPYRIGHT — BANANA SPLIT COPYRIGHT — TOOTHPASTE SMILE COPYRIGHT — PACIFIC OCEAN COPYRIGHTS — ABOVE AVERAGE COPYRIGHT — SHUT-EYE COPYRIGHT

ANOTHER "NOT-GETTING-IT-RIGHT-COPYRIGHT-FRIGHT" NIGHT.

novel into an interactive computer program. Since the program will be based on the novel, it will constitute a derivative work, and therefore cannot legally be marketed without the permission of the owner of the copyright in the novel. This is true not only in the U.S., but in all countries that have signed the **Paris Protocol** to the **Universal Copyright Convention**.

Although this example is relatively clear cut, there is a large grey area where difficulty exists in telling whether or not subsequent works are derivative of earlier ones.

Example:Tim writes a book in English that is similar to one written in French but that is not, strictly speaking, a translation. Is this a derivative work? Yes, if the court finds that Tim's book was "based" on the French one, and no, if the court finds that Tim's book was an "independent creation". Which of these results will occur depends on the degree of similarity between the works, whether Tim had access to the earlier work, the probability of Tim's independently creating a similar work, and so on. Related terms: **copyright** and **copyright infringement**.

display a work The exclusive right to display an **original work of authorship** is one of the **bundle of rights** that together form the overall copyright. If Marylou photographs Juan's copyrighted print for the purpose of using it in her art show, she must first obtain Juan's permission. The **Copyright Act of 1976** defines the concept this way: "To display a work means to show a copy of it, either directly or by means of a film, slide, television image, or any other device or process or, in the case of a motion picture or other audiovisual work, to show individual images nonsequentially" (as in movie previews) (17 U.S.C. section 101). Related terms: **copyright**.

dramatic works, copyrights A type of **original work of authorship** protectable by **copyright**. Dramatic works are usually defined to include works that carry a story line and are intended to be performed before a audience, either directly or through a tangible medium such as paper, film, videotape, or videodisk. Dramatic works include movies, plays, satires, comedies, and pantomimes.

Related terms: **original work of authorship**.

droit moral The french term for **moral rights**. These are rights that are considered personal to the copyright owner and cannot be assigned or licensed to others. They are not recognized to exist under the U.S. copyright laws, but they are recognized by all nations subscribing to the **Berne Convention**. Related terms: **moral rights**.

duration of copyrights Under the **Copyright Act of 1976**, **copyrights** on works first published after January 1, 1978 last for a defined period of time, as follows:

- If the "author" is an individual, and the work appears under that person's name, the copyright lasts for the life of the author plus 50 years.
- If the "author" is an employer, or the commissioner of a **work made for hire**, or uses a pseudonym, or remains anonymous, the copyright lasts for 75 years from the date of publication or 100 years from the date the work was first created, whichever comes first.

The value of works such as books, films, art and songs may last well beyond the term of the copyright. Computer-related works, on the other hand, seem more short-lived as a practical matter. Accordingly, copyright protection will probably last for more than enough time to protect them for their entire commercial life expectancy.

Under the **Copyright Act of 1909**, duration of the copyright lasted for an initial twenty-eight years. It was then renewable for an additional twenty-eight year period. The Copyright Act of 1976 changed this. Now, for any work that was renewed prior to January 1, 1978, the second period was automatically extended to forty seven years from the date of renewal, instead of twenty-eight. Any work that was published prior to January 1, 1978, but had a renewal date after January 1, 1978, must be renewed by the author or other **copyright owner**. Otherwise, the copyright will lapse. However, if it is renewed, the protection will extend for forty-seven additional years. The effect of these rules is that, properly renewed, a copyright under the 1909 act lasts for seventy-five years.

In a few countries, copyright protection lasts for a somewhat shorter period of time. The minimum time for copyright duration under the **Berne Convention** is the life of the author plus twenty-five years. All the nations that signed the **Universal Copyright Convention**, however, must offer protection for the life of the author plus 50 years, the same period as the current U.S. rule. In the event that a country is a member of both conventions (generally the case), it must offer the longer period of protection rather than the shorter. Related terms: **international copyright protection**.

exclusive copyright rights The entire **bundle of rights** that a copyright owner is exclusively entitled to exercise under the copyright laws. Related terms: **copyright** .

exclusive license A valid **contract** 5 in which a **copyright owner** authorizes another person or entity (called the **licensee** 5) to exercise exclusively one or more of the rights (or portion of such rights) that belong to the copyright owner under the **copyright**. If the license is in writing, the licensee is said to "own" the right granted in the license and is often referred to as a "copyright owner". Related terms: **copyright owner**.

Example: Jeanette Pulaski, a U.S. author, publishes a highly successful cookbook specializing in East African recipes. Aaron Smith believes the book will sell well in other countries, and approaches Jeanette for permission to sell it on the international market. Jeanette may then grant Aaron an exclusive license to copy, distribute, and translate (prepare **derivative works** from) the book for marketing in all countries outside of the U.S. or she might only license Aaron to market the book in several countries. Or, suppose Jeanette is looking for someone to help her market the book to cooking stores within the U.S. In this case, Jeanette might grant a prominent wholesaler in this field an exclusive license to make copies and distribute the book in U.S. cooking stores while exclusively licensing a cookbook publisher to publish and distribute the book to the book trade.

Under an exclusive license, the licensee, as "copyright owner", has the right to file an **infringement action** in court to stop all infringing activities (assuming that registration and recording requirements have first been satisfied). Related terms: **Transfers of Copyright Ownership** and **copyright owner**.

expression, protection of under copyright law See **original work of authorship** and **copyright**.

failure to deposit Under the **Copyright Act of 1909**, failure to **deposit** one's work with the Library of Congress, when asked to do so, could result in loss of the copyright. Under the **Copyright Act of 1976**, however, failure to deposit within three months after a demand is made by the Registrar of Copyrights can only result in a small fine. However, to register a copyright with the **U.S. Copyright Office**, making a deposit is mandatory. Related terms: **deposits with U.S. Copyright Office**.

failure to include copyright notice Under the **Copyright Act of 1909**, failure to place a **notice of copyright** on a **published work**, or the putting of a defective notice on the work, would both result in the copyright being lost. Under the **Copyright Act of 1976**, however, omission of notice or defective notice does not necessarily have this result if the number of copies are small or the copyright owner takes reasonable steps to cure the situation. Related terms: **defects in copyright notice, fixing of**.

fair use A rule permitting the use of a copyrighted work, without permission of the copyright owner, when done for private and non-commercial reasons.

The **Copyright Act of 1976** authorizes any person to make "fair use" of a **copyrighted work**, including the making of unauthorized **copies**, in the following contexts:

- in connection with criticism of or comment on the work
- in the course of news reporting
- for teaching purposes (including multiple **copies** for classroom use), or
- as part of scholarship or research activity

As a practical matter, the "fair use" principle is primarily used as a defense when a person or entity is sued for **copyright infringement** (e.g., no infringement occurred because the infringing activity was a ''fair use'' of the original work).

Whether or not a particular instance of copying without permission qualifies as a ''fair use'' is decided on a case-by-case basis and depends on a number of factors. These include:

- the purpose and character of the use, including whether such use is of a commercial nature or for nonprofit, educational purposes
- the nature of the copyrighted work
- the amount and substantiality of the portion used in relation to the copyrighted work as a whole, and
- the effect of the use upon the potential market for, or value of, the copyrighted work

Example: Tom, a teacher, makes twenty five photocopies of his favorite textbook, which was written by Samuel Scholar, and distributes them to his students for use during the semester. Samuel discovers this, and decides to take legal action, since royalties from the book represent his sole means of support. Samuel will probably win his lawsuit against Tom for copyright infringement. This is true even though the copyright act lists the making of **copies** of a copyrighted work by a teacher as a permitted fair use. Why? Because to qualify as a fair use, the use must also meet the other criteria mentioned above.

The first factor works in Tom's favor as he is not making money on the **copies** and is in fact using them for a non-profit purpose. However, the second criteria works against him, since the work is a textbook, and Tom's students would ordinarily be expected to buy it instead of receiving a photocopy. The third factor would definitely work against Tom, since he is copying the whole book. The fourth factor (market value) would also definitely be against Tom. So, in this example, Tom would almost certainly lose the **infringement action**.

If the facts of the example were varied somewhat, the result might be different. If Tom had only copied several paragraphs from Samuel's book, and provided a **credit line** as well as information about the publisher and price, this very probably would be ''fair use''.

What would happen to Tom if he mistakenly but reasonably believed that his use of Samuel's book was a fair use?

Tom would be considered an **innocent infringer** and could innocently be liable for any actual damages caused to Samuel prior to his being put on notice of the infringement. However, Tom would either have to stop his infringing activity altogether, or would have to pay Samuel a reasonable royalty for all future photocopies. Related terms: **innocent infringer status**.

false representation in copyright registration application A deliberate lie in a copyright **registration form** may operate to invalidate the legal effect and benefits of the **registration**. On the other hand, an innocent mistake should not invalidate the registration if timely moves are made to correct it. Related terms: **supplemental registration**.

first sale doctrine Under the **Copyright Act of 1976**, the purchaser of a **copyrighted work** is generally entitled to treat the work in any way he or she desires, as long as the **copyright owner**'s **exclusive copyright rights** are not infringed. This means the work can be destroyed, sold, given away, or rented. A common example is the rental of movie videotapes, where the store purchasing the tapes is entitled to rent them out without paying any royalties to the owner of the copyright rights in the movie. However, if copies of the movie were made and rented by the copier, the copyright would in fact be infringed. The term ''first sale doctrine'' comes from the fact that the copyright owner maintains control over a copy only until it is first sold.

In late 1984, Congress passed the **Record Rental Amendment of 1984** [P.L. 98-450]. This statute prohibits the owner of a **phonorecord** from commercially renting the record without the copyright owner's permission. This same type of statutory restriction on the ''first sale doctrine'' is being sought by owners of copyrights in movies and videotapes. Related terms: **copyright** and **copyright infringement**.

fixed in tangible medium of expression In the United States, and most other countries, an **original work of authorship** first qualifies for **copyright** protection when it is reduced to some physical form or representation (i.e., ''fixed in a tangible medium of expression"). Under the **Copyright Act of 1976**, a work is considered "fixed in a tangible medium of expression" when its embodiment in a copy or phonorecord, by or under the authority of the author, is sufficiently permanent or stable to permit it to be perceived, reproduced, or otherwise communicated for a period of more than transitory duration".

So, when a computer program is first reduced to paper or electronic patterns on a disk, it becomes "fixed in a tangible medium of expression" and is protected under the copyright laws. Similarly, when a song is recorded, a holograph photographed, a movie reduced to film, a game reduced to videotape, or an ornamental design molded in plastic, each is fixed in a tangible medium of expression and protected by copyright.

A work consisting of sounds, images, or both, that is being transmitted live, is considered "fixed" if some record of the work is being made simultaneously with its transmission. A live transmission of a baseball game is therefore subject to copyright protection at the instant of transmission, because the images being broadcast are captured on videotape or sound recording.

Even though copyright protection arises the instant a work becomes "fixed in a tangible medium of expression", additional steps, principally including a correct **notice of copyright**, must be taken in the U.S., and many other countries, to preserve this protection once the work is published. However, other countries, especially those that adhere to the **Berne Convention**, do not require these additional steps. Also in the U.S. and several other countries including Canada and Japan, **registration of a copyright** will provide even further (although optional) protection. Related terms: **copyright** and **international copyright protection**.

flow charts, registration of Flow charts that constitute **original works of authorship** qualify for copyright protection, and may be **registered** with the **U.S. Copyright Office**. When registering flowcharts, it is necessary to determine whether a **Form TX** or a **Form VA** is more appropriate. **Form TX** (for non-dramatic literary works) is used for flow charts which communicate information primarily through text. **Form VA** is used for charts which communicate information primarily

through a graphic arrangement of symbols and boxes. Related terms: **registration of copyright**.

Form CA A form issued by the **U.S. Copyright Office** to be used for making **supplemental registrations**. See **registration of copyright**.

(This and the following forms can be ordered through a "forms hotline" by telephoning 202 287-9100).

Form PA A form issued by the **U.S. Copyright Office** to be used for registering all works involving the performing arts, including **dramatic works** and **audiovisual works**, such as movies and training films. Related terms: **registration of copyright**.

Form RE A form issued by the **U.S. Copyright Office** used for **renewal of copyrights** on works first published prior to January 1, 1978. Related terms: **duration of copyright**.

Form SR A form issued by the **U.S. Copyright Office** to be used for registering all works consisting of serials, or periodicals such as magazines. Related terms: **registration of copyright**.

Form TX A form issued by the **U.S. Copyright Office** to be used for registering all works classified as **literary and non-dramatic**. These include books, poems, computer programs and documentation, essays and articles. Related terms: **registration of copyright**.

Form VA A form issued by the **U.S. Copyright Office** to be used for registering all **sculptural or graphic works**, such as paintings, photographs, and designs. Related terms: **registration of copyright**.

freedom of speech and copyrights
Although the First Amendment to the U.S. Constitution prohibits the government from placing restrictions on a person's freedom of speech, there are several exceptions to this rule. One of these is the Copyright law. Under this law, persons are prohibited from using speech when to do so would involve infringement on somebody's copyright. Thus, when appropriate, a court will issue an **injunction** preventing the **publication** of material that would constitute a

copyright infringement and thereby damage the copyright owner.

The *fair use* doctrine is often specifically relied on by the media when they publish portions of copyrighted materials they consider newsworthy. The degree to which this constitutes a defense to the charge of copyright infringement is currently in dispute.

grace period for registering copyright See *registration of copyright*.

grant of rights A phrase in common use whenever an *author* assigns all of his copyright rights to his publisher in advance, in exchange for an advance in royalties or other remuneration. Related terms: *grant of rights* 5.

graphic and pictorial works See *pictorial, graphic and sculptural works*.

ideas, no copyright but patent and tradesecret Ideas as such may not be protected through the copyright process. Only the actual expression of an idea is subject to copyright protection. For instance, suppose Janice La Beaux authors a new computer program that permits a homemaker to keep a running inventory of household goods. If Kim Rivera likes the idea and independently writes a competing program, no copyright infringement has occurred. Why not? Kim copied Janice's idea, but not her expression.

Some ideas may be protected through other legal doctrines, however. For example, an idea that adds to a business's competitive position and is not generally known or used in the trade may be treated as a *tradesecret* 1, and others may be prevented from disclosing or using it without permission. An idea may also qualify for a *patent* 4 if it otherwise fits the statutory qualifications. Related terms: *ideas and patents* 4 and *ideas as trade secrets* 1.

identifying material A portion or representation of an original *work of authorship*, which is *deposited with the U.S. Copyright Office* for the purpose of identifying the work being registered. Generally, to *register* a copyright, it is necessary to deposit at least one, and often two, complete copies of the work

with the copyright office. However, some kinds of works (e.g., holographs and computer programs) are not easy to deposit. In other instances, the author desires to maintain certain ideas as *trade secrets* 1, ideas which would be disclosed if a true or complete copy had to be deposited.

To accomodate the needs of the registrant in both of these situations, the copyright office will accept a deposit that only involves a portion of the work, or a representation of it, instead of the entire work. The portion deposited is labelled as ' "identifying material" in order to satisfy the deposit requirement in the copyright law. Examples of identifying material re: photographic prints, transparencies, photostats, drawings, or similar two-dimensional reproductions visable without the aid of a machine.

With regard to computer software, the Copyright Office allows the deposit of the first and last twenty five pages of a program as identifying material, if the program runs beyond fifty pages. For databases, identifying material consists of a portion of each file in the database.

In addition to these set policies allowing "identifying material " to be deposited, the U.S. Copyright Office is willing to provide *special relief* for individual deposits on a case by case basis. For instance, if a software developer wants to deposit *source code* but doesn't want to disclose certain trade secrets, the copyright office will allow the developer to black out certain portions of the code so that it cannot easily be understood and copied by potential infringers. Deposits accomplished under the special relief doctrine are also considered to be "identifying material". Related terms: *deposits with U.S. Copyright Office* and *special relief*.

importation of infringing works U.S. copyright and customs laws authorize the Customs Service to prevent material that infringes a U.S. Copyright from entering the U.S. It works like this:

- the *copyright owner* records his or her work with the U.S. Customs Service
- any imported copies that are the same or highly similar to the recorded works are temporarily seized, and
- the copyright owner is informed of the seizure, and provided time in which to

obtain a court order barring the materials from being imported

As a practical matter, this remedy is seldom used, due to the inability of the customs service to check imports carefully against recorded copyrights.

The U.S. Customs law also authorizes copyright owners to file a complaint with the International Trade Commission, to have infringing works excluded from the U.S., on the ground their importation would constitute an unfair method of competition.

inadvertent infringement of copyright, consequences of See *innocent infringement of copyrights.*

indecent or immoral works Copyright protection is not available for works that a court or the *U.S. Copyright Office* deems to be indecent or immoral.

Although in the past, the U.S. Copyright office was commonly willing to reject registration of works on these grounds, the tendency now is to accept registration for most doubtful material, and to let the courts decide the issue if anyone objects. Related terms: *registration of copyright*.

independent conception, defense to infringement action When an author independently creates a work, it is considered original, even though it may be highly similar to another work previously created by someone else. Accordingly, if a defendant in an *infringement action* can prove *independent conception*, the infringement action will fail, even though the plaintiffs have proved the necessary elements for such actions (similarity and *access*). Related terms: *copyright infringement*.

information in public domain See *public domain.*

infringement action A lawsuit brought in federal court by a *copyright owner* to obtain *damages* for copyright infringement, and/or *injunctive relief*, against a party who, without proper authorization, has exercised one or more of the *exclusive copyright rights* reserved to the copyright owner.

Under the *Copyright Act of 1976*, a *copyright owner* is entitled to file an action in federal court against a person who, without proper authorization of the owner, 1) makes copies of, 2) prepares derivative works from, 3) distributes, 4)displays, or 5) performs any *original work of authorship* protected by the copyright. However, before such action can be filed, the copyright must either be *registered with the copyright office*, or such registration must have been attempted and officially denied.

To prevail in an infringement action, a plaintiff must establish that:

• the infringing work is *substantially similar* to the infringed work (in all cases, a subjective judgment), and

• the alleged infringer could have had access to the infringed work in order to copy it

If these elements are proven, the defendant (the person who allegedly infringed the copyright) can defend on the ground that his or her work was the product of an *independent conception*, and is therefore an *original work of authorship*.

Infringement actions offer the successful plaintiff a wide variety of judicial relief, depending on the circumstances and the date of first registration. First, the court is authorized to grant both immediate and interim relief. This usually occurs in the form of a *temporary restraining order* and/or a *preliminary injunction*.

Temporary restraining orders (or TROs) are generally restricted to situations when the plaintiff is on the brink of suffering *irreparable injury* and needs the status quo to be maintained pending further consideration of the case. These generally only last for a week or two until the court can consider whether a preliminary injunction should be granted.

A preliminary injunction will be issued if the plaintiff makes a strong showing that he or she is likely to prevail in the case after the trial is eventually held, and 2) he or she will suffer greater economic harm than the defendant if such interim relief is not granted. Courts often do not demand the usual requirement of irreparable injury, since that is a presumed effect of nfringement. Whether or not such preliminary relief is granted, the court will determine after a trial whether injunctive relief is appropriate on a more permanent basis. Related terms: **injunctions, infringement action**.

In addition to court orders prohibiting further infringing activity, plaintiffs may be entitled (after trial) to collect a money award known as **damages**. Related terms: **damages in copyright infringement actions** .

An **innocent infringer** (a person who didn't know that a particular work was copyrighted) is not liable for statutory or actual damages, although the court may award the owner the infringer's profits, or require the infringer to pay a reasonable license fee for continued use of the work. Statutory damages may also be reduced to $100.00 or eliminated entirely if a non-innocent infringer reasonably but wrongfully, believed his use was a "fair use". Related terms: **innocent infringer**.

Copyright owners who register their copyright and/or record their ownership interest in a timely manner also qualify to have their **attorneys' fees** and court costs paid by the unsuccessful defendant in the event of a lawsuit. This alone can be a powerful incentive to register the copyright at the earliest possible time. Related terms: **registration of copyright**.

infringement of copyright See **copyright infringement**.

infringement suit, registration as prerequisite See **registration of copyright** and **infringment action**.

infringement, recovery of profits from See **profits**.

injunctions, copyright infringement
Once a **copyright infringement** is established, courts will often be willing to issue an order (termed an injunction) to prevent the infringer from making any further unauthorized **copies** of the original **work of authorship**. To the extent that the infringing work heavily relies on the infringed work, an injunction can have a severely adverse economic impact on the infringer. For example, when Apple Computer Corp. obtained an injunction preventing Franklin Computer from further copying the Apple Computer operating system, Franklin was effectively unable to market its computers, since

they would not work without using the infringing material. Related terms: **Apple v. Franklin case**.

Interim injunctive relief can be obtained immediately, once an infringement is discovered. This is fortunate, since a regular injunction, or "permanent injunction", can only be obtained as a part of a final judgment, which can take years. Accordingly, courts are authorized to issue "temporary restraining orders", (TROs), and "preliminary injunctions", to take effect pending the final outcome of the case. These are relatively easy to obtain, once substantial evidence has been presented to the court showing a probability that an infringement is occurring.

Time is obviously of the essence in many copyright **infringement actions**, especially those that are computer related. Accordingly, in computer-related suits, **preliminary injunctions** and the legal maneuverings that lead up to them have become a crucial stage. In fact, if a plaintiff obtains a preliminary injunction, this often means a victory as a practical matter and the case will commonly be settled on terms highly favorable to the plaintiff. Related terms: **infringement actions**.

innocent infringement of copyright
Because the copyright laws afford protection to a **original work of authorship** as soon as it has become **fixed in a tangible medium of expression**, copyright infringement can be, and often is, accidental. This is especially true if the copyright owner has failed to place a copyright notice on the work, but has taken the legal steps necessary to cure the default.

Example: Lester Lawyer decides to write a book about Robot law, and accordingly proceeds to collect a large mass of materials from diverse sources. Among these sources is a photocopy of a an article by a Timothy Witherspoon, describing the essentials of robotics. No copyright notice is attached, and Lester assumes (which he is entitled to do, failing notice) that the article is in the **public domain**. Accordingly, Lester includes large quotations from the article in his book, giving Timothy a full **credit line**, but no royalties. As it turns out, Timothy does in fact own a copyright in the article (omitting notice on a few copies does not negate a copyright) and Lester has in fact infringed that copyright.

Since Lester's infringement was inadvertent, however, Timothy will probably not be able to collect damages from him for his use of the work prior to being notified of Timothy's copyright. And, in fact, Timothy may not be able to prevent further publication and sales of the infringing work (the book on Robot Law). Rather, in such a case, the court can, as a condition of permitting the continuation of Lester's infringement, require Lester to pay Timothy a reasonable license fee. This arrangement is sometimes referred to as a judicially imposed **compulsory license**.

Whether any particular infringement will be considered as inadvertent or innocent varies from case to case. However, if a work has a proper copyright notice on it, or has been registered with the U.S. Copyright Office, an infringer cannot claim inadvertence. For this reason, if one wishes to make use of another's work of authorship even though it contains no copyright notice, it is still a good idea either to get the authorities permission, or at least check with the **U.S. Copyright Office**. Related terms: **fair use**.

innocent infringer One party who inadvertently infringes another party's **unregistered** copyright in a work, either because the work did not have a **notice of copyright** attached or because the infringing party reasonably belived he was making **fair use** of the work. Related terms: **innocent infringement of copyright**.

international copyright protection
Many nations have signed treaties in which they agree to extend reciprocal copyright protection 1) to works authored by nationals of the other signing countries, and 2) to works first published in one of the other signing countries. This is called "national treatment". Under one such treaty, for example, (**Universal Copyright Convention**) Japanese citizens enjoy copyright protection for their works in the U.S. on the same terms as U.S. nationals (citizens and permanent residents), and vice versa. Under this same treaty, if Ishmael Farah, who is a citizen of a non-signing country, first publishes his work in either Japan or the U.S. (or in any of the other signatory countries), he will enjoy protection for that work in all signatory countries.

Besides establishing reciprocal protection rights, these treaties also establish the minimum protections that must be afforded, and the formalities (if any) for gaining such protection. Generally, however, copyright treaties do not impose on any country a definition of what matter is and is not copyrightable. So, for example, it is conceivable that a particular computer-related product may be entitled to copyright protection in one signing country, but not in another. On the other hand, virtually all of the signatory countries fully protect such traditional items such as books, art works, and movies.

The two main copyright treaties are the **Universal Copyright Convention (U.C.C.)** and the **Berne Convention**. The U.S. has signed the first but not the second. Most industrial nations are members of both conventions, and, if any conflict in protection arises, an author is entitled to receive the best protection available under either. In addition, the **Buenos Aires Convention** establishes copyright reciprocity between the U.S. and sixteen Latin American nations. However, since all but three (Uruguay, Honduras, Bolivia) of the sixteen nations are also members of the U.C.C., the Buenos Aires Convention is of little importance. Related terms: **Universal Copyright Convention**, **Byrne Convention**, and **Buenos Aires Convention**.

joint work "A 'joint work' is a work prepared by two or more authors with the intention that their contributions be merged into inseparable or interdependent parts of a unitary whole" (17 U.S.C. section 101). Under this statutory definition, the **U.S. Copyright Office** will accept registration of a jointly authored work, and will treat the authors as having equal rights, whether or not the authors have made other arrangements among themselves.

For example, suppose Tom Maris and Mary Tiger have a partnership agreement, under which Tom owns three fourths of the copyright and Mary one fourth. If the copyright is registered with the U.S. Copyright Office, with Tom and Mary listed as co-authors, they will be treated as equal co-authors of the work for copyright purposes, regardless of their independent, unequal ownership arrangement. And, even if the work is not registered,

Tom and Mary are equally entitled to avail themselves of the benefits provided **copyright owners** under the **Copyright Act of 1976**.

Library of Congress, deposit requirement Under the **Copyright Act of 1976**, an author is required to deposit one copy of most types of works with the Library of Congress. This requirement is automatically met as part of the overall **registration of copyright** procedure. However, if an author decides not to register, he or she still has an obligation to make the Library of Congress deposit, except for computer programs and certain other types of works. Failure to make the deposit carries no penalty unless the Library of Congress makes a demand. Then, failure to deposit within three months may result in a fine. Related terms: **failure to deposit**.

license fee, payable by innocent infringer See **innocent infringement of copyright**.

licensing of copyrights A method under which the owner of a copyright gives permission for another to use or **copy** the **original work of authorship** . Because the essence of a copyright is the **exclusive right to make copies**, a **copyright owner** often needs to pass this and associated rights to others in order to exploit the product commercially. This permission, referred to as a **license** 5, can either be exclusive or non-exclusive and can be restricted by territory, by time, by media, by purpose, or by virtually any other factor desired by the parties. For example, in the software business, licenses are often restricted to certain machines or operating systems. Exclusive licenses almost always must be in writing to be valid and all licenses should be recorded with the Copyright Office. Related terms: **transfers of copyright ownership** and **exclusive licenses**.

literary works, copyrights "Literary works" is one of the categories of material protected under the copyright laws. The phrase has little legal significance, and is used primarily to classify materials that must be registered with the **U.S. Copyright Office** on a **Form TX**.

According to the copyright act, "Literary works are works, other than audiovi-

sual works, expressed in words, numbers, or other verbal or numerical symbols or indicia, regardless of the nature of the material objects, such as books, periodicals, manuscripts, phonorecords, film, tapes, disks, or cards in which they are embodied" (17 U.S.C. section 101).

Examples of literary works are computer programs, books, poems, plays, newspapers, magazines, software documentation, training films consisting primarily of dialogue and flowcharts consisting primarily of text. Related terms: **registration of copyright**.

litigation of copyright claim See **infringement action**.

mask work A multilayered three-dimensional template used for mass-producing semiconductor chips. Related terms: **Semiconductor Chip Protection Act of 1984**.

manufacturing clause A U.S. statute, in effect until July 1, 1986, that bars the importation of more than 2,000 copies of any non-dramatic literary material written in English by an American author, unless it has been manufactured in the U.S. or Canada.

methods, no protection under copyright laws Copyright protection extends to the actual expression found in **works of authorship**, but not to the content of such expression. So, if an article is published describing a particular method for reproducing holographs on two dimensional cards, the way the method is described is protected (e.g., the expression itself) but the method used can be copied by anyone unless it has been protected in a different way. The primary ways of protecting methods as **intellectual property** 5 are **trade secret** 1 and **patent** 4 laws.

mistakes in registration, correction of See **supplemental registration**.

money damages in infringement action See **damages in infringement action**.

moral rights Rights belonging to a copyright owner that are personal to the author and that cannot, therefore, be taken away or abridged. Sometimes referred to by the French term "Droits

Copyright

mask work

Moral", these rights include:

- the right to proclaim authorship of a work
- the right to disclaim authorship of a work, and
- the right of the author to object to any distortion, mutilation or other modification of the work that would be injurious to his or her reputation as an author

The **Berne Convention** requires its member countries to provide protection for "moral rights" whereas the Universal Copyright Convention (U.C.C.) does not.

motion pictures, copyrights According to the copyright act, "Motion pictures are audiovisual works consisting of a series of related images which, when shown in succession, impart an impression of motion, together with accompanying sounds, if any". Motion pictures are entitled to copyright protection under the *audiovisual work* category. To register these *works of authorship* with the *U.S. Copyright Office*, a *Form PA* is used. Related terms: *registration of copyright*.

multiple copies for classroom use, fair use The *Copyright Act of 1976* expressly allows a person, in some circumstances, to make "multiple *copies* " of a *copyrighted* work for use in the classroom without obtaining the permission of the copyright owner. Judgment on when this is permitted depends on a number of variables specified under the *fair use* law. Related terms: *fair use*.

musical works, copyright Musical works are among the categories of *works of authorship* that qualify for copyright protection. Musical works can consist solely of musical lyrics, or of a combination of music and words (as in operas and songs). Musical works may occur in a variety of physical forms such as sheet music, records, and tapes. When the music is in documentary form (i.e., sheet music) a *Form TX* is used for *registration* with the *U.S. Copyright Office* . When a record or tape is involved, a *Form SR* is required. When songs have lyrics containing an independent meaning (i.e., that aren't completely dependent on the music), the lyrics can be registered separately. Related terms: *registration of copyright*.

national treatment An international copyright protection arrangement, under which a country extends to nationals of other countries the same copyright protection as is extended to its own citizens. Related terms: *international copyright protection*.

news reporting, fair use See *first amendment and copyright* and *fair use*.

non-exclusive license An agreement in which a *copyright owner* authorizes another person or institution (the licensee) to exercise (on a non-exclusive basis), one or more of the rights belonging to the copyright owner under the *copyright*. This kind of agreement does not constitute a *transfer of copyright ownership* since the right involved is not exclusive. In other words, the transferee shares the right with the original owner and perhaps with one or more additional non-exclusive transferees. Related terms: *exclusive license* and *Licenses* 5.

Example: Steve Rogers builds an electronic legal dictionary for use in law offices. Rather than sell the dictionary outright, Steve distributes it under *non-exclusive licenses* that permit the law office *licensees* to use it in their office computers, and to make copies for use in personal computers belonging to the law office staff. The license prohibits a licensee from transferring the dictionary to another firm, and requires payment of a set amount each year for renewal of the license. Related terms: *non-exclusive license*.

notice of copyright Notification placed on an original *work of authorship* that informs anyone viewing the work of the date the work was first published and that it is protected by copyright in the name of the person on the notice. Often referred to as a "legend" or "bug" the basic copyright notice used most often in the United States is "Copyright © 1985 by Anthony Author." However, there are two other forms of copyright notice that are considered satisfactory in the U.S. These are:

1) Copyright 1985 by Anthony Author, or

2) Copr. 1985 by Anthony Author

Failure to fully enclose the c in a circle, or failure to capitalize the word

"copyright" may result in an invalid copyright notice. However, a "c" in enclosed parentheses is becoming increasingly common. Whether it will satisfy the U.S. copyright laws remains to be seen.

For **phonorecords** and **sound recordings**, a "p" in a circle replaces the "c" in a circle.

If a notice lacks any of the required elements it is not valid, and, any work published with a defective notice may lose its U.S. copyright protection if a large number of copies are involved and the owner does not take reasonable measures to cure the defect. Related terms: **omission of copyright notice** and **placement of copyright notice**.

Works for which **international copyright protection** under the **Universal Copyright Convention** is being sought may use only the following notice:

© (year of publication) (author or other basic copyright owner)

For this book, the correct U.C.C. notice would be:

© 1985 Stephen R. Elias

If international protection is being sought under the Berne Convention (The U.S. is not such a country) no copyright notice is required. U.S. authors who desire protection under the Berne Convention may **simultaneously register** their work in the U.S., and in either Canada or Mexico (both of which are Berne Convention countries). Related terms: **Universal Copyright Convention** and **Berne Convention**.

Finally, if international protection is being sought under the Buenos Aires Convention, the phrase "All Rights Reserved" must appear on the work. Although use of this phrase is only necessary for protection in three countries (Honduras, Bolivia and Uruguay), since the other Buenos Aires Signatories are also members of the U.C.C., the following notice is commonly found on all works first published in the U.S.:

© 1985 Stephen R. Elias All Rights Reserved.

object code, copyrights Many computers work under a process where the computer translates a program written by the programmer into a machine language that can be both reproduced on paper

and understood by the machine. This is similar to what happens when a written message is translated into the short and long Morse Code signals for telegraphic transmission. The program written by the programmer is called the **source code**, while the code that the machine can "understand" (i.e., the translation of the source code) is termed the **object code**. Because computers can normally only understand information that is reduced to **binary** form (i.e., ones and zeros, hexadecimal, or some similar form), object code usually takes that form.

Despite its basic unintelligibility to humans, the courts have held that "object code" qualifies for copyright protection as a form of expression. Further, when **registering** a program with the **U.S. Copyright Office**, an author may **deposit** all or a portion of the object code (referred to as **identifying material**) rather than the more humanly intelligible source code. However, because the object code deposit is not considered by the copyright office to be the **best edition** of the underlying work (source code is expressly favored as a computer program deposit) the registration proceeds under what the copyright office terms the **rule of doubt**. This means the copyright office expresses no opinion on whether the registration is valid.

This type of registration will typically preserve the underlying concepts in the program as a **trade secret** while accomplishing the end results of copyright registration. While the object code is open to inspection at the copyright office, which would seem to eliminate its status as a trade secret, its basic unintelligibility works to prevent it from being understood and/or copied by a prospective infringer. Accordingly, the program's status as a trade secret may be maintained after all. Related terms: **computer software, copyrightability of**.

omission of copyright notice **Publication** of a **work of authorship** without the proper **notice of copyright** may cause it to enter the **public domain**, and thus lose its copyright protection. Under the **Copyright Act of 1976** publication without notice will result in the loss of copyright protection unless 1) the number of affected copies is small, or 2) the author takes reasonable measures to correct the defect, or 3) the work is registered with the U.S. Copyright office within five years of its publication and an earnest attempt is made to have correct notices placed on all **copies** that have already been distributed.

Clearly, the more **copies** that are "out there", the harder this will be. If numerous **copies** have been circulated without the notice, and correction of the situation is impossible, a court may then consider the work to have entered the **public domain**. In essence, the test as to whether this has happened is based on common sense. The greater the likelihood of **innocent infringement of a copyright** caused by failure to place the notice on the work, the less protection the court will grant the copyright owner. Related terms: **notice of copyright**.

operating system, copyrights Computer programs that govern a computer's internal operation and govern such housekeeping tasks as 1) transferring information from peripherals to the central processing unit and back again, 2)organizing priorities when the central processing unit is asked to do more than one job at a time, and 3) deciding where information should be stored and in what format.

Operating systems may either be fed into the computer from outside (e.g., by floppy disk) or be located in a ROM chip (read-only memory) where the code is physically embedded in a silicon chip and the operating system forms a physical part of the computer. In either situation, the expression produced by the operating system is intelligible to the machine and unintelligible to human beings. Nevertheless, courts have held that the code generated by or found in an operating system is subject to copyright protection as an original **work of authorship**. Related terms: **Apple v. Franklin case** and **computer software, copyrightability of**.

original work of authorship With a few exceptions, any type of **expression** independently conceived of by its creator, and **fixed in a tangible medium** , qualifies for copyright protection under the **Copyright Act of 1976** as an "original work of authorship". As long as a particular expression has been independently arrived at, it need not be original in the sense of "new". For example, if Thomas Towel never heard of or read "One Flew Over the Cuckoo's Nest" by Ken Kesey,

but somehow managed to write a play very similar to it, Thomas's play would qualify as "original", and would thus be subject to copyright protection. Of course, when one work is very much like another, the odds favor the possibility that a copy was, in fact, made.

Among the many types of expressions that qualify as "works of authorship" are expressions found in sheet music, movies, records, tape recordings, video disk productions, laser disk games, cartoons, artistic designs, magazines, and (good old) books. Computer software also counts as a work of authorship, in both **source code** and **object code** form.

A few categories of expression do not qualify as "original works of authorship". Among these are titles, short phrases and slogans, printed forms, and works consisting entirely of information that is common property (e.g., standard calendars, height and weight charts, and lists and tables taken from public documents or other common sources). Related terms: **copyright**.

output of computer, copyrightability of Many computer programs produce **original works of authorship** on the screen that are protectable by **copyright** separate from the underlying program code. For example, the famous computer game "Pac-Man" produces a figure and maze that qualifies for independent copyright protection. Other examples of protectable output are computer-generated slides, music produced by a computerized synthesizer, and laser light shows.

overlapping transfers of copyright right Overlapping transfers of copyright rights occur when a **copyright owner**:

• transfers all or part of the same **exclusive right** to two or ore separate parties

• transfers an exclusive right when a **non-exclusive** license involving the same right has been previously made, or

• grants a **non-exclusive** license involving right that has already been transferred in an exclusive license. The following rules have been developed in the U.S. to determine who is entitled to what in these situations:

• in a case of conflicting exclusive rights, the first one granted is entitled to the protection if it is recorded (in the **U.S.**

Copyright Office) within one month of publication (two months if the right was granted outside of the U.S.)

- if **recordation** is late, the first transfer recorded is entitled to protection (even if it was the second one granted), as long as it was received in good faith (without knowledge of the earlier one)

- assuming it is in writing, whether recorded or not, a **non-exclusive license** will prevail over a) a later transfer of an exclusive right and b) over an earlier transfer of an exclusive right if the non-exclusive license is granted before the earlier transfer is recorded, and the recipient of the non-exclusive license did not know of the earlier exclusive-rights transfer. Related terms: **Recordation of transfers**. (See chart next page.)

ownership of copyright
See **author as owner of copyright** and **transfers of copyright ownership**, and **copyright owner**.

pantomimes and choreographic works, copyrights
Pantomimes and choreographic productions are among the forms of expression that can qualify for copyright protection when **fixed in a tangible medium of expression** (such as film, video, written score, or recording). To register these types of works with the U.S. Copyright office, it is necessary to use **Form VA**. See **registration of copyright**.

painting, copyrightability of
See **pictorial, graphic and sculptoral works**.

Paris Protocol
An amendment to the **Universal Copyright Convention** to which some, but not all, of the original members of the **U.C.C** have subscribed. Generally, the Paris protocol extends copyright protection to **derivative works** (called adaptations) and permits countries to issue **compulsory licenses** for translations after a work has been published for a period of time, but not yet made available in that country. Related terms: **Universal Copyright Convention** and **compulsory licenses**.

performing a work
The exclusive right to perform a work is one of the **bundle of rights** that make up a **copyright**.

Accordingly, the performance of a **copyrighted work** without obtaining permission from the copyright owner constitutes an **infringement of copyright**. The **U.S. Copyright Act of 1976** defines this term as follows: "To perform a work means to recite, render, play, dance, or act it, either directly or by means of any device or process or, in the case of a motion picture or other audiovisual work, to show its images in any sequence or to make the sounds accompanying it audible" (17 U.S.C. section 101). Related terms: **copyright, infringement of copyright**, and **public performance of a work**.

phonorecords
Under the **U.S. Copyright Act of 1976**, phonorecords are defined as follows:

"Material objects in which sounds, other than those accompanying a motion picture or other audiovisual work, are fixed by any method now known or later developed, and from which the sounds can be perceived, reproduced, or otherwise communicated, either directly or with the aid of a machine or device. The term 'phonorecords' includes the material object in which the sounds are first fixed" (17 U.S.C. section 101).

This definition applies not only to the traditional "record" but also to audio tape recordings.

An **original work of authorship** contained on a phonorecord may be **registered with the U.S. Copyright Office** on a **Form SR**. If the holder of a copyright in a musical composition has allowed the work to be recorded for general distribution to the public, he or she must also license others to make a recording on a non-exclusive basis. Failure to do so may result in a **compulsory license** being issued. Related terms: **registration of copyright** and **compulsory license**.

pictorial, graphic, and sculptural works
Works of expression that primarily involve graphic and physical representations of objects and ideas rather than text. Under the **Copyright Act of 1976**, this category includes "two-dimensional and three-dimensional works of fine, graphic, and applied art, photographs, prints and art reproductions, maps, globes, charts, technical drawings, diagrams, and models" (17 U.S.C. section 101).

Overlapping Copyright Transfers

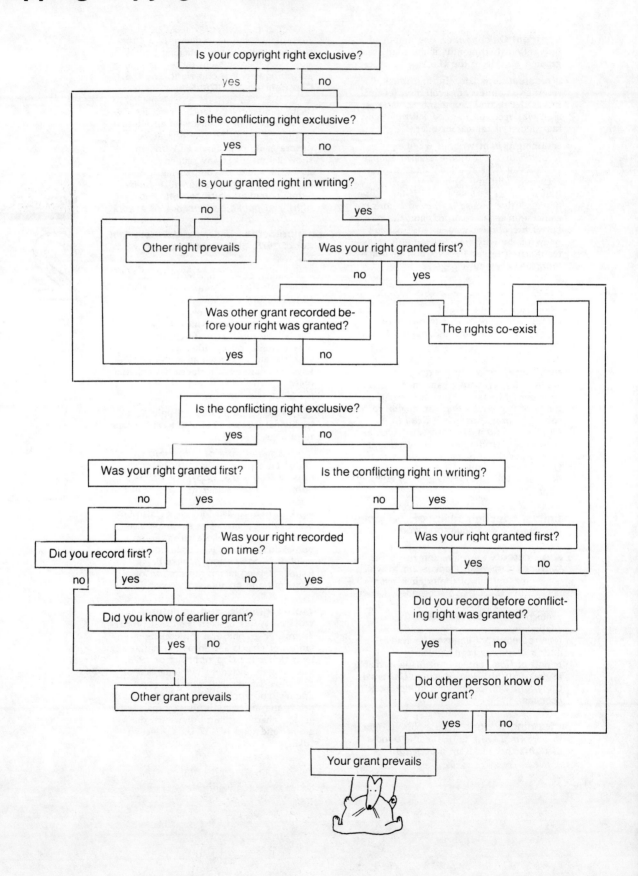

In this category of copyrightable works, the original design of a toy, package, implement, or other product can qualify for copyright protection if it is created for expressive rather than functional purposes. An ashtray designed as a unicorn may be subject to copyright protection as long as the unicorn shape is not directly related to the ashtray's function (i.e., the horn must not be used to pull up the cover over the ashtray inside the unicorn's body or something similar.) Whether or not a design is functional or expressive can only be decided on a case-by-case basis.

To register pictorial, graphic, or sculptoral works with the U.S. Copyright office, it is necessary to use a **Form VA**. Related terms: **registration of copyright** and **design patents** 4.

piracy A colloquial term without legal significance, used to describe the activity of willful copyright infringers. Related terms: **infringement of copyright**.

placement of copyright notice A **notice of copyright** must be placed where it will easily be seen by a person viewing the work (i.e., "reasonable notice of the claim of copyright".) For **literary works**, notice may appear on the front or on the back of the title page. For computer software, it can be on the disk or cassette, in the program itself, or may be placed to appear when the program appears on the terminal screen. For audiovisual works it can appear on the screen with the credits. For **phonorecords** it should appear on the cover or enclosure. There is no limit to the possible number of locations for a copyright notice, as long as it is prominently placed on the work so that no one can easily claim that they are **innocent infringers**.

preliminary injunctions See **injunctions, infringement action**.

principle, no copyright but patent See **copyrights and patents**.

printed forms, not copyrightable Printed forms do not usually qualify for copyright protection. However, flowcharts are definitely **copyrightable**. Related terms: **original works of authorship**.

priorities in conflicting transfers See **overlapping transfers of copyright rights**.

processes, no copyright but patent See **copyright and patents**.

profits The profit earned by a copyright infringer as a direct or indirect result of his infringing activity. Related terms: **damages in copyright infringement actions**.

programs, computer, copyright of See **Software Protection Act of 1980**.

protection of intellectual property The value of **intellectual property** 5 (product of a human intellect) comes from the ability of its owner to control its use. For example, the author or other owner of the intellectual property in a book has the legal right to exact royalties every time a copy is sold, or to sell the entire copyright, or to enter into any other compensation arrangement regarding the book's commercial treatment. If the author could not legally require payment in exchange for use, however, the intellectual property inherent in the book would have no value. The tangible book, of course, as a variety of regular property would probably have some instrinsic value.

Viewed this way, intellectual property only exists because the **copyright, trademark** 3 **patent** 4 and **trade secret** 1 laws protect **authors**, **inventors** and businesses in the event their intellectual property should be improperly taken by another. So, unauthorized copying of material protected by copyright will be stopped by a court upon request of the copyright owner. And, the use of a new mechanical device will be halted by judicial order if someone else can demonstrate that they have a patent on the device. Similarly, any photocopy business using the name "Xerox" will quickly be prevented from this use on the basis of trademark violation. And, any person improperly disclosing or acquiring a trade secret can be held liable for damages.

In sum, the value of intellectual property is directly related to the degree of protection it enjoys under the law. Related terms: **intellectual property** 5.

Of course I have every confidence in our group, but piracy is a possibility once the program leaves our hands

psuedonymous work A work whose *notice of copyright* and *registration* form refer to the author under a "nomme de plume" (e.g., pen name, alias, psuedonym) rather than her actual name. A famous example of this is Samuel Clemens, who wrote under the pseudonym, Mark Twain. Although an author is entitled to use a pseudonym, the copyright will last 75 years instead of the author's life plus 50 years. Related terms: *duration of copyright*.

publication of work An *original work of authorship* is only considered legally published under the *U.S. Copyright Act of 1976* when it is first made available to the public on an unrestricted basis. It is thus possible to display a work, or distribute it with restrictions on disclosure of its contents, without actually "publishing" it.

Example: Andy Author writes an essay called, "Blood Bath", about the war in Central America, and distributes it to five journalists under a *non-exclusive license* 5 that places restrictions on their right to disclose the essay's contents. In this event, "Blood Bath" would not legally be considered to have been "published".

Most works need to be published in order to exploit their commercial potential. The publication date is very important for several reasons. Once the work is published, copyright protection in the U.S. is dependent on each copy having a valid *notice of copyright* on it. Among other things that must be contained in this notice is the year of first publication. If the date is off by more than one year in the future, the notice is defective, and the copyright may be lost unless certain corrective measures are taken. The publication date also determines the *duration of the copyright* for *works made for hire*. Furthermore, the publication date can also be important in determining the right to protection in countries other than the U.S. Related terms: *international copyright protection* and *notice of copyright*.

public domain If any *original work of authorship, invention* 4, *idea* 1, *trademark* 3, *tradename* 3, *business information* 1 or other product of the intellect is not protected under the appropriate *intellectual property* 5 laws, it is said to fall within the "public domain". The arious statutory and judicial protections offered

intellectual property may be waived or forfeited by certain actions or, more commonly, inactions. For example, under many circumstances, *publication* of *original works of authorship* without a proper *notice of copyright* can operate to forfeit protection under the copyright laws if certain corrective action is not taken. Or, a *patent* 4 can be denied on the basis that the *inventor* 4 put his *invention* 4 into general use more than a year prior to applying for the patent. Or, a *tradesecret* 1 can be deemed to have been forfeited if a business doesn't maintain adequate internal security.

Once such a waiver of protection occurs, the product in question can be used by anybody without paying the creator, author, or inventor. In other words, the item belongs to the public. Of course, such property may continue to have great "value", as any reader of Shakespeare knows. Related terms: *protection of intellectual property*.

public performance of a work Among the *bundle of rights* making up a copyright is the exclusive right to publically perform or display an *original work of authorship*. According to the *Copyright Act of 1976*, to perform or display a work publically means: "1) to perform or display it at a place open to the public or at any place where a substantial number of persons outside of a normal circle of a family and its social acquaintances is gathered; or 2) to transmit or otherwise communicate a performance or display of the work to a place specified by clause 1 or to the public, by means of any device or process, whether the members of the public capable of receiving the performance or display receive it in the same place or in separate places and at the same time or at different times" (17 U.S.C. section 101).

Basically, any unauthorized performance or display of a copyrighted work, whether by direct or indirect means, which is aimed at a substantial but unspecified number of unaffiliated persons, qualifies as an *infringement of copyright*. Related terms: *copyright*.

recordation of copyright transfers When the transfer of one or more exclusive copyright rights occurs, it is important to record the transfer immediately with the *U.S. Copyright Office*. This is because the recordation date may determine who is entitled to protection in the event of **overlapping transfers**. And, once an exclusive right is transferred, it is possible for the owner of the right to file an **infringement action** against an infringer, as long as the transfer has been recorded first. Related terms: **transfers of copyright ownership** and **overlapping transfers of copyright rights**.

recordings, copyright of See **phonorecords**.

refusal of copyright registration by Copyright

Office See **registration of copyrights**.

registrar of copyrights The official title of the person who heads the **United States Copyright Office**. Established by Congress, the copyright office oversees the implementation of the U.S. copyright laws. It issues regulations, screens applications for **registration of copyrights**, accepts and stores **deposits** made in connection with registration, and issues opinions on whether certain types of items are subject to copyright protection. Related terms: **U.S. Copyright Office** and **registration of copyright**.

registration of copyright Although copyright protection automatically attaches to any **work of authorship** upon its being **fixed in a tangible medium of expression,** such protection can be subsequently weakened or lost unless certain affirmative steps are taken. One of these is attaching the correct **notice of copyright** to the work. Another is registering the work with the **U.S. Copyright Office**. In fact, when we speak of **copyrighting a work**, we often mean "registering it".

There are several distinct advantages to registration in the event court action later becomes necessary.

● Registration is required before filing an **infringement action** in court.

● if registration occurs either before an infringing activity has begun, or within three months of first **publication of the work**, the court is authorized to award **statutory damages** for the infringement, plus **attorneys fees**

● in an infringement action, the registered **copyright owner** is presumed to be the

actual owner, and the statements in the registration application are presumed to be true — such presumptions make it easy to present a viable case in court and put the burden on the other side to disprove the plaintiff's right to relief

Taken together, these benefits of registration can often make it worthwhile to go to court. Without them, such action might be too expensive to undertake, especially if high **actual damages** cannot be established.

The registration process is relatively simple. The copyright Office provides five preprinted forms for different types of works. Thus, a **Form TX** is used for all **literary works**, a **Form PA** is used for published and unpublished works of the performing arts (such as musical and dramatic works, pantomimes, motion pictures), and so on. Forms can be ordered through a "forms hotline" by telephoning (202) 287-9100.

Once the form is properly filled out, it must be returned to the U.S. Copyright Office accompanied by a proper **deposit** of the work itself, or material which satisfactorily identifies the work (called **identifying material**), and a nominal filing fee. The Copyright Office has specific regulations governing what form the deposit must take for different types of works and, in the case of items such as **computer software**, **phonorecordings**, and **mask works**, what kind of "identifying material" will be accepted. Related terms: **deposits with U.S. Copyright Office**.

In individual cases, upon application, the Copyright Office will afford the applicant **special relief** by waiving formal deposit or other registration requirements. This means, for example, that deposits in a different media or form than is normally required will be accepted. Related terms: **special relief**.

In the event that information provided in the initial registration is incorrect or needs updating, it is usually possible to file a **supplemental registration** form (Form CA).

Assuming that the appropriate form is used and properly completed, the Copyright Office will normally register the work and send a **certificate of registration**, unless the item to be protected does not qualify under the Copyright Act of 1976. If the work does not qualify, the registration will be denied. If information is either left out of the form or clearly erroneous on its face (e.g., the date of publication is one hundred years off) the Copyright Office will send the form back and indicate how to correct it. If the Copyright Office misses something it should have caught, a letter can be sent telling them to correct it.

In other countries, as in the U.S., registration is generally not required to obtain basic copyright protection. Furthermore, most countries do not even have a registration system. Related terms: *international copyright protection* .

registration process   The following chart details the steps involved in making a valid copyright registration in the United States.

remedies for infringement of Copyright   Congress has given the federal courts broad authority to protect copyright owners against actions by others that are inconsistent with the rights afforded by the copyright. To implement this, courts can:

- issue *temporary restraining orders* and *preliminary injunctions* (interim orders stopping infringement, pending final outcome of the trial) and permanent *injunctions* (similar orders that are final and permanent, assuming the case gets to trial rather than being settled earlier)
- award money for any actual harm caused to the owner by the infringment (*actual damages*)
- award the owner money in the amount of profits earned by the infringer as a result of the infringement (called *profits*)
- award penalties up to $50,000.00 (*statutory damages*), available in the event of timely *registration* and as an alternative to actual damages and profits
- award the *attorney fees* incurred in bringing the infringement action, assuming timely registration

Furthermore, in the event of an *innocent infringement*, the court is able to force the *copyright owner* to grant the *innocent infringer* a license to continue and pay for his or her activities. Related terms: *injunctions, infringement action* and *damages, infringement action*.

research, fair use   See *fair use*.

revocation of license   Most copyright *licenses* 5 contain conditions with which the licensee of the rights must comply. If these conditions are broken, the *copyright owner* generally has a right to revoke the license. Any exercise of the licensed right after such revocation will constitute an *infringement of the copyright*.

Revocation of a license should not be confused with the *termination of transfers* under the *Copyright Act of 1976*. In that situation, the original copyright owner has a legal right to terminate any transfer after 35 to 40 years have passed. Related terms: *termination of transfers*.

right to distribute copies to public   See *copyright*.

right to prepare derivative works   See *derivative works* and *copyright*.

right to publically perform work   See *public performance of works* and *copyright*.

right to publically display work   See *public performance of works* and *copyright*.

right to reproduce the work (make copies)   See *copies* and *copyright*.

ROM chips   See *computer software, protection of*.

rule of doubt   A policy of the *U.S. Copyright office* which allows *object code* to be *deposited with the U.S. Copyright Office* in connection with a computer program *registration*, upon the express understanding that doubt exists as to the legality and effectiveness of such deposit, in the event litigation later ensues. In essence, the Copyright Office is saying "we will let you deposit object code, but we won't commit ourselves as to its effectiveness or legality as a deposit". The reasoning is that since object code is unreadable by humans, the copyright office cannot determine whether the underlying program is registrable.

Although this appears to mean that the validity of this type of registration is in doubt, it is difficult to know what effect the rule of doubt will have in the real world, if and when it comes up in an actual case. One view is that since the copyright office agreed to register the work, object code deposit and all, the rule of doubt will have no practical effect. Another view is that a registration accomplished under the rule of doubt may prevent the **copyright owner** from obtaining a **preliminary injunction** in the event of an **infringement of the copyright**.

In order to help copyright owners protect **trade secrets** 1 in their software while depositing **source code**, the copyright office allows various partial deposits if **special relief** is requested. Such special relief deposits avoid the "rule of doubt" problem. See **registration of copyright** and **object code**.

scholarship, fair use   See **fair use**.

Semiconductor Chip Protection Act of 1984
A statute passed by the U.S. congress in 1984 that protects semiconductor chip manufacturers against the unauthorized copying or use of semiconductor chips and the templates (called **mask works**) that are used to manufacture them.

Semiconductor chips are a complex and very small combination of even smaller circuits that are designed to manipulate electronic data. They are mass-produced from templates that are called "chip masks" in the trade, and "mask works" under the new Act. Mask works (and the resulting semiconductor chips) are very difficult and expensive to design, but very easy to copy. Accordingly, semiconductor chip manufacturers have long sought protection of these devices as a form of **intellectual property** 5.

Because technological advances in these chips have been incremental in nature, most improvements have been considered **obvious** 4 and, therefore, not **patentable** 4. Nor, in the past, did the chips qualify for copyright protection, due to the fact that their design was considered functional rather than expressive. To plug this gap Congress passed this statute.

Under this Act, the owner of the exclusive rights in the mask work (generally, the manufacturer) is given an exclusive ten year right to:

- reproduce the mask work

- import or distribute a semiconductor chip product in which the mask work is embodied, and

- license others to exercise the rights described in 1 and 2.

These rights are forfeited in the event the owner fails to register the mask work with the U.S. Copyright Office within two years of its commercial exploitation anywhere in the world.

In the event a party innocently purchases a semiconductor chip product that has been manufactured in violation of these exclusive rights, that party is entitled to a **compulsory license**.

shrink-wrapped license
A practice, common in the mass-distributed software field, under which a purchaser of **copyrighted** software is informed that, by opening the shrink-wrapping on the package and using the program, he or she has agreed to possess the software under the terms of a license, rather than own it outright. Typically, this "license" is printed on the package and prevents the software "purchaser" from selling the diskette, making backup copies, making alterations in the software or disclosing any **trade secrets** 1 learned from the program.

Many of these restrictions are in conflict with the copyright laws, which allow software owners to make back up copies, and alterations for their own use, and to sell the original diskette. Also, to be valid, a license must meet the requirements for a valid **contract** 5. Given the contexts in which shrink-wrapped licenses usually occur (e.g., retail purchases in a software or book store) and the lack of negotiation over the license's terms, there is real doubt as to their validity as contracts. Related terms: **shrink wrapped licenses** 5 and **adhesion contracts** 5.

simultaneous publication
When an **original work of expression** is first **published** at the same time both in a country belonging to the **Universal Copyright Convention** and a country belonging to the **Berne Convention**. By doing this, the author obtains the combined international protections of both conventions. Because the U.S. belongs to the **U.C.C.** but not to the Berne Convention, it is common for a U.S. author to simultaneously first publish in both the U.S. and Canada (a

Berne Convention country). When this is done, a U.S. author may obtain such additional benefits (in Berne Convention countries) as *moral rights*, protection for works that lack a proper copyright notice, and basic copyright protection in those countries that don't belong to the U.C.C. (e.g., Cyprus, Romania, Thailand, Zaire). Related terms: *Berne Convention* and *Universal Copyright Convention*.

single registration rule A rule of the *U.S. Copyright Office* that allows only one registration for each *original work of authorship*. This means that if a second registration is desired for a particular work, because of changes, updates, or translations, such alterations must be substantial enough in quantity or quality to justify consideration of the new work as a "new edition" or "new version". If a new version or edition is registered, the registration only applies to the new material contained in the work. The material taken from the original work is still covered under the original registration.

There are two exceptions to the single registration rule. First, a new registration is permitted for a *published work* that was originally registered as an unpublished work. Second, a new registration is permitted when a substitution of the author's name is desired. Also, to make certain minor or technical changes in an existing registration, it is possible to file a *supplemental registration* .

software and copyrights See *computer software, protection of*.

sound recordings, copyrights See *phonorecords*.

source code, copyrights The computer program written by a programmer is usually called "source code". Source code is commonly written in a higher computer language (e.g., Fortran, Cobol, C, Forth, etc), and contains not only the commands for the computer, but also the programmer's comments regarding the purpose and meaning of the different lines of code. It is relatively easy for a skilled computer programmer to examine the source code for a particular program, and figure out how to produce the same result with a technically different program. Thus, access to source code can easily lead to a program's being legally

copied by a competitor. For this reason, programmers like to preserve their source code as a *trade secret* 1 if at all possible. Accordingly, when *registering* a program with the *U.S. Copyright Office*, many software authors prefer to keep their source code in the safe and *deposit object code* instead. Why is this? The *object code* contains no comments about the program and cannot readily be understood because it appears in the form of ones and zeros, hexadecimal, or some other inscrutable form.

The Copyright Office considers a program's source code to be the *best edition* of the work, and accordingly prefers it as a deposit. But the Copyright Office will accept a deposit of the object code under what is called the *rule of doubt* (i.e., the copyright office refuses to commit itself in respect to the benefits of registration, in the event litigation later ensues). Related terms: *registration of copyright* and *object code*.

special relief Permission given by the *U.S. Copyright Office* for a copyright *registration* and/or *deposit* to vary from the formal requirements established by that office. For many reasons, applicants for copyright registration often need a variance from the formal requirements for registration and deposits established by the Copyright Office. To obtain special relief, it is only necessary that the envelope containing the registration form and deposit contain a request that it be granted, and the reasons why. Related terms: *registration of copyright* .

statutory damages under copyright act See *damages in infringement action*.

substantial similarity, infringement See *copyright infringement*.

supplemental registration A method by which certain errors in a copyright *registration* can be corrected, changed or amplified, using *Form CA*, which is available from the *U.S. Copyright Office*.

Supplemental registration is appropriate when any of the following has occurred:

• the author's name has been misspelled, or

• an error in the author's birthdate has been made, or

- the title of the work has changed since the original registration
- the owner's address has changed

The first three of these situations are trivial and need not be changed for the copyright to remain valid. A change in the address need not be changed either, but it is usually a good idea, since anyone who wants to pay the **copyright owner** fort the use of the work needs to locate him first.

supplemental work See **works made for hire**.

termination of transfers Any exclusive copyright right that has been transferred by the author may be terminated by the author or his heirs either thirty five years after **publication** of the work, or forty years after the transfer is made, whichever comes first. However, such termination must occur within 5 years of the date the author or heirs become eligible for it. Otherwise the right of termination is lost forever.

Example: Twenty year old Walter Woodie composes a song protesting the takeover of American factories by robots. To get the song recorded and marketed, Walter makes a **grant of rights** to Ecotopia Enterprises (EE). The transfer takes place effective January 1, 1990. The song is first published in January 1991. It not only is a smash hit but also becomes a sort of American classic which is continuously recorded by a succession of artists. In 2026, Walter, who is then fifty six years old, will have the right to terminate the "grant of rights" and recapture full ownership of the copyright in himself. However, if Walter fails to exercise this option by 2031, he will lose it.

Although all copyright transfers can be terminated through this process, any **derivative works** that have been legally prepared in the meantime will continue to belong to their authors, rather than revert to the original copyright owner. For instance, if under its grant of rights Ecotopia had prepared and marketed a television series based on the song, all rights to the television series will remain with Ecotopia.

transfers of copyright ownership The **U.S. Copyright Act of 1976** defines "transfers of copyright ownership" as

follows:

"A 'transfer of copyright ownership' is an assignment, mortgage, exclusive license, or any other conveyance, alienation, or hypothecation of a copyright or of any of the exclusive rights comprised in a copyright, whether or not it is limited in time or place of effect, but not including a non-exclusive license" (17 U.S.C. section 101).

Under this statutory definition, any grant of an **exclusive right** by a **copyright owner** constitutes a transfer of ownership in the copyright. This transfer can involve the entire copyright or only a portion of it, since a copyright is really a **bundle of rights**. The right to make **copies** of an original work, the right to sell the work, the right to display the work, and the right to make **derivative works** of the work are all separate rights which make up, collectively, the "copyright".

Example: Ruth Gottried writes a book called "Nurse Ruth". Because Ruth is the author and did not write the book as a **work made for hire**, she is the owner of the copyright. Although it is possible that Ruth might want to publish and market the book herself, it is more likely that she will let others do the job for her. To this end, Ruth may find it profitable to grant certain exclusive rights to one or more different entities. Thus, she might want to give Able Publishers the exclusive right to sell, display and make **copies** of the book. If so, she would execute an exclusive written license to that effect. If she wishes, she may also transfer all of the remaining rights to Able, or she can choose to transfer some of them to Able, retaining only a few or even one, perhaps the exclusive right to make **derivative works**.

As long as Ruth retains at least one of the exclusive copyright rights, she remains the owner of the "copyright" as far as the U.S. Copyright Office is concerned, and continues to have her name on the **notice of copyright**. Although Able Publishers may own a number (but not all) of the rights and is considered a legal copyright owner, it only owns the exclusive rights tranferred in the license, and is not named as owner in the Copyright Office or on the notice of copyright.

However, if Ruth transfers all of her copyright rights to Able (including the right to make derivative works), then Able will become the new "owner" in the Copyright Office and on the copyright notice. But if Ruth transfers all rights to Able except the derivative works, which she transfers to someone else (her sister Edna, perhaps), Ruth will still be the "owner", even though she has transferred all her rights to other people. This is because the U.S. Copyright Office considers the original owner to continue as the owner unless all of the copyrightright rights are owned by another person or entity.

In addition to dividing up the separate rights among different people, a copyright owner can make transfers of exclusive rights on the basis of territory (e.g., the exclusive right to sell only in Hawaii), time (e.g., the exclusive right to sell for a five year period), use (e.g., the exclusive right to sell versions to be used on the Spiffy Computer), and so on. In fact, an almost infinite number of transfers can occur. The only prerequisites for a transfer of ownership are that 1) the transfer be in writing, 2) the transfer be signed by the owner, and 3) the right transferred be an exclusive one.

Although transfers can be valid without being recorded with the U.S. Copyright Office, it is better practice to make a **recordation** of the transfer. Then, if there is an argument about the scope of the rights being granted, this record will help serve as evidence. Also, once a transfer is recorded, the owner of the right being transferred can use the courts to prevent others from infringing on his or her exclusive right. Related terms: **overlapping transfers of copyright rights**.

translation rights   See **derivative works** and **compulsory licenses**.

unpublished work, copyrightability of   Any **original work of authorship** that is **fixed in a tangible medium of expression** but that has not yet been **published** (i.e. released to the public without restriction) is still entitled to copyright protection, and may even be **registered**. Previously, under the **Copyright Act of 1909**, unpublished works were not protected (except under the **common law**). Related terms: **copyright**.

U.S. Copyright Office   A branch of the Library of Congress charged with overseeing the administration of the federal copyright laws by establishing and running a registration system for copyrights. The Copyright Office provides its own forms for registering copyrights, issues regulations governing the registration procedure, and maintains copies of all copyright materials **deposited** as part of the registration process. Related terms: **registration of copyright**.

Universal Copyright Convention (U.C.C.)   An international copyright protection treaty under which copyright protection in a member country will be granted to works by authors who are nationals of other member countries and to works first published in another member country.

Over one hundred countries are signatories to the Universal Copyright Convention. They include the United Kingdom, most European Nations, Japan, the Soviet Union, Canada, Mexico, most Central and South American countries, and many African countries. Nationals of all U.C.C. countries may obtain copyright protection in the U.S. on the same basis as U.S. authors. And, any work first published in U.C.C. member countries is entitled to this same protection, regardless of its author's nationality. Equally, nationals of the U.S. can obtain protection in U.C.C. member nations on the same basis as their own nationals. Similar protection is available for works first published in the U.S.

In addition to creating these reciprocal rights (known as **national treatment**), the U.C.C. imposes limitations on the formalities necessary to obtain copyright protection. It requires only that the work carry this **notice of copyright**: © (Year of first publication) (name of the author)

Each member country must offer a minimum copyright duration of at least the life of the author plus 25 years. Each author is given the exclusive right to translate his or her own work, provided that if this work is imported to another U.C.C. treaty country, and not translated within seven years of the work's original publication, the government of that country has the right to authorize a translation into that country's language under a **compulsory licensing** system.

In addition to these basic protections,

the approximately one-half of the U.C.C. members who signed the **Paris Protocol** (an amendment to the original U.C.C.), including the U.S., now require that an author's economic rights in the work be protected, and that the author be given exclusive right to prepare **adaptations**. In fact, these protections are generally already afforded by those countries who have not yet signed the **Paris Protocol**. Related terms: **international copyright protection**.

violation of license restrictions, copyright infringement See **revocation of license** and **copyright infringement**.

work made for hire For purposes of the **U.S. Copyright Act of 1976**, a "work made for hire" is a work:

- created by an employee in the employment context, or
- created by an independent **author** under a written contract for certain types of projects specified by the copyright act, where the contract specifically states that the project is a work made for hire

Works made for hire most typically result when an employee authors an article, a computer program, or other original **work of authorship** on an employer's time with the employer's funds, tools, or facilities. Thus, if Ned Sugumoto uses company time to write a training manual for his employer, the employer will own the copyright in the manual as a work made for hire. On the other hand, if Ned uses his own time to write the manual, Ned would own the copyright, even though the manual's main purpose was to help Ned's employer.

The employment relationship does not have to be present for a work made for hire to occur. However, in a non-employment context, a work made for hire must basically be commissioned as part of a larger work. So, if the law-firm of Samuels, Samuels and Riley contracts with an outside company to create an entire software package to handle a large law suit the office is handling, the outside company will own the copyright to the program, even if a written work for hire contract is signed. On the other hand, if the outside company were only expected to program a portion of a larger litigaton support package being

used by the law firm, the law-firm would own the copyright as a work made for hire, assuming a written work made for hire contract was signed.

The U.S. Copyright Act defines "work made for hire" this way:

"A *work made for hire* is: 1) a work prepared by an employee within the scope of his or her employment; or 2) a work specially ordered or commissioned for use as a contribution to a collective work, as a part of a motion picture or other audiovisual work, as a translation, as a supplementary work, as a compilation, as an instructional text, as a test, as answer material for a test, or as an atlas, if the parties expressly agree in a written instrument signed by them that the work shall be considered a work made for hire" (17 U.S.C. section 101).

For the purpose of this definition, a "supplementary work is a work prepared for publication as a secondary adjunct to a work by another author for the purpose of introducing, concluding, illustrating, explaining, revising, commenting upon, or assisting in the use of the other work, such as forewords, afterwords, pictorial illustrations, maps, charts, tables, editorial notes, musical arrangements, answer material for tests, bibliographies, appendixes, and indexes, and an 'instructional text' is a literary, pictorial, or graphic work prepared for publication and with the purpose of use in systematic instructional activities" (17 U.S.C. section 101).

The overriding significance of "works made for hire" is this: the copyright protection in a work made for hire is owned by the person or entity doing the hiring rather than by the **author**. Also, the duration for copyrights on works for hire is different than that where the author is the owner. Related terms: **duration of copyrights**.

work of the United State government "A work prepared by an officer or employee of the United States Government as part of that person's official duties" (17 U.S.C. section 101). Basically, all such works are considered part of the **public domain**, and are not entitled to **copyright protection**.

World Intellectual Property Organization (WIPO) See this entry in Section 1.

Research Notes

2

This note assumes that you wish to delve deeper into the topics defined in this part of the dictionary. Instead of just providing you with a bibliography, we want to suggest a general research strategy. First, find some simplified background resources (often published as "self-help" law books) to obtain a general overview of your subject. Some of these are listed in **Step #1** below. Then consult more intensive background materials (listed in **Step #2**). These will go into greater detail and will also usually provide you with references (citations) to the primary law itself (**Step #3**). Finally, use *Legal Research: How to Find and Understand the Law* by Stephen Elias, Nolo Press, or another basic legal research guide, to assist you in understanding citations, using the law library, and understanding the law you find there.

Step #1: Simplified Background Resources

For copyright questions dealing with computer software and output, start with *How to Protect Your Software* by M.J. Salone, Nolo Press. Although not as detailed, *Legal Care for Software* by Dan Remer, Nolo Press will give you an overview of copyright protection for software. If your question involves copyright protection for literary authors, *Author Law and Strategies, a Legal Guide for the Working Writer* by Brad Bunnin, Nolo Press, is a good place to start. If your question involves copyright protection for musicians, consult *Musicians Guide to Copyright*, Erickson, Hearn and Halloran, Charles Scribner's Sons.

The U.S. Copyright Office publishes a series of pamphlets on numerous copyright topics as well as registration forms and instructions for using them. A listing of these publications is provided in Circular R2 (Publications on Copyright). This circular, as well as the other materials can be obtained by writing to: Information and Publication Section LM-455, Copyright Office, Library of Congress, Washington D.C. 20559 or call (202) 287-9100.

Step #2: Intensive Background Resources

Once you get your feet wet and become familiar with the basic concepts involved in your copyright question, it will usually be necessary to move to a more detailed and intensive source. Here are some recommendations. The library card catalog can be utilized to locate others.

Nimmer on Copyrights, published by Mathew Bender is a four-volume loose-leaf treatise on copyright law which contains discussions on virtually every legal issue connected with U.S. and international copyright law. Each volume has a table of contents for the entire set, each volume also has a table of contents for that volume. Each chapter has a synopsis of the information covered, and volume four has an extensive subject-matter index for the entire set. Appendices contain the federal copyright statutes, regulations, and the text of the major international copyright treaties. Each point made by Nimmer is supported by numerous citations to court opinions, sections of the U.S. Copyright Act, and Copyright Office regulations where appropriate. So, if you find something on point in Nimmer, it's easy to proceed to the primary source materials. Nimmer tends to be a little weak on computer-related copyright questions, due to the newness of the subject, and for this topic you might be better off using the *Copyright Law Reporter* (published by Commerce Clearing House) and/or *Index to Legal Periodicals* (or *Current Law Index*) all of which are discussed below.

An alternative resource to Nimmer found in most law libraries is *Copyright Law*, Boorstyn, Lawyers Cooperative, 1981. This resource is especially helpful for international copyright law.

Two national legal encyclopedias also contain extensive discussions of copyright law. These are *American Jurisprudence, Second Series* (AmJur.2d) and *Corpus Juris Secundum (CJS)*. By accessing either of these publications under "Copyright", you will find a complete discussion of U.S. Copyright law. The entire entry is preceded by a detailed table of contents and the publication contains a subject-matter index which you can access under the term "copyright". As is the case with Nimmer, these discussions are weak on computer-related copyright questions.

Copyright Law Reporter: This is a weekly loose-leaf service published by Commerce Clearing House (CCH). It contains the copyright statutes, Copyright Office regulations, the full text or summaries of recent copyright-related court decisions, relevant discussions of new developments in copyright law, and updates and amendments to all this material. This resource is extremely valuable if you are interested in computer-related copyright issues and recent trends in copyright law. Although it seems difficult to use at first, the first volume of the set contains easy to follow instructions. A few minutes of patience and you will have a valuable research resource at your finger tips.

Law review articles: Especially in regard to recent copyright issues such as software protection, protection of semi-conductor chips, international copyright protection, and licensing of videotapes, the best sources of information are often articles appearing in scholarly journals called "law reviews". By looking under "Copyright" in the *Index to Legal Periodicals* or *Current Law Index*, you will find frequent references to articles on current copyright topics of interest. These references refer you to law reviews. A key to the abbreviations used is located at the front of the index volume you are using. Law libraries always store law review publications alphabetically in one particular location. The reference librarian can help here.

Step #3: Access Primary Sources

Statutes: If you desire to directly access the primary law governing all copyrights in the United States on work created on or after January 1, 1978 is the Copyright Act of 1976. This collection of statutes is located in *Title 17* of the *United States Code*, starting at Section 101 [17 U.S.C. Sec. 101]. You can find these statutes in either *United States Code Annotated (U.S.C.A.)* or in *United States Code Service, Lawyers Edition (U.S.C.S)*. To find a specific statute, consult either the index at the end of Title 17, or the index at the end of the entire code.

Regulations: The United States Copyright Office has issued regulations which implement the Copyright statutes and create the procedures which must be followed to register a work. These regulations are located in *Title 37* of the *Code of*

Federal Regulations (CFR), a paperback service which is updated annually. *Title 37* has a table of contents, and the entire *CFR* set has a subject-matter index at the end of the set.

Court decisions: If you desire to go directly to cases relating to copyright law, you can find one-sentence summaries of federal court decisions interpreting the Copyright Act in West's *Federal Practice Digest* under the term "Copyright". Here you will find a detailed table of contents of the subjects covered by the summaries. This digest also has a very detailed subject-matter index at the end of the entire set. By looking first under Copyright, and then under your specific topic, you can access the summaries this way. Generally speaking, this method of research should not utilized unless you know of a specific case on your topic.

Introduction

This section defines the words and phrases commonly used to decide when and how a **mark** that is associated with the goods or services of a business can be protected from being used by others. We use the general term "mark" to refer to **trademarks** (used to distinguish products), **servicemarks** (used to distinguish services), **certification marks** (used to designate those who judge product quality) and **collective marks** (used to designate group members responsible for making a product).

A "mark" can be any word, phrase, logo, or other graphic symbol used by a manufacturer, merchant, or group that is associated with a product or service to identify and distinguish it from others. If a mark is understood by the public to refer to the product or service itself (e.g., escalator) rather than as a brand name (e.g., Kodak film) it is considered **generic** and not entitled to protection. If a mark is merely **descriptive** of a product or service (e.g., "Smooth Taste Coffee"), it will also be accorded little if any protection. Marks that are **strong** and **distinctive** (e.g., Exxon) are entitled to the most protection.

Weak marks may become distinctive by obtaining a **secondary meaning** through use over time, and marks that appear descriptive may be considered distinctive if they are **suggestive** of other meanings.

Under the **Lanham Act**, marks may be registered with the **U.S. Patent And Trademark Office** if they have been **used in interstate commerce**. Existing mark owners can **oppose the registration** or petition to have it **cancelled**, once it occurs. When an objection or cancellation petition is received by the Patent and Trademark Office, or if two pending applications claim the same mark, an administrative proceeding may be scheduled to decide the matter. This may result in only one business being entitled to register the mark, or in a **concurrent registration** where both parties can use the mark with specified limitations.

If a mark is distinctive, it will be placed on the main register (the **Principal Register**). If not, it may qualify for the **Supplemental Register**. Any mark on the Principal Register is presumed to be valid, in the event of a court dispute. Also, placement on the Principal Register serves as notice throughout the U.S. that the mark is already owned. And, if the mark remains on the Principal Register for five years, it may obtain **incontestable status**.

The central issue in all disputes involving marks is whether one business is entitled to the **exclusive use of a mark**. More specifically, whether a court will grant exclusive use of a mark to a business owner depends on a number of variables, including 1) whether the mark is strong or weak (i.e., distinctive or descriptive), 2) who first used the mark, 3) whether the party claiming exclusive use of the mark was the first to register it under the Lanham Act, 4) whether the second business to use the mark knew of the mark's prior use, and 5) whether **confusion to consumers** would likely result if both parties to the dispute were allowed to use the mark.

If a court finds that the use of a mark by one business infringes the right of another business to exclusive use of the mark, it will enjoin any further use by the infringing business and perhaps award money damages as well. If the court finds that no infringement has occurred, but that the public is likely to be confused, it can order concurrent use under certain restrictions.

Associated legal issues often lumped under "trademark law" are: 1) what protections are available under state laws, 2) when a business is guilty of **unfair competition**, and 3) what happens when a business name (**trade name**) raises the likelihood that the public will be confused between that and another business with the same or similar name.

Definitions

abandonment of mark Under certain circumstances, a U.S. mark owner's **exclusive right to use the mark** may be legally abandoned. Once a mark is abandoned, it is available for another's use. Abandonment commonly occurs when 1) the actual use of a mark ends and its owner intends to abandon it, or 2) the owner treats a mark in a manner as to cause it to lose significance as an indication of product or service origin.

If a mark is **registered** with the **U.S. Patent and Trademark Office**, its continual use anywhere in the country will preclude a finding of abandonment. However, if a mark is not used for two years or more, its abandonment will be presumed (i.e., taken as proven, absent evidence to the contrary). In this situation, if a court action should be brought by the mark's original owner against someone who began using it later, the original owner must explain why the two year non-use was not an "intent to abandon".

Such contingencies as temporary financial difficulty, bankruptcy proceedings, and the need for a product revision may all qualify as satisfactory explanations for non-use of a mark. In short, although the old adage about maintaining the ownership of a mark counsels "use it or lose it", the law often permits non-use for a considerable amount of time without loss of the exclusive right to use the mark. Nevertheless, a lapse of time in using the mark can prevent a mark from achieving **incontestable status**. Related terms: **continuous use of mark**.

Allowing others to use a mark without restrictions as to the product or service associated with it also operates as an abandonment to the extent that the mark no longer serves as a meaningful indication of a particular product's or service's origin. For instance, if a major fast food hamburger chain allows franchise operations to sell anything from chicken to squid under the company logo, the logo will soon become meaningless as a food service indicator. Related terms: **naked license** and **licensing of trademarks**.

accounting of defendant's profits
See **defendant's profits**.

affects interstate commerce, commercial activity which To "affect interstate commerce", a business, product, or service must have some connection with people or products from other states. Such a showing is necessary to obtain certain types of protection for a mark under federal laws. For instance, only businesses that affect interstate commerce may bring an **unfair competition** action under Section 43(a) of the **Lanham Act**. As a practical matter, most local businesses (e.g., restaurants, hotels, manufacturing concerns, computer companies, software houses) can easily be shown to meet this test, and therefore to affect interstate commerce.

The concept of "affecting commerce" should not be confused with the requirement that a **mark** be **used in interstate**

commerce in order to be registrable under the *Lanham Act*. Using a mark in interstate commerce means that the mark must be attached to goods, services, (or in some cases advertising copy describing such goods or services), that actually move between two or more states. Related terms: *unfair competition under Lanham Act*.

affidavit of continued use See *duration of registration on Principal Register*

anti-dilution statutes See *dilution of mark*.

anti-trust laws and trademarks See *unfair competition* and *unfair competition under Lanham Act*.

Anton Piller Order In the United Kingdom, a court order (named after a party to a famous case authorizing the order) that allows the plaintiff in a *palming off* case to enter the defendant's premises and seize offending goods, documents, and other evidence of product passing off (such as descriptive labels), and have them held in custody pending the trial.

arbitrary mark See *distinctive mark*.

assignment of mark The complete transfer of ownership in a *mark* to another person or entity. Assignment often occurs when a business is sold. In fact, including "good will" in the sale of the business automatically subsumes sale of the business's marks unless the *contract* 5 of sale indicates a contrary intent. Under the *Lanham Act* (15 U.S.C. Section 1058) an assignment of a mark must be in writing. Assignments can be filed with the *U.S. Patent and Trademark Office* can obtain new Certificates of Ownership in their names. Related terms: *assignments* 5.

attorneys fees in trademark infringement actions The *Lanham Act* authorizes attorneys fees in *infringement actions*, but only in "exceptional cases". Generally, an exceptional case is where the infringer is shown to have acted with full knowledge of his or her infringing activities. Also, attorneys fees are awarded when the infringement is a result of a violation of a *contract* 5 or

license 5 that provides for such fees. Related terms: *trademark infringement action* and *innocent infringer status*.

average consumer A hypothetical and reasonably prudent consumer whose probable viewpoint is invoked when courts must decide 1) whether a particular *mark* is *distinctive* enough to serve as a product or service identifier, and 2) whether a mark is likely to mislead or cause confusion to the public. If a mark is found to serve adequately as a product identifier, from the standpoint of the "average consumer", and its use would not mislead or confuse the average, reasonably prudent, consumer (and the mark is otherwise qualified), it will be placed on the *Principal Register* under authority of the *Lanham Act*. When a lawsuit arises from a dispute over the use of a particular mark, the parties will often conduct consumer polls to ascertain the actual views of the "average consumer", and will introduce the results of such polls in support of their case.

Bureau of Customs Under the U.S. Customs Act, a trademark owner whose mark is on the *Principal Register* may record the mark with the U.S. Customs Service (19 CFR Part 133 Subparts (A) and (B)). Once this is done, any products bearing *infringing marks* that are spotted by the customs inspectors will be seized, and the mark's owner contacted. If the importer agrees to remove the offending mark, or the mark's owner waives his or her right to object, the goods will be released. Otherwise, they will be destroyed.

cancellation of registration See *preventing registration of mark*.

certificates of registration on Principal Register Proof that a mark has been registered with the *U.S. Patent and Trademark Office* on the *Principal Register of Trademarks and Servicemarks*. The certificate reproduces the mark and sets out the date of first *use in interstate commerce*. In addition, it indicates the particular product or service on which the mark is used, the number and date of registration, the term of registration, the date on which the application for registration was received at the Patent and Trademark Office, and any conditions and limitations that may be imposed on the registration. Under the Lanham Act, the certificate for registration on the principal register must be different in appearance from a certificate for registration on the **Supplemental Register**.

In addition to proof of registration, the certificate is prima facie evidence (i.e., will be accepted as valid on its face) of the registration's validity, of the **registrant's ownership of the mark**, and of the **registrant's exclusive right to use the mark** in commerce, in connection with the product or service specified in the certificate. This basically means that in the event of court action involving an alleged infringement, proving ownership of the mark can be accomplished by presenting the certificate to the court.

However, if the defendant is able to introduce significant evidence challenging ownership of the mark, or the right of the plaintiff to its exclusive use, the plaintiff will need to respond with actual evidence showing his prior use, or that the mark is adequately **distinctive**, or whatever other fact has been challenged by the defendant. Related terms: **protection of marks under Lanham Act** and **ownership of mark**.

certification mark   A type of **mark** authorized by the **Lanham Act** to be used for the express purpose of certifying various characteristics or qualities of products and services manufactured or provided by others. Among the characteristics that may be covered by this type of mark are regional origin, method of manufacture, product quality, and service accuracy. Examples of certification marks are "Good Housekeeping Seal of Approval", "Roquefort" (a region in France), "Stilton" cheese (a product from the Stilton locale in England), and "Harris Tweeds" (a special weave from a specific area in Scotland).

Example: The Utah Teachers Federation (UTF) decides to endorse educational computer software it finds especially helpful to the learning process. It request that all educational software producers submit their educational programs to the UTF for analysis and possible endorsement. All programs endorsed by the UTF carry the legend "Approved by the Utah Teachers Federation". This would be a **certification mark**.

Certification marks must be retained by the persons or groups originating them.

Conversely, assigning or **licensing** a certification mark to others destroys any meaning the mark may have had, and thus constitutes an **abandonment of the mark**. Certification marks may be **registered** in the U.S. under the **Lanham Act** in the same manner as **trademarks** and **servicemarks**. Related terms: **protection of marks under the Lanham Act**.

changing marks   See **reverse palming off** and **palming off**.

classes of goods and services   All **marks** that are registered under the **Lanham Act** are classified by the **U.S. Patent and Trademark Office** according to a master list called the **international classification of goods and services**. Because a mark's meaning is inseparable from the product or service to which it is attached, all registered marks may efficiently be stored and retrieved according to the class assigned to such product or service.

In a more general sense, if a mark has been registered in connection with one type of product or service, and the mark's owner desires to use it in connection with another type of product or service, a new registration should be obtained. Put differently, a mark is always a proper adjective that has no meaning unless it is connected to a noun (the product or service). Accordingly, marks are classified according to the product or service (noun) described by the mark. Example: Sweets Inc., a candy manufacturer, attaches the **trademark** "TummyYummy Candies" to its line of chocolate candies. Later on, Sweets ecides to enter the fresh fruit-juice market. If it wants to use the trademark "TummyYummy FruitJuice", it should obtain a new registration, since fruit-juice and candy are different products.

cognates, use of as marks   See **phonetic or foreign language equivalents for descriptive terms** .

coined words   Words invented by the producer of goods or services to serve as specific product or service identifiers. Coined terms are generally considered **strong** or **distinctive**, and are thus afforded more protection, than are words that are **descriptive** or in **common use** . So, the easiest way to assure **protection**

Trademark

for a mark is to make up, or "coin", a word. Any coined combination of letters and/or numerals, not already in use to *identify* or *distinguish* another product, qualifies under this rule if it can reasonably be said to distinguish the product or service to which it is attached from others. Thus, "4711 water" is an example of a coined phrase which is used as the *trademark* for a particular brand of cologne. Other common examples of coined words or phrases are "Kodak" (cameras), "Exxon" (oil) and "Xenix" (computer operating system). Related terms: *distinctive marks*.

collective mark   A symbol, label, word, phrase or other identifying mark used by members of a group or organization for goods they produce or services they render. A "collective mark" differs from a *trademark* or a *servicemark* in that only the members of the group are entitled to use the collective mark. The primary function of a collective mark is to identify goods or services as originating from a group's members, and to distinguish them from the products of non-members. In addition, the organization itself, as opposed to its members, cannot use the mark on any goods produced by it. If the organization itself wants to identify its product, it must use a trademark or servicemark.

A common use of collective marks is to indicate membership in a union, association, or other organization. Thus the letters "ILGWU" on a shirt is a collective mark identifying the shirt as a product of members of the International Ladies Garment Workers Union. It distinguishes that shirt from those made by non-union shops. If the ILGWU actually started marketing its own products, however, the ILGWU collective mark could not be used to identify them. Collective marks are entitled to the same federal protection as other types of marks. Compare *certification marks*.

color, used as mark   A color in and of itself cannot constitute a protectable mark. This is because the number of available colors is limited, and giving any business the exclusive right to one would be an excessive restraint on commerce and expression. However, a color may serve as an integral part of a valid mark, and, when used with a *distinctive* word, symbol, shape or design, may qualify for

protection. For instance, a red dot on the rubber heel of a shoe, and a red crown painted on bowling pins have, been recognized as valid marks in the United States. When a color is used primarily for decoration rather than as an essential part of the mark, protection will only be provided if a showing is made (through surveys, advertising budgets, and the like) that the *average consumer* recognizes the decoration as a mark.

Thus, if it can be shown (and it probably could be) that the average consumer identifies a picture of a multi-colored apple with a bite taken from the top right-hand side as the mark of an Apple Computer product, the design, with the particular colors, will qualify for protection. In recent years, the exclusive right to use colors in capsules and pills to distinguish brand-name drugs from each other, or from generic drugs (i.e., drugs marketed under their medical rather than brand name), has been the subject of widespread court litigation, one argument being that color is the only way to distinguish one line of capsules or tablets from another. This question has not yet been resolved. Related terms: *distinctive mark* and *trademark*.

commerce   To qualify for *registration* and protection under the *Lanham Act*, a mark must have first been used in "commerce". Commerce is defined by the *Lanham Act* to mean any commerce (i.e., sales, advertising, distribution) subject to regulation by Congress. The only commerce subject to regulation by Congress is "interstate commerce". Accordingly, if a mark is attached to goods or services that in some way move across state lines, it qualifies as having been used in "commerce". Related terms: *use of mark in interstate commerce* .

commercial name   See *trade name*.

Commissioner of Patents and Trademarks   The administrative head of the *U.S. Patent and Trademark Office* (PTO), a division of the U.S. Department of Commerce. The Commissioner is responsible for operating the PTO, promulgating administrative regulations governing the patent and trademark application process, and deciding disputes presented to the PTO in *inter partes* proceedings.

common use When a once *distinctive* mark becomes the *generic* or *descriptive* name identifier for a type of product, is is said to have fallen into common use. Related terms: *generic marks*.

competing and non-competing products When the sale of one product might mean the non-sale of another, the products are said to be competing. For instance, the sale of a personal computer by one company might result in the non-sale of a sophisticated calculator by another company, and the products would thus compete. Products are said to be non-competing when consumers could reasonably purchase both items (i.e., the purchase of one is not at the expense of the other). For example, perfume does not compete with computers.

In the trademark context, if products compete and *infringement of a mark* is established, it is sometimes possible for the owner of the infringed-upon mark to be awarded money damages, measured by the amount of profits earned by the defendant from the infringing mark (called *defendant's profits*). This is because the sale, by the defendant, of a competing product with an infringing mark, can reasonably be said to be at the expense of the plaintiff's sales. On the other hand, if the goods are non-competing, profits are generally not awarded even though an infringement may be found to have occurred because the goods are *related*. Related terms: *related and unrelated goods*.

concurrent registration Two or more owners of identical or similar marks may legally, in some circumstances, both register their marks on the *Principal Register*. This can occur 1) if both marks were in *use in interstate commerce* before either owner applied for registration and 2) if the likelihood of customer confusion is slight either because the products or services to which the marks will be connected are *unrelated*, or the products and/or services will be marketed in sufficiently distinct geographic areas.

When such concurrent registrations are issued, the *U.S. Patent and Trademark Office* may specify marketing and use limitations to preclude *confusion of customers*. For example, the *PTO* may restrict the use of one mark to ten Western States and allow the use of the other

mark in the rest of the states. Or, the use of the respective marks may be restricted to their original products or services. Related terms: *related and unrelated products or services* and *competing and non-competing products*.

confusion of consumers A situation where an *average consumer* is likely to be confused by the use of same or similar marks on different products. This confusion can relate to source or origin, business affiliation, connection (e.g., putting the Olympic symbol on a product without authorization), or sponsorship.

In a lawsuit to determine whether *infringement of a mark* or *unfair competition* has occurred, a court must make several basic findings. Among these are 1) whether the allegedly infringing mark is the same as or similar to the mark allegedly infringed, and 2) whether the products or services are *related or unrelated*. How these issues are decided will be heavily influenced by the judge's opinion as to whether or not consumers might be confused by the simultaneous use of the two marks. One mark will be found to be similar to another if the average consumer might mistake the two. Similarly, a product or service will be considered related if this fictional average consumer would probably be confused in the event both products or services used the same mark. In short, the likelihood of consumer confusion is a key factor in the determination of whether trademark infringement and unfair competition has or has not occurred. Related terms: *trademark infringement action* and *unfair competition*.

constructive notice of mark under Lanham Act When a mark is placed on the *Principal Register* under the *Lanham Act*, the law assumes that all future potential users of the same or similar mark anywhere in the United States will have knowledge that the mark in question is owned by someone else. This assumed (constructive) notice precludes the use of the mark anywhere in the U.S., unless such use was begun prior to the *registration*.

While the courts will generally not act against an *infringing mark* if it is used in a *geographically separate market*, should the original *registrant* later choose to expand into such heretofore separate

Trademark

market, the infringer will have to cease using the mark, unless it was in use prior to the registrarion. Because of this rule, selecting a new mark often involves searching the Principal and Supplemental Register to make sure the proposed mark is still available.

Example: A California comedy group puts together a satirical review called Lawbotics, a series of skits about lawyers and their professional behavior patterns. As the review is performed in a number of Western states, the mark qualifies as being *used in interstate commerce*. The comedy group registers "Lawbotics" as a *service mark* under the *Lanham Act*. Because anti-lawyer jokes and skits are popular everywhere, a Vermont comedy group, which has never heard of the California "Lawbotics" review, names its act "Lawbotics" and starts packing them in along the Eastern Seaboard. In this situation, because the California "Lawbotics" group registered under the Lanham Act prior to the Vermont group's use of the term, the Vermont group has infringed the California group's service mark. And, because registration provides "constructive notice" of prior ownership, the Vermont group is a *deliberate infringer* from a legal point of view, even though it was actually unaware of the prior use. However, if the California group never goes East and the Vermont group never goes West the courts will probably never be called on to decide the issue. But if the California Lawbotics group starts getting bookings anywhere near the Eastern seaboard, or gains a national audience through television or radio, they may go to court to stop the Vermont group from further use of the mark.

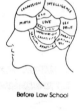

Fig 1 (Normal Brain)

Before Law School

Fig. 2 (Lawbotomized Brain)

After Law School

continued use of mark, affidavit of
See *duration of registration*.

continuous use of mark
To qualify for *incontestability status* (where a mark becomes immune from challenge except on certain specified grounds) a mark must first be in continuous use for a five year period subsequent to its being placed on the *Principal Register*. Any showing that the use of the mark was substantially interrupted during the five year period may prevent the mark from becoming incontestable. Related terms: *incontestability status* and *duration of registration on Principal Register*.

contributory infringement
Any act by a party that furthers or encourages the infringing activity of another. For example, a store that sells records carrying an infringing mark is considered a contributory infringer, as is the wholesale distributor of the records, the record company, and any other person or business whose actions contribute to the infringement.

Contributory infringers are not held liable for *damages* or *defendants' profits* as long as they qualify for *innocent infringer status* (e.g., they didn't know about the infringement), but they may be enjoined from any further contributory activity. Thus, the record store owner could be enjoined from selling the infringing records, unless the offending mark were removed. If a contributory infringer knows of the infringement, however, he or she can be held liable on the same basis and in the same amount as the principal infringer. Related terms: *trademark infringement action* and *innocent infringer status*.

counterfeit marks
According to the *Lanham Act*, a "counterfeit" *mark* is a mark that is identical with, or substantially indistinguishable from, a *registered mark*. For example, the term "Levi" on a pair of blue jeans not manufactured by Levi is a counterfeit mark. The legal difference between counterfeit marks and marks that merely infringe another mark is very hard to discern. Generally, the term counterfeit is reserved for situations where the infringer is clearly trying to *palm off* its goods as those made by another business (as in the Levi example). Related terms: *palming off*.

court orders
See *injunctions against infringement*.

Customs, Bureau of
See *Bureau of Customs*.

damages in trademark infringement cases
When the rights of a *registered mark's* owner are shown to have been *infringed*, and the owner has provided proper *notice of registration* when using the mark (i.e., ® or "Reg. U.S. Pat. Off."), a court is authorized under 37 USC Sec. 1117 to award the owner up to three times the actual money damages suffered as a result of the infringement (treble damages). Such damages may

consist of lost sales, loss of good will, or any other monetary losses directly attributable to the infringement. The court also has authority to award the plaintiff 1) **defendant's profits** (i.e., the profits made by the defendant from his or her infringing activity), and 2) **court costs** in addition to such damages. However, the court may not award **defendants' profits** and money damages on the same lost sales. Related terms: **trademark infringement action**.

deceptive terms as marks See **prohibited and reserved marks under Lanham Act**.

defendant's profits Profits earned by a defendant as a result of **infringing a mark** may be awarded to the **owner of the mark** under 37 USC Sec. 1117, if the owner provided proper **notice of registration** (i.e., "®" or "Reg. U.S. Pat. Off.") in connection with the mark. To qualify for this recovery, the plaintiff (the party bringing the infringement action) only needs to prove the amount realized by the defendant from the sales of his goods or services. Then, the defendant is given the opportunity to establish his costs (e.g., cost of production, sales attributable to other factors, etc.) and deduct them from the gross sales amount to arrive at the amount of his profit.

Awarding "defendant's profits" to the injured party prevents an infringer from realizing any gain from his or her infringement. Generally, courts will only award profits in the event that the defendant had full knowledge of the infringement (i.e., was a **deliberate infringer** rather than an **innocent infringer**), and therefore presumably intended it to occur. Also, profits will not be awarded if the products or services are not competing with each other. Related terms: **competing and non-competing products and services** and **damages in trademark infringement cases**.

defensive registration A type of registration in the United Kingdom where a trademark is registered not only for the product on which it is being used, but also for products on which the **registrant** may potentially use the mark in the future. This type of registration is used to keep other companies from using the mark on products that might be related in

the public mind to those already being marketed by the **registrant**.

Example: A large household supply manufacturer registers the trademark "Laserclean" in connection with a new dishwashing detergent. It might also register "Laserclean" with a laundry detergent, a bath soap, and a car polish, even though it is not currently manufacturing any of those products. These additional registrations will then preclude other companies from using Laserclean for such products, and allow the **registrant** an opportunity to expand its trademark into those areas if it desires.

deliberate infringer Any party who uses a mark with actual or **constructive notice** that the mark is owned by someone else. Deliberate infringers are generally liable for the harm their infringement causes to the mark's rightful owner, and for the **profits** that they have made from their infringing activity. In addition, deliberate infringers may be liable for **treble damages** if the infringement was particularly willful. Related terms: **innocent infringer** and **contributory infringement**.

descriptive mark A mark that is primarily used to describe the nature or characteristics of a product or service. Descriptive marks are generally viewed by the courts as **weak** and thus not deserving of much, if any, judicial protection. This is because a description of the characteristics of a product or service does not serve to distinguish it from similar products or services offered by others. Therefore, protecting such marks does not fulfill the primary purpose of the trademark laws, which is to afford protection to marks that operate as indicators of origin. Accordingly, descriptive marks do not usually qualify for placement on the **Principal Register** under the **Lanham Act**. Instead, they are placed on the **Supplemental Register** (which offers much less protection than the Principal Register). Related terms: **Supplemental Register**.

Among the examples of marks considered too descriptive for placement on the Principal Register are "Beer Nuts", "Chap Stick", "FashionKnit" sweaters, "Bufferin", "Tender Vittles" and "Rich 'n Chips". In each of these examples, the names focus more on describing some aspect of the product than they do on

distinguishing it from others in the public's mind.

What happens, however, if a descriptive mark is mistakenly placed on the Principal Register by the **U.S. Patent and Trademark Office**. In that case, the validity of the mark may be challenged up until the time the mark achieves **incontestability status**. Once that occurs, however, the mark is immune from a challenge on the ground that it is descriptive. Related terms: **incontestability status**.

Even if a descriptive mark does not make the Principal Register, if it is used over a period of time and can be shown to have become associated in the **average consumer's** mind with the source of the product or service, a descriptive mark may become **distinctive**, and thus may qualify for the Principal Register under the **secondary meaning** rule. Related terms: **secondary meaning**.

dilution of marks The use of a **strong mark**, owned by another party, in a manner that causes a reduction in the mark's distinctiveness, uniqueness, effectiveness, or prestigious connotation. Mark dilution normally arises when an already owned mark is used by someone else on an **unrelated product** in a situation where the **confusion of customers** is likely to be low or non-existent. In such a situation, the courts may hold that no **infringement of the mark** has occurred. But if use of the mark can be said to harm the value of the already owned mark in some way, a court may rule (in the states that recognize this legal doctrine) that "trademark dilution" has occurred, and enjoin the further use of the mark.

For example, on the ground that its mark was being diluted, the Hyatt Hotel Chain obtained an Illinois state court order preventing the Hyatt Legal Services from using the term "Hyatt" in Illinois. In the words of one court decision, "Dilution refers to a loss of distinctiveness, a weakening of a mark's propensity to bring to mind a particular product, service, or source of either". Generally, the courts will only apply the dilution concept to **strong marks**, since **weak marks** cannot be diluted in any meaningful way.

Example: Quick and Dirty Paint Company produces a line of cheap and decidedly inferior house paints which it labels

"IBM spectrum". Since house paints and electronics are unrelated and the likelihood of customer confusion as to origin is slight, the courts might find that no trademark infringement occurred. However, the use of a mark such as "IBM", which stands for quality high-technology products, in a context that is extremely mundane, may result in a finding of trademark dilution. If so, the court will probably issue an **injunction** to prevent further dilution by Quick and Dirty and award damages to IBM for any loss of business or goodwill caused by the dilution.

The **Lanham Act** does not cover trademark dilution, but a number of states have "anti-dilution statutes" providing for judicial relief in the case of dilution. Among these are New York, California, Illinois, Massachusetts, Connecticut and Florida.

disclaimer of unregistrable material
When a person or business seeking **registration of a mark** under the **Lanham Act** formally declares that part of the mark is not protectable. This is required of a **registrant** when a mark is comprised partially of registrable matter and partially of unregistrable matter. Before the **U.S. Patent and Trademark Office** will register such a **hybrid mark** , the **registrant** must disclaim the part that doesn't qualify. Then, although the mark will be registered in its entirety, the mark's owner will only have the exclusive right to use the portion not disclaimed.

Example: The Exotic Perfume Company manufactures a line of fragrances named for various wildflowers. One of these is called "California Snapdragon". If Exotic wants to register this mark, it will have to disclaim the "California" part of it, since California is a **geographic term** and thus not registrable. If Exotic refuses to disclaim "California", the Patent and Trademark Office will probably refuse registration. If disclaimer is made, however, the entire mark can be registered. But, only the "snapdragon" portion will qualify for protection, and only in relation to perfume or **related goods**. Then, if a competing fragrance company comes out with ' 'California Wild Rose" fragrance, there will be no infringement. On the other hand, if the competitor produces "Oregon Snapdragon" fragrance it is possible that a court will find infringement. Related terms: **protection of mark under Lanham Act**.

discontinuance of business, effect on mark   See **abandonment of mark**.

disparaging mark   See **prohibited and reserved marks under Lanham Act**.

distinctive mark   A **mark** capable of distinguishing the product or service to which it is attached from competing goods and services, thus qualifying it for maximum judicial protection under state and federal laws. The more distinctive the mark, the stronger it is considered to be for protection purposes. This means that the courts will be more willing to find that other similar marks are likely to result in the **confusion of consumers**, and are thus **infringing marks**.

For example, any mark used by a camera-related business that even hinted at the term "Kodak" would be considered infringing, since "Kodak" is a very **strong mark**. On the other hand, the use of the term "data" in a mark will probably not be considered to be infringing, since that word is already in wide use among large numbers of high-technology businesses.

A mark must be distinctive to qualify for placement on the **Principal Register** under the **Lanham Act**. As a general matter, marks that are **coined**, **fanciful**, or **arbitrary** are considered distinctive whereas marks that tend to describe the product (**descriptive marks**) are considered **weak marks** and thus **non-distinctive**.

Non-distinctive marks may become distinctive over time through widespread use of the mark, and association of it with a particular product in the **average consumer**"s mind. This is referred to as the mark assuming a **secondary meaning**. Also, marks that appear to be descriptive on their surface may in fact suggest another meaning and thus be considered distinctive on that basis. For example, if a personal robot manufacturer uses the trademark "Android" (as in "Android Kitchen Helper' ", or "Android Yard Cleaner"), the word Android is not meant in its descriptive sense but instead suggests such valid marketing concepts as high-technology and, generally, the future.

On the other hand, marks that are

originally distinctive, such as aspirin, monopoly, cellophane, etc., may become used in such a manner that they no longer serve as product or service identifiers. In that case they lose their status as protectable marks. Related terms: **generic marks** and **suggestive marks**.

distinctiveness acquired through use of mark over time   See **secondary meaning**.

duration of registration on Principal Register   In the U.S., once a **trademark** or **servicemark** is registered on the **Principal Register**, the owner receives a **certificate of registration**, good for twenty years. However, under the **Lanham Act** (15 USC sec. 1058), the mark is subject to **cancellation** by the **Commissioner of Patents and Trademarks** at the end of six years unless the **registrant** files a statement under oath (affidavit) showing that the mark is either still in use in **interstate commerce** or that the non-use of the mark is not for reasons of **abandonment**. This **affidavit of continued use** must be filed within the last year of the six year period. Registration may continually be renewed in this manner in perpetuity.

Example: Andrenae Associates, Inc. operates a graphics design business under the servicemark "Nae's Displays". If this mark carries a registration date of May 1, 1986, the registration is good for 20 years, or until 2006, as long as Andrenae files the appropriate "affidavit of continued use". Andrenae must file this affidavit between May 1, 1991 (five years after her registration date) and May 1, 1992 (the expiration of the six year period).

exclusive right to use mark   In the U.S., the exclusive right to use a mark begins on the date the mark is first used publically to identify particular goods or services in a **distinctive manner**. This right may last unless or until the mark is **abandoned**, **cancelled**, or becomes **generic** (i.e., becomes so popular that it serves to identify or define a whole product field instead of a particular product or product line). Under certain circumstances, the owner of the right to exclusive use of a mark may require a later user to stop use of an **infringing mark** and in some situations may be awarded **money damages**.

Although this exclusive right to use the mark initially exists in the area where the mark is being used, how broad is the scope of this right in the event the same or similar mark is used by another party somewhere else? In the U.S., the answer to this question depends primarily on the following factors:

• which mark was first used anywhere in the United States

• which mark was first registered under the **Lanham Act**

• whether the first **registrant** under the **Lanham Act** was the **junior user** or the **senior user**

• if the first **registrant** under the **Lanham Act** was the junior user, whether that party knew of the mark's prior use by the senior user

• whether there is geographical proximity between the areas in which two conflicting marks are used

• whether the types of products or services to which the marks are attached are **related** or **unrelated**, and

• generally, whether **confusion of consumers** is likely to result from the use of the the two marks

Example: Marylou Inc. restricts the marketing of its marshmallow cookies, "Marylou's Marvelous Mallows", to California. Since there is no interstate use, Marylou is only entitled to protection under state trademark laws. Accordingly, if MaryJean, who lives in Nevada, decides to market cookies exclusively in Nevada under the name of "MaryJean's Marvelous Mallows", Marylou will probably have no recourse, due to the geographically separate market for MaryJean's product, unless she can show that a number of customers are likely to be confused by the similar marks.

Suppose, however, that Marylou Inc. markets its cookies in even one other state besides California, and registers the mark under the Lanham Act, prior to MaryJean's use of her mark. In that case, Marylou Inc, can file an infringement action in court to stop MaryJean from using her mark, on the ground that Marylou Inc's prior registration gave MaryJean **constructive notice** (i.e., legally presumed notice) of Marylou Inc's national ownership of the mark, thereby precluding MaryJean from using her confusingly similar mark.

Suppose, now, that Marylou Inc. markets its cookies in a large interstate market prior to MaryJean starting business, but registers after MaryJean has used her mark in Nevada. Although Marylou Inc. was the first user, it can only force MaryJean to stop using her mark if it can show either that MaryJean knew or should have known of the prior use by Marylou Inc., or that a likelihood of customer confusion exists. The fact that Nevada and California are geographically close would weigh in Marylou Inc's favor on this point. If Marylou Inc. cannot establish either of these facts, it is possible that MaryJean will be able to

continue the use of her mark in Nevada.

If MaryJean uses her mark in New York rather than Nevada, while Marylou Inc. restricts its marketing to the Western states, even prior federal registration and first use would not allow Marylou Inc. to stop MaryJean's use of the mark. Nor, we might add, will she need to, since MaryJean's enterprise is not in competition with her own. However, if Marylou Inc. later decides to market in the eastern part of the U.S., Marylou's exclusive right to market nationwide, which arises from her prior registration, will require MaryJean to stop using the mark.

What, however, if MaryJean registers before Marylou Inc.? In this situation, if MaryJean did not know (either actually or constructively) of Marylou Inc.'s prior use, MaryJean will become entitled to exclusive use on a national basis except where Marylou Inc. is already marketing. If MaryJean does know of Marylou's prior use, however, her registration may be deemed fraudulent and set aside.

These priorities can be confusing and highly dependent on the facts of each case. This discussion is only meant to provide the reader with an idea of what is involved. The following chart puts these various factors in visual perspective. (See chart next page.)

failure to provide notice of registration See **notice of registration**.

false advertising under Lanham Act See **unfair competition under Lanham Act** and **palming off**.

National Priorities for Conflicting Marks

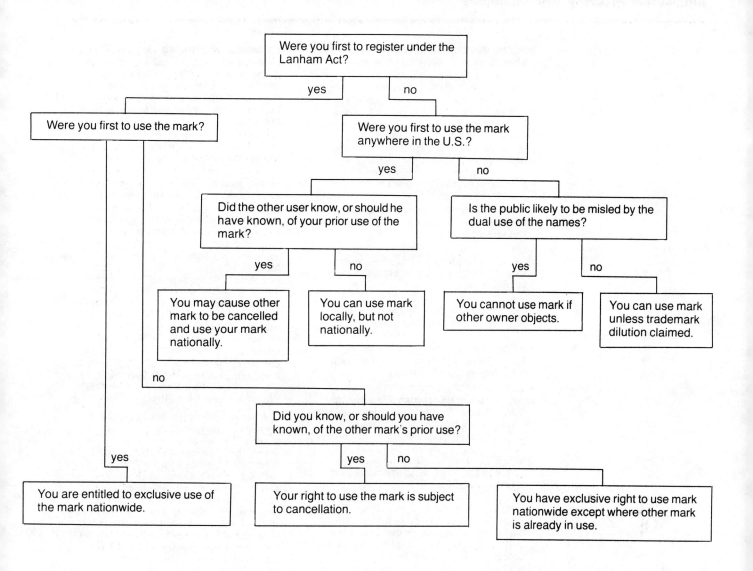

Were you first to register under the Lanham Act?

yes — Were you first to use the mark?

no — Were you first to use the mark anywhere in the U.S.?

Were you first to use the mark anywhere in the U.S.? → yes:
Did the other user know, or should he have known, of your prior use of the mark?

- yes → You may cause other mark to be cancelled and use your mark nationally.
- no → You can use mark locally, but not nationally.

Were you first to use the mark anywhere in the U.S.? → no:
Is the public likely to be misled by the dual use of the names?

- yes → You cannot use mark if other owner objects.
- no → You can use mark unless trademark dilution claimed.

Were you first to use the mark?

- yes → You are entitled to exclusive use of the mark nationwide.
- no → Did you know, or should you have known, of the other mark's prior use?
  - yes → Your right to use the mark is subject to cancellation.
  - no → You have exclusive right to use mark nationwide except where other mark is already in use.

fanciful words and phrases See *trademarks* and *distinctive marks*.

federal registration A process whereby marks are listed with the U.S. Patent and Trademark Office so that potential second users will know that someone else owns them. For the rules concerning which marks may be registered, the protection they will receive, and the procedures involved in the registration process, see *protection of marks under Lanham Act*.

first registration See *exclusive right to use mark* and *protection of marks under Lanham Act*.

first use of mark in U.S. See *ownership of mark in U.S.* and *exclusive right to use mark*.

flags as marks See *prohibited and reserved marks under Lanham Act*.

foreign language equivalent terms See *phonetic or foreign language equivalents for descriptive terms*.

foreign nationals, registration by in U.S. A non-U.S. national or business is entitled to register in the U.S. under the *Lanham Act*, provided that his, her or its country of origin affords reciprocal rights to U.S. citizens, and that the mark has been *used in the U.S.* in *interstate commerce*. In addition, if the person or business is a national of a country with which the U.S. has a reciprocal treaty, a mark registered in such a country may be *registered* in the U.S. without prior use in the U.S. However, to qualify for registration, the mark must have been used somewhere in the world. Also, after registration of such a mark in the U.S., the mark must be used in *interstate commerce* within a reasonable time. Otherwise it may be considered as *abandoned*. Related terms: *Paris Convention* and *Inter-American Convention for Trademark and Commercial Protection*.

franchising, service marks See *naked licenses*.

fraudulent registration of mark See *registration under Lanham Act* and *incontestibility status*.

free words or phrases Words or phrases that may be used by anyone in the world to describe goods or services, and that are thus not eligible for *trademark* protection in a specific country. *Generic terms* and *words in common use* such as "A OK" and "Hunky Dorey" are usually considered "free" under this test. Related terms: *generic marks* and *words and phrases*.

generic marks Words or symbols commonly used to describe an entire type of product or service rather than to distinguish one product or service from another. Generic marks are almost always refused protection on the ground that all-descriptive terms no longer fulfill the function of a mark (to distinguish goods or services from competing ones) and therefore belong in the public domain rather than to an exclusive owner. For example, "Raisin Bran" is considered a *generic* phrase in that it describes a kind of cereal (it defines the product itself rather than its source). So, several different cereal manufacturers produce raisin bran, but each imposes its own mark on it (e.g., Post Raisin Bran, Kellogg's Raisin Bran, Skinner's Raisin Bran).

A term formerly protectable as a mark may lose such protection if it becomes generic. This often occurs when a mark is assimilated into common use to such an extent that it becomes a general term defining the entire type of product or service. For example, "escalator" was originally a protected trademark used to designate the moving stairs manufactured by a specific company. Eventually, however, the word became synonymous with the very idea of moving stairs and thus lost its protection. Xerox is another example of a mark which originally was understood to refer to one product line but which now is commonly used to describe both the process of photocopying and the result. Other examples of marks that have become generic are kleenex, q-tips, and jello. Accordingly, "Xerox" is probably close to becoming generic.

What happens if a term used as a mark becomes generic as we saw, it no longer qualifies as a *protectable mark*. Assuming, for example, that Xerox does become generic, does this mean you can go out and call your photocopy service "Xerox, Inc."? The answer is no, since this would probably result in *confusion of consumers*, and therefore constitute *unfair competition* under federal and state law. However, if you called your company "Acme Xeroxing Corporation", you might be on safe ground, again assuming that the term has become generic.

How can a company keep a mark from becoming generic? Xerox has spent millions of advertising dollars advising the public that Xerox is in fact a *registered mark*, should only be used as a proper adjective in connection with a noun (i.e., Xerox brand photocopier), and should not be used as a verb (i.e., to xerox something) or as a general noun indicating the result of the photocopying process (i.e., a xerox). If later on someone challenges the Xerox Corporation's right to the exclusive use of the word "Xerox", on the ground it has become generic, Xerox may prevail if it can show that people understood these advertisements, and continued to consider the term "Xerox" as a brand, rather than generic, name.

In many countries, including the United Kingdom and members of the European Economic Community (EEC or Common Market), terms can never "become generic" once they have qualified as *protectable marks*. Related terms: *unfair competition* and *unfair competition under Lanham Act*.

geographically separate market
When products or services carrying a mark are sold in a part of the country that is definitively separate from an area where competing goods and services are being marketed. *Infringement of a mark* is not generally found when markets for similar goods with conflicting arks are geographically separate. Related terms: *exclusive right to use mark*.

geographic terms as marks Geographic words are generally considered to be *free words* (i.e., words that are *commonly used* and thus non-protectable). When such terms are used descriptively as part of a mark, they are not reserved for *exclusive use* by the mark's owner under the trademark laws unless they become *distinctive* (i.e., closely identified with a particular product in the minds of consumers) through the *secondary meaning* rule.

For example such words as "American", "Texan", "Antartica", and

"Nationwide" are generally not eligible for protection. However, "American" as in "American Airlines", "Nationwide" as in "Nationwide Move-it-yourself" and "Hershey" as in "Hershey Bar" are all examples of geographic terms that have become distinctive by use over time.

The *Lanham Act* provides that terms not "primarily" geographical in nature (not referring to defined locations) may be used and protected as marks. Examples of such words are "Northern", "Southern", "Metropolitan", and "Globe". Also, geographical terms are acceptable in *certification marks*. Related terms: *prohibited and reserved marks under Lanham Act* and *disclaimer of unregistrable material*.

good trademark A "good" or "valid" mark is one that is properly used by its owner and can be protected in the courts. For example, if I were to use the word "Sodapop" as a *trademark* on my new line of flavored mineral waters, I would have a "trademark", but not a good one. Why? Because "Sodapop" is highly *descriptive* and *generic* and therefore not enforceable as a trademark in court.

good will, sale of See *assignment of marks*.

hybrid marks Marks that consist of partially *registrable matter* and partially *unregistrable matter*. Related terms: *disclaimer of unregistrable material*.

identify and distinguish In order to receive judicial protection against *infringement*, a *mark* must serve to identify and distinguish a product or service from others. Related terms: *distinctive marks* and *trademarks*.

immoral marks See *prohibited and reserved marks under Lanham Act*.

incontestability status When a mark is in *continuous use* for five years after being placed on the *Principal Register*, it becomes immune from legal challenge, or uncontestable, provided that 1) no final legal decision adverse to the mark owner's claim has been rendered in the meantime, 2) no challenge to the owner's claim is pending, 3) an *affidavit of use* is filed on a timely basis, and 4) the mark is not and has not become *generic* (37 USC Sec. 1065). In essence, "incontestability

AmericanAirlines
Something special in the air"

Trademark

status" means *ownership of the mark* is conclusively established in terms of the uses specified in the "affidavit of use".

The question of whether a mark is incontestable generally arises in an *infringement action* where the defendant seeks to challenge the validity of the plaintiff's mark. If the plaintiff can establish that the mark is incontestable, then the mark is presumed valid unless the defendant can establish one or more "incontestability defenses".

Paradoxically, there are a number of contexts in which the incontestability of a mark may be contested. The very number of these "incontestablity defenses" means that the term "incontestable" really means "somewhat difficult to contest". Incontestability status may be challenged on any of the following grounds:

- the registration or the incontestable right to use the mark was btained fraudulently
- the mark has been *abandoned* by the *registrant*
- the mark is being used to misrepresent the source of the goods or services with which it is being used (i.e., use of the *mark* involves *palming off*)
- the infringing mark is an individual's name being used in his own business (i.e., a *tradename*), or is a mark prohibited or reserved under the Lanham Act
- the infringing mark was used in interstate commerce first, and prior to the incontestable mark's registration
- the infringing mark was registered first, or
- the mark is being used to violate the anti-trust laws of the United States [37 USC Sec. 1115(b)]

Even though an incontestable mark can still be challenged on these grounds, it is safe from attack on the ground it lacks distinctiveness. Thus, when Park "N Fly, Inc. sued Dollar Park and Fly, Inc. for trademark infringement, the U.S. Supreme Court ruled that because the Park 'N Fly mark had obtained incontestability status, it's validity as a descriptive mark could not be challenged by Dollar Park and Fly, Inc., as a defense.

incontestability defenses Circumstances that permit a trademark's *incontestability status* to be challenged in court. See *incontestability status*.

infringed See *infringement of marks*.

infringement action A lawsuit filed by a party claiming to own a mark (the plaintiff), against another user of the same or similar mark (the defendant), for the purpose of 1) preventing any further such use and 2) collecting damages suffered by the plaintiff as a result of such use. Related terms: *injunctions against infringement* and *damages in trademark infringement actions*.

infringement and unfair competition as a tort *Infringement of marks* and *unfair competition* (a collection of commercial wrongs) are considered to be torts (personal injuries) and therefore generally subject to the laws and doctrines applicable to other types of torts, except when statutes dictate otherwise. Thus, *contributory infringers* may be held liable on the same basis as the main infringer (when adequate knowledge of the infringement is present), and liability may accordingly be imposed on a joint and individual basis. Related terms: *contributory infringement* and *deliberate infringers*.

infringement of mark Under the *Lanham Act*, basic infringement occurs when any party makes commercial use of "any reproduction, counterfeit, copy, or colorable imitation of a registered mark in connection with the sale, offering for sale, distribution, or advertising of any goods or services on or in connection with which such use is likely to cause confusion, or to cause mistake, or to deceive" [15 USC Sec. 1114]. In other words, infringement is any use of a mark belonging to another in a commercial context where *confusion of consumers* is likely to result. A mark need not be identical to one already in use to infringe upon the owner's rights. If the proposed mark is similar enough to the earlier mark to risk confusing the *average consumer*, the use of it will constitute infringement.

Determining whether an *average consumer* might be confused is the key to deciding whether infringement exists. The answer to this question depends on whether the products or services carrying the disputed mark are *related* to those allegedly infringed upon, and if so, whether the marks are sufficiently similar to create the likelihood of consumer confusion. Related terms: *confusion of con-*

sumers and *related and unrelated products and services*.

injunctions against infringement and unfair competition Court orders that prevent further *infringing* activity or *unfair competition*. Under the state and federal laws applicable to *trademarks*, *servicemarks*, and *unfair competition*, courts have authority to require or prohibit any action or inaction necessary to protect the *owner of a mark* from economic harm.

Typically, if a court finds that infringement or unfair competition has occurred, the defendant will be ordered to stop using the *infringing mark* and will be required to destroy items or labels carrying the offending mark if it cannot be properly altered or replaced. In some cases, especially if the defendant has *innocent infringer status*, the court may allow some continued use of the mark in a particular locality, but bar it in other parts of the country.

The courts have broad power (called their *equity* 5 power) to fashion their injunctions so as to obtain justice under varying circumstances. Thus, even though an injunction is addressed to the parties in a case, its terms may be enforced against anyone. Because lawsuits often take years to resolve, the courts have power to issue *temporary restraining orders* 1 and *preliminary injunctions* 1 to prevent an infringement from occurring pending the final outcome of the case. Related terms: *injunctions in trade secret cases* 1 and *trade secret infringement action*.

innocent infringer status The status accorded a mark infringer by a court when he or she had no prior knowledge that the mark was being infringed, and when the mark was not previously *registered* under the *Lanham Act*, or in the state(s) where the infringement occurred. If the mark was registered prior to the beginning of the infringing activity, however, the law considers that the infringer received *constructive notice of the mark* (he or she is deemed to have been informed that the mark was owned by someone else). Such notice precludes the possibility of the infringer being innocent. But, if the registration occurred after the infringing activity began, then the infringer may still be "innocent" until he

or she learns of the registration.

When an infringer is considered innocent, the owner of an infringed mark will usually not be able to collect *money damages* or *defendants' profits* , and in some cases may not be able to prevent the infringer from continuing to use the mark, at least in a limited geographical area. Related terms: *infringement action* and *injunctions under Lanham Act*.

intent to abandon mark through non-use See *abandonment of mark*.

inter-partes proceeding An administrative hearing conducted by the *Trademark Trial and Appeal Board* to resolve 1) *interferences* (i.e., conflicts) between pending applications, 2) the merits of *opposition* and *cancellation* petitions, and 3) disputed decisions by the *Commissioner of Patents and Trademarks* in regard to applications for registration under the *Lanham Act*.

Inter-American Convention for Trademark and Commercial Protection A treaty providing reciprocal trademark relations between the U.S. and several Latin American nations that are not signatories to the *Paris Convention*. These are: Colombia, Cuba, Guatemala, Haiti, Honduras, Nicaragua, Panama, Paraguay, Peru, Brazil and the Dominican Republic.

interference, trademark When two or more marks awaiting *registration* in the *U.S. Patent and Trademark Office* appear to overlap or conflict with each other, an "interference" exists. In this situation, if any applicant requests it, the Patent and Trademark Office will set up an interference hearing in which the *ownership of the mark* in question will be determined. Interference hearings tend to be expensive and lengthy, and in many cases one applicant will simply withdraw his or her application and devise a new mark rather than suffer through one. For this reason, trademark interference proceedings are relatively rare. When they do occur, however, certain established priorities are utilized to determine who is entitled to *exclusive use of the mark*. Related terms: *exclusive use of a mark*.

international classification of goods and services A method of classifying goods and services in respect to which marks are customarily used. The first international classification list was drafted as part of the Nice Agreement of 1957, and has subsequently been updated and revised. This classification system is used by the *U.S. Patent and Trademark Office* to keep track of mark registrations. Related terms: *classes of goods and services*.

International Convention for the Protection of Industrial Property of 1883 See *Paris Convention*.

International Trade commission, complaints to See *Bureau of Customs*.

interstate commerce, affecting See *affecting interstate commerce*.

interstate commerce, use in See *use in interstate commerce*.

junior user When a dispute exists over *ownership of a mark*, the person or entity who was second to use the mark is called the junior user. Related terms: *senior users and junior users* and *exclusive right to use mark*.

Lanham Act A group of federal statutes covering such matters as 1) when *owners of marks* may be entitled to federal judicial protection against *infringement of a mark* by others, 2) the types of protection that the federal courts are authorized to provide (e.g., *money damages*, *defendant's profits*, or *injunctive relief*), 3) procedures for registering marks with the *U.S. Patent and Trademark Office* (on the *Principal Register* or *Supplemental Register*), 4) when trademarks become *incontestable*, and 5) remedies for activity that constitutes *unfair competition*.

The two basic purposes of the *Lanham Act* are: 1) to eliminate deception and *unfair competition* in the marketing of goods and services, and 2) to provide a means for the owner of a mark to be protected against the use of a confusingly similar mark by others. The Lanham Act is contained in 15 United States Code Sections 1050 and following. Related terms: *protection of marks under Lanham Act* and *unfair competition under Lanham Act*.

Madrid Agreement

licensing of trademarks When an *owner of a mark* authorizes another party to use it for commercial purposes. Such *licenses* 5 must be very carefully drafted, since allowing someone to use a mark without adequate restriction and supervision may result in the mark being considered *abandoned*. Related terms: *naked license*.

loss of trademark Ownership of an otherwise valid trademark may be lost in several situations. These may be when there is an *abandonment of a mark*, a loss of distinctiveness (i.e., the mark becomes *generic*), an improper use of a mark (e.g., an *anti-trust* 5 violation), or an unfavorable decision in a *cancellation* or *interference* proceeding.

mark, defined As used in this dictionary, "mark" is a generic reference to *trademarks*, *servicemarks*, *certification marks* and *collective marks*. Thus, when we speak of "protection of marks under the Lanham Act", we refer collectively to these different types of marks. The term "mark" is also generally used to refer to any means by which a service or product is identified and distinguished from others.

Madrid Agreement on International Registration of Trademarks An international treaty under which trademark owners in the member nations can submit their national trademark registrations to the International Bureau of the World Intellectual Property Organization for registration. Then, the mark is protected in all the member countries on the same basis as a national trademark. Each member country has one year from the date of such international registration to reject the mark for coverage in that country. If the year passes without such rejection, however, and the mark is used for five years after the international registration, it becomes good for an additional fifteen years, and longer if it is renewed.

Neither the U.S. nor the United Kingdom are members of this treaty. However the following countries are: Algeria, Austria, Belgium, Czechoslovakia, Egypt, France, West Germany (Federal Republic), East Germany (Democratic Republic), Hungary, Italy, South Korea, Liechtenstein, Luxembourg, Monaco, Switzerland, Tunisia, USSR, Vietnam, and Yugoslavia.

mark dilution   See *dilution of marks*.

marks as good will   See *assignment of marks*.

misuse of mark   See *proper use of mark*.

money damages for mark infringement   See *damages for trademark infringement*.

naked license   "Naked license" is a term used in the event an owner of a mark allows others to use it without adequate safeguards or restrictions as to the underlying goods or services. In some situations, especially those involving franchise operations, the grant of a "naked license" can operate as an *abandonment of the trademark*. This is because a mark is intended to identify and distinguish specific products and services from competing ones, and to indicate a particular level of quality attached to some product or service.

For example, the "McDonald's" *servicemark* is intended not only to distinguish McDonald's from its competitors generally, but also to call to a consumer's mind such characteristics as a specific level of service, a specific type of meal at a specific price, and a specific level of cleanliness. How is this accomplished? Every owner of a McDonald's franchise is required to operate the franchise under certain rules and restrictions, designed to insure that the characteristics associated with the McDonald's mark are always present.

If such restrictions were not placed on the franchisee, the McDonald's servicemark soon would stand for nothing, since each McDonald's operation would have vastly different characteristics, dependent on the individual quirks of the franchisees. In this situation, the trademark would cease to provide the consumer with meaningful information about a specific product or service, and would therefore be considered abandoned, just as if it were no longer used.

Accordingly, to maintain protection of a trademark or servicemark, especially in franchise situations, the owner must carefully control the product or service supplied under his mark. Related terms: *abandonment of mark* and *trademark*.

names of people as marks   See *prohibited and reserved marks under Lanham Act*.

non-competing goods   See *competing and non-competing goods*.

non-distinctive marks   Marks that do not serve to identify specific products or services, or distinuish them from others. Related terms: *distinctive marks*.

non-related goods   See *related and non-related goods*.

non-use of mark   See *abandonment of mark* and *continuous use of mark*.

notice of registration   A symbol placed next to a *mark* informing the world that the mark is *registered* under the *Lanham Act*. The most commonly used symbol in the U.S. is an "R" in a circle — ® — but "Reg. U.S. Pat. Off." is also used on occasion, with equal validity. In the United Kingdom, the only recognized notice is "Registered Trademark".

If a mark's owner fails to use one of these symbols to identify a registered mark when the mark is displayed in connection with a product or service, the owner will be unable to collect *treble damages* or *defendants' profits* for an *infringement*, unless he or she can show that the infringer actually knew the mark was registered. That is, in the absence of a proper notice, the *constructive notice* provided to potential infringers by a *federal registration* does not operate.

Example: While searching for a name for his new word processing program, Phil Programmer sees an advertisement in the newspaper for a new database manager called "Sorcerer's Apprentice". There is no "notice of registration" displayed in the advertisement, so Phil decides the mark is probably not registered and proceeds to use it as a trademark for his program. The work is in fact registered. While the owners of the mark "Sorcerer's Apprentice" could sue Phil for infringement, they probably will be unable to collect treble damages or defendants profits. Related terms: *constructive notice*, and *damages for trademark infringement*.

Trademark

Official Gazette of the U.S. Patent and Trademark Office An official publication of the *U.S. Patent and Trademark Office* for trademarks, in which marks proposed for registration on the *Principal Register* are published so that other mark owners can file an *opposition to the registration* in the event they believe an infringement would result.

opposition to registration under Lanham Act See *preventing registration of marks*.

ownership of a mark, international
In a number of countries, such as Japan or Taiwan, ownership of a mark can be acquired by prior registration rather than by use. For example: Berkeley Robotics Inc., which manufactures and sells a domestic U.S. robot under the mark "Robohobo", wants to market its product in a "prior registration" country. If the mark "Robohobo" is already registered in that country, Berkeley Robotics is out of luck. This is true even if Berkeley Robotics was first to use the mark, and the organization registering the mark (in the other country) has never manufactured a robot. The "prior registration" system often allows people to anticipate marketing trends, and to register the rights to valuable marks in advance of production.

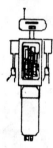

ownership of a mark in the U.S.
When a mark acquires protectable status, it also attains the status of intangible (intellectual) property. As is the case with other types of property, some marks are extremely valuable while others are worth little or nothing. Basically, in the U.S., the first party to use a mark in association with a product or service is considered the mark's owner. *Federal registration* or state registration of the mark by the owner confers actual title to the mark on its owner. In this situation, it is often said that a mark has "registered trademark" status. One advantage of registering a mark is that its owner will have a much easier time in court, in the event litigation is needed to protect it from use by others.

The primary benefit of "owning" a mark is the right to its exclusive use. As a practical matter, the extent of this right will depend on whether the mark is registered or unregistered and whether, under the U.S. system, it is registered on

Paris Convention

the Principal Register or *Supplementary Register*. Generally, the owner of a mark may protect it from *infringement* by competitors, or from *counterfeit marks*, so long as the owner has not misused it. In the U.S., this protection may include *injunctive relief* , *money damages*, *defendants profits* for domestic infringement, and exclusion orders for imported goods carrying counterfeit or infringing marks. Related terms: *exclusive right to use mark* and *Bureau of Customs*.

palming off Any act intended to confuse one product or service with another for commercial gain. Substituting one product for another (e.g., representing a computer as having one kind of microprocessor when it has another) and *deliberately infringing* a mark belonging to another (e.g., using IBN as a mark on a new computer line) are both examples of palming off activity. Although the phrase is usually applied only in situations where there is an intent to confuse, it is sometimes used more generally to designate any infringement where there is a likelihood of confusion, even though the infringer may not have intended it.

Paris Convention The primary treaty regulating trademark relations between the U.S. and other countries is colloquially called the "Paris Convention". The Paris Convention provides that each signatory country will afford to members of other signatory countries the same protections regarding marks and unfair competition that it affords its own nationals. The following countries are Paris Convention signatories: Algeria, Australia, Austria, Belgium, Brazil, Bulgaria, Burundi, Cameroon, Canada, Central African Republic, Republic of Chad, Republic of Congo, Cuba, Cyprus, Czechoslovakia, Denmark, Dominican Republic, Egypt, Finland, France, Gabon, Federal Republic of Germany, Ghana, Great Britian, Greece, Guinea, Haiti, Hungary, Iceland, Indonesia, Iran, Iraq, Ireland, Israel, Italy, Ivory Coast, Japan, Jordan, Kenya, Korea (North), Korea (South), Laos, Lebanon, Libya, Lichtenstein, Luxembourg, Malagasy, Malawi, Malta, Mauritania, Mauritius, Mexico, Monaco, Morocco, Netherlands, New Zealand, Niger, Nigeria, Norway, Philippines, Poland, Portugal, Rumania, San Marino, Senegal, Southern Rhodesia, Spain, Sri Lanka, Sweden, Switzerland, Syria, Tanganyika,

Togo, Trinidad, Tobago, Tunisia, Turkey, Uganda, Union of South Africa, U.S.S.R., United Arab Republic, United States of America, Upper Volta, Uruguay, Vatican City, Vietnam, Yugoslavia, Zaire, Zambia, and Zimbabwe.

passing off   See *palming off.*

phonetic or foreign equivalents for descriptive terms   If a word or phrase used in a mark is not eligible for protection under the trademark laws because of its *descriptive* or *generic* nature, then the phonetic or foreign equivalent of this word or phrase is also usually not eligible for protection. For example, if Rapidcompute is too descriptive a term to qualify as a mark when applied to calculators, Raapydcalmputte won't work either. Or, if the term Yellow Pages is considered too descriptive to qualify as a mark when applied to a phone directory, then using the French *Jaune Feiulles* will not help. Related terms: *words and phrases used as mark.*

pictures and symbols used as marks   Pictures and symbols may be protectable as marks if they are *distinctive* rather than *descriptive* . For example, the Quaker man on Quaker Oats cereals is a strong, distinctive pictorial mark. Similarly, the apple on Apple computer products is very distinctive and non- descriptive. On the other hand, a picture of a cow on a milk container, or a scales of justice on law firm's stationery is "descriptive" and therefore not protectable. If, however, over time, the particular cow or scales of justice become intimately connected with the product or service in the mind of numerous consumers, these pictorial symbols may become protectable under the *secondary meaning* rule.

preliminary injunction   See this heading in Section 1.

presidents names and likenesses as marks   See *prohibited and reserved marks under Lanham Act.*

presumption of ownership   An assumption made by the court that the holder of a *certificate of registration* on the *Principal Register* is the owner of a mark. This assumption (termed a pre-

sumption) will stand unless the defendant offers evidence to the contrary. If that happens, the certificate holder will need to introduce evidence of his or her own to back up the ownership claim. Related terms: *infringement action.*

presumption that mark has been abandoned   See *abandonment of mark.*

preventing registration of marks
Under the *Lanham Act,* there are several ways a party claiming ownership of a mark can either 1) prevent another party from placing an identical or similar mark on the *Principal Register* or 2) cause the offending mark to be removed from the *Principal Register* or *Supplemental Register* if registration has already occurred. These are known as 1) "opposition", 2) *interference,* and 3) "Cancellation".

• **Opposition:** If a party believes that he or she might be economically damaged if another party's proposed mark is placed on the *Principal Register,* a written *opposition* to the registration may be filed with the *U.S. Patent and Trademark Office* within thirty days of the date that the proposed mark is published in the *Official Gazette of the U.S. Patent and Trademark Office.* Extensions of the thirty-day period may be granted by the Patent and Trademark Office, upon written request.

• **Interference:** If it appears that two or more marks awaiting registration overlap or conflict with each other, and if the U.S. Patent and Trademark Office is presented with a petition showing extraordinary circumstances, an interference (i.e., conflict) may be declared, and the matter set for hearing. [15 USC 1066].

• **Cancellation:** Cancellation proceedings take several forms:

• if a party believes that he or she might be damaged or harmed if the proposed mark is placed on the Supplemental Register, an application to have the registration cancelled may be filed by this party with the Patent and Trademark Office [15 USC 1092]

• any person who believes he or she will be damaged by future or continued placement of a mark on the *Principal Register* may petition the Patent and Trademark Office for cancellation [15 USC 1064] — this may be done:

Trademark

3

- within five years from the date the mark is published in the Official Gazette, or

- any time, if the mark becomes **generic**, is **abandoned**, or its use becomes fraudulent in some way, or

- any time, if the mark is a **certification mark** and it is being misused (e.g., the **registrant** no longer exercises control or the **registrant** begins to manufacture goods subject to the certification)

When a petition for opposition or cancellation is filed, or the Patent and Trademark Office declares an interference, an **inter partes proceeding** to resolve the dispute will be scheduled before the **Trademark Trial and Appeal Board** [15 USC 1067]. At the conclusion of this hearing, the **Patent and Trademark Commissioner** may take any of the following actions:

- refuse to register the opposed mark (in an "opposition" case),

- cancel the registration of a mark or place restrictions on its use (in a cancellation case)

- refuse to register any one mark, or all of several marks (in an interference case), or

- register the opposed mark or marks of persons who are found to be entitled to ownership

Also, the commissioner may order **concurrent registration** of marks so long as the conditions of and restrictions on their use are established.

Principal Register of Trademarks and Servicemarks The primary federal listing of **trademarks** and **servicemarks** that meet the statutory requirements for **registration** with the **U.S. Patent and Trademark Office**. Basically, the requirements necessary for registration on the **Principal Register** are that a mark be **distinctive** and not **infringe** a mark that is already registered. Also the use of certain types of pictures, words and symbols disqualify a mark for registration on the Principal Register. Examples are the U.S. flag, other federal and local governmental insignias, names of living persons without their consent, names or likenesses of dead U.S. Presidents without their widows' consent, words or symbols that disparage living or dead persons, institutions, beliefs or national symbols, or marks that are judged immoral, deceptive, or scandalous. Also, marks consist-

ing primarily of **surnames** or **geographical names** may not be placed on the **Principal Register**. Related terms: **prohibited and reserved marks** .

If a **trademark** or **servicemark** is registered on the Principal Register it will be afforded several significant protections in the event it is misused or infringed by another party. These include:

- a presumption, in the event of litigation, that the **registrant** owns the mark — this means the challenger must prove that the mark is not owned by the **registrant** — placing the burden of proof on the challenger can often make the difference between winning and losing the lawsuit

- the right to file an **infringement action** in court

- the right to seek an award of **money damages** (including **treble damages**) and **defendant's profits**

- the right to **international protection** as a U.S. **registrant**

- the right to **exclusive use of the mark** in all parts of the U.S., unless the mark was being used by another at the time of registration, and

- the right, after the mark is on the Principal Register for five years, to file for **incontestability status** — if this is granted, a challenger will thereafter be prevented from arguing that he or she owns the mark (or that the **registrant** doesn't) unless certain specified showings are made (called **incontestability defenses**)

printers, injunctions against under Lanham Act If the party printing an infringing mark is an **innocent infringer**, the **Lanham Act** [15 USC Sec.1114] exempts him from liablity for **money damages** or **defendant's profits** , and only authorizes injunctions to prevent future printings of the mark.

prior registration countries Countries where ownership of a mark is determined by who registers first instead of who uses it first. Related terms: **ownership of mark, international**.

profits See **defendants profits**.

prohibited and reserved marks under Lanham Act Under the **Lanham Act** [15 USC Sec. 1052] no mark "by which the goods of the applicant may be distinguished from the goods of others" shall be refused registration on the **Principal Register** unless it falls into one of the following categories:

- If the mark comprises "immoral", "deceptive" or "scandalous" matter. For example, a mark resembling a sex organ would be considered immoral; a mark suggesting miracle properties in a product that are not substantiated would be deceptive; and, a mark showing a mutilated corpse would be scandalous.

- If the mark disparages or falsely suggests a connection with persons (living or dead), institutions, beliefs, or national symbols. **Example:** A mark showing a picture of the United States President standing on the American flag would constitute a disparagement of a person, of an institution (the presidency), and of a national symbol. A baseball-related mark suggesting a connection with Babe Ruth would also not qualify, unless authorization were given by Babe Ruth's heirs.

- If the mark comprises the flag or coat of arms or other insignia of the United States, or of any State or municipality, or of any foreign nation, or any simulation thereof.

- If the mark consists of or comprises a name, portrait, or signature identifying a particular living individual (except with his or her written consent), or the name signature, or portrait of a deceased President of the United States during the life of his widow, if any, except with the written consent of the widow.

- If the mark so resembles a mark previously registered with the **U.S. Patent and Trademark Office** that it is likely to cause confusion or mistake, or to deceive consumers.

If the mark is merely **descriptive**, a **surname** or a **geographical name** . But this last category of marks may be placed on the **Supplemental Register**.

In addition to these prohibitions, certain organizations, such as the Boy Scouts, are granted the exclusive right to use their marks and symbols by statute. Similarly, the use of the character/name "Smokey the Bear" is reserved to the Department of the Interior. Related terms: **Principal Register** and **Supplemental Register**.

proper use of mark   To retain its protectable status, a mark must be properly used by its owner. If a mark is used by its owner in violation of the **anti-trust laws** 5, or for fraudulent purposes, or in a **naked license**, the courts may refuse to protect it. Related terms: **incontestability status** .

protectable marks   Any **mark** that entitles its owner to obtain judicial or administrative protection against the unauthorized use by another of the **same or a similar mark**. Such protection may be available in state courts and administrative agencies, and in federal courts and administrative agencies, under a variety of statutes and legal doctrines. Related terms: **infringement of a mark** and **unfair competition**.

protection of marks under Lanham Act   The degree of protection offered to a mark under the **Lanham Act** depends on many variables, such as 1) whether the **mark** is listed on the **Principal Register** or the **Supplemental Register**, 2) the length of time the **registration** has been in effect, 3) whether the **registrant** is the **senior user** or the **junior user**, and 4) whether the **infringer** had either actual knowledge or **constructive knowledge** of the **registrant**'s mark.

Protection for a given mark under the **Lanham Act** can vary from preventing persons in other countries from using the **same or a similar mark** in connection with their goods or services, to preventing an identical mark from being used only in the specific part of a state where the mark is already in use by the person claiming **ownership of the mark**. The owner of a **strong mark** (**coined words**, arbitrary words, or fanciful words or symbols) that is properly placed on the Principal Register under the **Lanham Act** can prevent other, later users in the U.S. from using even a similar mark if such usage would be likely to cause the **average consumer** to be confused as to the source of the product.

Although state statutes and court decisions on **trademarks**, **servicemarks**, and **unfair competition** offer some local protection against mark infringement, this protection is greatly expanded under the **Lanham Act**, In fact, in some instances the failure to register under the **Lanham Act** can mean a loss of protection that

otherwise existed under such statutes and court decisions. Related terms: *exclusive use of mark*, and *state protection for marks*.

Obtaining protection under the Lanham Act basically involves taking the following steps:

1. *Using the mark in interstate commerce*

2. Filing an application for *Registration* of the mark on the *Principal Register*; or, if the *PTO* (Patent and Trademark Office) rules the mark inappropriate for the *Principal Register*, applying for placement of the mark on the *Supplemental Register*, assuming the mark has been in use for one year and is not *generic*

3. Publishing the mark in the *Official Gazette* if it qualifies for the Principal Register, and there is no opposition from the *U.S. Patent and Trademark Office*

4. If a petition showing extraordinary circumstances is filed with the *PTO* by a party claiming *ownership of a mark*, and if that office believes the proposed mark is the same or similar to another mark awaiting registration, the validity of the mark must be established in an *interference proceeding*, or use of the mark must be *abandoned*

5. If step 4 is not applicable, and no *opposition* from an owner of the *same or similar mark* is timely filed after the publication in Step 3, a *Certificate of Registration* on either the Principal or Supplemental Register is issued by and received from the PTO. Once a mark is thus registered, an R in a circle (which stands for *registered trademark*) or "Reg. U.S. Pat. Off." should be placed next to the mark whenever it is used. Otherwise, the owner may be prevented from collecting *money damages* or *defendant's profits* in the event of n infringement. Related terms: *Notice of registration* . (See chart next page.)

protection of marks under state law and common law
The English common law as brought into the U.S., and the laws of all states, have long afforded *trademarks* judicial protection against unauthorized use of the marks by others. The underlying theories under which protection of trademarks and *servicemarks* is provided in the various states vary from general rules and statutes barring *unfair competition*, or unfair

business practices, to statutes specifically barring trademark infringement. Although the federal *Lanham Act* has generally replaced state law as the most important source of protection for good and services that move interstate, the state systems are the only source of protection for businesses, craftspersons, dance and artist groups, theatre companies and restaurants that only operate on a local basis. Also, because the laws of many states provide for *punitive damages*, whereas the Lanham Act does not, it is common for an infringement action to claim violations of both federal and state statutes. Related terms: *state protection for marks* and *unfair competition*.

PTO
The standard abbreviation for the *U.S. Patent and Trademark Office*.

publication of mark in Official Gazette
When an application is made for *registration of a mark* that otherwise qualifies for registration on the *Principal Register* under the *Lanham Act*, the *U.S. Patent and Trademark Office* publishes the mark in a newspaper called the *Official Gazette of the U.S. Patent and Trademark Office*. If there is no negative response within thirty days by another claimant to the mark, the Patent and Trademark Office will register the mark. If, however, another trademark owner claims likelihood of confusion, mistake, or deception to the public, and files a timely *opposition* to the registration, the Patent and Trademark Office will schedule an administrative (*inter partes*) hearing to resolve the dispute. Related terms: *preventing registration of mark*.

publishers of advertising matter, injunctions against under Lanham Act
If an *infringement of a mark* occurs in advertising copy carried in a magazine, newspaper, or other periodical, and the publisher is unaware of the infringement (i.e., is an *innocent infringer*) the *Lanham Act* [15 USC Sec. 1114] exempts the publisher from liability for *money damages* or *profits*, and only permits *injunctions* as to any future advertising copy carrying the infringing mark. Further, no injunction shall be issued, despite the infringement, if the effect of the injunction would be to delay the normal publication, delivery, or distribution of a scheduled issue. Related terms: *intellectual property protection*

Nationwide Protection of Marks Under Lanham Act

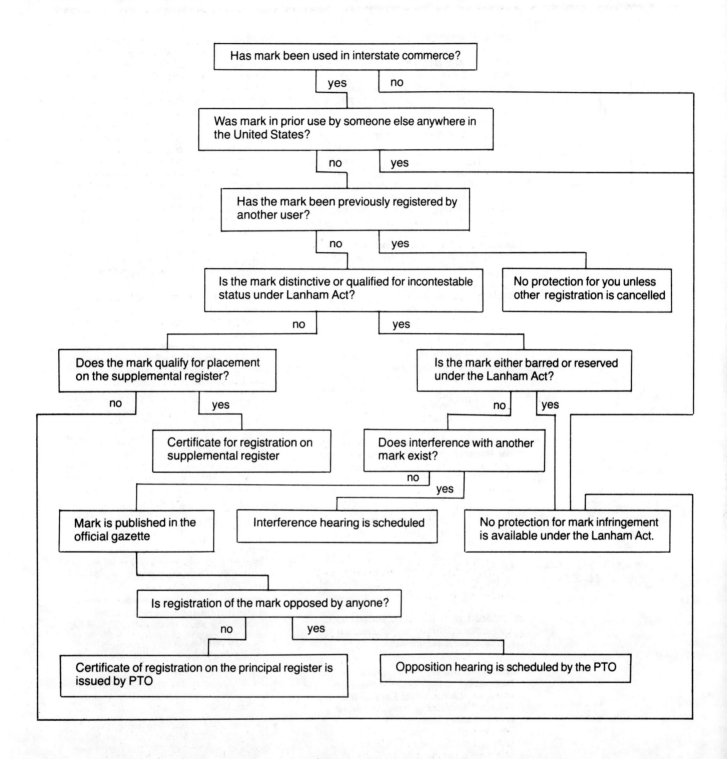

and first amendment 2.

punitive damages   Civil damages that are intended to punish a wrongdoer and serve as an example to future potential wrongdoers (termed *punitive damages* 5) may not be awarded by a court under the *Lanham Act*. However, the *Lanham Act* provides for *treble damages* in some instances. Also, the *unfair competition* and related laws of many states provide for either punitive or treble damages. For this reason, it is common to charge an alleged infringer with violations of both the Lanham Act and any applicable state laws.

reasonably prudent consumer   See *average consumer* and *confusion of consumers*.

Reg.U.S.Pat.Off. or ®   These abbreviations are used to denote *trademarks* or *servicemarks* that have been registered with the *U.S. Patent and Trademark Office* on either the *Principal Register* or the *Supplemental Register*. Related terms: *notice of registration* .

registered mark   Used colloquially, any *trademark*, *servicemark*, *certification mark*, or *collective mark* that is registered under the federal *Lanham Act*. This registration may be on either the *Principal Register* or the *Supplemental Register*. A '"registered mark" is entitled to many types of protection not afforded an unregistered mark.

In a literal sense, a mark registered under a state registration system is also a "registered mark". However, because state laws provide a mark much less protection than is afforded under the *Lanham Act*, the phrase "registered mark" is more generally only applied to federally registered marks.

registered with the U.S. Patent and Trademark Office   See *protection of marks under Lanham Act*.

registrable matter   The part of a mark that meets the standards for protection under the *Lanham Act*. Related terms: *Principal Register* and *disclaimer of unregistrable matter*.

registrant   Any person or business who registers a mark under a state registration law or under the *Lanham Act*. Related terms: *registered mark*.

related and unrelated products and services   When a *confusion of customers* is likely to result from the use of the *same or a similar mark* on two different products or services, the products or services are said to be related. Conversely, when the same or similar mark can be used on different products or services without causing such, if any, confusion, the goods are unrelated.

Confusion is more likely to result when *strong marks* (i.e., *distinctive marks* such as "Exxon") are involved than when *weak marks* (i.e., *descriptive marks* such as "Tasty Treat") are at issue. Thus, if an allegedly infringed mark is "strong", goods or services using the same or a similar mark must be very different to avoid being considered related. It follows that the weaker the mark claiming infringement, the less different goods or services carrying an allegedly infringing mark need to be, to be considered unrelated.

A number of criteria have been developed (mostly through court decisions) which are used by courts to determine when one product or service is related to another. These are:

- the likelihood that the goods or services of one business will be mistaken for those of the other

- the likelihood that one business may expand its activities so that its goods or services will be in competition with those of the other business

- the extent to which the goods or services of the two businesses have common purchasers or users

- the extent to which the goods or services of the two businesses are marketed through the same channels

- the market relationship, if any, between the goods produced, or the services provided, by the two businesses

- the degree of distinctiveness of the mark in question when compared to a competing mark

- the degree of attention usually given to trade or service marks in the purchase of goods or services of the two businesses

- the length of time during which the allegedly infringing business has used the designation, and
- the intent of the allegedly infringing business in adopting and using the mark in question

When products or services are considered to be totally unrelated, the courts will generally find that use of the same or similar mark does not constitute infringement. If the products or services are found to be related, on the other hand, infringement may be found to exist as well, assuming the other requirements for infringement are also present.

Whether a product or service is considered related or unrelated depends on the exact facts of the case, how the criteria listed above are weighed in light of the facts, and the subjective perceptions of the judge, based on the evidence before him, as to whether the **average consumer** might be confused by the use of the same or similar marks on the different products. In short, there is no firm dividing line between those marks that are ruled to be too similar, and those that are not.

Example: Ethereal Fragrance Company produces a line of products carrying the strong registered trademark "Ekbara Scents" for perfume. These products are marketed primarily to middle and upper-income women in boutiques throughout California and several other Western states. One day, Rubin Santiago of Oakland California, opens a small printing company specializing in business cards, and calls his product "Ekbara Cards". The cards are marketed to small businesses in the San Francisco Bay Area. Ethereal claims infringement. In deciding whether infringement has occurred, the court will probably engage in something like the following analysis: "It is not likely that purchasers of business cards will think a fragrance company is involved in the printing business. In addition, neither business is likely to go into competition with the other, the purchasers of the two products as well as the distribution channels are ifferent, there is no relationship between the functions of the two goods, there is little attention given to the origin of business cards, there is no indication Rubin Santiago intended to cash in on the mark used by Ethereal, and time of use is not a factor. Therefore, I conclude that the uses were unrelated and that there is no infringement. The only thing going for Ethereal is the strength of its mark. This is simply not enough to overcome all the other factors."

On the other hand, if Rubin Santiago creates a line of flavorings for ice cream, calls them "Ekbara Delights", and franchises them for sale in shopping malls containing the boutiques that carry Ethereal's products, he may be held liable for infringement. Related terms: **exclusive right to use mark** and **competing and non-competing goods**.

Although the use of the same or a similar mark might not result in a finding of infringement under the "related/unrelated" analysis, this does not mean that the alleged infringer may continue to use the mark. Although no infringement is found, the court may rule that the use of the allegedly infringing mark constitutes **dilution of trademarks** and restrict further use of the mark on that ground. Related term: **dilution of trademarks**.

reservation system for acquiring ownership of mark See **ownership of mark, international**.

reverse palming off The usual way in which goods are palmed off (i.e., marketed in a way that makes people think they are really manufactured by someone else) is to use the true trademark on substitute goods. Reverse palming off occurs when a non-infringing label is placed on someone elses goods and the goods are then sold under the non-infringing name. Either way, the public is being deceived. Related terms: **palming off**.

same or a similiar mark Any mark that is enough like another mark in appearance or meaning to lead the **average consumer** to confuse the two under the circumstances. For example, the **trademark** "Pineapple Computers" was held to be similar enough to "Apple Computers" in appearance and meaning to risk customer confusion and thus warrant its prohibition as a mark. Whether any mark is deemed the same as or similar to another mark is necessarily decided on a case-by-case basis. Related terms: **infringement of a mark** and **confusion of customers** .

secondary meaning When a mark that, by itself, merely describes some characteristic or function of a product or service (such as "White Out") comes to *identify and distinguish* the product or service from competing products or services, because of the mark's widespread use over time, it is considered to have become *distinctive* by assuming a "secondary meaning". In such a situation, the mark becomes qualified for placement on the *Principal Register* and is entitled to all the protections that such registration brings.

Example: "Dollar a Day", as used by a car rental firm, was initially purely descriptive of the service being provided — car rentals for a dollar a day. However, over time, and with the help of an advertising campaign and virtually exclusive use by the firm, the phrase lost its sole meaning as a description and instead became associated with the actual owner of the mark.

Although a descriptive mark is entitled to be placed on the *Principal Register* whenever a showing can be made that it has acquired a "secondary meaning", a mark that is in continuous and exclusive use by its owner for a five year period will be presumed to have acquired such secondary meaning. It will be qualified for *registration* on the *Principal Register*, and will be afforded protection as a *distinctive mark*.

Secondary Register See *Supplemental Register*.

seizure of imported goods containing counterfeit or infringing marks See *Bureau of Customs*.

selecting a protectable mark In selecting a mark for a product or service in the U.S., a business must find one that 1) is not being used by someone else 2) is *distinctive* (e.g., a coined arbitrary or fanciful term) rather than *descriptive*) and 3) is not currently registered on the *Principal Register* or *Supplemental Register* in the *U.S. Patent and Trademark Office*.

Generally, selecting a mark involves a process something like this. Stage one involves brainstorming for general ideas. After several possible marks have been

senior users and junior users

selected, the next step is often to use formal or informal market research techniques to see how the potential marks will be accepted by consumers. Next, a "trademark search" is conducted. This means that an attempt is made to discover whether the same or similar marks are already in use.

The trademark search is extremely important, because it should discover if the chosen mark is already owned and/or registered by someone else. Obviously, no-one wants to spend money on marketing and advertising the new mark, only to discover it infringes another mark and must be changed. In addition, if an earlier mark was *registered* under the *Lanham Act* prior to the infringing use, the infringing mark's owner may have to pay *defendants profits*, earned in connection with the infringing mark, to the mark's rightful owner.

Usually a trademark search is conducted by an attorney or professional search agency. Both federal and state registers are checked. Then, the Yellow Pages are checked in main cities, and trade journals, and other relevant publications are reviewed. The search report will note who, if anyone, is using the *same or a similar mark*. Assuming that the search fails to disclose use of the *same or similar mark* by anyone in a *related* business, the mark is then put into actual use, and, assuming the use is interstate, federally registered . If no interstate use is made, registration is accomplished under the appropriate state laws. Related terms: *trademark*.

selling goods or services with infringing marks See *contributory infringement*.

senior users and junior users When a dispute exists over ownership of a mark, the person (or entity) who first used the mark is called the "senior user" and the second person or entity to use the mark is termed the "junior user". Although the senior user is generally considered the *owner of the mark* in dispute, this may not be so in situations where the junior user did not know of the senior user's use, and is first to register the mark under the *Lanham Act* , or under state laws. Related terms: *exclusive right to use mark* and *ownership of a mark*.

service marks and franchising See *naked licenses*.

service marks A word, phrase, or graphic symbol used by the provider of a service (e.g., a law firm, medical group, hamburger stand, computer repair co.) to distinguish its service from similar services provided by others. Examples of servicemarks are "McDonald's", "Blue Cross", "Blue Shield", and "Greyhound". Titles, character names or other distinctive features of television and radio programs may also be registered as servicemarks. The rules for determining when and how servicemarks qualify for protection are the same, in the U.S., as the rules applicable to *trademarks*.

On the other hand, the United Kingdom and some other countries do not extend protection to servicemarks at all. For specific information on U.S. servicemarks, the *trademark* entry should be read, and the word "service" should be substituted for the word "product'", where appropriate.

similiar marks, use of See *same and similiar marks* and *exclusive right to use mark*.

simultaneous registration See *state protection for marks* and *concurrent registration*.

slogans, use as trademarks See *words and phrases, used as trademarks*.

state law protection for marks In addition to the *Lanham Act*, all states have laws under which marks may be *registered* and receive judicial protection should *infringement* occur. Generally, these laws are only utilized for marks used exclusively within the particular state (i.e., intrastate), since marks used interstate should receive national protection under the Lanham Act. However, it is possible to *simultaneously register* under both state and federal systems. That way, should there later be a problem in enforcing rights under the Lanham Act, there is still some state protection to fall back on.

In addition to trademark infringement laws, most states have laws prohibiting *unfair competition* (business practices that confuse or deceive the consumer public). As *infringement of a mark* is often also considered to be unfair competition, the law of most states recognizes at least two theories under which a business's mark will be afforded protection. Related terms: *protection of marks under state law and common law* and *unfair to competition*.

strong mark A mark that substantially functions to identify the origins of a product or service, rather than its characteristics. Accordingly, *distinctive* marks are considered strong, whereas *descriptive marks* are considered *weak*. The weaker the mark, the more reluctant a court usually is to find that it has been infringed, and the less protection it receives. The stronger the mark, the greater the likelihood of an infringement being found to exist. Related terms: *distinctive marks* and *related and unrelated goods and services*.

suggestive mark A mark that escapes being *descriptive* because its primary meaning is suggestive of qualities or concepts associated with the product or service, rather than directly descriptive of the product. It is often difficult to tell in advance whether a mark is descriptive or suggestive, since this determination is highly subjective and can therefore vary from judge to judge and case to case. One good example of a suggestive mark is "Piney Woods" air spray, or "Ambrosia Scents" for perfume.

supplemental register A secondary register maintained by the *U.S. Patent and Trademark Office* for the registration of *trademarks* and *service marks* that do not qualify for placement on the *Principal Register*. To be placed on the Supplemental Register, a "mark may consist of any trademark, symbol, label, package, configuration of goods, name, work, slogan, phrase, surname, geographical name, numeral, or device or any combination of any of the foregoing" [15 U.S.C. sec. 1091]. However, such mark must still be capable of distinguishing in some way the applicant's goods or services from others. Accordingly, *descriptive marks* qualify for the Supplemental Register, while *generic marks* do not, since by definition a generic mark defines a type of product rather than a particular product (e.g., "Blue Jeans" means a type of pants made of a particular material, rather than a specific clothing product

Trademark

originating from a particular manufacturer). Except for **surnames** and **geographical terms**, both of which may be placed on the Supplemental Register, the types of marks that are barred from the **Principal Register** are also barred from the Supplemental Register. Related terms: **prohibited and reserved marks under Lanham Act**.

Marks on the Supplemental Register do not receive as much protection as do those on the Principal Register. Unlike registration on the Principal Register, placement on the Supplemental Register does not serve as **constructive notice of ownership**, does not provide a **presumption of ownership** in the event of infringement litigation, does not support a later claim of **incontestable status**, is not evidence of the right to **exclusive use of the mark**, and does not allow the mark's owner to request exclusion of imports by the **Bureau of Customs**.

On the other hand, there are some benefits that may result from such registration, both in the U.S. and abroad. Placement of a mark on the "Supplemental Register" allows its owner 1) to use the circled ® or **"Reg.U.S.Pat.Off."** abbreviation to discourage would-be infringers), 2) to obtain reciprocal **international protections** in countries that belong to one or more of the **international trademark treaties** , and 3) to seek **injunctive relief**, **money damages**, **treble damages**, and **defendants profits** in the event of an infringement action (assuming that proper **notice of registration** was provided along with the mark in question).

However, it is often difficult to prove infringement of a mark on the Supplemental Register, since such registration is an admission by the mark's owner that the mark is **descriptive** rather than **distinctive** (otherwise it would have been placed on the **Principal Register**), and thus not entitled to significant protection under the trademark laws. But protection may be available under **unfair competition** laws, if customer confusion is likely to result. Related terms: **unfair competition** and **unfair competition under the Lanham Act**.

Before a mark can be placed on the Supplemental Register, it must be **used in interstate commerce** for one year. However, if registration is necessary for an owner to enforce his or her right to exclusive use of a mark in a foreign country, this one-year period may be waived. It is not necessary for an applicant to choose which register to place her mark on. Her first application should be for the Principal Register. If this is rejected, she will be provided an opportunity to apply for the Supplemental Register.

surnames used as marks   A mark that is "primarily" a surname will not qualify for protection under the **trademark** and **servicemark** provisions of the **Lanham Act**, unless it has become **distinctive** through **continual use** (i.e., assumed a **secondary meaning**).

However, under state **unfair competition** laws, and under the **unfair competition** provision of the **Lanham Act** [15 USC 1125], surnames used as marks may be entitled to protection if a later conflicting use is held likely to confuse consumers.

Example: Henry Landberry constructs a roadside stand at one end of a famous California seaside highway, and starts a booming business in "Landberry's Homemade Cherry Cider". One day, several years later, Paul Landberry (no relation) drives past Henry's stand and the proverbial lightbulb goes on. Paul immediately establishes a "Landberry's Homemade Cherry Cider stand" at the other end of the same highway, hoping to cash in on Henry's reputation. If Henry can establish that Paul's stand creates a reasonable possibility of customer confusion between the two products, he can use the unfair competition laws in California (and in most states), and possibly the unfair competition provision in the **Lanham Act**, to force Paul either to shut down or at least to change his mark to a non-confusing variant of his name.

except as we have noted, they can be used for protectable **tradenames** under state **unfair competition** laws and laws governing corporate name registrations and reservations. Related terms: **tradenames**.

symbols and pictures as marks   See **prohibited and reserved marks under Lanham Act**, and **pictures/symbols, used as trademarks**.

TM   This symbol is used to denote 1) marks registered on a **state** basis only, and 2) marks which have not yet been officially placed on the **Principal Register**

or **Supplemental Register** with the **U.S. Patent and Trademark Office**. The symbol is used to give notice to potential infringers that the word or symbol is considered a **protectable mark** by its owner. When a mark appears several times on a page, it is not necessary to use "TM" every time the mark appears. Since the first use of the TM identifies the word or symbol as a mark, adequate notice is provided. Using "TM" is not required to obtain basic protection from a court, but it will enhance the possibility of collecting **damages** because its use makes it difficult, if not impossible, for an infringer to claim **innocent infringer status**.

trade dress The part of a product's packaging that designates the product rather than serving a utilitarian function. For example, many liqueur bottles have a unique shape designed for advertising rather than for any particular function. The tall, tapered shape of the bottle used for Galliano, for example, is not necessary to hold the product, but helps to identify it. The trade dress aspect of packaging may be protected under state **unfair competition** laws and under the **unfair competition provision of the Lanham Act** [15 U.S.C. Sec. 1125] if a showing can be made that, were another product allowed to appear in similar dress, the **average consumer** might be confused as to product origin. Related terms: **confusion of customers** and **trademarks**.

trademark A word, phrase, logo, or other graphic symbol used by a manufacturer or merchant to distinguish his or her line of products from the products of others. In common usage, the term trademark is also used to refer to the broad body of law that covers how businesses distinguish their products and services from those of others. Thus, "trademark law" is typically used to include such narrower legal areas as **service marks**, **tradenames**, "commercial misappropriation", **unfair competition**, "unfair business practices" and **palming off**. In this definition, however, we focus on the narrower meaning of "trademark" as defined above.

The idea behind what we know as the modern doctrine of trademark law arose in Europe as early as the middle ages, when craftsmen began using distinctive stamps or symbols to mark goods so customers could associate particular items with their makers. Today, customers are not so much concerned with the identity of the person who actually makes a product, as they are with the identity of the business that manufactures the product or **line of products** (e.g., Ford autos, Kellog cornflakes, Apple computers, Microsoft software). Accordingly, the concept of trademark has evolved to refer to any visual mark (e.g., letters, words, numbers, color, symbol, design, or shape) that accompanies a particular product, or line of goods, and serves to identify it and distinguish it from those produced by competitors.

The ability of a trademark to distinguish one line of products from another is termed **distinctiveness**. Since the economic value of a product line commonly depends on the degree to which customers are familiar with the trademark associated with it, distinctive trademarks are themselves valuable property (often called **intellectual property** 5) and as such, will be protected from unauthorized use by others.

Protection for a trademark may mean different things, depending on the country or trading area, the type of mark, the scope of prior use, the intent of the person who uses a mark belonging to another, and the degree of compliance with certain formalities. Generally, trademark protection consists of a court order to a business that is using the **same or similar mark** to stop using it in any context where the public might be confused between the two products. If the mark is particularly distinctive, or the business improperly using the mark does so with knowledge that the mark belongs to someone else, or if the mark was properly registered under the U.S. **Lanham Act**, the court may also award damages. Basically, a court will do what is necessary to 1) protect the trademark owner's right to **exclusive use of the mark** and 2) make sure the trademark owner is properly compensated for any harm caused by the wrongful use of the mark by others.

Trademarks are divided into several basic types, depending on the degree of their distinctiveness. A very distinctive mark (e.g., Exxon) is considered to be **strong**, whereas a much less distinctive mark (e.g., "Easy Word" word processing software) is considered to be **weak**. Generally, the law provides that a strong

Trademark

trademark cannot easily be appropriated (i.e., copied or simulated) by a competitor, whereas a weak trademark is more vulnerable to use by others.

Traditionally, the most distinctive trademarks are those that are either **coined** terms (e.g., Kodak, Exxon) or **arbitrary** (i.e., have no logical connection with the type or characteristics of the product, such as "Mom's" computers or "Elf" Bulldozers), or **fanciful** (Double Rainbow Ice Cream). A good rule of thumb posits that the more "off the wall" a mark is in the context of the particular product, the stronger it is. This, of course, is because such arbitrariness provides the best possible way to identify the particular product, and distinguish it from others. Related terms: **distinctive marks**.

As mentioned, trademarks that have little or no distinctiveness are entitled to little, if any, legal protection as trademarks. This means that the **same or a similar mark** may be used by others, as long as there is no showing of a likelihood that the public will be confused. For example, a trademark that is also a generic name for a product (i.e., defines the product itself rather than serving as a brand name) will not be entitled to protection. This is because this type of mark necessarily refers to all similar products rather than to a specific and distinct product. An example of this is "Robot", a term that describes the product itself, rather than distinguishing one kind of robot from another.

Sometimes a once-distinctive trademark evolves into a common term over time. If this happens, the mark may be deemed to have become generic and to have lost its trademark status. Aspirin, which used to be a trademark for a particular brand of analgesic, eventually became a generic term commonly used to describe all brands of the same kind of analgesic. Once Aspirin became generic, it was no longer entitled to protection. Related terms: **generic marks**.

Somewhere between **strong marks** (entitled to the maximum protection as trademarks) and **generic marks** (marks which are entitled to no protection as trademarks) are **descriptive marks**. Descriptive marks are those that contain a description of some aspect or characteristic of the goods or services to which they are attached. While they may serve to identify and distinguish the product from

others, at least to some degree, they are not entitled to registration on the **Principal Register**, unless they have been in continuous and exclusive use by the owner for a five year period. However, they may qualify for the **Supplemental Register**. Also, most state laws permit state registrations of descriptive marks as well as distinctive marks. Related terms: **descriptive marks**.

Sometimes trademarks are "descriptive" in one sense, but also suggestive of a different quality or meaning. "Sugar 'n Spice", for example, identifies the ingredients of a product but is also suggestive of the phrase "Sugar and spice and everything nice" taken from a child's nursery rhyme. Because the suggestiveness of a mark can serve to identify a specific product apart from the mark's descriptive aspects, suggestive marks can qualify for placement on the Principal Register. Related terms: **suggestive marks**.

Descriptive marks that are at first disqualifed from being placed on the Principal Register can become distinctive over time, and can later qualify for such registration if the public comes to associate the mark with the particular product. **Example:** Upswept Electronics invents a vacuum straw that shoots liquid into the user's mouth, and calls it "Vacstraw". This name might be considered descriptive, and therefore not qualified for placement on the Principal Register. However, if "Vacstraw" is used over a period of time (say two years) and the public comes to associate the term "vacstraw" with Upswept's product, Upswept may be able to place the mark on the Principal Register. Further, if Upswept is used continuously and exclusively for a five year period, it is presumed to be qualified for placement on the Principal Register. When a descriptive mark becomes distinctive through use over time, it is said to acquire a **secondary meaning**. Related terms: **secondary meaning**.

trademark dilution   See **dilution of marks**.

trademark infringement action   See **infringement action**.

trademark owner   See **ownership of a trademark**.

trademark protection, registration of trademarks See *protection of marks under Lanham Act* and *state protection of marks*.

trademark search See *selecting a trademark*.

Trademark Register A privately published book published in Washington D.C. that lists all registered trademarks by their classifications.

trademark trial and appeal board An administrative arm of the *U.S. Patent and Trademark Office* consisting of the Trademark Commissioner, the Deputy Commissioner, the Assistant Commissioners, and members appointed by the Commissioner. This body hears and decides *inter partes* disputes (those involving the registrability of, or conflicts between, marks). Related terms: *preventing registration of marks*.

trade name Trade names are used to identify businesses, while marks are used to identify goods and services produced by businesses. The *Lanham Act* defines "trade name" and "commercial name" as follows: *"individual names and surnames, firm names and trade names used by manufacturers, industrialists, merchants, agriculturists, and others to identify their businesses, vocations, or occupations; the names of titles lawfully adopted and used by persons, firms, associations, corporations, companies, unions, and any manufacturing, industrial, commercial, agricultural, or other organizations engaged in trade or commerce and capable of suing and being sued in a court of law".*

Trade names, as such, cannot be registered under the *trademark* and *servicemark* provisions of *the Lanham Act*. However, they may be entitled to protection under state *unfair competition* statutes and court decisions, if the public is likely to be confused when someone else uses them. Related terms: *unfair competition* and *confusion of consumers*.

The unfair competition provision of the *Lanham Act* [15 USC Sec. 1125] also provides some protection for tradenames if their use with other products or services would be likely to confuse the public. Related terms: *unfair competition under Lanham Act*. Commonly, a company also uses its trade name as a trademark or servicemark. Apple Computer Corporation uses the trade name "Apple" as a trademark, and the McDonald fast food chain uses "McDonald's" as a servicemark. In these situations, the tradename may be registered in its capacity as a mark, and may receive additional protection under the Lanham Act's provisions applicable to *infringement of marks*.

treble damages Three times the actual amount of damages incurred by the plaintiff and proven in court. In the context of a trademark *infringement action*, a court is authorized by statute (but not required) to award treble damages consisting of three times the amount of monetary harm proven by the plaintiff. Generally, treble damages are awarded only when the infringement appears to have been intentional. Related terms: *damages in trademark infringement action*.

U.S. Patent and Trademark Office (PTO) The federal governmental body (part of the U.S. Department of Commerce) that processes trademark registration applications and therefore, as a practical matter, determines the initial degree of protection that a mark is likely to receive in the courts. In the event that registration of a mark is disputed, the *Trademark Trial and Appeal Board*, an arm of the PTO, will hold hearings and rule accordingly. Applications for federal registration of trademarks and information on the procedures for registration may be obtained by writing to the Commissioner of Patents and Trademarks, Washington D.C. 20231. Related terms: *protection of trademark through federal registration*.

unfair competition A general phrase used by the courts to describe any commercial activity that actually or potentially causes confusion among consumers regarding the source and characteristics of goods or services offered to the public. Such diverse activities as *trademark infringement*, *trade name* infringement, simulation of *trade dress* and packaging, *palming off*, false advertising, and *theft of trade secrets* ⫮ have all been held by various courts to constitute "unfair competition". Once a court defines any given activity as "unfair competition" it generally is authorized to enjoin (i.e., judicially prevent) any further such activity from occurring, and to award *money*

Trademark

3

109

damages.

State unfair competition laws are often used to obtain judicial relief in situations where a mark or trade name has been copied or simulated, but, for one reason or another, a federal or state trademark infringement action cannot be brought. In fact, in most cases where trademark or servicemark infringement is alleged, unfair competititon claims are also raised as an alternative basis for judicial relief.

Although most unfair competition law in the U.S. has been fashioned by legislatures and courts at the state level, the **Lanham Act** also contains a statute that prohibits a broad range of activity generally treated as unfair competition. Related terms: *unfair competition under Lanham Act*.

unfair competition under Lanham Act Section 43(a) of the **Lanham Act** (15 USC Sec. 1125) prohibits two basic types of commercial activity which are, in most cases, also treated as *unfair competition* under state laws. These are: 1) the use of a mark or label to designate falsely the origin of any product or service, and 2) the description of a product or service in false terms (i.e., false advertising). Anyone who engages in such activity may be sued in federal court by a person or business who can prove resulting economic injury, as well as the fact that the goods or services carrying the false designation or description were *used in interstate commerce*. It is possible to bring this type of unfair competition action in federal court for *infringement* of marks that are not registered under the **Lanham Act**. Although such actions are not technically *trademark infringement actions* (due to the absence of registration), they do enable the owner of an unregistered mark to use the federal courts to stop the use of a similar mark that is likely to lead to consumer confusion. However, such benefits as *presumption of ownership*, *constructive notice*, *treble damages* and *incontestability*, which result from having registered under the **Lanham Act** are not available to plaintiffs in this type of action.

Example: New Age Electronics Corp. builds a human-appearing personal robot and markets it nationally under the trademark "Android Robots." Because this mark is highly descriptive, it will probably not qualify for registration on the

Principal Register. Although it probably would qualify for registration on the **Supplemental Register**, New Age decides not to bother. Several months later, another robot manufacturer starts nationally marketing a similar product called "Mandroid Robot". New Age is entitled to file a federal court action alleging violation of Section 43(a) of the **Lanham Act** (affixing a label falsely designating origin). If the court finds that New Age suffered any loss of sales or goodwill as a result of the second mark, damages may be awarded accordingly. In addition, the second company may be enjoined from further use of the mark. In this situation, therefore, New Age may be able to obtain adequate judicial relief in federal court without first registering under the **Lanham Act**, and without bringing a "trademark infringement action" as such.

However, suppose the facts are the same, but New Age only markets its product on the Eastern Seaboard of the U.S. If the second company decides to market its product nationwide, New Age will only be entitled to protection for "Android Robots" in the geographical area where it has already been marketed. Had New Age been able to register the mark on the **Principal Register**, however, it could claim the use of the name and stop anyone else from using it in any part of the country where it might plan to market. Related terms: *constructive notice of ownership* and *unfair competition*.

unregistered mark Any mark that has not been registered under the **Lanham Act**. Unregistered marks may be entitled to protection under state trademark and *unfair competition* laws, and under the federal unfair competition law contained in the **Lanham Act**. However, they are not entitled to 1) the nationwide *constructive notice* of ownership, 2) the *presumption of ownership*, or 3) the presumption of right to exclusive use afforded by registration on the **Principal Register**. Related terms: *state law protection of marks*, *unfair competition*, and *unfair competition under Lanham Act*.

unregistrable material See *disclaimer ofunregistrable material*.

unrelated product or service See *related and unrelated products and services*.

untrue marks, lack of validity Any mark that is misleading or just plain false is not entitled to protection under the *Lanham Act*, nor under most *state law trademark protection* statutes. For example, a trademark that suggests chocolate in a product that contains no chocolate is not protectable as a valid trademark. Related terms: *prohibited and reserved marks under Lanham Act* .

use it or lose it See *abandonment of mark*.

use of mark in interstate commerce To be eligible for *federal registration*, a *trademark* must actually be used (i.e., "moved") in interstate commerce. An item or service to which the mark is attached must be marketed in more than one state. So, if Geraldine Smith starts a small business that brews a unique kind of honey wine called "Wine of Geraldyne", she will not be able to register this *trademark* with the *U.S. Patent and Trademark Office*, unless the mark has actually been shipped across state lines (on legitimate advertising copy or on the product itself), pursuant to an actual business transaction, not just to Uncle Albert in New Jersey for the purpose of satisfying the "interstate commerce" requirement.

The reason a trademark or service mark must actually be used in interstate commerce to be eligible for federal registration is that Congress passed the *Lanham Act* (the statute providing for registration) under its constitutional power to regulate interstate commerce. Since Congress has no power under the "commerce clause" to affect marks which remain within a single state, the regulation of such marks has been left to the individual states.

United States Trademark Association (USTA) A private organization founded to promote the use of trademarks and to provide guidelines for proper trademark usage.

weak marks *Marks* that describe characteristics of products or services rather than serving as *distinctive* identifiers of the products' origins or manufacturers.

Related terms: *descriptive marks* and *trademark*.

words and phrases used as marks Words, phrases, and acronyms are commonly used as *trademarks* and *service-marks*. In order to qualify for state or federal protection such marks must usually be *distinctive* rather than *descriptive*. This means that they must serve primarily as identifiers of the product line, rather than as descriptions of the product's function or characteristics. However, *distinctive* words need not be *coined* or invented, and may have independent meanings when used in non-trademark contexts.

For example, "fantastic" is a word commonly used to describe something pleasantly out of the ordinary. However, it might be acquired as a trademark when used on a specific brand of spray cleaner ("Fantastic"). While "fantastic" might be considered somewhat descriptive (i.e., this product is wonderful), the term is not concrete enough to destroy its distinctive flavor when used with spray cleaner. However, if the product were named "Goodcleaner", there would be no question of the term's descriptive nature. Related terms: *descriptive Mark*.

The use of the *phonetic or foreign equivalent* of an otherwise descriptive or *generic* word will not necessarily confer on it the status of a *protectable trademark*. Thus, trademark protection has been denied for "Kwixtart" (electric storage batteries) and "Flor-Tile" (tile flooring). "Yo-Yo" is generic, and thus not a proper trademark, because it is the Filipino word for that type of toy.

When phrases or slogans are used as marks, some words that comprise the phrase may be distinctive enough to qualify for federal registration on the *Principal Register* (and thus fully protectable) while others may not, because of their descriptive or *generic* nature. In these situations, the owners will acquire *exclusive rights* to the distinctive portions, but not to the non-distinctive portions. Indeed, as part of the registration, the owner is required to *disclaim* the non-distinctive portion as a trademark. Related terms: *disclaimer of unregistrable matter*.

Some words and phrases are prohibited by law for use as or in Trademarks. Related terms: *prohibited and reserved*

marks under Lanham Act.

words in common use   See *generic marks*.

Research Notes

This note assumes that you wish to delve deeper into the topics defined in this part of the dictionary. Instead of just providing you with a bibliography, we want to suggest a general research strategy. First, find some simplified background resources (often published as "self-help" law books) to obtain a general overview of your subject. Some of these are listed in **Step #1** below. Then consult more intensive background materials (listed in **Step #2**). These will go into greater detail and will also usually provide you with references (citations) to the primary law itself (**Step #3**).[ntFinally, use *Legal Research: How to Find and Understand the Law* by Stephen Elias, Nolo Press, or another basic legal research guide, to assist you in using the law library and understanding the law you find there.

Step #1: Simplified Background Resources

Unfortunately, there is no single basic background guide to trademark law. The trademark chapter in *An Intellectual Property Law Primer* by Earl Kintner, published by C. Boardman Co. (1982) probably provides the best overview. *Legal Protection for Software* by Dan Remer, Nolo Press (1984), *How to Copyright Software* by M.J. Salone, Nolo Press,(1984) and *Patent it Yourself* by David Pressman, formerly published by McGraw-Hill, 1979 and now by Nolo Press,(1985), all provide general overviews of this subject. Probably the best general discussion of unfair competition and trade practice laws (although somewhat out of date in its specifics) is *A Primer on the Law of Deceptive Practices* by Earl Kinter, pubished by Clark Boardman (1978).

Step #2: Intensive Background Resources

The most comprehensive resource for trademark law research is a two volume treatise *Trademarks and Unfair Competition* by J. Thomas McCarthy (Bancroft Whitney-Lawyer's Coop)(1983). As books written for lawyers go, this one is quite understandable and contains discussions of virtually every trademark question likely to arise. Each discussion is supported by references (citations) to the federal statutes (collectively known as the Lanham Act) governing the major part of trademark law in the U.S., and to the federal cases interpreting this statute. In short, the McCarthy set is an excellent way to get to primary law sources.

Comprehensive discussions of trademark law can also be found in *American Jurisprudence, Second Series (AmJur.2d)* under "Trademarks and Tradenames", and in *Corpus Juris Secundum (CJS)*, under "Trademarks, Tradenames, and Unfair Competition."

Patent and Trademark Forms, Clark Boardman, is a good source if you are pursuing your own trademark registration and need the correct forms.

Step #3: Accessing Primary Sources

Statutes: The basic law governing federal trademark protection in the United States is known as the Lanham Act, a collection of federal statutes located in *Title 15* of the *United States Code* beginning at section 1050 [15 USC Sec. 1050]. This can be found in the *United States Code Annotated (U.S.C.A.)* or in the *United States Code Service, Lawyers Edition (U.S.C.S.)*.

Regulations: The United States Patent and Trademark Office has issued regulations implementing the registration portion of the Act. These are located in *Title 37* of the *Code of Federal Regulations (CFR)*.

Cases: To find summaries of cases dealing with trademark law issues, use the *West Digest* series (choose the volume that contains a discussion of "trade regulation" This has a table of contents at the beginning of the case summaries (organized according to the West Key system). If you wish, you can begin with the detailed subject-matter index at the end of the whole digest.

Introduction

In this section we define the words and phrases commonly used in deciding when and how an *inventor* can prevent others from making, using and selling his or her *invention* without permission. This entire subject is referred to as patent law.

A *patent* is a statutory monopoly on the use and commercial exploitation of an invention. The U.S. Constitution provides for such protection, and, in the U.S., patent law is governed exclusively by federal statutes. These establish what kinds of items are patentable, the kinds of characteristics an invention must have to qualify for a patent, and the procedures which must be utilized to apply for and receive a patent.

A patent is obtained by filing a *patent application* with the *U.S. Patent and Trademark Office*. This application must contain a number of components including a *specification* (an overall description of the invention), patent *claims* (extremely specific sentence fragments delineating the exact scope of the invention to be covered by the patent), *drawings* showing each element of the invention, an *abstract* and an *information disclosure statement* telling the Patent and Trademark Office what prior developments in the field (*prior art*) the inventor is aware of to assist the examiner in determining if the invention qualifies for a patent.

Between the initial application for a patent and the granting of it, there is generally a stylized exchange of communications between the Patent Office and the applicant. This process normally leads to the substantial amendment of one or more of the claims in the application. Also, in the course of this application *prosecution* process, the applicant has the opportunity to file additional or *supplementary applications*.

Only those inventions that strictly meet the statutory requirements for a patent are entitled to receive one. In the U.S. there are five basic categories of items that qualify for a patent. These are 1) *processes*, 2) *machines*, 3) *manufactures*, 4) *compositions of matter*, and 5) *new uses* of any of the above four items. In addition, patents may be granted on asexually reproduced plants and ornamental *designs*.

Once an invention is determined to fall in one of these categories, the Patent Office must determine whether the invention is *novel* (i.e., not anticipated), *non-obvious* (i.e., an unexpected and surprising new result given the general

Patent

knowledge available in the field of invention), and useful in some way (has **utility**).

If the invention passes these tests, a patent will be granted unless another pending application involves the same invention. Then, the Patent and Trademark Office will declare an **interference** and a hearing will be held to determine who is entitled to the patent. The result depends on such variables as 1) who first conceived of the invention, 2) who was the first to actually build and test, and 3) who was first to file for a patent.

Once a patent is granted, the statutory monopoly may be enforced in the courts through patent **infringement actions**. If a patent infringement is claimed, the validity of the patent is likely to be challenged by the person claimed to have infringed it. Assuming the patent is upheld, however, the court will probably enjoin further use or sale of the infringing device and award damages to the patent owner.

In the U.S. a patent lasts for seventeen years unless it becomes unenforceable through **misuse**, **antitrust** violations, or unless the owner fails to pay **maintenance fees** required every four years or so. In other countries this period varies somewhat, usually downward. Once a patent has expired, the invention falls into the **public domain** and the patent owner is no longer entitled to protection.

Under the **Patent Cooperation Treaty** and the **Paris Convention**, U.S. inventors are entitled to **international patent protection** if they take certain steps specified in those international agreements.

Definitions

abandonment of patent application
When the *U.S. Patent and Trademark Office* considers a *patent application* to be legally abandoned because of the applicant's inaction in certain contexts. In the course of applying for a *patent* (*prosecuting a patent application*), there are many points where the failure of the applicant to act in a timely manner will be taken by the *PTO* as a legal abandonment of the application. For instance, if the *PTO* rejects a patent *claim* in its *first office action*, failure by the applicant to amend within three months (extendable up to six months with payment of a fee) will result in legal abandonment. Similarly, abandonment occurs when an applicant fails within three months of a *final office action* rejecting patent claims to 1) cancel the rejected claims or make any recommended corrections, or 2) successfully request a *reconsideration* of the application.

In the event that an application is considered abandoned, the applicant has three basic options:

- petition the *Commissioner of the PTO* (for a $60.00 fee) to set aside the decision to treat the application as abandoned

- file a *substitute application* — the application will receive a new (later) *filing date*, or

- abandon the attempt to obtain a patent and utilize another available method of protection

    Related Terms: *prosecuting a patent application*.

abstract of patent The portion of a U.S. *patent application* that summarizes the general nature, structure and purpose of the *invention*. The "abstract of patent" contained in each patent application is commonly used when conducting a *patent search* to quickly assess whether the invention described by the "abstract" is relevant *prior art*, that must be considered in determining whether an invention is patentable. Related terms: *patent search* and *patent application*.

abstract scientific principles See *non-statutory subject matter* and *algorithm*.

actual reduction to practice Building or implementing an *invention* so that its workability can be demonstrated. Generally, it is not necessary to actually reduce an invention to practice to obtain a patent. Rather, it is much more common to obtain a patent on an invention that has never been tried, but that appears workable on paper. The filing of the *patent application* technically constitutes a *reduction to practice* (sometimes termed "constructive reduction to practice" since no "actual reduction to practice " has occurred). However, should the invention consist of something generally thought improbable, such as a *perpetual motion machine*, the *PTO* may ask that its operability be demonstrated.

The issue of when an invention was first "actually" reduced to practice can be extremely important if two or more pending applications should claim the same underlying *invention* (this usually results in an *interference*). In this situation, the *inventor* who was first to actually reduce the invention to practice will be entitled to the patent, unless the other inventor was the first to conceive of the invention and can show *diligence in reducing it to practice*.

The inventor who files his patent application first is considered to be the first to reduce it to practice, unless the other inventor can establish that he "actually" reduced it to practice first. This can be proven by *swearing behind* a cited *prior art reference* (the inventor who actually reduced to practice first states under oath that the actual reduction occurred before the invention became relevant *prior art* by way of the other inventor's patent application).

Example: Bob in Idaho and Alain in Vermont both independently invent a new type of ski binding which releases when sensors on the skier's leg muscles indicate potential for severe muscular or skeletal strain. Bob files his patent application one day earlier than Alain. Because both patent applications cover the same underlying invention, the *PTO* declares an *interference*. Since Bob filed his application one day earlier than Alain, he will be awarded priority (and the patent) unless Alain can establish that he "actually reduced his invention to practice" first (and before Bob filed his application).

Even if Alain is held to be the first to have reduced the invention to practice, however, he will not necessarily be awarded the patent. If Bob can show that he was the first to conceive of the invention and was diligently working to reduce the invention to practice at the time the "lightbulb" went on in Alain's head, then Bob may be awarded the patent instead of Alain. Related terms: *interference* and *reduction to practice*.

adding matter by CIP application See *continuation in part application*.

additional claims fee When a *patent application* is amended by the *inventor* after the *PTO* has rejected one or more of the original patent *claims*, it is necessary to pay an additional application fee if the amendment includes more than three *independent claims* or more than twenty claims in all. See *amendment of patent*

application.

admissions by inventor Statements (admissions) made by an *inventor* in a *patent application*, or in any subsequent correspondence with the *PTO*, that are used to contradict a contrary position taken by the inventor in a court proceeding involving the validity of his or her *patent* . Related terms: *file wrapper estoppel*.

agents, patent See *patent agents*.

algorithms and patents An algorithm is a collection of two or more steps in a problem solving process. For example, $2 + 2 = 4$ is technically an algorithm because it involves at least two steps (addition and comparison). Of course, in the industrial and scientific world, complex formulae (algorithms) govern everything from making steel to putting satellites into orbit. Computer software can also be viewed as collections of algorithms, since all computers are made to work through the meticulous step-by-step instructions we call programs.

Algorithms, as such, are traditionally not considered to be *statutory subject matter* (i.e., within the categories of patentable items established by Congress), even though they may meet the other qualifications for a patent (i.e., are *novel*, *non-obvious*, and *useful*). Why not? Because the courts have always held "abstract ideas" and "pure thought" to be laws of nature belonging to the public domain, and to be unpatentable, therefore, by themselves.

However, to the extent that an algorithm is used in combination with a physical instrumentality of some kind, the combination may be independently patentable. For example, many types of software (otherwise considered to be algorithms) are now being developed for use in such special-purpose computerized systems as gas mileage analyzers in cars, heat regulation mechanisms in homes, and medical devices able to inject tiny amounts of drugs into patients on a continuous basis. Because these devices combine algorithms with physical devices, their patentability is not precluded by the "law of nature" rule. Furthermore, patents are also being granted on software programs that enable general purpose computers to process information in special inventive ways.

In short, if the software inventor **claims** the program in a way that relates the program to the physical computer, a patent may issue if the other patent requirements are met. Related terms: *algorithms as trade secrets* 1 and *software protection through copyright* 2.

allowance of patent application

When the **PTO** approves a **patent application** in the course of the application process (i.e., the **prosecution** stage). Related terms: *prosecuting a patent application*.

amendment of patent application

In the course of the **patent application** process, the **PTO** will commonly reject some of the **claims** as they appear in the original application. It is then necessary to either contest the rejection, or file an amendment that either alters such claims, or contains new ones.

When the **PTO** rejects claims, it explains its reasoning and sends the applicant copies of any **prior art references** that have contributed to the rejection. Accordingly, when filing an amendment it is important for the applicant to explain why any changes and/or additions both overcome the objections, and/or can be adequately distinguished from any relevant **prior art references** sent by the PTO.

Amendments that don't affect the substance of an application may also be made even after the PTO has decided to issue a patent. Related terms: *prosecuting a patent application*.

anticipation of invention

An **invention** for which a U.S. **patent** is being sought is considered to have been "anticipated" in either of the following circumstances:

- when all of the invention's elements have been described in one printed publication, described by a previous patent, known about by the public, used in the U.S., or found in a prior invention prior to the date the invention was conceived of by the inventor, or

- when the invention has been described in a printed publication, subjected to a public use or demonstration, placed on sale in the U.S. or described by a previous patent, at least one year prior to the patent application being filed

To say that an invention has been "anticipated" is really the same as saying that prior developments and/or public knowledge rule out the invention as being truly **novel**. Anticipation of an invention can occur in any of the following specific ways:

- By publication in news articles, trade journals, academic theses, and prior patents. For example, High Tech Mechanics, Inc., invents a low-cost kit that permits a car's driver to monitor ten different engine functions while driving the car. If all of the primary characteristics of this kit had been described by someone else in a trade journal, newspaper article, advertisement, or patent, prior to High Tech's creating the invention, then the invention would be considered "anticipated" by this published reference, and would be barred from receiving a patent.

- By public use or display of the invention. For example, if High Tech spent more than a year publicly demonstrating its kit prior to filing for a patent, the invention would be considered "anticipated" because of the late filing (often referred to as a violation of the **one year rule**). But if the public demonstrations had been predominantly for experimental purposes, the one-year period might not apply. Anticipation through public use or display rarely occurs.

- By placing the invention "on sale" more than one year prior to an application's being filed. "On sale" can mean not only actual sale, but any offer of sale, or

- By prior inventions. In the far most common form of "anticipation", a prior invention is said to "anticipate" a later one when all the elements of the later one are found in the earlier one. For example, suppose Sammy "invents" an electric generator that is driven by the kinetic energy of a car's moving wheels. If all the basic elements used by Sammy in his "invention" can be found in a prior invention (whether patented or not), Sammy's generator has been anticipated.

As mentioned, an invention is not anticipated by a printed publication or prior invention unless all of the later invention's basic elements are contained in at least one invention or publication (termed a **prior art reference**). For example, if a news article describes some elements of an invention, and a prior

Patent

4

invention shows the rest, no anticipation has occurred, since no single reference contained all the elements. Anticipation only occurs when all elements of an invention are described or found in one place, or are known about publicly (through public use), so that all of the later invention's elements have been *fully met* by a single prior art reference.
Related Terms: *prior art references* and *novelty*.

anti-shelving clause A *contract* 🖐 provision, negotiated into some *patent licenses* and *assignments*, that requires the licensee or assignee to exploit the patent commercially rather than "put in on the shelf". For obvious reasons, this type of provision is especially important when the license or assignment is made in exchange for the payment of royalties computed on the number of products sold.

anti-trust law and patents A *patent* is a seventeen-year legal monopoly over the production, use and distribution of an *invention* covered by the patent. This monopoly is an exception to the laws of the United States, and of many other industrialized countries (including the member nations of the *European Economic Community*), which generally prohibit businesses from engaging in monopolistic activities (activity designed to drive all or most competitors out of business).

Example: Bionics, Ltd. develops and patents a brace that provides 360 degree support for the human knee. Because this invention is a great improvement over existing knee braces, any company that has the exclusive right to make and sell the brace will have a great advantage over competitors. If Bionics markets its invention in such a way that one company gets the lion's share of the knee brace business, and the other knee brace manufacturers are eliminated from competition, the courts may hold that Bionics's patent has been used in violation of the anti-trust laws (prohibiting monopolistic practices), and is therefore invalid. If, on the other hand, Bionics grants non-exclusive licenses to other knee brace manufacturers on a non-restricted basis, anti-trust violations will probably be avoided.

Anti-trust laws also prohibit business practices that restrain the free flow of commerce (called restraint of trade). Among the more common types of patent-related activity that may potentially cause such violations are:

- *vertical price fixing* (e.g., a patent owner requires the licensee of the patent to charge certain prices for goods manufactured under the patent)

- *exclusive dealing agreements* (e.g., a patent owner encourages patent licensees not to deal with certain customers)

- "tying agreements" (e.g., requiring a customer to purchase other goods as a condition for purchasing those covered by the patent)

- *requirements contracts* 🖐, whether mandatory or encouraged by price reductions (e.g., a purchaser of goods covered by a patent is prohibited from purchasing comparable items from another source)

- *territorial restrictions* (e.g., licensees are restricted to certain geographical areas in their marketing of the goods covered by the patent

- *concerted refusal to deal* (e.g., some potential customers are excluded from use of the device or process covered by the patent while others are included)

Practically speaking, anti-trust law should not be a concern for most inventors, as few patents have a large enough impact on the related market or industry to raise the anti-trust warning flag. If, however, an invention is so important that the actual ebb and flow of commerce might be affected by it, there is no substitute for a good knowledge of anti-trust law. See the Research Notes directly following this Section.

Especially when important inventions are involved, it is common in patent *infringement actions* for the defendant to charge that the plaintiff committed an anti-trust violation and cannot therefore enforce the patent. Related terms: *misuse of patents* and *defenses to patent*.

articles describing invention, publication of See *anticipation of patents*.

assignment of patents A *patent* is a type of property, and as such can be sold to others outright (usually termed an *assignment* 🖐) or licensed to parties for specific uses and periods of time. A license is a permission to use or do what one could not otherwise do legally.

attorneys fees, infringement action
See *infringement actions*.

attorneys, patent See *patent attorneys*.

attorneys and agents registered to practice before the United States Patent and Trademark Office A publication by the *PTO* listing all the patent attorneys and patent agents who are licensed to prepare patent applications and to practice before the *U.S. Patent and Trademark Office*. Related terms: *patent attorneys* and *patent agents*.

automated patent search systems
See *computerized patent searches*.

base-issue fee Formerly, the basic fee that had to be paid to the *PTO* in the event it decided to issue a *patent*. Now called the "issue fee", this fee must be aid within three months (or up to six months if extension fees are paid) after receipt of the "Issue Fee Due" form that normally accompanies the formal *notice of allowance* (the notice from the patent office that a patent will be issued).

best mode disclosure requirement A *PTO* rule requiring a *patent applicant* to disclose the best embodiment of his or her invention or in the best light possible (i.e., in the way it will work best). Related terms: *disclosure requirement for patents* .

biotechnology and patents See *genetic engineering and patents*.

Board of Appeals Formerly, an administrative body within the *U.S. Patent and Trademark Office* that handled appeals from decisions by *patent examiners* to disallow one or more *claims* in *patent applications*. Now these appeals are handled by the *Board of Appeals and Interferences*. If a *patent applicant* wishes to appeal any other type of decision by the patent examiner, he or she must directly petition the *PTO Commissioner*. Related terms: *final office action*.

Board of Appeals and Interferences
A new administrative body within the Patent and Trademark Office that combines the former function of the *Board of*

Appeals and the *Board of Patent Interferences*.

Board of Patent Interferences Formerly an administrative body within the *U.S. Patent and Trademark Office* established for the purpose of deciding who is entitled to a *patent* when an *interference* occurs (i.e., when two or more *inventors* lay claim to the same *invention*). Related terms: *interference* and *prosecuting a patent application* .

breaking a patent Establishing that an *in-force patent* (i.e., an existing patent) is *invalid* or *unenforceable* because 1) it was improperly issued by the *PTO* in the first place, or 2) it was *misused* by the patent owner. Normally, a patent is broken in the course of defending against a patent *infringement* charge brought by the *patent owner*. Related terms: *infringement action* and *defenses to patent*.

broad claims See *claims*.

broadened claims in reissue patent
See *reissue patent*.

broadening paragraph in specification See *specification*.

building and testing of invention See *actual reduction to practice*.

CCPA Abbreviation for "Court of Customs and Patent Appeals", title for the court that formerly handled appeals from determinations by the *U.S. Patent and Trademark Office*. Now combined with the former Court of Claims and renamed the "U.S. Circuit of Appeals for the Federal Circuit" (usually called Federal Circuit Court of Appeals or CAFC — pronounced "Kafka"), this court not only continues to handle all appeals from the *PTO*, but also decides all appeals taken from U.S. District Court judgments in *patent infringement actions*.

certificate of correction A form issued by the *PTO* when an inventor wishes to make minor corrections of a technical or clerical nature in an application after the PTO has decided to issue the patent. Related terms: *prosecuting a patent application*.

Patent

4

chemicals, invention of as patentable subject matter   See *composition of matter*.

CIP   See *continuation in part application*.

claiming an invention   Describing the essence and scope of an invention by precisely reducing its elements into one or more sentence fragments, called *claims*. Related terms: *claims*.

claims   Formal single-sentence fragments in a *patent application* , which circumscribe and delineate the true nature of the *invention* in question. A patent's "claims" are the primary means by which a court can tell whether the *patent* has been *infringed* by a later device. Related terms: *infringement of patent*.

Most *patent applications* contain *multiple claims*, each of which describes the invention's elements from a slightly different viewpoint. These can be "independent claims " (i.e., they stand on their own without referring to other claims for their elements or limitations), or "dependent claims" (i.e., they depend on and refer to other claims for their meaning). There has to be at least one independent claim in a patent application. In the United States, the fee for filing a patent application permits the inclusion of up to three independent claims and up to twenty claims in all. An extra fee must be paid if the application contains more than twenty claims, or three independent claims.

In the U.S., each claim must "particularly point out and distinctly claim" the subject matter claimed to be the invention for which the patent is being sought. To meet this requirement, the Patent and Trademark Office requires that each claim must:

- be stated in one unit (a sentence fragment without a verb which can and almost always does have numerous clauses and subclauses)

- be very specific

- be clear

- be distinct from other claims, and

- be consistent with the narrative description of the patent contained in the *specification* portion of the patent application (See chart next page.)

Because it is the claims that define the scope of the invention for the purpose of preventing others from using, manufacturing or selling it, the broader the claims are, the broader the reach of the patent.

Example: A claim to a new type of writing implement states that the invention is "a hand-held device containing a means by which marks may be made on a surface". Since the language of this claim literally reaches every writing implement that ever has been or ever could be manufactured, it would be considered extremely "broad". Conversely, the narrower the scope of a patent claim, the more restricted is the reach of the patent, and the easier it is for another inventor to come up with a somewhat similar invention that would not infringe the claim.

Returning to our "writing implement" example, suppose our inventor now claimed his invention as follows: "A 3-inch by 1/2-inch plastic tube containing liquid and for making an indelible 1/32 inch line on a flat paper surface." If another inventor made a "4-inch by 1/4 inch metal tube containing a charcoal substance capable of making variable width lines on any flat surface", the later device would not infringe a patent granted on the earlier invention. Why not? Because the elements of the invention described in the first claim are different from the elements in the later one. And, as a general rule, any patent claim that recites fewer or different elements than are found in another device do not *read on* (i.e., fully describe) that device for infringement purposes. A patent's reach only extends as far as the elements and limitations contained in its claims and its equivalents.

Although broad claims clearly appear to give the patent owner more protection, there is a rub. Claimed subject matter (i.e., the invention for which a patent is being sought) must be *novel* (different in some way from previous inventions or developments) and *non-obvious* (an unexpected or surprising result from the standpoint of what a *person with ordinary skill in the art* knew about the technology involved in the invention at the time it was made). Broad claims run a high risk of either being *anticipated* by a prior invention (i.e., not being novel) or being rendered *obvious* by *prior art*.

In the example given, our first

Example of Independent and Dependent Claims

I claim:

1. A target comprising substrate means and target pattern means formed on one side of said substrate means in a layer substantially covering said one side of said substrate means, said substrate means and said target pattern means being mutually contrasting visually, said substrate means and said target pattern means being arranged such that when struck by a high speed projectile, a substantially larger-than-projectile-size portion of said target pattern means at the projectile's point of impact will be physically separated and remove from the rest of said target pattern means, and a hole, of a size smaller than said removed portion of said target pattern means, will be made in said substrate means, whereby a portion of said substrate means around said hole will be exposed by the impact of said projectile.

— independent

2. The target of claim **1** wherein said substrate means is contrastingly colored to said target pattern means by means of a fluorescent dye.

3. The target of claim **1** wherein said substrate means comprises a transparent film backed by a layer of material having a contrasting color to said target pattern means.

4. The target of claim **1** wherein said substrate means comprises an ionomer resin and said target pattern means comprises an ink layer.

5. The target of claim **4** wherein said ionomer resin is transparent and is backed by a layer of material having a contrasting color to said target pattern means.

6. The target of claim **4** wherein said ionomer resin has a contrasting color to said target pattern means.

7. The target of claim **1** wherein said substrate means has a target pattern congruent with the target pattern on said target pattern means.

8. The target of claim **7** wherein said substrate means comprises a transparent film backed by a layer of material having a contrasting color to said target pattern means, said congruent target pattern being formed on said layer of material.

9. The target of claim **8** wherein said layer of material is paper which is dyed with a brightly-colored fluorescent ink.

10. The target of claim **1** wherein said target pattern means comprises at least one substaintially larger-than-bullet-size flat member adhesively secured to said substrate means.

11. The target of claim **1** wherein said target pattern means comprises a mosaic of substantially larger-than-bullet-size flat members adhesively secured to and covering said substrate means and carrying a target pattern thereon.

— dependent

writing-implement claim was so broad that it clearly **read on** (described) prior inventions (pencil, chalk, pen, quill, crayon, etc.) But the narrower version of the writing-implement claim excluded some of these prior inventions (e.g., by claiming a liquid means, the claim excluded pencils and chalk). For any claim to be approved by the Patent and Trademark Office, it must be narrow enough to make the invention different from prior inventions or developments (i.e., novel) and unexpected or surprising enough an advance over prior developments to be non-obvious. The primary goal of all patent claim drafters is to draft claims as broadly as possible, given the constraints of the state of prior knowledge (inventions and developments — e.g., *prior art*). Related terms: *prior art*, *anticipation of invention* and *infringement of patent*.

Class Definitions Manual   A manual published by the *PTO* that provides brief definitions of each classification and subclassification used by the PTO to categorize the underlying *inventions* on which *patents* have been issued. If you are performing a *patent search*, this volume can teach you what the different classes and subclasses mean, so you can figure out which one applies to your invention and thus search only for relevant patents. Related terms: *classification of patents, patent search*.

classification of patents, patent search   *Patents* are maintained by the *U.S. Patent and Trademark Office* according to certain definitive classifications and subclassifications assigned to the underlying inventions. To conduct a *patent search* efficiently, it is necessary to first ascertain the class and subclass within which an invention falls. There are more than three hundred (300) main classifications and more than two hundred (200) subclasses for each main class. So, an invention will fall within at least one of 60,000 separate classifications (actually, 66,000).

Fortunately, the classes and subclasses are indexed alphabetically in the *Index of Classification* maintained by the *U.S. Patent and Trademark Office Office*. There is also a *Class Definitions Manual*, which provides brief definitions of the classes and subclasses, and a *Manual of Classifications*, which goes into more depth about the characteristics of each

classification. Related terms: *patent search*.

co-inventors   In cases where there is more than one inventor, each person who makes creative contributions to an invention, as described in at least one *claim* in the *patent application*.

Example: Tom Haberfeld and Bonnie Rand jointly conceive of and design a miniature EEG machine (a machine that measures brain waves) that allows its wearer to monitor his or her own brain waves on a wrist watch. To make sure the concept is viable, Tom and Bonnie get their engineer friend, Clark Bromsky, to build a test model according to their specifications. Once the invention is proven, to Tom and Bonnie's satisfaction, a patent application is drafted that includes three *independent claims*, all of which relate to the invention's miniature structures and means for monitoring brain waves. In this situation, Bonnie and Tom would be listed as "co-inventors" of the invention since they were the sole creative contributors. Clark would not be considered a co-inventor since his contribution was made according to set specifications and did not therefore encompass creative additions to the invention. However, if while building the test model, Clark signficantly altered the invention's basic specifications and design, Clark also might qualify as a co-inventor.

When filing a patent application, it is extremely important to be accurate about the identity of the inventor or co-inventors. Leaving an inventor out or putting someone in who doesn't qualify may later cause an issued patent to be declared invalid and unenforceable. Related terms: *inventors* and *defenses to patent*.

combination patent   A colloquial phrase for patents on inventions that are combinations of prior existing inventions or technology. Suppose an inventor combines a bicycle frame with a movable tread design previously utilized on a snowmobile, to create a device that travels efficiently on sand. Because the invention combines two previous patented inventions, a patent issued on it will commonly be referred to as a "combination patent".

Earlier court decisions in patent cases suggested that a combination invention must demonstrate a new or surprising result, called "synergism", before it could qualify for a patent. However, the **Court of Appeals for the Federal Circuit** has ruled that the phrase "combination patent" has no meaning under the patent laws, and that virtually all inventions can be said to be combinations of prior existing technology. As long as an invention meets the basic requirements for a patent (**statutory subject matter, novelty, non-obviousness**, and **utility**), the fact that it is a "combination" of prior developments has no legal effect, and no showing of synergism is required.

Commissioner of Patents and Trademarks See section 3.

community patent A patent issued by the **European Patent Office** to an **inventor** from one of the nine member nations of the **EEC**. Community patents enjoy equal status and protection in all nine countries.

composition of matter Compositions of matter are one of the five statutory categories of things (collectively, **statutory subject matter**) that qualify for a patent. Generally, compositions of matter consist of chemical compositions, conglomerates, aggregates, or other chemically significant substances that are usually supplied in bulk, in liquid, gas, or solid form. They include most new chemicals, new forms of life created by gene splicing techniques (the genetic mixing comprises the composition), drugs, road-building compositions, gasoline, fuels, glues, and paper. Related terms: **statutory subject matter** and **non-statutory subject matter**.

compulsory licensing of patent Forcing a **patent owner** to allow others to utilize his or her **invention** in exchange for reasonable compensation. In the U.S., a patent owner has the right never to produce, manufacture, create or implement his or her invention. This, of course, means that the public may never benefit from the invention at least until the patent has expired. Because the primary purpose for awarding an inventor a statutory monopoly over his invention is to provide such benefit, Japan and many other countries, require inventors to **actually reduce their inventions to practice** and to market them within a specific period of time. If this is not done, the

inventors may be forced (compelled) to license others to develop and use their invention in exchange for reasonable royalties or other compensation. Related terms: **working a patent**.

computer programs and patents See **algorithms and patents**.

computerized patent searches In recent years, it has become possible to conduct at least part of a **patent search** using a computer terminal. This is because **databases** containing either the full text of a **patent** (LEXPAT) or just the patent **claims** or **abstracts** (DIALOG) have been constructed and made available through subscription telecommunication services.

At the present, the LEXPAT database contains the full text of all U.S. patents issued since 1975. For some inventions, this date is too modern, and they will require a search of older patents. However, in the fields involving such technologies as computers, semiconductors, integrated circuits, alternative energy, robotics, modern medicine and biotechnology, it is highly unlikely that many patents issued earlier than 1975 will prove to be relevant (i.e, contain a **prior art reference**).

Computerized searches under LEXPAT are carried out by typing certain key words at a computer terminal, and instructing the computer to produce a list of all patents that contain those words in the order that you specify. For example, if your search involves a bicycle chain, you might ask for a listing of all patents that contain the words "bicycle" and "chain' ", where "bicycle" comes before "chain". When the list appears on your terminal, you can then view the full text of any entry on the list or any selected portion (such as the **abstract of patent**, **drawing**, **claims** or **specification**). If you are told that no patent contains the words bicycle and chain in that order, then you will need to reformulate your request (try "bipedal vehicle" and "wheel pulling device"). Sometimes it takes a number of attempts to cover all the actual words used in all relevant patents. Unless you do come up with all the correct words, you may miss patents, and thus perform an incomplete search. For this reason, many patent searchers also choose to conduct a manual search, were the

Patent

4

patents can be reviewed by **classification of patents** rather than by key words.

Other databases exist as well. Examples:

- a database called "Claims" (operated by Dialog), which contains the abstracts and claims for patents issued since 1950

- a database called PATLAW, which contains sources of intellectual property decisions by the Federal Courts, as well as administrative decisions pertaining to patents, trademarks, copyrights, and unfair competition laws, and

- a database called Claims/Class, which provides a classification code and title dictionary for all classes and selected sub-classes of the U.S. patent-classification system

concerted refusal to deal When two or more businesses jointly boycott (e.g., discriminate against, refuse to buy from, or refuse to sell to) one or more other businesses. Such activity can be an **anti-trust** violation if commerce has been significantly affected. If a concerted refusal to deal stems from the selective use of one or more patents, these patents may be declared invalid if the anti-trust laws have been violated, or they become unenforceable because of **misuse**, even though the anti-trust laws are not involved. Related terms: **anti-trust law** and **misuse of patents**.

Example: The three largest genetic engineering laboratories agree to share their patents through a **patent pool** arrangement. Competitors are not allowed to use the patents. This exclusion of competitors may constitute a "concerted refusal to deal", resulting in either invalidity or unenforceability of the patents.

confidentiality of patent application See **disclosure of patent application** and **patents and trade secrets** 1.

continuation application An application that is filed after an earlier **patent application** has been disallowed by the **PTO**. This second application must be filed within three months (unless an extension is obtained) if it is being made in response to a **final office action** by the PTO. It requires a new fee and new **claims**. The continuation application will receive a new serial number and **filing date** . However, in the event an **interfer-**

ence occurs, and for purposes of determining the existence of **prior art**, the **inventor** will be entitled to the benefit of the original **filing date**. Related terms: **prosecuting a patent application** and **continuation in part application** .

continuation in part application (CIP) A second subsequent application for the same invention which includes new material not covered in the original application. CIPS provide a way for an inventor to supplement an earlier patent application with new matter to cover improvements that have been made in the meantime. The CIP has the same **filing date** for matter that it and the original application have in common. However, any **claim** in the CIP that covers the new subject matter is entitled only to the filing date of the CIP. This type of application should be distinguished from **continuation applications**, where the applicant reformulates his or her claims after a disallowance by the PTO. In practice, CIPs are seldom used. Related terms: **continuation application** and **prosecuting a patent application**.

constructive reduction to practice **Reduction to practice** is legally (constructively) assumed to occur on the date when a patent application is filed. This will also be presumed to be the first date of reduction to practice, should an **interference** occur, unless a showing is made that an **actual reduction to practice** occurred at an earlier time. Related terms: **reduction to practice** and **actual reduction to practice**.

contributory infringement of patent The sale of an item that has been especially configured to work as a material part of a patented invention may be considered an **infringement** of the patent (called a "contributory infringement"), if the item itself has no independent non-infringing use. Contributory infringement can occur even when the item being sold is itself not patentable.

Example: Bionics, Inc., a manufacturer of artificial human organs, patents and manufactures an artificial kidney containing several unique (but **non-patentable**) valves. If Empire Hospital Equipment Ltd. starts selling the modified valve separately, they may be held to be a contributory infringer of the kidney patent, unless they can show that the part does, in fact, have an independent use that does not infringe the kidney invention.

In essence, the contributory infringer doctrine recognizes that items especially modified for a patented invention will not generally be sold unless they are being used for an infringing purpose. Related terms: *infringement action* and *rights of patent owners*.

convention application An application for patent protection in other countries, filed in accordance with the *Convention for the Protection of Industrial Property*, sometimes known as the *Paris Convention*. Under this treaty, a *patent application* must be filed in every country where patent protection is desired, within one year of the date that an application is first filed in any other member country. So, if a U.S. patent application has a filing date of February 5, 1985, all additional filings in other countries under the "Convention" must be made by February 5, 1986. Each convention filing must be made in the language of the country where it takes place, and separate filing and search fees must be paid. Generally speaking, convention applications utilize a different, more costly procedure, than do applications under the *Patent Cooperation Treaty*. Related terms: *Patent Cooperation Treaty*.

Convention for the Protection of Industrial Property See *Convention Filing*.

Court of Appeals for the Federal Circuit The federal court of appeals responsible for hearing and deciding all appeals from patent *infringement actions* decided in the U.S. District courts, and all appeals from decisions by the *Board of Appeals and Interferences*. This court sits in Washington and also travels around the U.S.

Court of Customs and Patent Appeals See *CCPA*.

cross-licensing A licensing arrangement under which two or more owners of separate *patents* cooperate so that each may use the other's invention. Because such technologies as automobile manufacturing, genetic engineering, and semiconductor chip fabrication depend heavily on

many inventions from a variety of sources, these sources commonly share their patents through cross-licensing agreements so that all may benefit from the ' 'state of the art''. Related terms: *patent pools* and *improvement patents*.

damages for patent infringement See *infringement actions*.

declaration for patent application A statement made under penalty of perjury by a patent applicant, acknowledging that 1) the applicant is the first and true inventor, 2) that he or she has reviewed and understands the specification and claims, and 3) he or she has a duty to disclose all information material to the examination of the application. Related terms: *patent application* and *prosecuting a patent application*.

declaration of prior art See *Information Disclosure Statement*.

declaratory judgment of non-infringement, invalidity and unenforceability of patent If a business desires to utilize commercially a device or process arguably described in a patent owned by another party, and if it is unable to reach a satisfactory licensing agreement with the other party, and if it feels the patent is invalid or infringed, then the business can file an action in court, requesting a judge to declare (issue a declaratory judgment) that the patent is either invalid or unenforceable, or that it doesn't apply to the device or process in question. If such judgment is granted, the business can then use the device or process without risking liability for *infringement of the patent*.

defective patent See *defenses to a patent*.

defenses to a patent When a *patent owner* attempts to enforce his or her *patent*, by alleging that it has been infringed (i.e., that the *invention* described in the patent has been made, used, or sold without the patent owner's permission), the alleged infringer may raise a number of potential defenses, depending on the facts. Some of these defenses can render the patent unenforceable. Others challenge its basic validity. The primary difference between an unenforceable patent and an invalid patent is that an unenforceable patent's owner can usually take steps to make it enforceable, whereas an invalid patent cannot be made valid. In either event, if a party accused of *infringement* can establish that at that time the patent is either invalid or unenforceable, he or she will win the *infringement action* .

A patent may be declared unenforceable if the patent owner has *misused* the patent in some way. Among the specific types of misuse that can render a patent unenforceable are:

- false marking of an invention (i.e., putting a *patent number* on it that doesn't apply)
- illegal or unfair licensing practices
- extended delay in bringing the infringement action to the detriment of the defendant (called *laches* 5), and
- *fraud on the Patent and Trademark Office* (such as failing to include a pertinent *prior art reference* in a *statement of prior art*)

Patents may be declared invalid if the court finds:

- that relevant prior-art references exist that the PTO didn't discover or analyze properly, and that affect the *novelty* or *non-obviousness* of the invention
- that an invention doesn't or won't work
- that the disclosure of the invention in the patent application contains insufficient information to teach an *ordinary person skilled in the art* to build the invention
- that the patent claims are too vague and indefinite
- that the patent was issued to the wrong inventor
- that *anti-trust* violations have occurred, or
- that any other set of facts exist that operate to retroactively invalidate the patent

Because of the variety of potential defenses in a patent infringement action, many observers feel that a patent is not worth a great deal if there is significant economic motivation to infringe it. Basically, the more valuable an invention is, the more difficult it is to enforce a patent on it. This is because large economic interests are almost sure to mount a fierce and expensive court challenge to the patent's validity. And the more difficult it

is to enforce a patent, the less it is worth to its rightful owner. (Sounds like a paradox? Welcome to the law.) It should also be pointed out, however, that billions of dollars are awarded to patent owners every year as a result of infringement actions, and numerous inventors, both small and institutional, make good money from patents issued on their inventions. Related terms: *misuse of patents*.

defensive publication This means to prevent others from obtaining a patent on one's invention by publishing a description of the invention in the *Official Gazette* or any other publication. By publishing the details of an invention prior to obtaining a patent, an inventor can transform the invention into *prior art*, which will preclude others from obtaining a patent on it. This type of pre-emptive publication is useful when an inventor who has filed a *patent application* decides not to pursue it further, but still wants to make, use or sell the underlying invention. To publish defensively, an inventor must file a paper with the *PTO* that:

- requests the PTO to publish the patent application's *abstract* in the Official Gazette
- formally abandons the patent application, and
- authorizes the PTO to open the patent application to public inspection

Example: Lou Swift invents a new form of portable energy source that allows most residential users of electricity to disconnect from the common electrical grid. After Lou applies for a patent, she comes to believe that the cause of peace and freedom would best be served by the invention being placed in the *public domain* (and becoming, therefore, unpatentable). She therefore utilizes the procedures described above to turn her application into a *prior art reference* that precludes anybody else from obtaining a patent on her invention. Related terms: *prior art reference*.

dependent claim A particular type of patent *claim* that refers to another claim for part of its substance, and which is therefore conceptually dependent on this other type of claim. Dependent claims must be read (interpreted) in the light of the claims to which they refer (which can be either **independent claims** or other dependent claims), and must also be read to contain all the limitations of these claims. The typical **patent application** contains several ''independent claims'', and each of these may in turn have several ''dependent claims'' which refer back to it. Related terms: **claims**.

deposit account with PTO An account established with the **PTO** by an **inventor** or **patent attorney** who expects to submit a number of **patent applications** over time. Instead of the inventor's submitting a check every time a fee is called for under the patent application rules, the fees are simply deducted from the current account balance. At present, a $1000.00 minimum balance must be maintained, or a charge of $2.00 a month is levied.

design patent A patent issued on an inventive design that is purely ornamental or aesthetic in nature. The requirements for a design patent are that the design be **novel, non-obvious**, and ornamental rather than useful. If a new personal computer were designed to resemble a classical robot, it might qualify for a design patent as long as the robot characteristics played no functional role. But if the robot characteristics were primarily functional, so the computer could actually move across the room or perform other functions associated with robots, rather than ornamental, a design patent would be precluded.

Often, two patents will be submitted for the same device. One is a **utility patent** , which covers the device's functional characteristics while the other will be a ''design patent'', to protect the device's ornamental characeristics. In our robot computer example, it might be possible to obtain both a utility patent and a design patent, if the device primarily acts as a computer, but is made with ornamental robotic features.

Although design patents are relatively easy to obtain, they provide little protection since designs are generally very easy to **design around**. Related terms: **design around** .

design around To design or build a device or process that is similar to an **invention** protected by a **patent**, but that avoids **infringment of the patent** by utilizing one or more different elements.

The scope of protection acquired under a given patent is determined by the wording of its **claims**. Thus, any device, process, or substance containing the same elements as those described in the claims of a patent can be said to infringe the patent. Conversely, any device or process that contains fewer elements, or different ones, than those described by the patent claims, does not infringe the patent (i.e., the patent's claims do not ''read on'' the infringing device). By studying the claims associated with a specific patent, it is often possible to design or build a highly similar device or process that is sufficiently different in its elements to avoid infringing the patent. In this way it is possible to ''design around'' a patented invention.

Example: Akama Bathroom Designers (ABD) invents and patents a small radiator-type device that uses hot water to dry and warm towels. The claims for this invention describe it as consisting of plastic. If Bonanza Bathroom Products (BBP) creates a similar device, but uses a metal alloy that doubles the ability of the device to retain heat, they probably have not infringed ABD' 's patent since they ''designed around it'' by using a different element that produced a different result. But if a court decided that the type of substance used in the invention and the extra heat retention were immaterial (i.e., unimportant) to the overall invention, infringement might be found to exist under the **doctrine of equivalents**, which allows infringement to be found when two inventions with somewhat different elements are are substantially equivalent in result.

Of course, to prevent such ''designing around'' activity, a carefully drawn claim would probably have been much broader, and would not have specified plastic as the main material. Instead, the claim might have described something like ''a hard, inflexible means through which hot water can be channelled at normal domestic water pressures, the heat retained over a period of time, and towels folded over for the purpose of drying''. Related terms: **claims** and **doctrine of equivalents**.

DIALOG The name of a computer **database** 1 that lists **abstracts of patents**, and **claims**, for U.S. patents issued since 1950. Related terms: **comput-**

Patent

4

erized patent searches.

diligence in reducing to practice

Continuous and sincere efforts by an inventor either to build and demonstrate an invention, or to file a *patent application*. If two or more *inventors* apply for a *patent* on the same underlying invention, the inventor who is first to file a patent application (or first to actually build the invention) if this occurs earlier) will get the patent, unless the other inventor can show that he conceived of the invention first and was diligent in reducing the invention to practice. Related terms: *interference*.

direct infringement of patent   See *infringement of patent*.

disclosure of patent application by PTO   See *non-disclosure of patent application by PTO*.

disclosure requirement for patents

A *patent application* must disclose enough about the *invention* to enable a *person with ordinary skill in the art* to build or develop it. To the extent that an application fails to make this disclosure (often called an "enabling disclosure" because it enables the invention to be built), the *patent* may later prove to be unenforceable, should an *infringement action* need to be brought. However, the fact that the *PTO* approved the application in the first place is generally relied on by courts to reject this particular defense.

The reason for the disclosure requirement is simple. The complete disclosure of the technology and ideas involved in an invention is the condition by which an *inventor* earns the grant of his or her seventeen-year monopoly over the right to make, use and sell the invention. Related terms: *patent application*.

divisional application   A *patent application* that has grown out of (i.e., been divided from) an earlier application that *claims* two or more *inventions*. Only one *patent* may be issued per invention. If a *patent application* claims two or more inventions, in the informed opinion of the patent examiner, the applicant is required to restrict the application to one invention and has the option to file a separate "divisional application" for each addi-

tional invention.

What happens if the patent examiner is wrong and a court later finds that there was only one invention and that two or more patents issued on the same invention? Even though this violates the statutory rule against *double patenting*, the patents will be upheld because restriction was required by the PTO.

The *filing date* for the original application will be considered the filing date for the divisional application(s) as well. This date is extremely important in deciding such issues as 1) whether the invention has been *anticipated* by *prior art* (the application date shuts the door on all subsequent developments from being considered as prior art); 2) whether the patent application has been filed within one year of the invention's being used in public or described in a printed publication; 3) when an application for patent protection in other countries must be filed; and 4) when was the invention first *reduced to practice* in the event of an *interference* . Related terms: *date of application* and *anticipation*.

doctrine of equivalents   A rule allowing patent *infringement* to be found when an allegedly infringing device or process does the same work in substantially the same way, to accomplish the same result as the *invention* protected by a *patent*, even though the patent's claims do not expressly describe the device. In this case, an "identity of inventions" is said to exist. The rule is intended to prevent the *designing-around* of patents on hyper-technical grounds. Unfortunately, there is no logical dividing line between 1) non-infringement based on the legitimate designing around an invention, and 2) infringement based on the "doctrine of equivalents". It is up to the courts to decide, on a case-by-case basis, when inventions are or are not "substantially equivalent".

Related terms: *design around* and *infringement of a patent*.

double patenting   Applying for and/or obtaining two *patents* on one *invention*. Double patenting is not allowed under the patent laws and both patents can later be invalidated in the event they claim a single invention but slipped by the *PTO*. If double patenting results from *divisional applications* being required by

the PTO, this rule does not apply and the patents will be considered valid.

drawings, patent application *Patent applications* involving inventions that can be visually represented, including machines or articles of manufacture, must contain drawings showing features of the *invention* that are different from those known in the *prior art*. A drawing for a *process* should consist of a flowchart showing its sequence of steps. The drawings should show all the features *recited* (described) in the claims.

Drawings are generally not required for inventions consisting of *compositions of matter* unless the inventions consist of structures that can be shown in a cross-sectional representation. Related terms: *patent application* and *disclosure requirements for patent*.

duty of candor and good faith in disclosure to PTO Under rules issued by the *U.S. Patent and Trademark Office*, every *patent applicant* has a "duty of candor and good faith" in connection with the information and disclosures contained in the *patent application*. This means that the applicant must disclose:

• all known instances of *anticipation* (events or references that might constitute a *statutory bar* to the patent)

• pertinent *prior art* that might bear on the question of *non-obviousness*

• the *best mode* of the invention, and

• any other information known to the applicant that bears on the patentability of the invention and the proper scope of the *patent claims*

Failure to comply fully with this duty can result in rejection of the *patent application* by the Patent and Trademark Office, or a later finding of *fraud on the Patent and Trademark Office* in an *infringement action*. In the latter case, the patent may be declared invalid even though the information that was not disclosed would not have invalidated the patent as such. Related terms: *defenses to infringement* and *disclosure requirements for patent*.

Example: In 1984, Patricia invented a device and a process that allowed differential wind velocities to be conveniently measured by the square yard. The results

of the measurements could then be fed into a computer, and the best placement for windmills could be determined. Patricia made the invention for her own home in the country and decided not to patent it, due to the plentiful supply of centralized electrical energy at that time. However, Patricia shared her invention with two of her neighbors for experimental purposes only and made them promise not to talk about it with anybody.

Two years later, in 1986, oil prices soar, and Patricia decides to apply for a patent. In her patent application, she mentions that she first built the invention in 1984 but "forgets" to mention the use of the device by the neighbors. The PTO grants the patent. In 1989, a leading power company begins to market Patricia's device across the country. If Patricia sues for infringement, she may find that her patent cannot be enforced. Why not? Because she failed to disclose information to the PTO bearing on the question of *anticipation*. This might be the case even though the information in question, if disclosed, may not have barred issuance of the patent.

elements of invention See *claims*.

enabling disclosure A *patent application* must describe (i.e., disclose) the *invention* in sufficient detail to "enable" a *person with ordinary skill in the art* to build or develop it (i.e., *work* it) without the exercise of inventive faculties. Related terms: *disclosure requirements for patents*.

equivalents, doctrine of See *doctrine of equivalents*.

estoppel See *file wrapper estoppel*.

European Patent Convention A treaty primarily covering patent law relationships among the members of the *European Economic Community* (the common market), plus a few other countries. Under the European Patent Convention (EPC), an *inventor* need make only one filing and undergo one examination procedure to obtain patent protection in the member countries. Filings and examinations are conducted by the "European Patent Office" in Munich, Germany and Den Haag, Netherlands. A patent issued under the EPC lasts for 20 years from the

Patent

date of application.

European Patent Office See *European Patent Convention*.

examiners, patent The *PTO* employs a large number of patent examiners whose job it is to examine patent applications, correspond with applicants, and initially decide whether to issue a patent. All patent examiners must have technical degrees in some field such as electrical engineering, chemistry, or physics. Many are also attorneys. Related terms: *U.S. Patent and Trademark Office*.

exclusive dealing agreements Agreements between two or more businesses that work to shut out competitors. If a *patent owner* engages in this type of conduct, it may result in his patent later being declared unenforceable or invalid because of patent misuse or violation of the *anti-trust* laws. Related terms: *anti-trust law and patents*.

exclusive license of patent rights A *contract* 5 in which a *patent owner* grants to another party the sole (exclusive) right to make, use, and/or sell the *invention* covered by the *patent* . Sometimes the grant of rights is for all purposes, but often it is limited to a specific context. For example, a patent owner could grant one company the exclusive right to make and sell the invention in the United States and another company the exclusive right to make and sell it in the Common Market. The essence of an *exclusive license* 5 is that within the context defined in the license (e.g., for sales restricted to the U.S., or to a particular period of time, or for a particular purpose), the right is granted exclusively to the person or business receiving it. Related terms: *exclusive licenses* 5 and *anti-trust law and patents*.

exhibiting an invention Exhibiting an unpatented *invention* in an unrestricted context constitutes a *public use* which may later bar a *patent* from being issued, under the *anticipation* doctrine. Related terms: *public use as anticipation*.

experimental use An unpatented *invention* may be sed experimentally in public without this use being considered a *public use*, or a *disclosure*, that will later

bar a *patent* under the doctrine of *anticipation*. This is because many inventions must be actually tested in public one or more times before the inventor is ready to file a *patent application*. However, if the public use is not truly experimental in nature (i.e., not actually done for the purpose of testing or improving the invention), such use may bar a patent unless an application for the patent is filed within one year of the use. Related terms: *public use as anticipation*.

false marking of invention See *marking of invention*.

Federal Trade Commission proceeding An administrative process under which a patent owner can bar articles that infringe the patent from being imported into the U.S.

field of invention Used colloquially to distinguish different types of inventions from each other. An invention involving gene splicing would be in the "genetic engineering field", while an invention involving computers would fall within the "electronics field". These terms have no legal significance, although the similar phrase *field of search* does have a precise legal meaning relating to how patents are categorized for search purposes. Related terms: *classification of patents, patent search*.

file wrapper The collection of papers constituting the prosecution history of the patent in the Patent Office. A file folder is maintained by the *U.S. Patent and Trademark Office* for each individual patent application. Thus, if a letter is sent to the patent office regarding a pending application, it will be added to the applicant's "file wrapper". Related terms: *file wrapper estoppel*.

file wrapper estoppel A rule of court under which a *patent applicant* is bound by the statements made in his or her *patent application* as well as in his subsequent correspondence with the *PTO* in the course of *prosecuting* the application. This rule becomes pertinent if the patent owner should ever seek enforcement of his or her patent in court. If this occurs, the inventor will be prevented from describing the scope of the invention differently from how he earlier described it in documents now located in the PTO patent file (colloquially referred to as the *file wrapper*). In short, a patent owner is stuck with what he's already told the Patent and Trademark Office, and he cannot recapture coverage surrendered by amendment or argument, whether or not the examiner was correct when insisting upon the changes. Because of "file wrapper estoppel", it is good practice not to say anything negative about an invention for which a patent is being sought, and to draft patent claims as broadly as possible in light of the pertinent *prior art*. Related terms: *claims* and *prosecuting a patent application* .

Example: Otto Makespence invents a medical tool that uses a fiber optic strand, laser light, specially cloned antibodies, and certain chemicals to detect the presence of various substances in human tissue. In his patent application, Otto drafts his claims extremely broadly, and without a *limiting reference* to his use of fiber optics. After the PTO rejects the initial claims, Otto amends his application so that the claims now specify fiber optics as the method of transmitting the laser light. The patent is then granted.

Ten years later, Lewis Opalenik, a famous heart surgeon, makes and uses a similar diagnostic tool, using a magnetic rather than fiber optic means for transmitting the laser light waves. If Otto brings an *infringement action* against Lewis, alleging that his invention is sufficiently broad in scope to preclude Lewis's device, the court will prevent Otto from proving this. Instead, the court will hold Otto to the terms of the amended claim, as found in the file wrapper, which clearly is limited to a fiber optic means.

However, in this instance, a court might apply the *doctrine of equivalents* , and find an *infringement*, if the change from fiber optics to magnetism added little to the original invention. Related terms: *doctrine of equivalents*.

filing date   Each *patent application* is assigned a "filing date". The date is usually one to four days after the patent application has been mailed or the date it's mailed if sent by express mail, and is indicated on a "filing receipt" that the PTO sends to the applicant. The filing date is crucial for a number of reasons, which include the following:

• The filing date starts the period within

which a *patent application* must be filed in other countries. If a *convention application* in Germany, for instance, is not filed within one year after the U.S. filing date, and the applicant does not opt to file under the *Patent Cooperation Treaty* (which allows a longer time), German patent protection will be precluded.

• The filing date closes the year period during which an inventor can *publically use*, *work*, describe, or place *on sale* in the U.S. his invention without engaging in *anticipation*

• The filing date is when the law considers an invention to be first *reduced to practice*, absent evidence that it was *actually reduced it practice* at an earlier time. Thus, in the event of an *interference* (i.e., pending applications by different *inventors* covering the same invention), the inventor who filed first will be entitled to the patent, unless the other inventor can either show that he *actually reduced his invention to practice* first, or that he conceived of the invention first and then diligently set about to *reduce it to practice* (i.e., file a patent application or build the invention). Related terms: *anticipation*, *international patent filings* and *interference*.

final office action   When the *patent examiner* makes a "final" determination about whether or not to issue a patent. Normally, the final office action occurs after the patent applicant has been afforded one opportunity to amend your application in response to the *first office action* denying all or some of your *claims* .

Despite the name, "final office actions" are not necessarily final. A patent examiner can be petitioned to *reconsider* the application. And, if the decision remains final, it can be appealed to the *board of appeals*, or a *continuation application* can be filed, or the rejected claims can be excluded.

first office action   The first substantive *PTO* response to a *patent application*. Often, this involves the rejection of all or most of the *claims* in an application (humorously termed a *shotgun rejection*) on the ground that one or more *prior art references* render the *invention obvious*. A response may then be filed within 3 months (extendable for up to six months) that either amends the claims, or satisfactorily explains to the **patent examiner** why the prior art references are not pertinent. Related terms: **prosecuting a patent application**.

foreign patents and publication, anticipation of U.S. invention   See **anticipation**.

fraud on the Patent and Trademark Office
Any behavior by the applicant in the course of **prosecuting a patent application** that attempts to mislead (or withhold relevant information without consciously misleading the **PTO** in regard to whether the **invention** deserves a patent. The usual type of fraud is failure to inform the PTO about one or more relevant **prior art references** known to the applicant. Fraud on the Patent and Trademark Office usually results in an issued patent being judged unenforceable or invalid. Related terms: **defenses to a patent** and **duty of candor and good faith in disclosure to PTO**.

fully met
When any single previous development or publication (**prior art reference**) contains all of the specifics (elements and limitations) found in a **claim** contained in a current **patent application**, the claim is said to be "fully met" by the prior art and thus **anticipated**.

Example: Unaware of prior developments, Gary invents a mechanical match. When he tries to patent it, however, the **PTO** points out a prior patent which shows (**teaches**) all of the elements in Gary's device (i.e., fully meets the device). In this situation, Gary's device has been "anticipated" and is not entitled to a patent.

functional means and structure as patentable matter
When preparing a **patent application**, it is necessary to describe accurately those aspects of the **invention** that are to be covered by the patent. Although the overall **specification** of the invention must contain a description of what the invention does and how it works, the patent **claims** themselves need only describe the invention in terms of how and by what means it accomplishes a given inventive result. A patent on the "means" described in the claim will then support all possible structures that can perform the function inherent in the means.

For example, the claim for a pencil would describe in specific detail the exact means by which the materials in the pencil are used to make lines on a surface. The patent on this means would then extend to whatever structure used the same means to accomplish the result. Related terms: **claims**.

genetic engineering and patents
Ordinarily, patents will not be issued on "inventions" consisting of items or substances that are found to exist in a natural state. The reason for this is obvious. Something occurring in nature without human intervention cannot have been the product of inventive activity. In other words, the discovery of natural substances and processes does not qualify as an invention.

There are several categories of patentable inventions that do involve "natural" materials, however. One of these is novel and non-obvious plants created through asexual breeding. **Plant patents** are specifically authorized by statute for these "inventions". In this case, however, human inventiveness (i.e., breeding skill) is required as an indispensible aspect of the product being patented.

Genetic engineering is another field where "natural" materials (i.e., bacteria, DNA, RNA) have been manipulated by humans through gene splicing and cloning techniques to produce new organic materials and life forms. These new substances and forms, and the processes used to create them, also are considered patentable, this time under authority of the U.S. Supreme Court [Diamond v. Chakrabarty, 447 U.S. 303 (1980)], as long as they meet the basic patent requirements of **novelty**, **non-obviousness**, and **utility**. However, some restrictions are being placed on such patents. For example, one court decision held that claims describing (**reciting**) new bacterial strains resulting from recombinant DNA techniques cannot be broader than the specific strains deposited deposited with the patent office.

Because Congress wants basic research in biotechnology to develop as quickly as possible, federal law permits a company to utilize biotechnical inventions patented by another company if the purpose of the use is strictly for research. This is an exception to the general rule that a patent prohibits the manufacture or use of an

invention covered by an *in-force patent*. If, however, the company doing the research desires to commercially utilize the substance or process being utilized, it must obtain permission from the patent owner (usually accomplished through standard licensing techniques).

geographic patent licenses Any *license* 5 that grants its holder the right to make, use or sell a patented invention within a specified geographic region. For example, one license might allow its holder to exploit the invention commercially in the U.S., while another license might provide similar rights to another company, to be exercised solely in the Common Market countries. Related terms: *exclusive patent licenses*.

Graham v. John Deere A famous Supreme Court case (often called the "John Deere" case), decided in 1966, that created the basic guidelines for determining when an invention satisfies the statutory requirement that an invention be *non-obvious* to be patentable. To address this issue the John Deere case requires that we:

● determine the scope and content of the *prior art*

● determine the *novelty* of the invention

● determine the skill level of artisans in the pertinent technology (art)

● against this background, determine the obviousness or *non-obviousness* of the inventive subject matter, and

● consider relevant secondary factors, such as commercial success experienced with the invention, long-felt but unsolved need for the invention, or failure of others to produce the invention

In practice, these guidelines boil down to a determination whether, taking all relevant factors into account, a *person reasonably skilled in the art* involved in the invention would find the invention to be a surprising or unexpected development at the time it was made. The text of this case can be located in 383 U.S. 1, 86 S.Ct. 684 or 15 L.Ed.2d 545. Related terms: *non-obviousness*.

grant of patent When the *U.S. Patent and Trademark Office* issues a patent on an invention, this is sometimes called a "grant of the patent".

human-made structures with inventive characteristics A phrase sometimes used to define the total universe of items that may qualify for a *patent* if they fit within one of the statutory classes of patentable items and meet the other patent qualfications. Because *inventions* must be human-made, an interesting question is whether an article "invented" by a machine will ever qualify for protection. Although machines are still presently tools of human beings, it is not difficult to envision an intelligent machine with the capacity to diagnose its own needs, and invent new products to meet them. Related terms: *statutory subject matter* and *non-statutory subject matter*.

illegal licensing practices as defense to infringement action See *misuse of patent* and *defenses to a patent*.

improvement inventions A colloquial term for inventions that "improve upon" other prior inventions. Technically, almost all inventions are "improvement inventions". It is easier to obtain patent protection for small improvements on existing inventions if the *field of invention* is well developed (i.e., lots of technological developments). Conversely, if a field is relatively new, such as *genetic engineering*, small improvements may be considered too trivial or *obvious* to be granted a patent. A patent on an "improvement invention" only covers the improvement itself, and is thus subject to the rights of the holders of *in-force* patents on the other technology involved in the overall device or substance.

Example: A computer manufacturer makes an unexpected and novel improvement on an existing patented data bus (a device included in most microcomputers to move electrical impulses in an orderly way). The value of this "improvement patent" will depend heavily upon the degree to which appropriate arrangments can be made with the owner of the patent on the original data bus. Because mutual cooperation is to everyone's benefit in such a situation, the "improvement patent" would probably result in a *cross-license* agreement under which both patent owners would be permitted to use each other's inventions for agreed upon remuneration. If there are two *in-force patents* covering the original data bus, then the *improvement patent* owner would have to come to terms with both

Patent

of them to exploit his invention. Cross-licensing is extremely common throughout the industrial world. Related terms: *cross-licensing* and *patent pools*.

incomplete disclosure in patent application If an applicant for a patent fails to disclose certain aspects of his or her invention in the *patent application*, the application can be rejected by the *PTO* and any patent subsequently issued on the invention may later be declared invalid for "incomplete disclosure". Related terms: *disclosure requirement for patents*.

independent claim A patent claim that stands by itself in expressing the essence of the invention for which the patent is being sought. This should be compared with a *dependent claim*, that depends in part on an antecedent independent or other dependent claim for its meaning and effect. Related terms: *claims* and *dependent claims*.

index of classification An index maintained by the *PTO* which lists all 66,000 categories used to classify patented U.S. *inventions*. Related terms: *class of patents, patent search*.

in-force patent A patent that has not expired because of age (seventeen years from the time the patent was issued) or failure to pay *maintenance fees*, or invalidation (successfully challenged in court, used to violate the anti-trust laws, etc).

information disclosure statement The new name for the *statement of prior art references* that must be filed as part of each *patent application*. Related terms: *statement of prior art references*.

infringement action A lawsuit alleging that one or more parties has, without permission, made, used, or sold an invention protected under a patent owned by the person (plaintiff) bringing the lawsuit. Patent infringement actions must be filed in the U.S. District Court within a maximum of six years after the date the infringement occurred, but sooner if a delay in filing would cause undue hardship to the defendant. To determine whether infringement has occurred, the court will:

• examine the *claims* in the patent issued

by the *PTO*

• compare the elements *recited* in these claims with the elements of the device or process that is accused of infringing the patent, and

• decide whether the claims cover the defendant's device or process (i.e., fully describe the elements contained in the device or process)

If the claims cover the device or process, then infringement is found, unless the court applies the doctrine of *negative equivalents* (i.e., determines that the two devices are sufficiently dissimilar in what they accomplish or how they work to warrant a finding of no infringement).

If the claims do not cover the defendant's device or process, then no infringement has occurred, unless the court applies the *doctrine of equivalents* (i.e., determines that the two devices are sufficiently equivalent in what they do and how they do it to warrant a finding of infringement).

If infringement is found to exist, the court may:

• issue an injunction (court order) preventing any further infringement

• award the patent owner damages for loss of income or for profits resulting from the infringement from the time the invention was properly marked (i.e., when the word "patent" and the patent number were affixed to the invention) or from when the infringer was first put on actual notice of the infringement, whichever occurred first, and

• in the event the infringement was willful or flagrant (e.g., continued without a reasonable defense after notification by the patent owner, or occurred through a direct copying without any ground to believe the patent was invalid or not infringed), the court may award the plaintiff "smart money", i.e., punitive damages in order to make the defendant "smart" — these damages can be treble damages (three times the actual damages established in court) and reasonable attorneys fees

Historically, patent infringement suits have been difficult and expensive to win, even if the patent's claims squarely cover the infringing device, or the patented invention and the allegedly infringing device are substantially equivalent. This is because an infringer who is well financed is typically able to mount a serious challenge to the validity of the patent by alleging **anticipation**, **non-obviousness**, **lack of novelty**, failure to meet the **disclosure requirements for a patent** application, failure to disclose relevant **prior art** known to the applicant(i.e., **fraud on the PTO**) and a number of other **defenses to a patent**.

Even though the **PTO** may have already determined some of these issues in favor of the patent owner by granting the patent, a court must determine them anew if asked to do so by the defendant. In short, when a patent owner brings an infringement action, the underlying validity of the patent is placed in issue. Until recently, courts ruled against the validity of the patent in over one-half of all patent infringement cases. Lately, however, under leadership of the U.S. **Court of Appeals for the Federal Circuit**, the courts are tending to uphold more patents than they strike down. Related terms: **defenses to a patent**.

infringement of patent   A situation that occurs when a party makes, uses, or sells an item covered by the claims of an **in-force patent** without the patent owner's permission.

Example: Owens Organic Products invents and patents a simple computerized sprinkler system that turns on and off according to the moisture level of the soil. Although Phil Prendergast has been independently working on the same invention, he failed to beat Owens to the Patent and Trademark Office. However, figuring that Owens will probably never find out, Phil **licenses** Garden Development Corp. to construct and market his invention in exchange for royalties. Garden Development distributes the system on a wholesale basis to a chain of retail garden-supply stores, which then sell the sprinkers to consumers, who use them in their gardens.

In this situation, Phil, Garden Development, the retail stores, and the consumers are all guilty of patent infringement. This is true even if none of them knew about Owens' patent except Phil. Every patent infringer can be ordered by a court to stop all infringing activity. Some or all of the infringers may also be found liable to Owens for money damages.

However, an infringer who had no reason to know that a patent was being infringed cannot be held liable for **treble damages** as a willful infringer. Thus, Garden Development, the retail stores, and the consumers would not be liable for such damages unless they knew or should have known that activity infringed Owens' patent.

Related terms: **infringement action** and **contributory infringement**.

infringement search   A **patent search** conducted for the purpose of discovering whether an invention infringes any **in-force** patent. Related terms: **patent search** and **validity search**.

injunctions and injunctive relief   See **infringement action** and **equity** 5.

interference   When the **PTO** determines that two or more pending **patent applications** (or, a patent application and a patent issued within a year of the application's filing date) describe and want to monopolize the same **invention**, an interference is declared and a hearing scheduled before the **Board of Appeals and Interferences** to resolve the conflict, unless the application of one of the **patent applicants** is withdrawn or amended. The Board of Appeals and Interferences resolves the dispute according to the following analytical steps:

- the Board decides which inventor was the first to **reduce the invention to practice** — this will be the inventor who first filed a **patent application**, or the inventor who first **actually reduced the invention to practice**, whichever occurred first

- the Board then decides whether the inventor who was second to reduce to practice has proven that: a) he or she was first to conceive of the invention, and b) he or she was also diligently attempting to reduce the invention to practice, either by filing a patent application, or by actually building the invention, at the time when the inventor who first reduced to practice, first conceived of the invention

- if the inventor who was second to reduce to practice can prove prior conception and diligence in reduction to practice, he or she is awarded the patent — if that inventor cannot prove these two facts, then the inventor who was first to reduce to practice gets the patent. (See chart next page.)

Because it may someday become neces-

Patent

Patent Interference Priorities

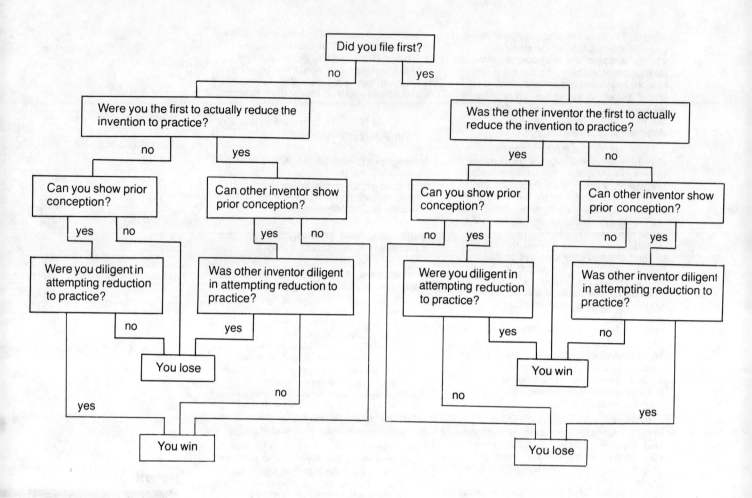

sary to retroactively prove when an invention was first conceived, and what steps were taken to reduce it to practice, most inventors maintain detailed records of their inventive activities in *patent notebooks*.

Example: Bellingham Medical Supplies and Boca Raton Pharmaceuticals simultaneously apply for a patent on a pain-killing device designed to allow patients to self-medicate small doses of certain opiates, without running the risk of an overdose or addictive reaction. An interference is declared and a hearing scheduled. At the hearing, the research scientists at Bellingham Medical produce their patent notebooks showing that they were the first to conceive of the invention, and claim entitlement to the patent on this basis. Boca Raton, on the other hand, establishes that it filed its patent application first, and was thus the first to *constructively reduce the invention to practice*.

If Bellingham then establishes that it *actually reduced the invention to practice* before Boca Raton filed its application, or if it proves that it was diligently seeking to reduce the invention to practice at the time Boca Raton first conceived of the invention, Bellingham will be awarded the patent. If neither of these showings is made, however, Boca Raton will be awarded the patent, even though it was the "junior inventor", since it was the first to reduce the invention to practice and Bellingham failed to make the required showing of diligence.

The reasoning behind these priorities is relatively simple. The patent laws are designed to encourage an inventor to apply for a patent at the earliest possible time, so that the statutory monopoly will not be extended unnecessarily beyond the seventeen year period. Accordingly, a senior inventor may still lose out to a junior inventor who has shown greater diligence in pursuing the patent and/or in developing the invention.

International Bureau of the World Intellectual Property Organization

An administrative arm of the World Intellectual Property Organization (WIPO) in Geneva Switzerland, designated by the Patent Cooperation Treaty of 1970 (PCT) as the clearinghouse for *international patent applications*. Related terms: *Patent Cooperation Treaty*.

international patent protection for U.S. inventions Patent protection in countries outside the U.S. can be obtained in two different ways. The first is to file separately in every country where protection is desired. This can be accomplished under certain rules established by the *Paris Convention*. Related terms: *convention filing*.

The second method to obtain international protection is to file an "international application" with the *International Bureau of the World Intellectual Property Organization*, an office established under the *Patent Cooperation Treaty* (PCT). As of December, 1984, thirty seven countries had become members of the PCT. Related terms: *Patent Cooperation Treaty*.

While there are other treaties between the U.S. and certain countries pertaining to reciprocal patent protection, the two mentioned above provide the primary international protection for U.S. patents.

international searching authority See *Patent Cooperation Treaty*.

international search report See *Patent Cooperation treaty*.

intervening right The right of a business to continue *working* a device or process that originally did not *infringe* a *patent* under its *claims* as worded at the time, but that later became infringing when the scope of the claims changed under a *re-issue patent* or a *continuation-in-part application*.

When the scope of a patent claim is changed because of later amendments, there exists the possibility that someone relied on the wording of the original claims, and developed or used a device that would not have infringed the patent under such original wording, but that does infringe the patent under the claims as redrafted. When this occurs, the infringing business's rights to use the infringing device are said to be "intervening" and will be upheld against the patent, even under the new claims. However, these "intervening rights" are considered personal to the business in question and cannot be transferred to another business or owner. Related terms: *reissue patent* and *continuation in part application*.

Patent

139

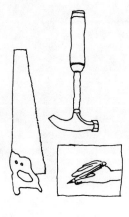

invention As defined by patent attorney David Pressman, an invention is "any thing, process or idea which is not generally and currently known; which, without too much skill or ingenuity, can exist or be reduced to tangible form or used in a tangible thing; which has some value or use to society; and which you or someone else has thought up or discovered". In addition to this description of "invention" as a noun, an "invention" is said to happen when the thing, process or idea being invented is first conceived of, if efforts are then continually made to reduce it to practice.

inventor A person who contributes significant creative input into one or more *inventions*. Only the inventor(s) can apply for and receive a patent on an invention. Failing to accurately name the inventor in a patent application can result in an issued patent later being declared invalid. Related terms: *co-inventors* and *shop rights*.

inventor's publication of invention as prior art See *anticipation*.

issue-fee The fee that must be paid for a patent to issue. This formerly was called the *base-issue* fee. Related terms: *base-issue fee*.

joint inventors See *co-inventors*.

Journal of the Patent and Trademark Office Society A monthly publication that contains articles on patent law and advertisements by patent services (patent searchers, graphic reproducers, etc). Subscription information can be obtained by writing to Box 2600, Arlington VA 22202.

journals as prior art See *anticipation* and *prior art references*.

junior filer in interference proceedings An *inventor* who files a *patent application* after another patent application describing the same *invention* has been filed by another inventor. Related terms: *interference*.

junior inventor The second *inventor* to conceive of an *invention* in a context where an *interference* exists. Junior inventors may still be entitled to the *patent* if they were the first to *reduce*

their invention to practice and if the *senior inventor* failed to exercise *diligence in reducing the invention to practice*. Related terms: *interference*.

laboratory notebook See *patent notebook*.

lapse of patent See *abandonment of patent*.

laws of nature exception to patents Patents may not be obtained on any invention that consists primarily of a law of nature, such as "2+2" or "E=MC2". Laws of nature are considered generally to consist of discoveries rather than products of human inventiveness. Related terms: *algorithms*.

lay judge A term used by patent law practioners to refer to any judge sitting in a patent case who is not a patent attorney or especially experienced in patent law.

lay patent searchers See *patent agents*.

licensing of patents A party may be given permission by a *patent owner* to make, use, or sell an *invention* covered by the *patent*, as long as the patent is not used to violate the *anti-trust laws*. Related terms: *exclusive patent licenses* and *anti-trust*.

limiting reference Any element in a patent *claim* that operates to both define the invention and, by defining it, limit it's scope. When analyzing a *dependent claim*, the court will read into such claim every "limiting reference" contained in the claim on which it depends.

machines as patentable subject matter One of the five categories of *statutory subject matter*, machines generally include any device with moving parts. However, electronic circuits are also considered machines, even though their parts, strictly speaking, don't move. Related terms: *statutory subject matter*.

maintenance fees Fees that must be paid to a patent office for continued processing of a *patent application*, and to maintain the validity of the *patent* once it has been issued. A number of industrialized countries require an *inventor* to pay hefty maintenance fees, reaching into the thousands of dollars per renewal period, in order to maintain the validity of his or her patent.

In 1982, maintenance fees were instituted in the U.S. for the first time. Although the basic patent lasts for seventeen years, it can be forfeited if maintenance fees are not paid. The primary patent period lasts for four years (years 1-4). After that, for small entities, a $200 fee must be paid to extend the patent for another four years (years 5-8). A $400 fee is required (for small entities) for an additional four years (years 9-12). And, for the last five years of the 17 year period (years 13-17), for small entities, the fee is $600.00.

Manual of Classification A manual containing considerable detail about the types of *inventions* found in each classification and subclassification used by the *PTO* to categorize them. This manual is used to assign the proper classification and subclassification to inventions, so that efficient *patent searchs* can be made. Related terms: *class of patents, patents search*.

Manual of Patent Examining Procedure (MPEP) A large, looseleaf manual of internal procedures to be followed by the *PTO* examiners when processing patent applications. Many large libraries carry this volume (often termed "The Examiner's Bible"), which will provide the answers to most questions that arise in the course of applying for a patent.

manufacture patents Patents granted to articles belonging in the class of *statutory subject matter* known as "Manufactures". Sometimes called "articles of manufacture", manufactures are relatively simple objects that don't have working or moving parts as prime features. Still, there is some overlap between the *machine* and "manufacture" categories. Examples of typical manufactures include: erasers, desks, houses, wire, tires, books, cloth, chairs, containers and transistors. Related terms: *statutory subject matter*.

march-in rights Inventions often result in the course of a U.S. Government contract being performed. Although a resulting patent may belong to the person performing the services, the U.S. government retains the right to "march in" and use the invention for their own purposes if the inventor fails to *work the patent* sufficiently.

marking of an invention After a *patent application* has been officially filed, the *inventor* is permitted to mark his or her *invention* with "Patent Pending" or "Pat.Pend." This mark has no immediate legal significance. However, it does place potential infringers on notice that, should a patent ultimately issue, they will not be allowed to make, use or sell the invention without the *patent owner's* permission. In essence, marking an *invention* for which a patent is pending discourages many would-be infringers from making or selling it, due to the possibility of a major hassle should the patent go through, and the specter of a wasted tooling-up effort. However, if infringement does occur prior to issuance of the patent, the infringer is entitled to keep any profits made up until that point.

After a patent is issued, the inventor may mark the invention with the patent number (e.g., patent #4,040,387, or pat. #4,040,387). This number puts infringers on notice that any use of the invention may result in an *injunction* and damages. If, later on, an *infringement action* is required, the patent owner will be able to collect damages from the date when he or she began properly marking the invention. If the invention is not marked, damages can only be collected from the time the infringer received actual notice (usually a demand letter from the patent owner), or from when the suit was first filed, whichever occurred earlier.

Many inventors prefer not to place the patent number on their invention. Why? Because this makes it easier for a competitor to obtain a copy of the patent and *design around* it. Absent the number, the competitor may have a much more difficult time in locating the patent. However, just the term "patent", without an accompanying number, does not provide the type of notice that starts the period for which damages may be recovered. Instead, as indicated above, damages will then only be recoverable for the period after the infringer received actual notice, or after the suit was filed.

Patent

mathematical forumula, nonpatentability of See *algorithms*.

means clauses in claims See *functional means and structure* and *claims*.

methods, patents on See *statutory subject matter* and *processes*.

minimum statutory damages for design patent infringement If a *design patent* is found to have been infringed, the plaintiff is entitled to at least a minimum damage award of $250.00.

misuse of patent The illegal expansion of the scope of the patent monopoly. Misuse of a patent can result either from *anti-trust* activity (e.g., using the patent to restrain trade or for monopolistic purposes), or from other activity that is unfairly designed to push the coverage of the patent beyond its legal limits.

If a patent owner is found to have misused a patent, a court will not enforce the patent unless the owner can show that the misuse was voluntarily and completely cured (i.e., "purged"). If the misuse was an anti-trust violation, no such cure is possible and the patent will simply be declared invalid. Related terms: *defenses to a patent* and *anti-trust*.

multiple claims Two or more *claims* in the same *patent application*, which describe a single *invention*. An application for an invention may and often does contain more than one *claim*. This is because there is often more than one view on how an invention is *novel* and/or useful. As with most things in life, the true essence of an invention can assume different characteristics depending on one's perspective, much the same as a glass can be seen as half full or half empty. For example, a robotics invention that keeps a running account of a kitchen's ingredients can be viewed as a device for maintaining general inventory, a specific process of managing a kitchen's stock of food, and a new physical manifestation of certain robotics principles. In such a case, at least three different independent claims could be contained in the application for the patent. In addition, each of these claims could be claimed narrowly and broadly, and each might support several dependent claims.

Another example: An engineer working for Sleeptight Bed Company invents a new hospital-type, kingsize bed, which has separately adjustable sides, which, when in use, create two single beds, but when lowered, create a single kingsize bed. The broadest independent claim for this invention would emphasize the means by which the bed functions equally well as separately adjustable beds, or a single kingsize bed. Additional claims might add such subparts of the invention as the means by which the two separate top mattresses are automatically joined when the sides are down, the new material utilized in the joining parts of the mattresses that enables the binding to occur, and so on. Related terms: *claims* and *independent claims*.

monopoly from patent grant See *anti-trust law and patents*.

narrowing a claim See *claims*.

naturally occurring substance See *non-statutory matter*.

negative doctrine of equivalents A legal rule stating that a device or process will not be held to infringe a *patent* on an *invention*, even though the patent's claims fully cover the device or process, if the device or process, and the patented invention, are substantially different in structure, function, or result. This rule is the mirror opposite of the one that requires a finding of infringement when an invention and a later item are basically the same, even though the patent's claims do not, strictly speaking, cover the later item. Related terms: *doctrine of equivalents*.

new and useful improvement patent See *improvement patents*.

new combinations of old inventions See *combination patents*.

new-use inventions One of the five large categories of *statutory subject matter* wherein a new use of an existing material, device, or process may be *patentable*, even if the original item is not.

Example: Tony invents a new process for transferring color patterns into textiles, by utilizing a known physical property of colors that causes them to expand at a different rate when applied to cloth. Assuming that the process is considered **non-obvious**, it will be entitled to a patent as a "new use" of an old principle. Related terms: **statutory subject matter**.

non-disclosure of patent applications by PTO   **patent applications** are maintained in confidence by the **U.S. Patent and Trademark Office** (PTO) until a decision is made to issue a **patent** and the **inventor** pays the **issue fee**. Then, the application becomes available to the public, and the **abstract** and **drawing** of the **invention** submitted by the inventor are published in the **Official Gazette**.

If a decision is made to reject the application, or if the inventor decides not to pay the base issue fee, no disclosure to the public is made. Because of this policy of confidentiality, it is possible to treat and maintain a new invention as a **trade secret** 1 while simultaneously applying for a patent. If the patent is granted, then the trade secret aspect of the invention will be destroyed through the PTO's disclosure. If the patent is denied, however, the inventor may continue to treat the invention as a tradesecret.

The PTO policy of nondisclosure can result in a **patent search** that misses **prior art** (e.g., a prior invention), since nondisclosed patent applications can take up to two years to process. Related terms: **patent searches** and **patents and tradesecrets** 1.

non-elected claims   Claims that a patent applicant has voluntarily chosen not to prosecute in his or her **patent application**. However, the non-elected claims may be prosecuted in a **divisional application**. When **prosecuting a patent application** a **patent applicant** may be required to restrict his or her application to one invention if the **PTO** determines that the original application contained two or more **inventions**. In such a circumstance, the applicant must elect which **claims** he or she desires to remain with the original application. The remaining "non-elected" claims are then either put in the divisional application(s) or cancelled.

non-exclusive licenses   Contracts 5 between **patent owners** and those who wish to use the **patents** (licensees). These licenses allow a number of users to share use, rather than granting one user an **exclusive license**. For example, the **inventor** of a new, more efficient, fuel injection system would most likely grant non-exclusive licenses to all the major car companies able to utilize the system, rather than just license it to one company on an exclusive basis. Related terms: **exclusive licenses of patents** and **non-exclusive licenses** 2.

non-obviousness   To qualify for a patent, an invention must produce unexpected or surprising new results from the viewpoint of a **person with ordinary skill in the art** (technology) involved in the invention. This quality of unexpectedness is termed "non-obviousness" (i.e., it would not have been obvious at the time that the invention would occur). Thus, if a video engineer could honestly state that a particular invention involving video technology was to be expected, a patent could be denied on the ground the invention was "obvious". Conversely, if the invention would have caught the engineer by surprise, it would probably be characterized as "non-obvious."

The concept of non-obviousness is among the most difficult concepts to grasp in patent law. Normally, the question of whether a particular invention is non-obvious is addressed several years after the invention actually occurs, (because of delays in filing the patent application, and additional delays inherent in the patent **prosecution** process. Accordingly, the PTO (and the courts, should a dispute over the patent "s validity later arise) must attempt retroactively to assess the knowledge of someone skilled in the relevant art at the time of the invention, and to judge whether the invention would have been obvious in light of such knowledge.

The **PTO** generally determines this question by examining all pertinent **prior art references** that existed at the time the invention was first conceived of. In a court action, both sides typically produce experts who testify both ways. The inventor will also attempt to establish that the invention enjoyed commercial success or solved an unperceived need and should therefore be considered to be non-obvious on the basis of actual developments. In addition to this evidence, the court will also consider the **prior art** existing at the

Patent

4

time of the invention, in determining whether the invention was or was not obvious. Such Monday-morning quarter-backing necessarily occurs with every patent examined by the PTO, and (usually) whenever a patent *infringement action* is brought.

Example: Future Enterprises invents a machine that is able to analyze chromosomes for multiple types of genetic damage and abnormalities. Such an invention would probably qualify for a patent at the present time since current analytical procedures permit only one analysis at a time, and, it's difficult to anticipate exactly how multiple-analysis techniques will work. However, several years from now, when genetic knowledge and robotics techniques are far advanced over the present, patent examiners or a court may look back to the present and conclude, with the "wisdom" of hindsight, that now-existing robotic technology and genetic engineering techniques made such an advancement *obvious* from the standpoint of a present-day genetics engineer. They will therefore probably either deny the patent or (if a court is involved) rule the patent retroactively invalid.

non-statutory subject matter Any item that does not logically fall in one of the five categories of *statutory subject matter* that qualify for a *patent*, assuming the other requirements for a patent are also met. These categories are *compositions* , *processes*, *machines*, *manufactures*, and *new uses*). The phrase non-statutory subject matter is also commonly used to refer to any invention that does not qualify for a patent period at all. Thus, under this definition, even if an invention fit within one of the above categories, it would still be considered "non-statutory subject matter" if it failed to meet the basic patent qualifications of novelty, non-obviousness and utility.

Examples of non-statutory subject matter that do not fall in any of the five statutory categories are:

- processes done entirely by human motor coordination (e.g., break dancing routines)
- processes done by hand with simple tools (e.g., hair-styling processes)
- methods of doing business (but see *trade secrets* 1)
- printed matter that has no unique physical shape or structure associated with it

(but see *copyright* 2)

- naturally-occurring matter, even though its external characteristics may be modified (but see *plant patents* and *genetic engineering*), and
- abstract scientific principles, natural laws, or ideas unconnected to any physical means for carrying them out (see *algorithms*)

Related terms: *statutory subject matter*.

non-staple articles and contributory infringement Articles that are especially modified to work as a material part of a patented *invention* (i.e., not staple items useful in their own right) may not be sold without the *patent owner's* permission. If they are, the seller may be liable for *contributory infringement* of the patent. Related terms: *contributory infringement* .

not invented here (NIH) syndrome A general policy in many big companies of rejecting all inventions by outside inventors (inventions that are "not invented here"). One reason for this is corporate ego. The argument is also made that the company wants to avoid potential and expensive disputes over who owns the patents held or applied for by the company.

notice of allowance A notice sent by the *PTO* to a *patent applicant* informing him that his *patent application* has been allowed as currently written. This notice is usually issued only after a *first office action* has rejected all or most of the application's claims, and the inventor has amended the application accordingly. Related terms: *prosecuting a patent application*.

notice of patent number See *marking of invention*.

notice of references cited A form sent by the *PTO* to the *patent applicant* as part of its *office action* on a *patent application*. The form lists the various *prior art references* used by the PTO as a basis for rejecting *claims* contained in the application. Copies of the references are enclosed with the office action so the applicant can intelligently either explain why they don't apply, or amend the rejected claims. Related terms: *prosecut-*

ing a patent application.

novel See *novelty requirement for patents*.

novelty requirement for patents To qualify for a *utility patent*, *design patent* or *plant patent*, (the main types of patents) an *invention* must be "novel" (in addition to several other qualifications). In this context, "novelty" means the invention must differ in some respect from prior products and devices, and that the technology used must differ from or add to existing public knowledge of the invention's main elements. However, this difference need not be great. As long as no one single product, device, or printed publication contains all the elements of the invention, it will be considered novel. Once an invention is determined to be novel, however, it faces the considerably more difficult hurdle of *non-obviousness*. Related terms: *anticipation* and *non-obviousness*.

number, patent See *marking of invention*.

obvious When a *person with ordinary skill in the art* could reasonably believe that an invention was to be expected, the invention is termed "obvious", and a patent is denied because the invention lacks *non-obviousness*. For instance, if a new metal is invented that is significantly lighter and stronger than current alloys, it is perfectly "obvious" that someone will build a bicycle containing the material, since lightness is a desirable aspect of high-quality bicycles. Thus, while the inventor of the metal may be entitled to a patent, the developer of the new-metal bicycle is not. Related terms: *non-obviousness*.

office action A letter sent by the *PTO* in respect to a *patent application*. Generally, there are two main "office actions" taken per patent application — the *first office action* and the *final office action*. Related terms: *prosecuting a patent application*.

Official Gazette An official weekly publication of the *U.S. Patent and Trademark Office*. There is one edition for trademarks and another for patents. The patent edition contains summaries of

issued patents, and a variety of official announcements concerning patents and trademarks. Related terms: *Official Gazette*, *patent search* and *Gazette* ③.

Official Gazette, patent search The Official Gazette for patents is a weekly publication by the *U.S. Patent and Trademark Office* which, among other information, includes *abstracts* and the main figure or *drawing* for each *patent* issued that week. Anyone wishing to keep up with the patents being issued in his or her field should habitually read the "Official Gazette". Many major libraries subscribe to this publication and file back issues. In fact, it is possible to use the Gazette to conduct a superficial *patent search* in your local library (and Patent Repository), assuming that you either know what classification your *invention* belongs in, or the library has an *Index of Classifications*. Related terms: *patent search*.

omission of elements in later invention If all the elements (essential characteristics) *recited in* the *claims* of a *patent* to an earlier *invention* are not found in a later device, the later device will not infringe the patent. Conversely, if all of the elements of a device are found in the patent claims associated with the earlier invention, the later device will probably be held to be infringing.

The decision as to whether or not a later invention incorporates all of the elements of an earlier invention is generally not a subjective one. Despite this, there is no sure way to predict how an *infringement action* will turn out since such questions as *obviousness* and *misuse* are subjective. Related terms: *infringement of patent* and *infringement action*,

one year rule A rule that requires a *patent application* to be filed within one year of:

- any *public use* of the *invention* by the *inventor*
- placement of the invention *on sale*, or
- any description of the invention by the inventor in a *printed publication*

Failure to file a patent application within this one year period results in the invention passing into the public domain. Related terms: *anticipation*.

Patent

on sale statutory bar to patentability
If an *invention* is placed "on sale" more
than one year prior to the filing of the
patent application, the *patent* is barred
by statute from issuing. "On sale" can
mean not only actual sale, but also any
sale effort or solicitation. Related terms:
anticipation.

**operability of invention, requirement
for** To qualify for a *patent*, an *invention* must be operable. This does not
mean that it has to be actually built and
operating. Rather, it means that the
patent application must disclose sufficient
information to demonstrate the theoretical
operability of the invention. If the Patent
and Trademark Office believes an invention will not work (e.g., a perpetual
motion machine) it can require further
evidence of its operability, such as a
demonstration, before the patent application will be allowed. Related terms: *statutory subject matter*.

opposition proceeding In almost every
country outside the U.S. and Canada,
patent applications are published, and
anyone can then register their opposition.
If the opposing party is able to establish
that relevant *prior art* exists, an *opposition proceeding* is held to determine
whether a patent should be issued. This
process opens up the initial patent determination to all interested parties. In the
U.S. and Canada, on the other hand,
patent applications are kept secret and
third parties are only afforded the opportunity to challenge a patent's validity after
it has been issued.

ordinary skill in the art The usual way
of determining such "ordinary skill" is by
requesting a person thoroughly amiliar
with the particular technology or knowledge involved in the invention to give his
or her subjective reaction. If possible, the
person asked is one who actually prac-
ticed the "art" (the technology) at the
time the invention was made. Related
terms: *person with ordinary skill in the
art*.

ornamentality and design patents
See *design patents*.

ownership of patent See *patent owner*.

PCT A common abbreviation for the
Patent Cooperation Treaty. Related
terms: *Patent Cooperation Treaty*.

PTO A common abbreviation for *Patent
and Trademark Office*.

parent application An original *patent*
application in a context where a subsequent application, such as a *divisional
application*, a *substitution application*, a
continuation application, a
continuation-in-part application, or a
reissue patent has been filed. Often, in
the course of *prosecuting a patent application*, it is necessary to file a related
application. Sometimes this occurs when a
single application has claimed two or
more *inventions*, in violation of the rule
against this practice. In this instance, the
original or "parent" application is prosecuted with one of the inventions, while a
new "divisional application" is filed for
each additional invention. At other times,
a new application based on the parent
application is filed to pursue new or
modified *claims*, or to make other
amendments. Other terms commonly
used for "parent application" are "prior
application", "basic application", and
"original application".

Paris Convention See *convention filing*.

patent Legally, a patent is a
government-backed right of protection
granted to an *inventor* which can be used
to exclude others from manufacturing,
selling or using his or her invention as it
is specifically described in the patent
claims allowed by the *U.S. Patent and
Trademark Office*.

Physically, the basic patent consists of
the following:

• a cover sheet bearing the patent number,
the name of the invention as provided by
the inventor, a list of the *prior art references* found by the *patent examiner* to
be pertinent to the invention, and the
patent *abstract* (a concise summary of the
invention)

• one or more pages containing drawings of
the invention submitted by the patent
applicant

• the patent specification as submitted in
the patent application, and

- the patent *claims* as finally approved by the patent examiner

The original physical patent issued by the *PTO* is termed a "patent deed" or "letters patent" and has a blue ribbon and gold seal for adornment. The physical patent as retained by the PTO and others interested in the patent is often termed a "patent copy" or a "soft copy" and lacks the adornment found on the patent deed.

Physically, as with a college diploma, the patent in any of its forms has no intrinsic value. Rather, the patent derives its value from the protection it provides in the event of an *infringement*.

patent, abandonment of See *abandonment of patent*.

patentability search The search initially carried out by an inventor to discover whether his or her "bright idea" is patentable in the event it can be transformed into an invention. This determination is necessary to prevent the waste of time and money spent in developing an idea that is not patentable. Related terms: *patent search*.

patent agents Non-attorney patent experts who are licensed by the PTO to represent clients before the *Board of Patent Interferences*, and conduct patent *prosecutions* on their behalf. However, if a patent case gets to court, only *patent attorneys* are authorized to appear.

Patent and Trademark Office See *U.S. Patent and Trademark Office*.

patent applicant Any person (usually the inventor) who applies for and *prosecutes* a patent application with the *U.S. Patent and Trademark Office*. Although this is usually done through a *patent agent* or *patent attorney*), many inventors are now applying for patents without an attorney (pro se) with the help of such legal self-help books as *Patent it Yourself* by David Pressman, published by Nolo Press.

patent application A voluminous packet of papers mailed to the *U.S. Patent and Trademark Office* in order to obtain a *patent*. Included in a patent application are the:

- *specification*
- *claims*
- formal or informal patent *drawings*
- *abstract*
- completed *declaration* form
- self-addressed receipt postcard
- transmittal letter
- check for the filing fee
- *information disclosure statement* and references (can be sent three months later)

One to two weeks after an application is mailed, the applicant receives his or her postcard back from the *PTO* with the *filing date* and number stamped on it. This means that the *PTO* has established a separate file (called a *file wrapper*) in which it retains the application and all future correspondence between the applicant and the PTO. Once an application is on file, the applicant is said to be in the patent *prosecution* stage, which can last up to two or three years. Often, the patent examiner will reject all or most of the *claims* as first submitted (this is called a "shotgun rejection"), for a variety of reasons. However, the applicant is afforded at least one opportunity to redraft his or her claims. If, the PTO rejects them again, this rejection is generally considered final. After that, if the applicant wishes to pursue the claims as written, he or she must either:

- request *reconsideration* from the Patent examiner
- comply with the rejection and/or make the suggested changes
- appeal the rejection to the *Board of Appeals*, or
- file a *substitution application* or *continuation application*

Related terms: *prosecuting a patent application*.

patent attorneys Persons who are admitted to the practice of law in at least one state or Washington D.C., and who are also licensed by the *U.S. Patent and Trademark Office* to practice before the *PTO*, to prepare and prosecute *patent applications*, and to represent clients in interference proceedings. Patent attorneys generally have a technical education as well as legal background. A complete listing of all licensed patent attorneys can be obtained in the PTO's publication, *Attorneys and Agents Registered to Practice Before the U.S. Patent and Trademark Office.*

patents as prior art See *prior art references*, *anticipation*, and *prior art*.

patents, breaking of See *breaking of patents*.

patent claim See *claim, patent*.

Patent Cooperation Treaty (PCT) An international agreement, first reached in 1970, which has been ratified by 37 countries (as of December 1984) and which establishes streamlined procedures for obtaining uniform patent protection in those countries.

To utilize the procedure established under this treaty, a PCT request form and a separate "International Application" must be filed with either the *International Bureau of the World Intellectual Property Organization* in Geneva, Switzerland, or, in the case of U.S. patents, with the *U.S. Patent and Trademark Office*, which has been designated a "receiving office" of the *International Bureau*.

The International Application must be prepared according to a specified format, and must list the countries for which the applicant desires protection. The request and application will then be forwarded to the "International Searching Authority", where an "international search report" will be prepared. For U.S. applicants, a branch of the PTO will conduct the international search, and prepare the report. Once the report is completed, it, is forwarded, along with the application, to the countries listed in the application.

For each country, it will eventually be necessary to translate the application into that country's language, and to pay any fees that are generally required for patent filings in that country. Although the international search report is generally given great credence, it is possible that any individual country will deny the patent on the basis of *prior art* not uncovered in the international search.

The primary advantages of using the procedures established under the PCT are:

• the member countries will rely heavily on the one international search, thus saving

the applicant the great expense and delay that can result from separate prosecution of a patent application in each country under a *convention filing*, and

• the applicant need not decide whether to prosecute the international application in the individual countries until eighteen months after the initial patent application filing date in his or her original country

As of December, 1984, the following countries are members of the PCT: Australia, Austria, Belgium, Brazil, Bulgaria, Cameroon, Central African Republic, Chad, Congo, Denmark, Finland, France, Gabon, Germany (Federal Republic), Hungary, Japan, Korea (Democratic People's Republic), Korea (Republic), Lichtenstein, Luxembourg, Madagascar, Malawi, Mauritania, Mali, Monaco, Netherlands, Norway, Romania, Senegal, Sri Lanka, Sudan, Sweden and Switzerland.

For more specific information on filing under the Patent Cooperation Treaty, a booklet called the PCT Applicant's Guide can be obtained from the *World Intellectual Property Organization (WIPO)* 2.

Patent Deed The formal written patent issued by the *U.S. Patent And Trademark Office*, which contains a gold seal and a blue ribbon. This is also sometimes termed a "letters patent". Related terms: *patent*.

patent depository library A public or special library that contains copies of patents and the reference tools necessary to carry out a reasonably informative *patent search*. The Patent and Trademark Office library in Arlington, Virginia is the only place in the country where a complete patent search may be undertaken. Accordingly, most professional patent searches are conducted by *patent searchers* living in the Washington D.C. area. However, a number of libraries around the countries have been designated as Patent Depository Libraries (PDLs). These contain enough pertinent materials to enable an inventor or other *patent searcher* to get a reasonably complete picture of the relevant *prior art*. But, not all PDL's have all patents issued from No. 1 to the present. And more seriously, no PDL has patents physically separated by classification, as does the PTO in Arlington.

To get around this problem, it is necessary to first get a list of patents in the selected classes and subclasses. Many of the PDLs have lists of patents in each class and subclass on microfilm. If a PDL doesn't, it is necessary to order one from the PTO in Arlington, which may take several weeks to arrive. The depository library staff explains how to order.

Once a list has been obtained, the abstract for each patent

can be located in the **Official Gazette** volume, or (in some PDLs) the entire patent can be located in a numerically-arranged stack.

The Official Gazette will probably be in large bound volumes, each containing issues for one month (4 or 5 issues). If the Official Gazette is being used, the following information is available for each patent: 1) the patent's number, 2) the inventor's name(s) and address(es), 3) the name of any assignee(s) (usually a company which the inventor has transferred ownership of the patent), 4) the patent application's filing date, 5) the patent application's serial number, 6) the patent's international classification, 7) the patent's U.S. classification, 8) the main figure or drawing, 9) the number of claims, and 10) a sample claim or abstract. Thus, it is possible to gather much information about a prior patent without having the actual **patent copy** on hand. However, if the drawing and claim appear relevant, then the actual patent can be scrutinized further, or, a copy of the patent can be ordered for later study.

It is important to remember that the patent claim reproduced in the Official Gazette is not a summary of the patent's description. Instead, it is the essence of the invention. The full text of the patent contains far more technical information about the invention than the claim contains.

If a PDL is not handy, most libraries around the country subscribe to the Official Gazette, which is published by the PTO each week. This, along with an Index of Classification, permits a search there, but facilities are usually far inferior to those at a PDL. Related terms: **patent search**.

patent examination process   See **prosecuting a patent application**.

patent examiners   See **examiner, patent**.

patent infringement actions   See **infringement actions**.

patent invalidity as defense to infringment action   See **defenses to a patent** .

patent license agreements   See **exclusive patent license** and **non-exclusive patent licenses**.

patent notebook   A journal maintained by most **inventors** where they record all procedures, dates, actions, failures, successes, contacts, and other events that occur in the course of the **invention's** development. Because of the extreme importance that such information might assume in the event that another inventor claims he or she invented first, or if an **interference** occurs, every inventor is well advised to maintain such a journal, diary or notebook, and get the entries signed, dated and witnessed. Related terms: **interference**.

patent number   The unique number assigned to each patent by the **PTO**. Related terms: **marking of invention**.

patent number marking   The placing of one's patent number on an invention to give notice to potential infringers that the invention has been patented. Related terms: **marking of invention**.

patents of addition   A colloquial term used in Japan for **improvement patents**.

Patent Office Board of Appeals and Interference Proceedings   The administrative arm of the **U.S. Patent and Trademark Office** that initially determines who should prevail in the event of a patent **interference** (when two or more pending applications essentially **claim** the same invention). Related terms: **interference**.

patent owner   A **patent** must in the first instance be filed in the names of the original and true **inventor** or inventors. Once an inventor files a patent application, he or she owns a resulting patent outright, and can either personally keep and develop it, or transfer full or partial

Patent

control over it to others through *licenses* and *assignments*.

It is not uncommon for large companies, universities, and laboratories to require employees to assign (transfer ownership rights on) their patent applications to the institution as a condition of employment. However, in California, such requirements are prohibited for inventions that:

- were made on the employee's own time, and

- did not involve the use of the employer's equipment, supplies, facilities, or trade secret information, and

- do not relate to the business of the employer, or result from any work prepared by the employee for the employer, or relate to the employer's actual or demonstrably anticipated research or development

Generally, employers retain the right (called "shop rights") to make and use an invention created in the course of the employment relationship, and with the employer's tools and facilities , even though the inventor retains actual ownership of the patent.

patent pending notice See *patent pending status*.

patent pending status Once a *patent application* has been officially filed in the *U.S. Patent and Trademark Office*, the underlying invention is said to have a "patent pending" status. If the inventor then places a "patent pending notice" on the invention, potential competitors may be deterred from copying it, since any investment they make in it may be wasted if the invention should later receive a patent. However, unless and until a patent is actually issued, an inventor has no right to prevent others from making, using, and selling the invention. In other words, simply applying for a patent does not earn the applicant the right to behave like a *patent owner*. Related terms: *marking of invention*.

patent pools An arrangement between two or more companies wishing to share their *patents* in which the companies assign their patents to a third party, who, in turn, *licenses* any or all of the patents back to a requesting company. This provides the participating companies with access to each other's patents on a reciprocal basis. Patent pools run a substantial risk of violating the *anti-trust* laws in the event they are not open to all competitors. Related terms: *concerted refusal to deal* and *anti-trust and patents*.

patent search A broad term generally used to mean an examination of all prior relevant *patents* and *printed publications* in order to determine the extent to which an *invention* is *novel* and *non-obvious*. If the *claims* or *specification* of a prior patent substantially *teach* (i.e., describe) the elements of a current invention, the current invention may either be found to be *anticipated* (i.e., found to be not novel), or *non-obvious* (i.e., not a surprising or unexpected new development in light of the relevant *prior art*) and therefore not qualified for a patent. Even if a prior patent does preclude a current invention from being patented, any other type of prior printed publication, or prior public knowledge of the invention's elements, or prior published foreign patent, may have the same result.

There are normally two specific types of patent searches conducted in the course of seeking a patent. The first one is conducted by the *inventor* (either in person, or, more generally, through a *patent attorney* or *patent agent*. The primary purpose of this initial search is to determine whether it is worthwhile developing the invention and/or applying for a patent in the first place (i.e., whether the current invention is barred by prior patents). Sometimes termed a *patentability search*, or "pre-examination" search, this initial search familiarizes the inventor (or his attorney or agent) with the way that claims for similar inventions have been worded, and therefore assists in the application drafting process. Also, this search informs the inventor about the relevant *prior art* in the specific *field of invention*.

The second patent search is conducted by the *PTO* itself, to determine whether the invention is patentable. In both searches, the primary object is to discover and analyze any prior patent or other printed publication that can be considered as relevant *prior art* (i.e., prior developments, discussions, or disclosures bearing on the issues of novelty and non-obviousness).

In addition to these searches, if the

validity of an issued patent should be challenged in a patent *infringement action*, a more extensive *validity search* will be conducted by the defendant to see whether the patent is capable of being invalidated (called *breaking a patent*).

A complete classification breakdown of all the patents ever granted by the U.S. Government is only maintained in the PTO located in Arlington, Virginia. Therefore, that is the best place to conduct a complete patent search. However, a number of libraries around the country (called *patent depository libraries*) contain enough patent information to allow reasonably thorough patent searches. Also, it is increasingly possible to conduct *computerized patent searches*.

The procedure for manual patent searches in the PTO library is relatively straightforward. Patents are stored according to 66,000 pre-set classifications and subclassifications. If the searcher knows which classifications and subclassifications apply to the invention in respect to which the search is being performed, he or she can fairly easily inspect all similarly classified patents. If the classifications and subclassifications are not known, the searcher can use the *Manual of Classifications*, the *Index of Classification*, and/or the *Class Definitions Manual* to find out.

Although each patent can be read in its entirety (in Arlington, Virginia and in most patent depository libraries) the more common technique in the patent depository libraries is to read the *abstract* for each similarly-classified patent to screen those that appear to be relevant from those that obviously are not.

Each possibly relevant patent must then be investigated further to see 1) whether it's *specification* or *claims* describe all the elements of the current invention (which may result in the invention being *anticipated*), or 2) whether the patent substantially *teaches* the current invention (i.e., indicates the likelihood of it occurring), thereby creating a serious obviousness problem.

To the extent that pertinent patents may be found, they must be copied and included in the *patent applicant*'s *Information Disclosure Statement* that accompanies the *patent application*. If any of these patents actually threaten the patentability of the invention, the applica-

tion should be amended before it is sent in, or the PTO will have to be convinced that the prior patents do not bar the desired patent from issuing. Related terms: *class of patents, patent search,* and *patent depository library*.

patent searcher An individual or firm specializing in conducting patent searches. Because the *PTO* library in Arlington, Virginia is the best place to conduct a patent search, patent searchers tend to be concentrated in that area.

patent term extension Under Section 155 of the patent laws [35 U.S.C. Section 155] the 17-year period for a patent may be extended if the inventor's ability to realize gain from the invention (i.e. a new drug or food) is held up because of the requirement that the Food and Drug Administration approve such items as being safe and effective.

patentable subject matter See *statutory subject matter*.

patentability The standards an *invention* must meet to qualify for a patent. For *utility patents* inventions must 1) fit within one of the statutory subject-matter classes, 2) have *novelty*, 3) be *non-obvious* and 4) have some usefulness. For *plant patents* the plant must meet the first three qualifications listed above. For *design patents*, the designs must meet the first three qualifications, and must be ornamental. Related terms: *statutory subject matter* and *non-statutory subject matter*.

patents and anti-trust See *anti-trust law and patents*.

pending patent application From the date a *patent application* is filed with the *PTO*, until the time the patent is either issued or abandoned, it is said to be pending. Inventions for which a patent is pending may be marked accordingly. Also, pending *patent applications* are considered to be confidential, and the information in them may be maintained as trade secrets up until the time the patent is issued. Related terms: *prosecuting a patent application*, and *marking an invention*.

Patent

person with ordinary skill in the art
Among the questions that must be answered in deciding whether a *patent* should issue, or whether an *in-force patent* is valid, are:

• whether a hypothetical "person with ordinary skill in the art" would find the invention an obvious development in light of the technology and knowledge existing at the time the invention was first conceived of (i.e., the *prior art*), and

• whether the *patent application* sufficiently discloses the nature of the invention to permit a hypothetical "person with ordinary skill in the art" to build it in a routine manner without time constraints or inventive faculties

This hypothetical "ordinary person skilled in the art" is generally defined as someone whose educational or occupational credentials theoretically make him or her professionally competent in the field related to the patent. So, an electrical engineer would be a person with ordinary skill in the art relating to integrated circuits, whereas a prosthetics engineer would be a person with ordinary skill in the art of designing knee braces. Related terms: *non-obviousness* and *disclosure requirements for patents*.

plant patents The Plant Variety Protection Act specially authorizes seventeen-year patents for any *novel*, distinctive, and *non-obvious* new variety of plant produced by asexual breeding (e.g., grafting, budding, cutting, layering, or division). Only one claim is allowed for any one plant, and color *drawings* or photos can be used instead of, or in combination with, words to claim the plant.

Plant Variety Protection Act The statute authorizing patent protection for certain types of plants. Related terms: *plant patents*.

practicing an invention See *actual reduction to practice* and *working an invention*.

preliminary look Before investing time and money in developing an invention, many inventors conduct an initial (preliminary) look at stores, catalogs, reference books, product directories, etc, to discover whether their proposed invention already exists. If this preliminary look finds no significant previous development, then the invention may be developed, with a more serious *patentability search* to follow. Related terms: *patentability search*.

presumption of validity A *patent* issued by the *U.S. Patent and Trademark Office* is presumed to be valid. This means that a *patent owner* does not have to prove the validity of the patent in the event he or she finds it necessary to file an *infringement action*. Rather, once infringement is proven by the patent owner, the alleged infringer will have the burden of showing either that the patent is not, in fact, valid, or that it is otherwise unenforceable, in order to escape judgment. Related terms: *infringement action*.

price fixing and anti-trust When two or more businesses enter into a formal or informal agreement to maintain their prices at a certain level, they engage in price fixing. Price fixing is considered a restraint of trade, and a violation of the *anti-trust* laws. For instance, if a *patent owner* requires parties who are authorized to *work the patent* to charge a certain price, the patent owner may be guilty of *misusing the patent* and the patent may become invalid or unenforceable. Related terms: *anti-trust and patents*.

printed publication as statutory bar
Under the *patent* laws, any printed publication that discusses or describes the essential ideas, functional means, or structures that underly an *invention* may operate as a *statutory bar* to a *patent* on the invention. This will happen if 1) such publication is made by someone else prior to the date of an invention, or 2) such publication is made by the inventor more than one year prior to his or her filing a *patent application*. Related terms: *anticipation*.

prior art The general level of knowledge in the area of expertise involved with an invention that existed prior to, or is available at the time of, the invention. The relevant *prior art* (i.e., the prior art that *teaches* all or some aspects of the invention in question) is the benchmark used to determine whether an invention is really "inventive". Prior art generally includes:

- any relevant description or discussion of the invention's essential characteristics in prior printed publications anywhere in the world, in any language, that was made available to the public before the invention was conceived of
- any relevant printed publication prepared by the inventor and published more than one year prior to the *filing date* of the *patent application*
- any relevant public knowledge of the invention in the United States that can be shown to have existed at the time the invention was first conceived of, or
- any relevant foreign or U.S. patent issued before the inventor conceived of the invention for which a patent is being sought, or any U.S. *patent application* made prior to such conception

Prior art is used by the PTO and by the courts (in the event of an infringement action) to determine whether inventions are a) *novel* and, b) if so, whether they are also *non-obvious*. Any specific instance of "prior art" is generally referred to as a *prior art reference*.

prior art reference Any printed publication, prior patent, or other document that contains a discussion or description relevant to an *invention* for which a *patent* is currently being sought or enforced. When applying for a patent, an applicant is required to submit a *statement of prior art* in which all known "prior art references" must be listed, and to which copies of these references must be appended. In the event an *office action* results in one or more *claims* being rejected on *prior art* grounds, the *PTO* sends out a *notice of prior art references* (and copies of the references) which lists the references found relevant to the application by the PTO. Related terms: *prior art* and *statement of prior art*.

prior conception of invention in interference proceedings See *interference*.

prior domestic patent by anyone as statutory bar Under the U.S. patent laws, a U.S. *patent* showing all the elements of a current invention, that was issued prior to the date of invention, will bar a patent on such invention on the ground of *anticipation*. Also, a prior patent that does not anticipate the current invention may still constitute relevant *prior art* for the purpose of determining its *non-obviousness*. Related terms: *anticipation*.

priorities in interference proceedings See *interference*.

processes One of the five large categories of *statutory subject matter*, processes are ways of doing or making things. Processes always have two or more steps, each expressing some activity or occurrence. Examples are: heat-treatment processes, chemical reactions, surgical techniques, gene- splicing procedures, applied robotics, and so on. To be *patentable*, a process must relate to some physical product or physical work. Thus, an educational process such as teaching speed reading, or study skills, is not generally considered to be a "process" for purposes of obtaining a *patent*. Related terms: *statutory subject matter* and *non-statutory subject matter*.

proper inventor See *inventor* and *ownership of patent*.

prosecuting a patent application Engaging in the full gamut of procedures that are generally followed to obtain a patent on an invention.

The first step in prosecuting a *patent application* is to mail it (along with the application fee) to the *PTO*. After a week or two, the self-addressed stamped postcard submitted with the application is returned to the inventor with a *filing date* and a *patent number* and a file (called a *file wrapper*) is opened in the PTO. Then, sometimes up to a year later, a PTO *patent examiner* assigned to the application will send a written form called the *first office action*. This typically will deny all or most of the application's *claims* on a variety of grounds.

Some claims may be rejected because of pertinent *prior art*. If so, the *office action* will list the *prior art references* in a *notice of prior art references*, send copies of the references, and designate which claims the references are pertinent to.

Other claims may be rejected because

they are too broad, or formulated incorrectly. If so, the inventor will be provided the opportunity to make the suggested amendments.

On occasion, the patent examiner will determine that the application actually covers two or more patents. Since an application may only cover one invention, the applicant will be informed in the first office action that he or she may "elect" to retain the claims covering one of the inventions in the *parent application*, and file one or more *divisional applications* for the *non-elected claims* that recite the additional inventions.

Sometimes, an inventor will improve his or her invention while the application is pending and want to broaden or better define his or her claims. If so, he or she can file a *continuation-in-part* (CIP) application incorporating the changes.

Whatever the recommendations made by the patent examiner, and the reasons given for the claims being rejected, the applicant must either file a response to the first office action within three months or obtain a three-months extension for a fee. If he or she fails to do either, the application will be deemed *abandoned*.

Once the applicant has responded, the patent examiner will respond again, usually with a *final office action*. This will either reject all of the claims with suggested modifications that would make them allowable, or reject some of the claims and accept others. Any pertinent prior art references that were not cited the first time around by the patent examiner will be listed (and copies sent) if amended claims are rejected on *anticipation* or *obviousness* grounds. Suggestions will be made for how to narrow claims that are too broad.

After the final office action, the applicant will have four basic choices:

- the applicant can amend the claims as suggested by the patent examiner

- the patent examiner can be petitioned to reconsider one or more of the decisions contained in the final office action

- the applicant can appeal to the *Board of Appeals*, or

- the applicant can file a *continuation application* (essentially a new application with new claims, with the benefit of the original filing date for certain purposes)

Whatever the choice, it must be carried out within three months of the final office action, or a three-month extension must be obtained. Otherwise, the application will be deemed legally abandoned.

Assuming that the final action results in an allowance of one or more claims, either as drafted or as amended in response to the final office action, the applicant will receive a *notice of allowability* . This will be followed by a formal "notice of allowance" and a form specifying the *issue fee* that is due.

At this time it is still possible to file minor amendments. Also, if any amendments to claims that have occured in the course of prosecution are not covered by the formal *declaration for patent application* signed by the applicant, a *supplemental declaration* should also be filed.

If the issue fee is sent to the PTO within three months of the formal Notice of Allowance, the applicant will receive a *patent deed* and a *patent copy*. Although the formal patent prosecution process is now over, the inventor may later wish to amend his or her *in-force* patent in some material way. If the amendment *broadens* one or more claims, and the application is filed within two years of the patent issue date, a *reissue patent* may be obtained. This will carry the same issue date as the original patent but will incorporate the claims as amended. (See chart next page.)

public domain Any *invention* that is published, put in public use, or placed on sale more than one year prior to a *patent application* being filed, and inventions whose patents are no longer *in-force*, both fall into the public domain. Public domain inventions can be used or sold by anyone.

publication of invention as anticipation See *anticipation*.

public knowledge, prior See *anticipation*.

public use as anticipation When an *invention* is *worked* (i.e., used) by the *inventor* before one or more members of the public in an unrestricted manner (not on a confidential or experimental basis), it is considered to have been "publicly

Prosecuting a Patent Application

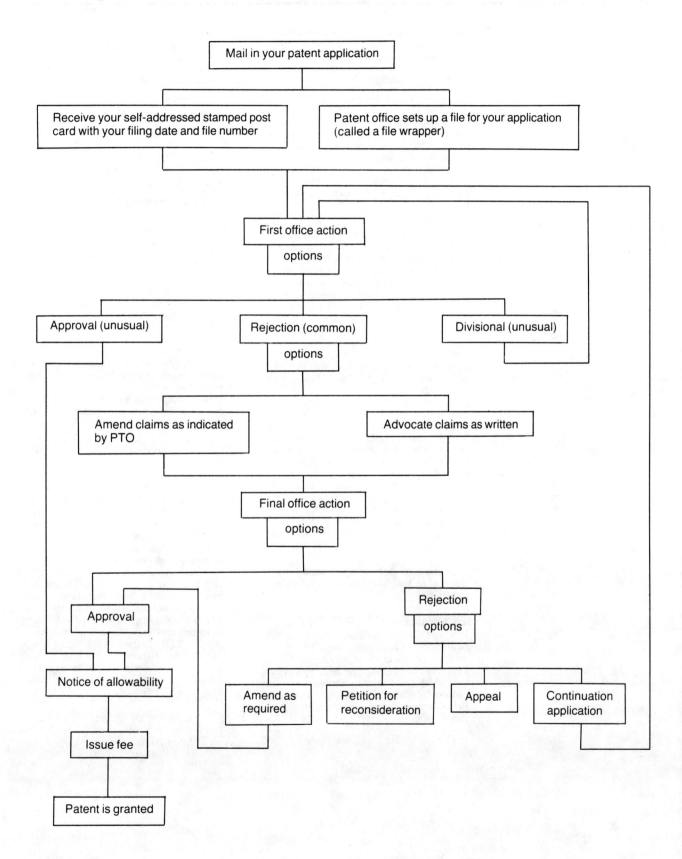

used". Public use of an invention constitutes a **statutory bar** to a patent under the **anticipation** doctrine, unless the use occurs within the one year period prior to the **patent application** being filed.

There is an exception to the "public use" rule for "experimental tests" (to develop and improve the invention) and for uses in a context where the members of the public have signed **non-disclosure agreements** 1, or are otherwise required to maintain secrecy. Whether any particular use of an invention is a public use must be determined on a case-by-case basis.

Example: Julian David, a motel keeper, invents a counterweighting device that allows a kingsize bed to be easily moved on very thick carpets. Julian actually constructs such a bed that uses the device and tries it out in his motel for a little over a year. If Julian then attempts to obtain a patent, the **PTO** will probably deny it if this public use comes to light. Why? The use of the bed in the motel would be considered a public use, and therefore a statutory bar to the patent, since the **patent application** was not filed within one year of the "use". What about the exception for experimental uses? If Julian can show that he was engaged in both monitoring the experiences had by cleaning personnel with the bed, and actively modifying the bed's basic design according to what he learned, he might escape the statutory bar. What if Julian only allowed one customer to use the bed, and only for two nights, but he still failed to file the patent application within one year? He will be barred from the patent unless he can establish that the two nights use was really for experimental purposes. Related terms: **anticipation**.

publication of patent application as defensive publication See **defensive publication**.
-

race statutes In all countries but the U.S. and Canada, an inventor who is the first to file an application for a patent on an invention is given absolute priority over other inventors. The laws providing for this absolute priority are termed "race statutes", because they award a patent to the inventor who wins the race to their patent office.

Because the first to file is the one who gets the patent, **interference** hearings do not exist in the countries with race statutes. If two or more inventors file an application for the same invention on the same day in Japan, for instance, no patent will issue unless the parties reach a settlement.

read on In the patent context, this means "literally describe". So, a patent is infringed if the patent's claims ' 'read on" all the elements of the infringing device. Related terms: **infringement of patent** and **anticipation**.

recite When the **claims** of a prior **patent** literally describe the elements of a later invention, they are said to "recite" such elements.

reconsideration request When a **final office action** has rejected claims in a **patent application**, it is possible to request that the **patent examiner** reconsider the application. If the request is rejected, it is then possible to amend the claims in the manner suggested by the patent examiner (if this option has been presented to the applicant), appeal to the **Board of Appeals and Interferences**, or file a **continuation application** . Related terms: **prosecuting a patent application**.

records of invention See **patent notebook**.

reduction to practice An **invention** is legally considered to be first **reduced to practice** (i.e., to exist in fact rather than just theoretically) on the date a **patent application** is filed. This type of "reduction to practice" is sometimes termed "constructive", because the law says the invention is reduced to practice whether or not it is in fact. When an invention has been actually been built or developed, it is called **actual reduction to practice** . When an invention was first "reduced to practice" can often determine who is entitled to the patent in the case of an **interference** (when two pending patent applications **claim** the same invention) Related terms: **actual reduction to practice**, and **interference**.

re-examination of patent A formal proceeding in which the **PTO** re-examines an **in-force patent** to determine whether *newly-cited prior art references* adversely affect the validity of the *patent*. This re-examination procedure was introduced by the 1980 Patent Act Amendments. This is how it works:

- Any person can call to the *PTO*'s attention any *prior art reference* that pertains to an *in-force patent*. If the person adequately demonstrates why the prior art reference is relevant, the reference will be placed in the patent's file (the *file wrapper*). The identity of the person providing the reference can be kept confidential upon request.

- Any person can request a "re-examination of the patent", if a) they describe the way in which the *prior art references* specifically bear on claims contained in the patent, and b) they pay a re-examination fee of $1500.00.

- Once a re-examination has been requested, the PTO must decide within three months whether a "substantial new question of patentability has been raised". If it has, then a re-examination will be ordered. If it has not, then the requestor will be refunded $1200.00 (the $300.00 balance will be retained by the PTO).

- If a re-examination finds that the patent claims are still valid, then the PTO will issue a "Certification of Validity". If it finds that one or more claims are not valid as drafted, the inventor will have an opportunity to redraft the claims to the *patent examiner's* satisfaction. In the event of such a change, the patent will enjoy the same status as a *reissue patent*.

The patent re-examination process can be useful in several common situations. For instance, if a *patent owner* discovers that a competitor is *infringing the patent* and the competitor counters on the ground that the patent is invalid in light of certain *prior art*, the owner can refer the prior art in question to the PTO and request a "re-examination" either before or during an infringement lawsuit. If the PTO then upholds the claims as drafted, the owner can feel much more secure about bringing the *infringement action*. Or, if a business wants to use an invention covered by an in-force patent, and believes that the patent is invalid because of certain prior art, the re-examination process is a relatively inexpensive way for the business to "test the water" without actually infringing the patent.

references   See *prior art references*.

reissue patent   If a *patent owner* desires to change the *specification* or *claims* of his or her *in-force patent* , it is possible to apply for a "reissue" patent that will take the place of the original patent and expire when that patent would have. If the owner desires to *broaden the claims* of the original patent, the reissue patent must be applied for within two years of the date the original patent was granted. In fact, reissue patents are relatively rare, since the broadening of claims typically occurs in the course of the original patent *prosecution* process.

request for international patent application   See *Patent Cooperation Treaty*.

reverse engineering   Figuring out how an invention works. Related terms: *reverse engineering* 1.

same invention, claim of two inventors to   See *interference*.

search of patentability   See *patentability search*.

search of patent validity   See *validity search*.

secrecy of patent applications   See *disclosure of patent application*.

senior inventor   When two or more *inventors* file separate *patent applications* on the same invention, the inventor who first conceived of the *invention* is termed the "senior inventor". The senior inventor may or may not be entitled to the *patent*, depending on other, additional, factors. Related terms: *interference* and *junior inventor*.

shelving of invention   See *anti-shelving clause* .

shop rights   The traditional right of employers to an irrevocable, non-assignable, and non-exclusive, royalty-free license to use an employee's invention, if the invention was accomplished primarily on company time with company facilities and material. The theory is that since such inventions are developed with the employer's funds or property, the employer should at least be able to use them in the business. However, the employee still qualifies as the **patent owner** (assuming the patent was obtained in his or her name) and has an exclusive right to issue **non-exclusive licenses** to others to use and manufacture the invention in exchange for royalties or other compensation. Related terms: **patent owner**.

shotgun rejection of claims When the **PTO** denies all **claims** in its **first office action** (its first formal response to the original patent application) on the premise that the applicant can submit amended claims or a more detailed explanation of why the existing claims should be allowed. See **prosecuting a patent application** and **first office action**.

single application rule See **divisonal application**.

smart money A colloquial phrase used by patent attorneys to describe punitive damages imposed on infringing defendants to teach them a lesson and make them "smart". Related terms: **infringement action**.

specification As commonly used, the narrative portion of a **patent application** that includes descriptions of:

• the type of **invention**

• the pertinent **prior art** known to the applicant (e.g., previous developments in the technology utilized in the invention)

• the purpose of the invention

• the invention itself (how it's constructed, what it's made of, etc)

• the operation of the invention (how it works), and

• any accompanying **drawings**

As defined by the patent laws, the "specification" also includes the patent **claims** and **abstract**.

Essentially, the specification must provide enough information about the invention so that a **person having ordinary skill in the art** (i.e., proficient in the particular area of expertise involved in the invention) could build it without having to be "inventive" himself. Because the specification is where the fullest disclo-

sure of the invention is made, it, rather than the claims, is commonly used to determine whether the patent has anticipated a later invention. Related terms: **disclosure requirements for patent** and **patent application**.

standards of patentability See **patentability**.

statement of prior art An applicant for a **patent** must file a statement with the application that contains 1) all relevant **prior art references** known to the applicant, and 2) actual copies of such references. Recently renamed as an "information disclosure statement", this statement provides the **PTO** with a head start in determining whether the **invention** deserves a **patent**. If the applicant knowingly fails to disclose any known and relevant prior art reference, it is considered **fraud on the PTO**, and a patent, if granted, may later be held unenforceable, even though the omitted reference might not have resulted in any **claim** being disallowed. In most cases, such an omission of a prior art reference will never be brought to light. But in the event of an **infringement action** to enforce a patent, the defendant will attempt to prove fraud in order to **break the patent**. Related terms: **defenses to a patent** and **duty of candor and good faith in disclosures to PTO**.

statute of limitations, infringement action An **infringement action** must be brought within six years of the infringing activity for which damages are being sought. However, if, under the circumstances, the failure to bring suit sooner has lulled the infringer into believing his or her activity to be permissible, all or part of the action may be barred by the legal doctrine known as **estoppel** 5.

statutory invention registration In the event a patent applicant desires to abandon the application, it is possible to file an invention registration form with the PTO. This will then be published and operate as a **defensive publication**, except that if another inventor files an application on the same invention within a particular period of time, the invention may be subjected to **interference** proceedings.

statutory bar   An occurrence or fact requiring the *PTO* or a court to determine that an *invention* does not qualify for a *patent* under the U.S. patent laws. Among the most common types of statutory bars are:

- prior patents, or other *printed publications*, describing the invention
- prior invention
- *abandonment of an invention* by the inventor, and
- prior *public use* or *on-sale* status of the invention

   Related terms: *anticipation*.

statutory subject matter   The kinds of *inventions* that qualify for a *patent* under the patent statutes. As commonly used by *patent attorneys*, the term ' 'statutory subject matter'' refers to any invention that is at least one of the five types of items established by the patent laws as entitled to a patent (assuming the other qualifications are met as well). These categories are: 1) *compositions*, 2)*manufactures*, 3) *machines*, 4) *processes* and 5) *new uses* of any of these. Any invention not falling within one of these categories is not patentable no matter how *novel* or *non-obvious* it may otherwise prove to be.

   Example: Einstein's special and general theories of relativity are considered to be among the most important advances in scientific thought ever accomplished. Yet, they did not qualify for a patent because they are considered as abstract scientific principles and *algorithms* and thus do not qualify as ''patentable subject matter''.

   In addition to falling in one of the five statutory categories, an invention must be *novel*, *useful*, and *non-obvious* to qualify for a patent. The phrase ''statutory subject matter'' is thus often used to refer not only to inventions that fall within one of the five statutory classes, but also to those that satisfy these other patent requirements as well. Related terms: *non-statutory subject matter*.

subclass of patents, patent search   See *class of patents*.

substitute patent application   A *patent application* that is filed after an earlier application on the same *invention* has been *abandoned*. For example, if an application is abandoned because of the applicant's failure to respond to the *PTO's first office action* within three months, the applicant can refile a ''substitute application''. However, the substitute application does not obtain the benefit of the original *filing date*, and any *prior art* that has surfaced in the meantime may operate to *anticipate* and thus bar the patent from issuing.

suit on patent   See *infringement action*.

supplemental declaration   A declaration (statement under oath) that should be filed with the *PTO* by a successful *patent applicant* when *claims* have been changed or *broadened* in the course of *prosecuting the patent application*. The declaration should 1) specify which claims have been altered in the course of the *prosecution*, and 2) declare that the applicant was the *inventor* of the subject matter contained in the altered claims, and knows of no *prior art* that would *anticipate* the claims as altered. Related terms: *prosecuting a patent application*.

swearing behind a prior art reference   When a *patent applicant* offers evidence to the *PTO* that his or her *invention* was conceived of or *reduced to practice* early enough to 1) effectively remove an earlier filed *patent application* as relevant prior art, or 2) preclude other *prior art references* from operating as *statutory bars*.

   The evidence to establish these facts typically consists of the inventor's testimony under oath, and appropriate entries from his or her *patent notebook*. Here are some specific examples of times when an inventor might need to ''swear behind a prior art reference'':

- When a pertinent *prior art reference* is any publication dated less than one year prior to the patent application's *filing date*, a showing by the applicant that the invention was conceived of prior to the publication date (and *diligent attempts were made to reduce it to practice*) will eliminate the reference as a *statutory bar*.

   Example: An article appearing in the November, 1984 issue of a leading popular science magazine details an efficient portable photovoltaic cell, able to run various electronic devices. Lou Swift has already conceived of such a cell, and has been busy designing it so that a patent

Patent

application can be filed. Lou may still be able to obtain a patent if she files a patent application within one year of the article's publication date and shows (swears behind) that she conceived of her invention prior to such publication date and was diligently engaged in *reducing it to practice*.

- When a *prior art reference* consists of any U.S. patent with a filing date preceding the applicant's filing date, and an issue date that is either within a year prior to the applicant's filing date, or anytime after such filing date, a showing by the applicant that he or she conceived of the invention prior to the patent's filing date (and thereafter exercised diligence to reduce it to practice), will eliminate the patent acting as a *statutory bar* to the application.

Example: Lou Swift invents a photovoltaic cell, but before she files a *patent application* she discovers that another inventor has patented the same invention (the patent issued on July 1, 1986). If Lou 1) files her application within one year of the date the patent issued (i.e., by July 1, 1987), and 2) is able to state that she conceived of her invention prior to the date the other patent application was filed, and 3) can show that she was diligently attempting to *reduce her invention to practice* at the time the other patent application was filed, Lou's application will be entitled to consideration, and will most likely be *thrown into interference* with the other invention (i.e., the PTO will declare an interference hearing). The outcome of this proceeding will depend on a number of additional variables. Related terms: *interference* and *statutory bar*.

teach   What any prior publication, invention, or patent shows (teaches) about the elements of, or technology associated with, an item for which a patent is being sought.

thesis as prior art   A college or university thesis may count as a *prior art reference* and operate as a *statutory bar* to a *patent*, if the thesis describes (*teaches*) the essential characteristics of the *invention* on which the patent is being sought.

Example: Fred Walker, an enterprising graduate student in computer science, writes a thesis on using certain protein molecules as a molecular computer memo-

ry. If a patent is later sought by someone else on an invention that utilizes the same principles and procedures described in Fred's thesis, the thesis may act as a *statutory bar* to the patent, unless it is Fred himself who is seeking it, and he has filed his *patent application* within *one year* of the date when his thesis was first published.

Because a thesis can count as prior art, a thorough *patent search* will usually cover listings of theses, as well as prior patents and publications in trade journals. Related terms: *prior art references*.

thrown into interference   When the PTO determines that 1) two or more *patent applications* are *claiming* the same invention, and 2) determines that the claims are allowable, it will schedule an *interference* hearing for the applications (i.e., throws them into interference) to determine who should be awarded the patent. Related terms: *interference*.

time for response to Patent and Trademark Office actions   In the course of *prosecuting a patent application*, an applicant will have several occasions to respond to actions by the *PTO*. Under Patent and Trademark Office rules, the time for such responses is three months. Failure to respond within this three-month period (or obtain an extension) will normally result in the *patent application* being considered legally *abandoned*. Related terms: *abandonment of patent application* and *prosecuting a patent application*.

Title 35   The section of the United States Code (U.S.C.) that contains the patent statutes. To locate these statutes, consult 35 *United States Code Annotated (U.S.C.A.)* or 35 *United States Code Service, Lawyers Edition(U.S.C.S.)* . See Research Note at end of this Part.

transfer of patent or patent application   See *assignment of patents*.

transmittal letter for patent application   See *patent application*.

treble (triple) damages for patent infringement   See *infringement action*.

treaties on international patent protection See *Patent Cooperation Treaty* and *convention filing*.

tying agreements as anti-trust violation See *anti-trust and patents*.

two inventions in one patent application See *divisional application*.

unenforceability of patent See *misuse of patents* and *defenses to a patent*.

unilateral refusal to deal as anti-trust See *anti-trust and patents*.

unobviousness See *non-obviousness*.

U.S. Patent and Trademark Office
An administrative branch of the U.S. Department of Commerce charged with the responsiblity for overseeing and implementing the federal laws on patents and trademarks. Also known as the PTO, or Patent Office, this agency is responsible for examining, issuing, classifying, and maintaining records of, all patents issued by the United States. The PTO publishes the *Official Gazette* (both the patent and trademark versions), a weekly periodical that describes newly issued patents, new regulations, and other information of interest to patent practitioners. The PTO also maintains a library in which a complete patent search may be conducted by classification. Related terms: *U.S. Patent and Trademark Office* 3.

usefulness, required for patents See *utility patents*.

utility See *utility patents*.

utility model A Japanese and German legal provision providing that inventions that do not qualify for a regular patent may nonetheless receive some protection for a shorter period of time. Related terms: *utility model* 1.

utility patents htPatents on *inventions* that are within one of the five classes of *patentable subject matter*, and that (in addition to the requirements of *novelty* and *non-obviousness*) are useful in some way, even if the use is relatively frivolous. Generally speaking, all patents obtained in the U.S. are considered utility patents unless they are specially obtained as *design patents* or *plant patents* , neither of which require utility. Related terms: *statutory subject matter*.

validity search A *patent search*, conducted after a *patent* has issued, for the purpose of discovering any fact that might be used to invalidate and thus *break the patent*. Generally conducted by the defendant in a patent *infringement action*, the validity search tends to be much more thorough than the initial *patentability search* conducted by the inventor prior to filing his *patent application*, in which he sought to determine whether his invention infringed a prior one. Related terms: *patent search*.

vertical price fixing See *anti-trust and patents*.

working a patent Actually developing and commercially exploiting the underlying *invention* covered by a *patent*. In many countries outside the U.S., the failure of a *patent owner* to work the patent within a specific period of time may result in the owner's being forced to grant a license (called a *compulsory license*), at government-set fees, to any party who desires to do so. Related terms: *compulsory license*.

World Intellectual Property Organization (WIPO) See *Patent Cooperation Treaty* and *World Intellectual Property Organization* 2.

Research Notes

This note assumes that you wish to delve deeper into the topics defined in this part of the dictionary. Instead of just providing you with a bibliography, we want to suggest a general research strategy. First, find some simplified background resources (often published as "self-help" law books) to obtain a general overview of your subject. Some of these are listed in **Step #1** below. Then consult more intensive background materials (listed in **step #2**). These will go into greater detail and will also usually provide you with references (citations) to the primary law itself (**Step #3**). Finally, use Legal Research: How to Find and Understand the Law by Stephen Elias, Nolo Press, or another basic legal research guide, to assist you in using the law library and understanding the law you find there.

Step #1: Simplified Background Resources

Patent it Yourself by David Pressman, (formerly published by McGraw-Hill and now by Nolo Press) is a clearly written, well-documented, up-to-date, and step by step guide for how to obtain your own patent. Because it is designed especially for inventors, rather than lawyers, it can serve as an excellent background resource for the beginning patent researcher. It has a good table of contents, an excellent, detailed index, and a focused bibliography.

Patent

Resources that are midway between *Patent it Yourself* and the most detailed secondary sources are the discussions of patent law found in the national legal encyclopedias known as *American Jurisprudence Second Series (AmJur.2d)* and *Corpus Juris Secundum (C.J.S.)* . These publications provide basic overviews of the law in respect to most issues that are likely to arise, although they tend to be a couple of years out of date, despite the update "pocket parts" at the end.

Step #2: Intensive Background Resources

The best intensive background resource for patent law is *Patent Law Fundamentals by Peter Rosenberg*, published by Clark Boardman Company, Ltd. This is a two volume set containing a table of contents, a table of cases (if you should happen to have the name of a patent case that you want to understand better), a detailed index, and annual supplements. This publication is generally considered by patent attorneys to be the bible of patent law. Because it is written for attorneys, it might somewhat difficult sledding for the non-lawyer. However, if you first obtain an overview of your topic from the Pressman book or the national encyclopedias, you should do fine.

Another potentially useful book, also published by Clark Boardman, is called the *Patent Law Handbook*. Currently authored by C. Bruce Hamburg, a new edition of this book is published each year in which new developments in patent law are discussed. So, if you are aware that your question involves some recent change in the patent laws, or court cases interpreting these laws, or you simply want to check to see whether your information has been recently superseded by any such changes, this publication can be useful.

In the event you are prosecuting your own patent application and get stuck at the stage where you are called on to draft proper patent claims, consult *The Mechanics of Patent Claim Drafting* by J.L. Landis, 2d ed. 1974, Practicing Law Institute, 810 Seventh Ave. N.Y. 10019. If you are stuck at other stages of the patent preparation or prosecuton process, consult the six volume set called *Patent Preparation and Prosecution Practice*, Patent Resources Institute, (1976) Washington D.C. 20006. If you are engaged in a patent search, see that entry in this dictionary for specific resources to use.

Law review articles: Especially in regard to recent developments concerning such topics as the patentability of software and the products of gene-splicing techniques. the best sources of information are often articles appearing in scholarly journals called "law reviews". By looking under "Patents" in the *Index to Legal Periodicals* or *Current Law Index* , you will find frequent references to articles on current topics of interest in the patent field. These references refer you to law reviews. A key to the abbreviations used is located at the front of the index volume you are using. Law libraries always store law review publications alphabetically in one particular location. The reference librarian can help here.

Step #3: Accessing Primary Law Sources

Statutes: The basic U.S. Patent Law is located in *Title 35 United States Code*, Section 101 and following [35 USC SEC. 101]. This can be accessed in the *United States Code Annotated (U.S.C.A.)* or in the *United States Code Service, Lawyers Edition (U.S.C.S)*.

Regulations: The U.S. Patent and Trademark Office has issued regulations contained in *Title 37* of the *Code of Federal Regulations (CFR)*. These regulations govern such details as what a patent application must contain, what happens if an interference is found to exist, how to file for a patent "reexamination", and how your applications will be processed and assessed by the Patent Office.

Introduction

This section defines the words and phrases commonly used to 1) describe the kinds of **contracts** commonly used in the **intellectual property** field, and 2) determine when and how agreements will be recognized and enforced by the courts, and the ways in which a party to an agreement can legally back out without having to pay up.

Contracts are very important to the intellectual property field. National and international **licenses** of copyright and patent rights, **non-disclosure** 1 and **confidentiality agreements** 1 to preserve trade secrets, and franchise agreements under nationally known **trademarks** 3 are all examples of how contracts are used to commercially exploit intellectual property. Authors and publishers daily enter into contracts, containing such provisions as **option** , **satisfactory in form and content**, **grant of rights**, **warranty and indemnity**, **right of first refusal** and **out of print** clauses. Performers and musicians enter into similarly comprehensive contracts with their producers and recording studios.

There are two basic types of contracts. One, called **bilateral contracts**, is where two or more parties are bound to do something in the future (i.e., you promise to pay, I promise to deliver). For this type of contract to be valid and enforceable, 1) there must be an **offer** and an **acceptance** (i.e., I offer to sell, you accept my terms), 2)the parties must come to a **meeting of the minds** (actually agree on the contract's terms from relatively equal bargaining positions), 3) each party must receive something of value (called **consideration**) from the other as part of the bargain, and 4) each party must be obliged to perform some act (called **mutuality of obligation**).

The other type of contract (termed a **unilateral contract**) is when one party becomes obligated only when another party performs an act (i.e., if you write a program for my computer, I'll pay you $1000.00). Here, the only factors necessary to make a binding contract is the performance of the act by one party in response to an offer by the other. After such performance, the offering party becomes bound to perform his or her part of the bargain.

In addition to bilateral and unilateral contracts, contracts can be both **express** (i.e., written down or orally agreed on) and **implied** (the law implies them to exist either because of the way the parties behaved — **implied in fact** — contracts, or because policy considerations dictate that they should exist — **implied in law** — contracts).

Contract and Warranty

5

In the event one party fails to perform a duty specified in a contract, and the other party files an action in court for **breach of contract**, there are a number of legally recognized defenses available to the defendant. Among these are: 1) no valid contract was formed (e.g., a proper offer wasn't made, the offer wasn't accepted, there was no meeting of the minds, etc.); 2) events arising after the contract make it impossible or unfair to perform contractual obligations (e.g., a natural catastrophe occurs, a party dies, changes in the law make the purpose of the contract illegal, etc.) or 3) the party claiming to be victimized by the breach failed to perform his or her end of the bargain.

In the event a breach of contract is found to exist, the court can award damages under several basic theories and can order a contractual obligation to be performed under certain circumstances. Even if the court finds that valid contract did not exist, it may still hold that a promise made to another party is binding if that other party justifiably relied on that promise to his/her detriment.

Definitions

acceleration clause   A contract provision or clause, commonly contained in **installment contracts**, that allows a creditor to demand payment of the entire sum due under the contract if an installment payment is late or missed entirely. For example, suppose W.W. Corp. borrows $5,000 from a bank to purchase a personal computer and peripherals, and then falls behind on the monthly loan payments. If there is an acceleration clause in the loan agreement, the bank can demand that the entire balance on the loan be repaid immediately. If W.W. Corp. does not comply, the bank can sue for that amount, not just the amount of the missed payment(s).

acceptance of a contractual offer

Where a legal offer to form a contract is agreed to in a way that forms a binding contract. Law students spend months debating the technical details of what constitutes the "offer" and "acceptance" of a contract. Basically, however, a contract is accepted if the party to whom an offer to contract is made says "yes" to the terms of the offer in timely fashion. However, if the second party proposes a new term or condition, that is, he or she says "yes, but", and attempts to vary the terms of the offer, there is no acceptance, and no contract has been formed. As a general matter, an offer may be withdrawn before a legal acceptance is made. Once an offer is legally accepted, however, a binding contract has been formed (assuming the other prerequisites for a valid contract are present). Related terms: *formation of contract*.

Example: Intelligent Design Corp. offers to build Acme Machine a custom-made industrial robot for Acme's machine tool shop, for the price of $20,000, payable half in advance and half upon completion. If Acme says, "That's fine with us, go ahead", Intelligent Design's offer has been accepted, and a contract exists. However, if Acme says "That's an interesting offer; how about the same robot for $15,000, 1/3 payable in advance?", Acme has varied the terms of the offer and has not, therefore, accepted it. Accordingly, no contract exists.

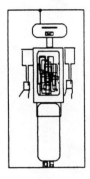

accord and satisfaction   An agreement to settle a dispute over a contract obligation (accord) and the actual performance of the accord (satisfaction). By definition, an "accord" always involves paying less money or agreeing to a lesser performance than that owed under the basic contract. Once the accord is satisfied (i.e., the sum paid or the performance tendered), the original debt is extinguished. For example, if Glenda Garulous contracts with a magazine to write an article for $1000.00, and the magazine says it will only pay $500.00 when the finished product is submitted, Glenda might agree to accept the lesser amount (an accord) and receive the $500.00 sum as satisfaction for the entire $1000.00 debt. Related terms: *settlement of contract disputes without going to court*.

Contract and Warranty

accounting and payment clause A standard publishing (books and computer software) contract clause that states the frequency and dates of royalty payments, as well as the details of the publisher's accounting duty to the author.

adequacy of consideration, determination of When a court examines whether the parties to a *contract* have each received, or will receive, enough of a *benefit of the bargain* to warrant judicial enforcement of the agreement as a contract. Related terms: *consideration* .

adequate assurance of performance See: *right to adequate assurance of performance*.

adhesion contracts A very unfair (*unconscionable*) agreement forced on one party because of the other party's superior bargaining position. In most jurisdictions, courts will refuse to recognize such agreements as contractually binding. Why? Because, for a contract to be valid, it must result from the mutual agreement of the parties. Thus, if, as a result of a seriously unequal relationship, the weaker party to a contract agrees to an "unconscionable" provision, a court should find an absence of genuine mutual agreement, and therefore not enforce that provision. Sometimes this will result in the invalidation of the entire contract while in other situations only the offending contract provision will be invalidated. Related terms: *unconscionable contracts and contract terms*.

A CHECK AT LAST!

advance breach of contract Related terms: *anticipatory breach or repudiation of contracts*.

advance clause A publishing (computer software and books) contract clause that provides the author with certain advance payments against expected royalties. These can be large or small, payable all at once or over a period of time, refundable under certain conditions, etc, depending on the publishing contract.

Example: Rasputin Publishing Co. agrees to advance author Nicolai Romanov $25,000.00 against royalties of 10% of the books cover price as part of its contract to publish Rasputin's forthcoming book "Might is Right". The advance is to be paid 1/3 at the signing of the contract, 1/3 when a manuscript *satisfactory in form and content* is delivered to Rasputin, and 1/3 when the book is published. The advance is not refundable, which means simply that Romanov gets to keep the $25,000 even if the book does not sell enough copies to equal the advance. Assuming that "Might is Right" sells for $25.00, it would have to sell 10,000 copies to pay off the advance (10% of $25.00 times 10,000 copies = 25,000). Once the advance is paid off, Romanov would receive his 10% royalties on any additional copies sold.

advertisements as offers to form a contract Normally, media advertisements "offering" merchandise or services for sale to the public on a general and unrestricted basis do not legally extend the kind of *offers* to contract that can be accepted and thereby turned into an *enforceable contract*. Rather, such "offers" are usually considered as invitations for the public to come in and offer to purchase the merchandise or services. Thus, if Ted calls a C.P.A. after seeing an ad in the yellow pages for "moderately priced tax accounting services", and says, "I accept your accounting offer", he has not created a binding contract requiring the accounting firm to do his taxes. Rather, by his action Ted has offered to retain the firm. If the C.P.A. is short of personnel, or sick, or just doesn't like Ted, it is not obligated to take Ted's business, under general contract law principles.

This does not mean that advertisements can never be offers. When an ad specifies a limited class of persons who qualify for the goods or services being advertised, the courts will find that an affirmative response by such person is an *acceptance of a contractual offer*. Suppose a C.P.A. firm offers $100.00 worth of free accounting software to the first ten businesses with sales of $200,000.00 or more who offer to retain the firm to prepare their tax returns. This would probably constitute a valid offer, since the total number of possible acceptances are restricted by the ad. In addition to normal contract rules, consumer protection laws in many states require retailers to provide "rain-checks" for customers if they run out of advertised merchandise, unless they indicate in the ad that quantities are limited. Related terms: *acceptance of a contractual offer* and *formation of contracts*.

agency The legal label applied to a variety of principles governing the relationship between businesses (generally termed masters, employers, or principals, depending on the relationship), those through whom the businesses operate (generally termed servants, employees, and agents, again depending on the relationship) and third parties. Among the common types of agency relationships are employees and their employer, partners and the partnership, corporate officers and the corporation, agents and their performers, and attorneys and clients.

All legal systems must deal with what happens when a person or business suffers damage or injury as a result of the activity of another person or business acting on behalf of a third person or business. In the contractual context, for example, if an employee purchases some office equipment on the employer's account, and the employer later refuses to pay for it, claiming that the employee was not an authorized purchaser, agency principles will determine whether the employer is liable (legally responsible) for the bill. The employer will be considered liable if the employee has either 1) "actual authority" to purchase the equipment (i.e., the employer has specifically given the employee the authority to make the purchase) or 2) "apparent authority" to purchase (i.e., from all external appearances the employee had the authority to make the purchase and the seller reasonably relied on these appearances).

In personal injury (tort) situations, an employer (or other principal) may be held liable if an employee (or other ' 'servant'') causes an injury while acting in furtherance of the employer. For example, suppose Tim, a computer installer for Pop's Computer Co., is on his way to install a new computer when his car rams a truck being driven by Tonya Veron, causing injuries to her. Because Tim's activity was directly in furtherance of Pop's business, Pop's would be held liable for Tonya's injuries, under general agency principles.

Whether or not one person or business is liable for the act of another is extremely important, since employees are usually often relatively short of cash whereas the underlying business is usually able to foot the bill or carries insurance. Assume, for example, that Aurora Publishers purchases a business computer for $30,000 from Acme Computers, after

being falsely told by the salesman that it was ideal for their needs. If only the salesmen were liable, Aurora might never recover its money or additional statutory penalties, since the salesman would very likely have insufficient assets to be be able to pay. Aurora, however, or its insurer, would more likely be able to come up with the funds.

agency clause A clause, found in many publishing and entertainment contracts, that authorizes payments of royalties or performance fees by the publisher or entertainment company directly to the author or performer's agent.

agent Any person or business entity authorized by another person or business (the "principal") to act on his or her behalf. This relationship is usually created under a written or oral *contract*. Attorneys, stockbrokers, and real estate salesmen commonly act as agents for their respective client-principals. In the intellectual property context, agents perform an extremely important role in assisting their principals (commonly, authors, software designers, artists, and performers) to sell their wares on favorable terms. The laws of many states regulate the conduct of agents and, in a few instances, even require them to register with a state agency. Related terms: *literary agencies* and *artists and managers contracts*.

When the relationship between an agent and his or her principal is based largely on trust (usually the case when an agent handles the principal's funds or performs personal services), the agent is said to have a *fiduciary duty* toward his or her principal, and must not act contrary to the principal's interests. Whether or not a person is an agent in any particular context is covered by the law of *agency*. Related terms: *fiduciary duty*.

agreements Oral or written indications between two or more parties that they have agreed to something. Agreements may or may not be enforceable as contracts, depending on a variety of factors. Related terms: *formation of contracts*.

anti-assignment clauses A contractual clause specifying that one (or both) parties may not legally give away (*assign*) their rights under the contract to another

Contract and Warranty

party.

Example: Cynthia Celebrity writes a novel, and assigns the movie rights to Serendipity Studios, an independent movie production company. Such a contract (assignments are a type of contract) would commonly include an anti-assignment clause prohibiting the assignee (Serendipity) from passing on the movie rights to another studio.

While the courts will usually enforce anti-assignment provisions in contracts involving personal or artistic services (such as the example above), they are often not enforced when fungible goods or money are involved.

Example: Montana Hides, Ltd., agrees to provide Leathercraft Saddle with a particular grade of leather for a year at an established price. If Montana Hides then assigns its rights to provide leather under the contract to Western Townes, Leathercraft will have to accept Western Townes as long as they provide the leather under the terms of the original contract. However, a court will hold the assigning party (Montana Hides) responsible for resulting damages if Western Townes fails to meet the terms of the contract. In practice, this means that if Western Townes turns out to be a poor leather supplier, Leathercraft could sue both Montana Hides and Western Townes for any damages suffered.

anti-competition agreements See *covenants not to compete* 1.

anti-competition clause Often referred to as a *covenant not to compete* 1, an anti-competition clause in a contract is where one party promises not to engage in economic competition with the other. These commonly arise in three situations. The first is when the seller of a business promises not to compete with the new buyer. The second is when a key officer or major stockholder of a corporation agrees not to compete with the purchaser of the corporation. The third is when an employee promises an employer not to compete with the employer's business after leaving his employment.

The first two kinds of anti-competition clauses are usually enforced by the courts on the ground that the buyer is purchasing not only the tangible assets of the business but *good will* 3 as well. If the

former owner were allowed to compete (e.g., by starting a new business), the value of the good will of the original business might be diminished or even eliminated. In other words, without the anti-competition agreement, the purchaser could be deprived of the benefit of his bargain.

Restraints on employees competing with the company after they leave it are viewed much more strictly by the courts. For a variety of reasons, including the fact that these clauses are often imposed on employees as a result of the employer's superior bargaining position, and can result in substantial hardship to the employee, the courts in most jurisdictions will often refuse to enforce them unless they are very narrowly drawn, so that the anti-competition restriction does not hamper the employee's ability to earn a living. The exception is when the employee has been given access to *trade secrets* 1 of some kind (e.g., a recipe for a special sauce or a specialized customer list) and would be likely to use such secret in his or her new employment without an anti-competition agrement. Related terms: *unconscionable contracts and contact terms, covenants not to compete by employees* 1 and *covenants not to compete by sold businesses* 1.

anticipatory breach or repudiation of a contract When a party who is obligated to perform a contractual obligation, unequivocally indicates an intention not to do so. For example, in June, Roger Roy contracts to write a number of new songs for ''Up and Running'', a rock-and-roll band, to be finished by December. ''Up and Running'' pays Roger a substantial advance. Then, in July, Roger informs ''Up and Running'' that he doesn't want to compose anymore, and is leaving the U.S. forever to join a religious community in India. What legal recourse does ''Up and Running'' have?

Ordinarily, a party may not sue for *breach of contract* until the actual breach occurs. However, in this situation, with a clear anticipatory breach, the law would allow ''Up and Runnng'' to go to court in July, to try to recover the advance, instead of waiting until December. Anticipatory repudiations can result from unequivocal behavior as well as language. Thus, even if Roger never told ''Up and Running'' of his intention to quit composing, his move to India, and his acceptance of an ascetic religion, might by itself constitute an anticipatory breach. Such behavior is sometimes referred to as "voluntary disablement".

When one party commits an anticipatory breach or repudiation, the other party is relieved from his or her obligations under the contract. Thus, if "Up and Running" had promised to pay Roger an additional third of the contract sum by September, they would be relieved of this duty, due to Roger's prior anticipatory breach.

arbitration   Arbitration is a formal proceeding designed to solve disputes. In the United States and most other countries, this type of dispute- resolution mechanism is generally offered as an alternative to the formal court system. However, in some parts of the U.S., arbitration is now being utilized as part of the general court system and procedures.

The first step in arbitration is to pick an arbitrator. This is generally accomplished in one of the two following ways:

- the parties to a contract pick (usually in advance) a third person or entity to decide any dispute that has developed or arisen under the contract — often, but by no means always, the American Arbitration Associaton is used, or

- the parties each select their own representative, and these then select a third arbitrator from a list by striking names until only one name is left

Each side's case is presented to the arbitrator in a more informal way than would be the case in court and the abitrator(s) render a decision. In the case of the three arbitrator system, the decision is made by majority vote.

As a general matter, people end up in arbitration as a result of business or employment contracts that require the parties to undergo arbitration if a dispute under the terms of the contract arises. For example, most labor management collective bargaining agreements contain mandatory arbitration clauses. Under most arbitration agreements, arbitration is final (i.e., what the arbitrator says, goes). However, under some agreements, it is merely a first step after which the losing party may bring an action in court (called a *trial de novo*) as if the arbitration had never occurred.

Arbitration is a faster and less expensive remedy than regular court, because many of the "lawyer" devices that slow the average court case to a turtle's pace are prohibited. Thus, in the usual contested court case, the attorneys often take months, or even years, using "depositions and interrogatories" in an attempt to discover what the other side does and doesn't know about the dispute. This process is greatly restricted in arbitration proceedings. However, arbitration is still a formal adversary proceeding, in which lawyers make arguments and present evidence. It should be distinguished from *mediation* where a mediator's role is normally to help the parties arrive at their own agreement. Related terms: *conciliation and mediation*.

arbitration clauses   Clauses commonly found in business, employment, and labor contracts that require *arbitration* if certain types of disagreements should arise. Some arbitration clauses allow a party who is unhappy with the result of an arbitration to seek a new resolution of the dispute in the courts. More often, however, these clauses provide that the decision of the arbitrator is final. In situations where arbitration clauses are claimed to be confusing or ambiguous, courts tend to look for a way to enforce them anyway, in part because arbitration reduces work for the courts. In most states, arbitration agreements must be put in writing to be enforceable. Related terms: *arbitration*.

arm's length negotiation   A negotiation process based on equal bargaining positions of the parties. The courts are much more willing to enforce contracts reached through "arms length egotiation" than those produced by personal (insider deals) or unequal relationships (*adhesion contracts*), which might involve *duress* or favoritism, and therefore produce *unconscionable* results. Related terms: *formation of contracts* and *adhesion contracts*.

artist and manager contracts   Comprehensive agreements between such performing artists as musicians and actors, and their agents, which regulate the respective rights and duties of each.

Contract and Warranty

171

assignment clauses Most contracts have clauses specifying the conditions under which the rights or duties under the contract may be assigned to others. Related terms: *assignments, assignors and assignees*.

assigning contractual benefits The process by which rights or benefits under a contract are transferred to someone else. This is often called an *assignment* of rights. Example: Jimmy agrees to provide Fastsoft twenty hours of programming time, in exchange for being able to use their computer for one hundred hours. If Jimmy transfers the right to use the computer time to his friend Kate, he would be making (executing) an assignment of contractual benefits (or rights).

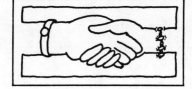

Assigning benefits under a contract is not the same as assigning the contract itself. Why? Because, by definition, parties to a contract have both *duties and rights* under it. The rights are the benefits they expect to receive. The duties are the obligations they have undertaken in exchange for the benefits. Assigning rights, therefore, does not necessarily involve the assignment of duties. For example, even though Jimmy gave away his computer time to Kate, he still has a contractual obligation to provide the 20 hours of programming. When contractual duties are transferred to another it is termed a "delegation". Related terms: *delegation of duties*.

Contract benefits can usually be assigned, with the following exceptions:

• Benefits are not assignable if there is a valid *anti-assignment clause* in the contract. This is common in many publishing, entertainment and computer software contracts. Benefits are not assignable if the burden or obligation of the person owing the duty (called the *obligor*) would substantially change. For example, Wonder Graphics agrees to design a cover and chapter-opening pages for five Westlake and Albert Publishing Company books, and W & A. assigns this right, under the contract, to Pop's Publishing. The assignment would be invalid if Pop's books were significantly more difficult to design. Or, for another example, John's being insured under a life or property insurance contract is usually not assignable, since such assignment would signficantly change the insurer's duties, especially if John, a young healthy person, assigned

the benefits under a life insurance policy taken out on his life to an eighty-year old heart disease sufferer.

• Benefits are not assignable by a party to a contract if the assignment decreases the chances of the other party receiving his or her benefits. For example, suppose Dan, a respected pioneer in journalism about artificial intelligence, agreed to write some articles for a leading computer magazine under a *work made for hire* ② contract. Dan could not assign his right to author the articles to somebody less skilled or knowledgeable, since this would substantially reduce the likelihood that the magazine would receive articles of the quality usually produced by Dan.

When the benefits of a contract are assignable, the consent of the other party need not be obtained unless the contract clearly calls for it. Once the other party receives notice that benefits have been assigned, the new owner of the benefits (the *assignee*) may require the party owing the duty to perform this duty in the assignee's favor. Without such notification, the benefits only need be provided to the original party (the *obligee*). Once a contract has been validly assigned, the original obligee has no further rights in the contract. Related terms: *anti-assignment clauses*, and *delegation of duties*.

assignment of contracts See *assigning contractual benefits*.

assignment of copyright ownership See this listing Section ②.

assignment of marks See this listing Section ③.

assignment of rights See *assigning contractual benefits*.

assignments, assignors, assignees Persons who transfer benefits or rights owned by them to someone else are called "assignors". Parties who are assigned such benefits or rights are called "assignees". The act of transferring contractual or statutory benefits or rights is called "assignment". The various types of *intellectual property* ① (i.e., trade secrets, trademarks, copyrights, patents) are often the subject of assignments. For example, the author of a book will typically "assign" *all rights* ② to the publisher. This means that all of the author's **exclusive copyright rights** 2 have been transferred to the publisher, usually in exchange for compensation in the form of royalties or the payment of a fixed sum. Similarly, when a business is sold, the sale should include the "assignment" of all **trademarks** 3 belonging to the business.

attorneys' fees in breach of contract actions Attorneys' fees are not usually recoverable in the U.S. by the prevailing party in a lawsuit as an element of damages for breach of contract, unless the contract or a statute specifically authorizes their recovery. Many types of contracts. such as those between businesses and custom software houses, or those that extend credit, routinely provide for reasonable attorneys " fees, should breach of the contract result in a lawsuit. Failing such a provision, however, many lawsuits involving modest damages, and resulting from a breach of contract, are generally not worth bringing (except in Small Claims Court, perhaps), since the non-recoverable cost of the prevailing party's attorney would probably be more than the sum in dispute.

When there is a provision in a contract for the recovery of attorneys' fees in the event of a contractual breach, the courts will usually enforce it. Further, the law in some states provides that when attorneys' fees are recoverable under a contract by one party, the other party may also be awarded such fees, if he or she prevails in the lawsuit.

auctions See *bids (at an auction)*.

audit clause A standard publishing and entertainment contract clause, giving the author the right (typically on an annual basis) to conduct an independent audit of the publisher's books. Normally, an audit clause establishes a number of notice and conduct requirements on the person requesting the audit, and requires that that person pay all costs unless substantial accounting irregularities are discovered.

authorization to sign trade secret agreements See *actual and apparent authority to make trade secret agreements* 1.

author's copies clause A common publishing contract clause entitling the author to a small number of free copies (perhaps 10, 20 or 25) and a fixed discount off the standard price for additional copies. This clause may or may not allow the author also to collect royalties on the books purchased by him or her at discount.

avoidable consequences, breach of contract as a result of See *duty to mitigate damages*.

bad faith A knowing and willful refusal to honor clear contractual or legal obligations without adequate justification. Courts are increasingly inclined to treat clear instances of bad faith as a kind of personal injury (tort), and accordingly to award *punitive damages* for this type of contract violation cases. Related terms: *breach of duty of good faith and fair dealing*.

bailment The legal relationship created when one person agrees to store property for another. When a bailment exists, each party has specific rights and responsiblities imposed on him or her by law. The person keeping the "bailed" property (called the "bailee") is considered to have "legal possession" of it, while legal title or ownership remains with the person who is storing it (called the "bailor"). Thus, if you store the model for your precious new invention in your Uncle Leo's garage, or rent space from a storage company for your newest metal sculpture, a bailment has been created.

The law of bailments is concerned with issues such as who bears the responsibility if your invention is stolen or your sculpture is ruined in a fire. If you pay money in exchange for the bailment, a "bailment for hire" has been created, and the "bailee" has a higher duty of protection than if the bailment were for free. In many cases bailment contracts contain express disclaimers of liability for your goods, and instead offer you an opportunity to insure your property by purchasing a policy for that purpose. Some courts consider such disclaimers invalid under some circumstances on the ground they are *unconscionable*.

The law of bailment is especially important in respect to *consignment contracts*,

Contract and Warranty

under which artists place their works with a gallery or shop in exchange for a share of the sales price in the event the work is sold.

bailors and bailees Persons who store their property with another are called "bailors". Those with whom the property is stored are called "bailees". Related terms: *bailments*.

beneficiaries of a contract Those who benefit from a contract made between two or more other parties. In some circumstances the beneficiaries of a contract actually receive some rights under it and may sue to enforce these rights. Related terms: *third party beneficiaries* and *public contracts, beneficiaries of*.

benefit of the bargain The rights or benefits that each party to a contract reasonably expects to receive under it. To the extent that a party does not receive the benefit of his or her bargain, it is sometimes possible for that party to escape performing duties specified in the contract. (i.e., back out of the contract). Related terms: *remedies for breach of contract*.

best efforts See *exclusive dealing contracts*.

bids (at an auction) Offering property for bid at an auction constitutes inviting the public to make an offer to form a contract. A contract between the auctioneer and the winning bidder is not actually formed (i.e., the bidder's offer is not accepted) until the gavel comes down or some other indication is made that the bid has been accepted.

bilateral contracts Contracts under which, during at least one moment in time, each party has a reciprocal obligation to perform an act, as opposed to *unilateral contracts*, in which only a single party is obligated to perform at any one time. Related terms: *unilateral vs. bilateral contracts*.

blue pencil doctrine Where courts will enforce part of a contract and invalidate (blue pencil) the rest. This is generally done because one or more provisions (the blue pencilled ones) are *unconscionable* (extremely unfair), illegal, or generally

against public policy. Many contracts contain specific provisions saying that if one or more clauses of the contract are found to be invalid, the rest of the contract is still enforceable. Related terms: *unconscionable contracts and terms*.

boilerplate clauses Contract clauses that are standard throughout the business or industry, and that are accordingly included in most contracts and not subject to much (if any) negotiation. For example, most contracts have clauses that a) require all *assignments* or consents to be in writing, b) provide how the parties to the contract must give notice to one another in case of a dispute, c) specify which state's law should govern in case a dispute arises, and d) provide for arbitration or mediation in case a dispute arises under the contract.

box-top license See *shrink-wrapped license*.

breach of contract The substantial failure to perform obligations required under a valid unilateral or bilateral contract. When a party breaches a contract, the other side is entitled to go to court (or arbitration if that is provided for in the contract) to recover damages suffered as a result. The phrase "breach of contract" covers a full spectrum of misbehavior and non-behavior. At one end is a total failure to perform. On the other are inconsequential deviations from minor contract terms. Accordingly, the important distinction in contract law is between "material breaches" (or major breaches) and "immaterial breaches" (or minor breaches). If a breach of contract is deemed to be material, the innocent party has a right not only to sue for damages, but also to suspend his or her own performance under the contract. If a contractual breach is less important, the innocent party still has a right to sue for damages, but must continue to perform his or her part of the bargain (called *counter-performance*) . If the breach is a minor or technical one causing no real harm, it will be treated as an immaterial breach, and the contract will be unaffected.

There are no hard and fast rules for distinguishing minor from major contract breaches. For example, a slightly late payment will normally be classified as minor, and thus be found not to excuse counter-performance. However, if the person making the late payment knows that the other party has a cash flow problem, or if the agreement specifies that *time is of the essence* when it comes to payment or performance, the late payment or performance might constitute a material breach. Late performance of a *personal services contract* (e.g., delivery of photographs to a magazine) or late delivery of goods that were to have been received for a specific occasion, such as an important trade show or a gallery opening, are also examples of situations where a major or material breach may have occurred.

In deciding this question, the court will generally ask whether the breach impairs the value of the contract as a whole under all of the surrounding circumstances. If so, the breach will be held to be material. Related terms: *defenses to breach of contract based on lack of contract formation* and *excuses for breach of valid contract*.

breach of duty of good faith and fair dealing The refusal by an insurance company to operate in good faith when denying an insurance claim or refusing to defend an insured against the claim of another. In an increasing number of states, every insurance contract is considered to contain a provision (called an *implied in law* provision) requiring the insurance company to exercise good faith in dealing with its insured and with third party claimants against the insured. If the insurer fails to deal in good faith, this provision is considered to be violated. Such violation is generally considered to be a tort (personal injury), which means the victim of the insurance company's breach can sue for *punitive damages*.

The courts in some states imply "good faith" provisions into other types of contracts (e.g., employment contracts and trust arrangements), where the purpose of the contract is to provide for a person's security and sense of well-being rather than for his or her commercial gain. Although common commercial contracts are not generally considered to contain an implied "good faith" provision, one state (California) considers all contracts to have an implied provision that the existence of the contract will not be denied in bad faith. In the event that such a denial

occurs, punitive damages for the breach of the implied contract term will be allowed. Related terms: *punitive damages in contract actions* .

breaching contracts in advance See *anticipatory breach or repudiation of contracts*.

breaking a promise Many contracts (called *bilateral contracts*) involve an exchange of promises (e.g., I promise to deliver you ten microprocessors and you promise to pay me $500.00 apiece for them). Other contracts (called *unilateral* contracts) only involve one promise (e.g., I promise to pay you $500.00 dollars if you write a publishable article on current developments in biotechnology). In either case, breaking such a promise can amount to a breach of contract, depending on the circumstances. Further, even if a promise is not contractually binding, if the other party justifiably relies on it and changes his or her economic position accordingly, the promise may be enforced under the doctrine of *promissory estoppel* Related terms: *breach of contract* and *unilateral and bilateral contracts*.

breaking contracts in advance See *anticipatory breach or repudiation of contract*.

changing existing agreements See *modifying xisting agreements*.

children and contracts Generally, children (another word for minors) are not allowed to enter into binding contracts. However, there are some exceptions to this, such as when the minor is emancipated under the law (e.g., married, a member of the armed services, living independently) or agrees to purchase certain personal necessities. Also, after a child legally becomes an adult, a contract he or she made while still a minor will be valid if the new adult recognizes it as such, carries out his obligations in a way that clearly indicates the contract is being adhered to, or continues to reap the benefits of the contract. For example, if a minor agrees to sell his rights in a computer game program to a software publisher in exchange for royalties, and after turning eighteen continues to receive the royalties, the contract will be treated as valid.

Contract and Warranty

Even though minors cannot enter into binding contracts it is common in the entertainment and fashion industries for minors to contract through their parents. Related terms: *defenses to breach of contract based on lack of contract formation* and *void and voidable contracts*.

collective bargaining agreements A contract between a labor union and an employer, setting forth the terms and conditions of employment. These contracts are negotiated by the union on behalf of the represented employees, and are thus referred to as "collective bargaining agreements" (i.e., the union bargains for all the represented employees at one time). Often a collective bargaining agreement will involve many employers and various local unions. These are called "multi-employer agreements". Since the 1930s, the process by which collective bargaining occurs has been heavily regulated by such federal laws as the National Labor Relations Act, the Taft-Hartley Act, and the Landrum-Griffin Act.

Collective bargaining agreements are extremely important to the world of the performing arts. For example, musicians' and actors' unions typically enter into multi-employer collective bargaining agreements for minimum union rates that can be paid to a performing artist or actor. Then, each artist is free to negotiate his or her own performing rate, as long as it is above the minimum.

competing works clause A standard publishing contract clause, prohibiting the author from creating new works, without the publisher's permission, that might impair sales of the work the author has already sold to the publisher. As these clauses can be interpreted quite broadly to prohibit the author from publishing anything else in the same field as the original work, they can seriously impair an author's ability to make a living. For this reason, many authors attempt to make the competing work clause of a publishing contract as narrow and specific as possible.

Example: Vanae Jermany, an expert steel drummer, contracts with a publisher to write a beginner's manual on steel drum playing. If the contract's competing works clause says that Vanae may not "create any new work that might impair sales of the work", Vanae might be pre-

vented from writing an intermediate, advanced, historical, or "how-to-make" book about steel drums. Accordingly, Vanae would be well advised to try negotiating a clause that would only prohibit her from publishing any new work that instructed beginners on how to play the steel drums.

compulsory license A license granted by a property owner because the law requires it. Generally, a *license* constitutes voluntary permission granted by a property owner (including an owner of *intellectual property*) for someone else to use the property under terms specified in the license. For example, in exchange for royalties or a fixed fee, a *patent owner* 4 might grant a manufacturer a license to develop and sell an *invention* 4 over a ten year period, in Canada. Or, a *copyright owner* 2 might grant a publisher a license (in exchange for some form of compensation) for exclusive distribution rights, for the work covered by the copyright, in a certain country or in a certain language.

In some situations, however, the law requires that certain types of licenses be granted, for either a reasonable compensation or a fee established by law. For example, Canadian law requires any drug company doing business in Canada to grant a compulsory license to a Canadian agency to market drugs in Canada on a generic (non-brand name) basis. This means that Canadian citizens get drugs at a fraction of what is paid in the U.S., and in many other countries. And in the U.S., composers of music may, under some circumstances, be required to grant compulsory licenses to parties wishing to record their songs.

compulsory license of copyright See this listing in Section 2.

conciliation and mediation Conciliation (often termed mediation) is a dispute resolution system designed to help the disputants arrive at their own compromise solutions. It is essentially the opposite way of settling disputes from the adversary system. Conciliation (mediation) expects the best result to be obtained from the parties trying to find common grounds for compromise with the help of the conciliator or mediator. The adversary system, on the other hand, has two or more parties argue in court in order to bring out the truth.

Because the conciliator (mediator) has no power to render a judgment (i.e., he or she cannot make decisions that bind the parties), the atmosphere tends to be more cooperative than it could ever be in a process where a decision-maker needs to be convinced of the rightness or wrongness of a party's case. A conciliation (mediation) approach is often used to try to settle child custody and visitation disputes, and is increasingly being tried in areas such as business and labor, where the parties have a need or desire to deal with each other on a continuous basis in the future.

Example: A west coast major league basketball team copies part of the year-book produced by an Eastern publisher for an east coast team. Instead of suing for copyright infringement, the Eastern publisher might enter into formal or informal mediation with the west coast team in an effort to settle the dispute in an mutually satisfactory fashion. The result might be that the west coast team is allowed to use the current yearbook without cost or penalty, and the Eastern publisher is hired to produce future year-books.

conditions precedent Contracts usually involve promises that are conditioned upon the occurrence of certain events. For example, a promise by a television station to pay an independent producer for a film is made on the condition that the film be made and delivered to the pub-lisher. The event that must occur for the promise to become binding is usually termed a "condition precedent", i.e., the promise will only be honored if the con-dition is met first.

confidentiality agreements See this listing under section 1.

confidential employment relationship See this listing under section 1.

consequential damages Unusual losses, such as lost profits or personal injuries, that result from a breach of contract. Related terms: *remedies for breach of contract*.

consideration The legal term for the value or quid pro quo that each party to a contract is supposed to receive from the other party in exchange for entering into the contract. Unless a contract provides some consideration for each party, the law will not usually recognize it as bind-ing.

Example: If Sellit Advertising Agency agrees to promote Genius Software in exchange for royalties per item sold, the consideration received by Sellit is the royalties, while the consideration Genius receives is the promotion of its goods. If mutual consideration exists, an agreement can be enforced by both parties, (assum-ing other requirements for a contract have been satisfied). If, however, Sellit prom-ises to promote the software without receiving anything in return, Genius probably could not force Sellit to keep its promise, since there was no consideration on Sellit's side.

There are a few notable exceptions to the rule that unless each party to a con-tract receives something (consideration) from the other, there is no legally enforceable contract. Related terms: *prom-issory estoppel* and *detrimental reliance*.

Consideration may consist of money, goods, acts, other benefits, or promises to deliver any of these things. Regardless of the particular type of contract involved, however, an act or promise must always possess the following qualities in order to constitute consideration. First, it must represent some type of benefit (actual or theoretical) to the person receiving it, and a detriment to the person giving it. Sec-ond, the consideration must be bargained for, that is, offered in exchange for the consideration being tendered by the other party. Contracts that lack "bargained-for consideration" are not contracts but rather only a pair of promises.

Example: Igor and Eugeny, the CEOs of two competing robot manufacturers, are having cocktails together after a busy day at an internationally attended elec-tronics show. In a rush of good feeling, and truly believing that Eugeny's com-pany is far behind his in technology, Igor promises to provide Eugeny with advance information about an expected robotics breakthrough. Eugeny responds that his programmers have been working double time on a new vision system, and that he will "open his shop" to Igor as soon as the project shows signs of success. On

Contract and Warranty

the face of it, this might appear to be a contract, since Igor and Eugeny seem to have exchanged promises to give each other a benefit. But on closer inspection, we can see that neither promise was conditioned on the other, and neither was induced by the other (motivation is not the same thing as inducement). They are merely two independent promises to provide reciprocal benefits, and even taking the promises together, there is no contract.

Consideration must be legally adequate, as well as "bargained for". This does not mean that the benefits to each contracting party must be equal. Indeed, the core of commercial activity is making deals involving unequal consideration. Rather, "adequate consideration" only means that some consideration must be present that the law recognizes as such. The law does not regard a clearly nominal payment as "adequate consideration". Your promise to give me your immaculate 1955 T-Bird in exchange for my promise to pay you $1.00 does not qualify as a contract. Whether a payment is nominal or not is determined on a case by case basis.

The law also refuses to recognize "past consideration" as adequate consideration. Past consideration is when the benefit to be conferred has already been conferred. For example, suppose Wilma Mullins, an elderly inventor, promises to leave her entire fortune to her assistant, Electra, "in exchange for your inspired help these past 20 years". No enforceable contract has been created by this promise. Why not? Electra has already provided the benefits, and Wilma's promise was thus not induced by Electra's loyalty. If, however, Wilma made the same promise in exchange for Electra's promise to provide up to twenty future years of such help, the promise would be an enforceable contract.

A variant of the "past consideration" rule is the pre-existing duty rule. If a party to a contract already has a duty to perform some act, again promising to perform it does not represent a benefit to the other party and cannot therefore constitute adequate consideration for a modification of the existing contract or for a second contract.

Example: Tom Quincy is a vice-president of NewBooks, a large publishing house. By virtue of his position, Tom has an *implied obligation of confidentiality* 1

not to disclose company *trade secrets* 1. One day, Tom is offered a new job by a competing company and decides to leave NewBooks. Recognizing that Tom "knows too much", NewBooks enters into a severance agreement with Tom under which NewBooks agrees to pay Tom $5,000 in exchange for Tom's promise not to disclose or use any of the NewBooks trade secrets in his new employment. Tom cannot enforce this agreement if NewBooks decides not to honor it, since Tom's agreement conferred no new benefit on NewBooks (due to Tom's pre-existing duty not to disclose the trade secrets).

The pre-existing duty rule commonly applies to situations where parties to an existing contract agree to modify it. Unless the modification involves an additional benefit for both parties, it probably won't be valid.

Example: The famous Australian rock band "Kangaroo" signs a contract with Illusion, a California recording company, to cut an album. The deal involves a $500,000.00 advance and royalties, in exchange for assignment by Kangaroo to Illusion of *all rights* 2 to the music and album. After the advance is paid and half the songs are recorded, Kangaroo decides it wants a 50% increase in its royalties. Not wanting to fall behind in its production schedule, Illusion agrees to the new terms, and the original contract is modified to reflect them. Such modification might not be valid, since no new benefit was conferred on Illusion. However, if Kangaroo promised to record two additional songs, or complete the existing work in a shorter time, adequate consideration to qualify the new agreement as a binding contract would exist. Related terms: *pre-existing duty* and *novation*.

Questions regarding consideration lie at the heart of contract law. Whenever a party wishes to escape from an agreement, consideration, or the lack thereof, becomes an issue. Related terms: *formation of contracts*.

consignment contracts Contracts between artists and galleries, under which art works are placed with (consigned to) the gallery for sale under certain conditions, specified in the contract. These might include the minimum sales price, the percentage of the sale price to be retained by the gallery, responsibility for any damage to the art work, financial responsibility for catalogues and advertising, and so on. In essence, a consignment contract is a type of **bailment** arrangement peculiar to artists and artisans.

continuing offer An offer by one party to fill all orders that the other party places for a particular product or service over a specific period of time. For example, Superchip Semiconductors might offer to fill any orders for its production model microprocessor chip at a set price that HighTech Computers will place over a six month period. Every time HighTech places an order, a valid contract will be created for the amount of the order.

Continuing offers are different from **requirements contracts** . The former can be terminated by their makers at any time between orders, whereas the latter are definite contracts to meet one party's needs over the period of time established in the contract, and cannot be terminated. Related terms: **requirements contract** and **options**.

contract A valid agreement between two or more parties that is enforceable in court. Related terms: **formation of contract** and **contract law**.

contract date clause A provision in virtually all contracts stating when the contract becomes effective. This may be at the time of signing or at some later time specified in the contract.

contract law The statutes and court decisions governing when agreements are enforceable, how a party can get out of them, and what happens if they are broken without adequate excuse. Modern contract law has been developing for about five hundred years, and has become quite complex. Yet the basic questions addressed by contract law are surprisingly few. They are: what actually constitutes a valid and enforceable contract?

- when are parties to a contract justified in not performing their duties under it? what types of relief can the victim of a contract breach obtain?
- under what circumstances can a person injured by a broken but non-contractual promise obtain relief?

- when does fairness require a court to intervene so that the original intent of the contracting parties can best be put into effect?
- in which forums (court, arbitrator, mediator, etc) does a party who has suffered from a contract breach have recourse?

these primary contractual concerns can be broken down into a number of secondary issues. First, in addressing whether a valid contract has been formed, the courts will ask: whether a valid **offer** has been made

- whether the offer has been **accepted**
- whether a true exchange between the parties has occurred (i.e., whether **consideration** and **mutuality of obligation** are present)
- whether the **consideration** is "adequate" and has been "bargained for", and
- whether the agreement constitutes a **meeting of the minds** (i.e., an absence of fraud or mistake on the part of both parties, relatively equal bargaining positions, and the presence of mental competency)

Related terms: **defenses to breach of contract based on lack of contract formation**.

In determining whether a party is entitled not to perform his or her end of an agreement, the court or arbitrator will look to such factors as whether the reason for the contract has ceased to exist, whether performance would involve an undue hardship, whether performance would cause a law to be broken, or whether performance has become factually impossible. Related terms: **excuses for breach of contract**.

If there are no sufficient excuses for the contract breach, the court will then decide whether the contract should be **specifically enforced** or whether the victim should instead be awarded certain types of damages for her resulting loss. This topic is generally referred to as **remedies**. Related terms: **remedies for breach of contract**.

Finally, if the technical requirements for a contract have not been met, or the contract, as written, does not reflect what the parties intended, the court or arbitrator will rely on the rules of **equity** to determine whether:

- the contract should be changed or

Contract and Warranty

reformed to meet the original expectations of the parties, or

- the contract should be cancelled (**rescinded**) and the parties restored to their original positions, or
- a legally non-enforceable promise should be enforced anyway under the doctrine of **promissory estoppel**

For a schematic picture of these general contract law principles see the chart on the next page.

contract provisions prohibiting assignment   See **anti-assignment clauses**.

contract requirements for non-disclosure agreement   See under Trade Secrets section 1.

contradicting the terms of a written contract   See **parol evidence rule**.

conveyance of copyright   See **transfers of copyright ownership** 2.

corporations' ability to contract   The law regards corporations as persons, and accordingly permits them to make contracts under the same rules applicable to individuals. Generally, corporation officers such as the President, Vice President, Secretary and Treasurer are permitted to sign binding contracts on behalf of the corporation. In addition, any number of other corporate employees may be delegated authority to sign all or just certain kinds of contracts.

counter-performance of a contract
One party's performance of his duties under a contract after the other party has performed his or her's. Thus, if Joe Lee performs his end of a film-making contract with Multiple Media by satisfactorily filming a designated sporting event, Multiple Media must "counter-perform" by paying Joe Lee for his work.

covenants   Promises contained in such documents as deeds, employment contracts, sales agreements, and mortgages. This term is also occasionally used as a synonym for any contractual promise. Thus, when Landlord Tim Tausy "covenants" in a lease to maintain the

studio roof, he has made the equivalent of a legally enforceable promise.

covenant not to compete signed by employee   See in Trade secrets Section 1.

covenant not to compete by sold business   See in Trade secrets Section 1.

creditor beneficiaries   See **third party beneficiaries to a contract**.

cross-collateralization clause   A publishing contract clause that permits the publisher to recoup (recover) advances that have been paid an author on one book, out of the royalties earned by the author on a succeeding book.

Example: Paula Prolific writes childrens books. On her first book, Paula's publisher gives her a $10,000.00 advance. The book doesn't sell well, and a year later the publisher has only recouped $3,000.00 of the advance. If Paula writes a later book that is covered by a contract containing a cross-collateralization clause, the publisher will be able to use Paula's royalties on the second book to recoup its advance on the first.

damages   A general word used for the various ways a court can monetarily recompense the winner of a lawsuit for wrongs suffered. Related terms: **remedies for breach of contract**.

date of delivery clause   See **delivery of manuscript or software clause**.

date of publication clause   A publishing contract clause that specifies an estimated date for publication of the work. This clause can provide a benchmark for determining whether the publisher's obligation to publish the work has been met or breached.

death and its effect on contracts   See **excuses for breach of contract** and **formation of contracts (termination of offers)**.

defenses to breach of contract based on lack of contract formation   Over the hundreds of years that contract law has developed (first in England and then

Basic Contract Principles

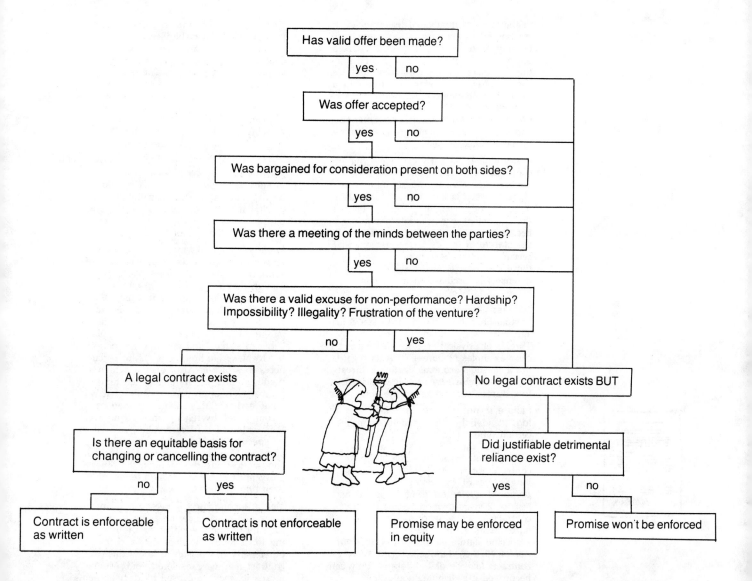

Has valid offer been made?
yes / no

Was offer accepted?
yes / no

Was bargained for consideration present on both sides?
yes / no

Was there a meeting of the minds between the parties?
yes / no

Was there a valid excuse for non-performance? Hardship? Impossibility? Illegality? Frustration of the venture?
no / yes

A legal contract exists

No legal contract exists BUT

Is there an equitable basis for changing or cancelling the contract?
no / yes

Did justifiable detrimental reliance exist?
yes / no

Contract is enforceable as written

Contract is not enforceable as written

Promise may be enforced in equity

Promise won't be enforced

in the U.S.), a number of legally valid reasons for escaping from an otherwise binding contract have developed. A major reason is if no valid contract existed in the first place. This is commonly discussed by experts under such headings as 1) "lack of adequate or bargained-for **consideration**", 2) "lack of a proper **offer**", 3) "lack of a proper **acceptance**" and 4) "void agreements" (e.g., a contract to have someone killed).

Additionally, a party can avoid the consequences of what otherwise may appear to be a valid contract if she can show that she lacked the legal capacity or intent to form a binding contract, or that the agreement was non-enforceable because of a legal technicality, such as the **statute of frauds** (a requirement that certain contracts be in writing). Each of these defenses (termed formation defenses) is discussed in more detail below.

- **Duress:** A party may escape from contractual obligations when his or her initial agreement was wrongfully coerced. Threats of physical or emotional harm are clear examples of duress. Threats regarding a person's economic status or threats to file a lawsuit may or may not constitute duress, depending on the facts.

- **Failure to put contract in writing:** Under the laws of many countries, certain types of contracts must be put in writing. In the U.S., these commonly include contracts for the sale of land, contracts for specific jobs that will take longer than one year to perform, and **personal service contracts** expected to last for 2 years or more. Some types of contracts, such as **work made for hire agreements** 2, must be in writing under a specific statute (such as the **Copyright Act of 1976** 2). However, many types of contracts may be oral as long as they can be proved if a dispute should arise. Related terms: **statute of frauds**

- **Illegality of contract:** Courts will not enforce a contract to do an illegal act. This prohibition is often expressed in terms of **consideration** , in that illegal consideration is held to be no consideration at all. Thus, a company that agrees to produce counterfeit software for a large sum does not have an enforceable contract since the consideration being offered by that company (pirated software) violates the **Copyright Act of 1976** 2 and is therefore illegal.

Mental incapacity

Contracts often contain one or more provisions that may be illegal. Leases, for example, often contain terms that are contrary to state laws governing landlord-tenant relations. The question commonly arises as to whether an entire contract is invalid because it contains one (or even a few) illegal provisions. The answer depends on the seriousness of the illegality, and the degree to which the illegal clause or clauses were central to the reason for making the contract.

If the primary **consideration** for a promise is illegal, the contract is void. If, on the other hand, the illegality is only incidental to the agreement, the court will normally strike the offending provision and enforce the rest of the contract.

- **Infancy:** Contracts made by minors (generally, those under eighteen years of age) are usually not enforceable, even though they may be valid in all other respects. However, in the **intellectual property** context, minors are subject to contracts that have been signed by their parents. In some states, further, people between sixteen and eighteen are permitted to make binding contracts for certain necessities of life. Also, once a person becomes "of age", he or she can ratify (retroactively approve) a contract that was made earlier. Ratification may often be accomplished by relying on the contract (i.e., acting as if it were valid), as well as by specifically affirming it (expressly agreeing to be bound). If the "new adult" chooses to ratify the contract, the other party must honor it. Related terms: **children and contracts**

- **Mental incapacity:** A person agreeing to a contract must have the adequate mental capacity to know what he or she is agreeing to. If he or she does not, and the other party has reason to know this, the contract may be considered void. Mental incapacity may be caused by developmental disabilities or by mental illness. If, after a contract is made, the mentally incapacitated person recovers, he or she may, under some circumstances, retroactively approve (ratify) the contract made earlier.

- **Misrepresentation:** When one party enters into a contract on the basis of a central fact that was misrepresented by the other party, the contract may be avoided by the party deceived by the misrepresentation. Thus, if a weatherman gets a job on T.V. on the basis of his statement that he graduated from M.I.T., and in fact he never went to college, the station could void the employment contract.

- **Mistakes:** Contracts can be avoided if both parties were mistaken about some fact critical to the agreement. Suppose that Peter Haliburton contracts to buy Lori Little's highly successful breakfast shop, largely because of its well known *servicemark* ③ "Lori's Porridge". However, it develops that this servicemark actually is owned by someone else and cannot either be sold by Lori or used by others. Because of this "mutual mistake", either party may back out of the contract. However, a mistake by one party that is really an error in business judgment does not allow that party to avoid a contract. Thus, an agreement to buy "Lori's Porridge" in the belief that its value will go up, cannot be avoided if the value goes down instead.

  If a mistake is made while reducing a contract to written form, the contract will usually be honored but the court will order the writing changed (**reformed**) to reflect the original intentions of the parties.

- **Unconscionability:** Contract law operates under the fiction that contracts result from two relatively equal parties each bargaining for some benefit until there is a true meeting of their minds. Although this may be true in some situations, it is not in many others (e.g., student loans, employment contracts, model releases, etc.). In some situations, these one-sided contracts (termed **adhesion contracts**) deviate so much from the contracting "ideal" of equality that the courts will find them too unfair to be enforced (i.e., unconscionable), and permit a party to back out when necessary to avoid hardship or injustice. Related terms: **unconscionable contracts and contract terms**

- **Undue influence:** A contract may be avoided if an agreement was obtained by means of undue influence, by a person who is close to the promisor and who herself stands to benefit. Thus, the relationship between a husband-manager and his performer-wife, who has no business experience, is one situation where undue influence might arise.

defenses for breach of contract lawsuits
Here are three legally valid reasons for failing to perform obligations under a contract:

- no legal contract was ever formed (e.g., no **offer** or **acceptance**)
- the contract lacks adequate or bargained for consideration, and
- events arising after the formation of the contract warrant the obligations not being enforced.

  Related terms: **defenses to breach of contract based on lack of contract formation** and **excuses for breach of contract**

delegation of duties
An agreement under which one party's obligations to perform duties under a contract are transferred to another. Unless the duties owed under a contract are personal in nature, such as a promise to write an article, program a computer or compose a soundtrack for a movie, they may usually be handed over (delegated) to someone else to perform. Thus, a housepainter might delegate her duty to paint a house to another housepainter of similar skill and reputation. As long as the new painter does the job correctly, all will be well. However, the person delegating duties under a contract usually remains responsible if the contract is breached by the person to whom the delegation was made.

Delegation of duties under a contract is different from another contractual arrangment called a **novation**, in which the original parties to a contract agree that a new person will step into the shoes of one of the parties for all purposes, including being solely responsible if there should be a contract breach. Related terms: **novation** and **settling contractual disputes without going to court**.

delivery of manuscript or software clause
A common clause in publishing and software contracts that sets the time by which the author or programmer must deliver a work to the publisher. In many cases the "delivery of manuscript" clause will also provide that the publisher has the right to terminate the contract and demand repayment of any advance royalties paid, in the event the author or programmer fails to comply with the the specified deadline. Related terms: **time is of the essence**.

Undue influence

Contract and Warranty

designated beneficiaries Persons who are expressly mentioned by the owner of an insurance policy as being entitled to receive the policy's benefits in the event of payment.

detrimental reliance Situations where one party justifiably changes his or her position in reliance on another party's offer or promise to contract, and would actually suffer economic detriment if the offer were taken back, or the promise withdrawn, before it became legally binding.

Example: XRC Robotics offers to pay Celestial Electronics $50,000.00 in the event Celestial develops adequate diagnostic and repair procedures for robots sold by XRC. Celestial foregoes other contracts, and has already sunk $10,000 and hundreds of research hours into the project, when XRC notifies it that XRC has decided to develop the procedures in-house. Although XRC is not contractually required to pay Celestial until Celestial has actually developed the procedures, because Celestial has foregone other business and "changed its position" in reliance on the XRC offer, a court will probably require XRC to let Celestial finish the job. Related terms: *promissory estoppel* and *unilateral and bilateral contracts*.

donee beneficiary See *third party beneficiaries to a contract*.

duress in formation of a contract See *defenses to breach of contract based on lack of contract formation*.

duties and rights Each of us has numerous restraints on our behavior and obligations towards others, automatically imposed on us by our legal system. Sometimes these restraints and obligations (collectively called duties) come from court decisons, other times from statutes and regulations, and in still other instances from binding written agreements (contracts). Whatever the source, if we violate or breach any of these duties, we may end up being held accountable (liable) to anyone injured, in any way, as a result.

Sometimes the duty creating our liability arises from the area of the law known as *tort* (personal injuries and wrongs). Other times, it is said to derive from

contracting principles. Either way, these are only labels placed on types of duties and do not change the fundamental fact that our accountability arises from the breach of a duty owed to another.

When the word "right" is used (e.g., "I have a right to be free from the invasion of privacy by others"), we usually mean that someone else has a duty to behave toward us in a certain way. For example, we have a right to a good reputation (if we desire it), and our neighbors have a duty not to tell lies about us. This duty is imposed on them by state statutes and court decisions defining "defamation" (e.g., libel and slander). Similarly, if an author has a right to receive royalties on time under a contract with a publisher, the publisher has a duty, under common law (court developed) contract principles, to pay them. Or to take one more example, I have a right to work where I choose without regard to my race, which means potential employers have a duty to consider me fairly under the Civil Rights laws. In short, rights and duties are two sides of the same coin.

When any type of action is filed in court, the primary determination that must be made is whether a right has been violated, or a duty breached. If so, the law usually provides the courts with several ways to recompense the injured party.

To decide this fundamental question, the courts examine relevant statutes, regulations, and opinions from previous court decisions, to see whether a right or duty has been recognized to exist under similar circumstances. If so, and the court goes on to find that one party has breached the duty or violated the right so as to cause personal injury or economic harm to another party, the damaged party may obtain some relief, depending on which court recognized the existence of the right or duty, and whether a relevant statute or regulation allows such a recovery. If, on the other hand, the court determines that no previous recognition of a duty or right has been made, recovery will usually be denied, no matter how dreadful the behavior of the defendant.

Because changing times require new legal approaches to both new and old problems, courts and legislatures may create new duties and rights, from time to time. When it's a court that strikes out on its own (especially the U.S. Supreme

Court and the top state courts), such "law reform" decisions often have a ripple effect, and the new right or duty is recognized as legally binding precedent by other courts. Similarly, when Congress or a state legislature decides to create a new right or duty through the statutory process, other legislatures tend to do likewise.

duty of trust   See section 1.

duty to mitigate damages   When an innocent party in a breach of contract situation attempts to collect damages for the breach, the court will inquire whether such injured party attempted to minimize the harm caused by the other party's breach. For example, if the Computer Boutique breaks a promise to deliver a computer to CBY video at a certain time, CBY cannot simply sit around for a year, calculate the damages to its business from not having the computer, and then sue. Instead, when it appears reasonably certain that the contract has been broken, other sensible arrangements, such as buying another computer, must be made. Computer Boutique can be sued for damages suffered in the interim. In other words, under rules designed to limit or lessen damages (the mitigation of damages rule), the non-breaching party cannot recover any damages that could have been avoided by reasonable effort without undue risk, expense, or humiliation. Related terms: *remedies for breach of contract*.

editorial control clause   A standard publishing contract clause, allocating final responsibility for what appears on the printed page. This clause usually gives the editor the final say, although authors commonly can retain control over the general sense and content of their works, and sometimes bargain for and get the right of final approval over what is printed.

enforcement of contracts   The legal methods by which persons or businesses can be required to perform their contractual duties. The most common of these is an action for *breach of contract*. Here, the party who breaks a contract is required to pay the other party for certain types of resulting injuries. In other types of cases, contracts can be enforced according to their terms. This is called **specific performance**. In still other situations, the actual words of a contract will be changed to fit the original intentions of the parties. This is called **reformation**. See *remedies for breach of contract*.

escalation clause   A common publishing and software development contract clause that increases the rate of royalty payable to the author in the event that sales exceed a certain specified level. For example, if Tim contracts with Flora Publishers to write a book on growing orchids in cold climates, the contract might contain an escalation clause providing that Tim would receive a 7% royalty for the first 10,000 copies sold, and a 9% royalty for the next 10,000 sold, and 10% royalty for all copies sold above 20,000.

equity   A set of principles used by the courts to resolve disputes and grant relief either in 1) situations that are not covered by regular legal principles, or 2) in situations where an injustice or unfairness would result if regular legal principles were applied.

As a general matter, remedies for contract-related disputes are divided into three classifications: legal remedies, equitable remedies, and arbitration. Legal remedies tend to only involve money damages, whereas equitable remedies can involve judicial orders requiring action or inaction of a party in addition to the payment of money. Over the years, **equity courts** have developed a number of additional remedies, to be employed under general guidelines tailored to achieve a just result under any circumstances. Equity rules traditionally operate where the damage being caused cannot be remedied by the award of traditional legal remedies (i.e., the payment of money). While the original idea of equity was to have more flexibility to do justice in a particular situation, most courts now adhere so closely to the equity guidelines (termed "rules of equity") that they too often fail to "do justice", in much the same way that the legal system's failure to do justice made it necessary to create the rules of equity in the first place.

Contract and Warranty

The most commonly encountered equitable remedies are *injunctive relief* (requiring a party to act or refrain from acting), *restitution* (requiring the return of property to its rightful owner), *reformation* (rewriting a contract to reflect the actual intentions of the parties when the contract was made), *specific performance* (ordering a contract to be performed where damages would not compensate for the breach), *laches* (preventing a party from benefiting as a result of his or her unreasonable delay in taking a matter to court), "equitable *estoppel*" (preventing one party from unfairly benefiting from another party's reasonable reliance on that party's words or actions) and *recission of a contract* (allowing a contract to be set aside, and restoring the parties to their positions prior to the agreement).

estoppel   Under certain circumstances, the law does not allow a party to raise an issue or prove a fact in a trial when it would result in unfairness to the other side. The rule that operates to prevent the issue or fact from being raised is called "estoppel".   Example: A performer is hired by a studio to appear in a film with the knowledge that he doesn't have a proper union card, and the studio later has to lay him off because of union objections. Equitable rules may prevent the studio (i.e., "estop" it) from raising the lack of the union card as a defense to a suit by the performer for payment, since such a defense would be unfair under the circumstances. On the other hand, had the studio not known about the lack of union membership, then this could possibly be raised as a defense, since the studio is entitled to assume that performers are in good standing with their union. Related terms: *promissory estoppel*.

exclusive agency contract   See *exclusive dealing contract* and *literary agencies*.

exclusive dealing contract   A contract in which one party gains the exclusive right to promote the services or goods of another. These are also sometimes referred to as "exclusive agency agreements". Actors, artists, musicians, writers, software programmers, and athletes commonly sign these contracts.

In many exclusive dealing contracts, the agent is not committed to the perfor-

mance of any specific duty. Because valid contracts require a *mutuality of obligation*, the courts tend to interpret these exclusive dealing contracts as containing an *implied promise* by the agent to exercise his or her "best efforts" to promote the goods or service in question.

exclusive and non-exclusive licenses   Licenses are *contracts* under which the owner of a *patent* 4, *copyright* 2, *trademark* 3, *trade secret* 1, or other type of property permits another party to use the property for a specific period of time, under specific conditions. Licenses are especially important in the *intellectual property* world, where much of the value of the property is often realized by licensing others to use it.

Licenses can either be exclusive or non-exclusive. An exclusive license gives the license owner (licensee) the exclusive authority to exercise the right being granted in the license. Then, if any other company attempts to exercise this right, the owner of the exclusive license can obtain protection and relief in court. A non-exclusive license, on the other hand, means that permission is being given to exercise the right specified in the license, but on a non-exclusive and shared basis.

Example: Supersell Software Company licenses the FXY and PCT corporations to use the same software in the same geographical area at the same time. These are non-exclusive licenses. If, on the other hand, FXY acquires the sole right to use the software east of the Mississippi while PCT has the sole right to use it West of the Missisippi, each has an exclusive license based on geography (often termed "exclusive territorial licenses"). Similarly, if FXY has the sole right to the software between 1986 and 1988 while PCT has the sole right to its use between 1988 and 1990, each has an exclusive license based on time ("temporal license").

exculpatory clause   A clause in a contract that exempts or releases one party from legal responsiblity to the other for certain types of conduct that that party might otherise have been responsible for. For example, contracts involving the sale and installation of business computers often contain a clause excusing or "exculpating" the seller from liability to the buyer for any damages caused to the buyer or his customers resulting from a computer malfunction. Depending on the circumstances, the courts will sometimes refuse to enforce such clauses, especially when one party is trying to escape liability for an intentional wrong or some responsibility specifically required by law, or when the clause is found by the court to be an **adhesion contract** (i.e., the unequal bargaining position of the parties prevented true negotiation from occurring).

executor-administrator provision See *statute of frauds*.

excuses for breach of valid contract
..legally recognized reasons why a party need not perform otherwise valid contractual obligations. When a party wishes to escape from a contract, there are several common ways to do so. One is to argue that a valid contract was never formed. Related terms: *defenses to breach of contract based on lack of contract formation*.

Another approach is to argue that events subsequent to the formation of the contract have made performance of the obligations impossible, impractical, or extremely unfair. These post-formation defenses are grouped under the categories of "impossibility", "commercial impracticability", and "frustration of the venture".

- **Impossibility:** The "impossibility" defense arises when performance under a contract is literally impossible. Thus, if the contract is for personal services (e.g., an in-house computer programmer), death of the person who was to perform the service renders the contract "impossible" to perform. In such a case, the deceased's estate would not be liable for a breach of contract action. Similarly, serious illness will excuse contracts in some situations (e.g., if a portrait painter becomes severely arthritic). In this same line, if the essential subject matter of a sales contract is accidentally destroyed, the contract will not be enforceable. For example, if SpaceDesign Inc. agrees to license certain **tradesecrets** 1 to NewAir Enterprises, and the tradesecrets are accidently disclosed to the public before the deal goes through, NewAir is released from its obligation under the license agreement. Finally, if a new law makes performance of a contract illegal, the contract will be excused unless the law was foreseeable at

the time the parties entered into the contract.

- **Commercial impracticability:** The "commercial impracticability" defense (only operative in some states) allows a party to escape from a contract if subsequent events make performance just too impracticable from a commercial standpoint, even though performance is not completely impossible as such. For example, the substantial destruction of its main laboratory by a tornado might release a biotechnology firm from its contractual obligation to deliver a new type of hormone. In states not recognizing this doctrine, on the other hand, the lab would still be held responsible for performance, and would either have to buy the item from other sources, if this were possible, or pay for any economic injury suffered by the buyer.

- **Frustration of the venture:** This may be held to occur if subsequent events make a contract useless to one of the parties, and if both parties assumed when they made the contract that such use was an important part of it. For instance, if Sally leases some space from Jeb for the expressed purpose of showing video movies to the public on site, and if Congress later passes a statute making such operations a copyright violation, Sally may be released from her obligation, since the original reason for her agreement has been extinguished.

executed contract A contract that has been fully performed by both parties.

executory contract A contract that has yet to be fully performed. For instance, if James promises to install a furnace in Grace's house, and Grace offers to pay James a set amount for this service, the contract is "executory" until James installs and Grace pays.

A contract may be "wholly executory" (i.e., neither side has performed, as in the example) or "partially executory" (i.e., one side has performed, but the other has not. If, for example, James has installed the furnace, but Grace has not yet paid, their contract would be considered partially executory.

Whether a contract is wholly or partially executory can make a difference in the available court remedies in the event a contractual breach occurs. Thus, if the

Contract and Warranty

contract is wholly executory, the court might order such relief as restores the parties to their original positions before the contract was made. If, on the other hand, a contract is partially executory, the court might order the non-performing party to complete his or her side of the bargain. Related terms: *remedies for breach of contract* .

expectation damages See *remedies for breach of contract* .

express and implied contracts Binding agreements primarily based on the actual expressions of the parties, whether oral or in writing, are termed "express contracts". The clauses containing these expressions are termed "express provisions". Examples of express contracts are: *leases* , sales agreements, *intellectual property licenses*, *literary agency* contracts, *publishing contracts*, *artist-manager* contracts and employment contracts.

Sometimes a contract may be arrived at by virtue of the conduct of the parties rather than by words. These are "implied-in-fact contracts". For example, if you consult a tax accountant, you are obligated to pay for his or her services, even though no mention is made of payment until you are leaving. Why? Because your agreement to pay is implied from the circumstances of the accountant-client relationship.

While most implied contracts are "implied-in-fact" (i.e., implied to actually exist, even though the parties never expressly talked about it), some are implied because the law says they should be. These are called "implied-in-law". Here, there really is no contract as such. Rather, the law imposes a duty on a party because of the surrounding circumstances. Sometimes this duty is imposed to prevent one party from experiencing *unjust enrichment*.

Example: Todd suffers a heart attack at the theatre, and a doctor in the audience administers first aid and follow-up treatment, all while Todd is unconscious. The law implied a contract between Todd and the doctor, and, accordingly, will permit the doctor to recover for his services. Otherwise, Todd would be unjustly enriched by receipt of the doctor's services. In other situations the law implies a contract because fairness requires it. In many states, every insurance contract is held to contain an implied contractual provision placing a duty on the insurance company to engage in good faith and fair dealing when dealing with the insured or a claimant against the policy. Related terms: *breach of the duty of good faith and fair dealing*.

The body of law governing instances when courts retroactively form contracts, which is basically what happens when courts find an implied-in-law contract to exist, is known as *quasi-contract*. The *quasi-contract* doctrine is a good example of how courts are willing to engage in creative (some say fictional) thinking to reach a fair result under circumstances where existing legal principles would otherwise produce an unacceptable result. When a court does this it exercises its "equitable powers". Related terms: *equity*.

failure to perform a contract See *breach of contract*.

fiduciary duty When a business or personal relationship commonly involves reliance by one party on the other's expertise or leadership, the person with the expertise or power is said to have a duty of trust, or "fiduciary duty", toward the other. The relationship between the two is called a "fiduciary relationship". Attorneys, insurance agents, literary agents, performers' managers, and bankers are examples of persons who have fiduciary relationships with their clients, since the clients rely heavily on their experience and knowledge. Recently, some courts have also recognized such a relationship to exist between a real estate agent and the seller of property.

When one person owes a fiduciary duty to another, his or her actions must always be taken in accord with, and never against, the other person's interest. A fiduciary duty is thus a "higher" or more serious duty than would be the case in the normal, arms-length, commercial relationship.

If a fiduciary duty is breached, the party owing the duty may be held to have inflicted a personal injury (tort) on the other party, and be liable for such types of damages as emotional distress and, in some cases, *punitive damages* .

film (or movie) rights clause A common publishing contract provision included where the book or article to be published has potential value as a film. This clause defines how ny money received from a film company is to be divided between author and publisher.

firm offers See *options*.

first refusal clause See *right of first refusal clause*.

force majeure clause A common contract provision that permits time requirements in a contract to be relaxed when a party has been rendered incapable of meeting them because of external circumstances beyond his or her control. See *time is of the essence* and *excuses for breach of contract*.

formation of contracts For a valid contract to be formed under most circumstances, one party must make an "offer" and another party must "accept" it. In many situations (including most commercial contexts) the acts or statements constituting the offer and acceptance are obvious. Pop's Computer Store calls up TrueLife Peripherals and orders fifty 8″ disk drives for stock. Pop's call is an offer to buy. Assuming that Truelife's response is "Fine, I'll send them out", the offer has been accepted, and a contract has been formed. Pops has promised to pay for the goods at Truelife's standard wholesale price, and Truelife has promised to deliver them at that price within a reasonable time. The terms of the contract (i.e., the price, the time of delivery, when payment is due, etc.) may be written, spoken, or simply understood between the parties from past dealings. If either party fails to deliver on its promise, a breach of contract has occurred.

In many situations, however, it is not clear who is doing the offering and who the accepting. Suppose that Frieda wants to apply for a loan to expand her business. She goes to the bank and fills out an application. The bank processes the application and sends Frieda some paperwork to sign, including a written promise to pay the loan back on certain terms (called a promissory note). Frieda signs the note, sends it back, and then receives a check. Who offered and who accepted? When did this occur? These questions can

become important when one party wants a contract to exist and one party doesn't. If a valid offer and acceptance have not occurred, there may be no contract. Further, if the offering party withdraws the offer before it's accepted, no contract has been formed. The issue here, of course, is whether an acceptance has occurred prior to the offer being withdrawn. The concepts of "offer" and "acceptance" are discussed in more detail below.

- **The offer:** Three elements are required to qualify a communication as a contractual "offer". **First:** it must be communicated to an identifiable person or entity (called an offeree). If you offer to sell your single copy of your database management software to an individual buyer for a certain price, you have made an offer. If, on the other hand, you simply list your desire to sell your copy at the same price on a computer bulletin board you have not made an offer. Why not? Your first offer was capable of being accepted by a definite offeree, whereas your bulletin board listing created the possibility of multiple conflicting acceptances. The listing, therefore, is treated as an invitation for an offer. *Advertisements* and *auctions* are also generally considered to be invitations for offers. **Second:** an offer must indicate an intent on the part of the person making it (the offeror) to enter into a contractual relationship. This does not mean the offeror's private intent, but rather his manifest purpose. Often, courts will ask whether a reasonable person in the position of the offeree would feel that the offeror intended to create a contract. For example, if you drunkenly offered to sell your million dollar business for $100.00 to your "best and only true friend Sal", whom you met in a bar for the first time ten minutes earlier, a court would probably decide that you had not, in fact, made an offer to sell. **Third:** to be valid, an offer must be sufficiently specific about who the parties are, the subject matter of the contract, the price, and the time for performance. However, if only one of these elements is lacking in specificity, the courts will tend to infer what was intended, if possible. Thus, if an otherwise valid contractual offer to sell wholesale merchandise does not specify the time for delivery of the goods, the courts may infer that the offer intended delivery to be "within a commercially reasonable time". Also, where these contract terms

force majeure

Contract and Warranty

can be implied from past dealings, published price and credit schedules, or general principles of the particular trade, they will be. and the contract will be upheld.

- **Termination or revocation of offer:** Once a valid offer is made, it can be taken back (revoked) or invalidated by some intervening event, if this occurs prior to the offer being accepted, except when the offer is "irrevocable". Most offers can be terminated by the death or insanity of the offeror, by the death or destruction of someone or something essential to the contract, by government action subsequently making the proposed contract illegal, by the passage of time, by a direct or indirect revocation of the offer, by a rejection of the offer, or by a counter-offer (which counts as a rejection). Once an offer has been properly terminated or revoked, a subsequent acceptance does not form a contract. For this reason, the timing of acceptance can be crucial. If the original offeror wants out of the contract, he may argue that he revoked the offer in some way before it was accepted.

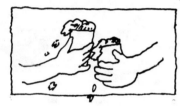

- **The acceptance:** Acceptance of an offer occurs when an act or statement clearly indicates such an intent. The acceptance must usually substantially mirror the specific offer (e.g., I accept your offer to sell your share of the film "Eve's Shoulder" to me for $200,000). An acceptance which varies the material (main) terms of the offer serves as a rejection and counter-offer. If the offer is for the sale of goods in a commercial setting, however, the acceptance can vary from the original offer somewhat without rejecting it. If this happens, the variation is considered a proposal for additional terms, which, if accepted by the offeror, become part of the contract. Related terms *acceptance of a contractual offer*,

frustration of the venture See *excuses for breach of contract*.

geographical licenses See *territorial restrictions and trade secret licenses* 1.

gift promises See *promises to make a gift*.

good will, sale of See *assignemnt of marks* 3.

grant of rights clause A clause found in virtually all publishing and promotion contracts, in which an author, composer, programmer, or artist agrees to transfer some or all of his or her *copyright rights* 2 to the publisher or promoter so that they can adequately produce and market the work. See *bundle of copyright rights* 2 and *copyright* 2.

gratuitous promises See *promises to make a gift*.

guarantors See *sureties*.

hold harmless clause A common contractual provision, under which one party agrees to reimburse the other party (hold him harmless) for any economic harm or liability that might be incurred as a result of the contract being performed.

Example: Ethan Lazarus asks Scandal Press to publish his muckracking book about the Motocross industry and associated culture. If Scandal Press agrees to publish, they might ask Ethan to "hold it harmless" for any liability arising from the publication, due to the possibility that one or more of the persons named in the book may consider portions to be libelous. Related terms: *warranty and indemnification clause*.

illegal contracts and contract terms Agreements that violate the law in some way. See *defenses based on lack of contract formation* and *excuses for breach of contract*.

illusory promises Promises that do not involve the assumption of a duty or the giving up of a right. Illusory promises do not constitute *consideration*, and cannot therefore give rise to enforceable contracts.

Example: Randy Ruler offers to sell Melbourne Paint Co. his patent on a new type of invisible drop cloth for $500,000, and Melbourne Paint promises to buy it *if* they go into the invisible drop cloth supply business. Since Melbourne Paint may never make the requisite decision, they have not given up any right nor undertaken any commitment. Thus, their promise confers no benefit on Randy. Accordingly, since Melbourne's promise is illusory, the agreement lacks *consideration*, and may not be enforced. Related terms: *consideration* and *promissory* estoppel.

immaterial breach of contract See *breach of contract*.

implied contracts Enforceable agreements that arise because certain facts are implied to exist, or because the law implies an agreement to exist, under the specific circumstances. See *express and implied contracts* .

implied duty not to disclose trade secrets See section 1.

implied-in-fact In contract law, a contract or provision that is implied to exist in fact because the context, or the actions of the parties, indicate this to be so. Related terms: *express and implied contracts*.

implied-in-law In contract law, a contract or provision that the law says exists, even though it really doesn't. Related terms: *express and implied contracts*.

impossibility of performance See *excuses for breach of contract*.

impracticability, commercial See *excuses for breach of contract* .

inability to perform contractual obligations See *excuses for breach of contract*.

incidental beneficiaries See *third party beneficiaries to a contract*.

incorporate by reference When a party to a contract wants to include the contents of another document, such as specifications or descriptions of services being offered, in the contract being drafted, but they don't want to retype the entire document, they can incorporate the document into the papers by reference. This is usually done by attaching it to the back of the contract, and referring to it in the contract with language such as, "Said manufacturing specifications are attached hereto as exhibit A, and incorporated by reference as if fully set out herein".

indemnification clause A standard contract provision providing that one party agree to pay another party for certain specified costs that might arise in the course of the contract. Among the types of costs commonly covered by indemnification clauses are those arising from lawsuits and those arising from the failure of a party to perform his or her duties or *warranties* under the contract. Related terms: *warranties and indemnification clause*.

independent contractor An individual or business is an independent contractor, as opposed to being "employed", when he or she 1) provides services under a contract, 2) is only responsible for the final result (as opposed to being accountable for how that final result is reached), 3) is not supervised by the business paying for the services, and 4) uses his or her own tools and expertise in performing the services.

Whether a business qualifies as an independent contractor in respect to the work being performed becomes extremely important 1) when determining liability in the event that an employee working for the independent contractor is injured or injures another, and 2) as far as unemployment compensation, and other tax and benefit rules are concerned. Accordingly, various state and federal agencies have developed detailed criteria as to whether a person or business qualifies as an independent contractor. These involve such questions as 1) whether the "contractor" has his own place of business, his own phone listing, his own tools, more than one "client", when and how payment is made, and who supervises the work. The decision as to whether any given person or business is an independent contractor is decided on a case-by-case basis, under these criteria. Generally, the courts will lean toward considering a person or business an employee, and will place the burden of proof on the party claiming that an independent contractor status exists.

infants A term often used in law to mean any child under the age of majority. Thus, when researching law that involves minors or children in some way, it is often a good idea to look under "infants". There are many laws protecting minors against being commercially exploited. Especially in the entertainment industries, where children are involved, it is common for contracts to cover such items as the hours to be worked, the rate

of pay, the method of payment, the means by which the child will receive an education, and so on. Related terms: **children and contracts** and **defenses to breach of contract based on lack of contract formation**.

injunctive relief Court orders preventing a party to a lawsuit from taking certain actions, or requiring certain actions to be taken. This kind of judicial relief is especially important in **intellectual property** cases, where the primary goal of the plaintiff is usually to prevent others from exercising rights exclusively belonging to the plaintiff under his or her **copyright** 2, **patent** 4, **trademark** 3, or **trade secret** 1. Related terms: **equity**.

installment contracts Contracts calling for one or both parties to perform over a period of time at definite intervals. Loan agreements where one party must repay the other a set amount on a certain date each month are the most common form of installment contracts.

MUTUAL LIFE; THE NEXT BEST THING TO LIFE ITSELF....

insurance contracts Contracts providing that in exchange for the payment of a fee (premium) by an insured, the insurer will pay a specified sum to the insured, or to his **designated beneficiaries**, in case a specified event occurs. Insurance contracts cover such events as death, illness, accidents, theft, loss of income in a personal context, and all sorts of business risks. For example, when publishers advance authors large sums of money for yet-to be-written books, it is common for them to take out insurance policies on the authors' lives.

The amount of the premium, the identity of the insured, the sum to be paid, and the events that will trigger payment are all covered in the insurance contract. Most states have extensive legislation governing which terms are permissible and fair, and which are not. As a result of this legislation, and of the fact that most insurance contracts are written by large national and international companies, insurance contracts are standardized to an extent not usually found in contract law. Unlike general commercial contracts, insurance contracts are often entered into for the purpose of providing a person with economic or emotional security against certain defined risks. Accordingly, insurance companies are often called on

to perform their contractual obligations when the insured or a claimant is in desperate need. Because of this, the law in many states automatically imposes on insurance companies a "duty of good faith and fair dealing", the breach of which may result in large damages against the company in a tort (personal injury) suit. Related terms: **breach of duty of good faith and fair dealing**.

integration of contract terms Jargon for "written down". A "mistake in integration" means a mistake that has occurred in reducing the terms of a contract to writing, and "complete integration" of a contract means that all the provisions agreed to by the parties are written down in the one document.

intellectual property Intellectual property is any product of the human intellect, such as an idea, invention, expression, unique name, business method, industrial process, or chemical formula, which the courts are willing to protect against unauthorized use by others. Intellectual property law is the collection of legal rules, procedures, and remedies that are available to owners of intellectual property for the purpose of obtaining such protection. Generally speaking intellectual property law is divided into categories according to the source of the protection and the type of property protected. Thus:

- **trade secret** 1 law protects trade secrets under the laws of the various states
- **copyright** 2 law protects forms of expression under the **U.S. Copyright Act** 2
- **trademark** 3 law protects labels and symbols that serve to identify commercial products and services, and
- **patent** 4 law protects inventions under the U.S. patent laws

In 1984, Congress created a new category of intellectual property law for the protection of semiconductor chips and the templates used in making them (called chip masks). This has not as yet been dubbed with a label, although the new law (The **Semiconductor Chip Protection Act of 1984** 2) has been placed among the copyright statutes.

intellectual property licenses Agreements by owners of intellectual property (i.e., **patents** 4, **trademarks** 3, **trade**

1, copyrights 2) permitting others to utilize some aspect of the property for commercial purposes. The core idea underlying an intellectual property license is that owners are afforded the exclusive right to use their property for commercial ends. Thus, the **copyright owner 2** has the exclusive right to copy, distribute, display, perform and adapt the work covered by the copyright. Similarly, the **owner of a trademark 3** has the exclusive right to use the trademark. A **patent owner 4** has a seventeen-year monopoly over the development and use of the invention covered by the patent. And finally, the trade secret owner has exclusive use of a trade secret, simply because the information has been kept secret.

In order to exploit their property commercially, intellectual property owners customarily permit (license) others to exercise some aspect of this exclusive right. The scope of these licenses can be as wide as **all rights 2** (e.g., a copyright owner transfers all of her rights to her publisher), and as narrow as transferring the right to use a patented invention or a trade secret in one plant for the manufacture of one particular item. Licenses may be exclusive (the licensee is the only recipient of the right granted in the license) or non-exclusive (the licensee is only one of many recipients of the license, a group which commonly includes anyone who will pay the license fee and adhere to the conditions established in the license contract). Licenses may be granted on a territorial basis (e.g., use of a trademark in one country only) or on a time basis (e.g., exclusive license to distribute record albums for a three year period). Simply put, intellectual property licenses can be as varied as are the needs and desires of the intellectual property owners and their customers.

In more abstract terms, these licenses are contracts in which owners of an intellectual property right permit others to exercise all or some part of those rights under specified conditions. A licensee promises to abide by the terms of the license, and to pay the licensor the sum agreed on for the issuance of the license. If the licensee fails to conform to the terms of the license, the licensor is usually entitled to cancel it. Related terms: **trade secret licenses 1, licenses of copyright rights 2, licensing trademarks 3,** and **licensing patents**4.

intended beneficiary See *third party beneficiaries to a contract*.

international rights clause Commonly found in publishing and in other types of intellectual property contracts, this clause authorizes the publisher (or recording company, manufacturer, promoter, distributor, etc.) to commercially exploit the **trade secret 1, copyright 2, trademark 3,** or **patent 4** on a worldwide basis. This clause may provide for a lump sum payment for such rights, or for royalties to be paid to the original intellectual property owner for each item sold or produced.

invitations to make offers See *formation of contracts*, *bids at auctions*, and *advertisments*.

irrevocable offers Offers which once made cannot be terminated or revoked. Related terms: *options* and *formation of contract*.

kill fees provision A contractual provision commonly found in magazine and other periodical publishing contracts, under which an author is guaranteed a certain percentage of her payment in the event that periodical chooses not to publish (i.e., kills) the article or work.

laches If delay in bringing a lawsuit has caused harm to the defendant, and the delay was unreasonable under the circumstances, the court has authority under the rules of *equity* to bar the suit on the ground of unreasonable delay (termed "laches"). This is a concept similar to barring a case because the *statute of limitations* has expired. However, "laches" is normally utilized where no statute of limitations exists for the particular issue or case, or where it would be unfair to allow the case to be brought to court, even though an existing statute of limitations is not yet up. See *equity*.

late performance of contractual obligations See *breach of contract*, *time is of the essence*, and *delivery of manuscript clause* .

lease A contractual agreement that establishes the terms under which one party, called the lessee, may possess personal property (e.g. a film) or occupy real

Contract and Warranty

estate (e.g. a building) owned by another party, called the lessor. The typical lease contains provisions specifying the time of possession or occupancy, the cost to the lessee in the form of regular payments (rent), the respective *duties and rights* of both the lessee and the lessor, the conditions under which either party can back out of the lease, and the events that will result in a cancellation of the lease. As with other types of contracts, a lease requires an *offer and acceptance, bargained-for consideration*, and a *mutuality of obligation*.

legally binding agreements Any agreement that the courts will enforce as a contract. Related terms: *formation of contracts*.

license See *exclusive and non-exclusive licenses*.

licensing of copyrights See this heading, section 2.

licensing of trade secrets See this heading, section 1.

licensing of marks See this heading, section 3.

liquidated damages A penalty agreed upon in advance in the event of a later breach of contract. These liquidated or "stipulated" damage provisions are sometimes not enforced by U.S. courts (they are readily accepted in Japan and many other countries) unless it is shown that at the time the contract was formed, 1) it appeared to the parties that actual damages would be difficult or impossible to calculate, 2) the clause was a reasonable estimate of probable damages, and 3) the damages stipulated were reasonable in terms of the injury that actually resulted.

Example: NorCal Publishing Company decides to computerize its operations, and orders the necessary hardware and software from Farallon's Computing, a local original equipment manufacturer. Because NorCal feels that it is critical that the computer be delivered and installed on schedule, Farallon's agrees that it will pay $500.00 a day in liquidated damages for each day it is late. Farallon's is nine days late, and NorCal sues for $4500 after Farallon's refuses to pay the liquidated damages amount. The courts would prob-

ably not enforce the liquidated damages provision, because the amount of these damages did not bear any relation to the injury NorCal suffered by the delay in starting its computerization project. On the other hand, if the damages were set at an amount measured in the estimated extra cost NorCal would actually suffer by processing its records by hand rather than by computer, or by some other actual measurable detriment, the liquidated damages provision might be upheld.

literary agency agreement A contractual arrangement between an author and her representative (termed a literary agent) authorizing the agent to find a publisher for the book on the best possible terms, and (often) to receive a portion of royalties eventually earned on the book. This arrangement can be, and often is, an "exclusive agency", in the sense that the author must channel all books through that one agent. Under "exclusive agencies", the author must pay the exclusive agent a commission on all sales of the book effectuated by others. Literary agent contracts generally last for an indeterminate period of time, depending upon mutual satisfaction and benefit. However, the agent ill often attempt to negotiate a long term agreement whereas the author will typically favor a shorter period with mutual options to renew.

major breach of contract See *breach of contract*.

mass market rights clause A contract clause used by hardcover and trade paperback publishers to define the financial plit between themselves and the author if the work is later sold to a mass market publisher to be reprinted as a pocket-sized paperback.

material breach of contract See *breach of contract*.

material terms (in a writing) sufficient to satisfy the statute of frauds See *statute of frauds*.

material terms in an offer See *formation of contracts*.

mediation A dispute resolution process in which a mediator or conciliator attempts to bring conflicting parties to a point of compromise. Related terms: *conciliation and mediation*.

meeting of the minds When two parties knowingly agree on all material terms in a contract. A meeting of the minds is generally held to be necessary for the formation of a valid contract. See *formation of contract*.

mental incapacity See *defenses to breach of contract based on lack of contract formation*.

merger clause See *parol evidence*.

minor breach of contract See *breach of contract*.

minor's capacity to form an enforceable contract See *defenses to breach of contract based on lack of contract formation*.

misrepresentation In the context of contract law, a misrepresentation is a statement that substantially distorts the truth of a fact or situation. Misrepresentations can be intentional(outright lies), negligent (highly careless misstatements not made "deliberately"), or innocent (made in good faith). Normally, when a contract is based on the substantial misrepresentation of facts by one party, it can be *rescinded* by the other party (a process in which the contract is cancelled and the parties restored to the same situation they were in before the agreement was made). When misrepresentations are deliberate or reckless, and relied on by the other party to his or her detriment, the result may constitute tort fraud and support a suit (in tort) for *punitive damages*. Related terms: *defenses to breach of contract based on lack of contract formation*.

mistake See *defenses to breach of contract based on lack of contract formation*.

modifying existing agreements
Parties wishing to legally modify a valid existing contract often experience a particular difficulty. By definition, in order to establish the existing contract, each party has provided some contractual *consideration* (e.g. a duty has been imposed on them in exchange for a benefit provided by the other party) requirement. In order for the existing contract to be modified and a new contract formed, each side must furnish new consideration. If only one side furnishes the new consideration, the modification is technically invalid.

Example: F.M. Sound Co. has agreed to build a computerized sound board for Radio Station KOOO for $50,000. Subsequently, F.M. Sound says that it greatly underestimated the task, and asks KOOO to modify the agreement to stipulate an additional $15,000 payment. If KOOO agrees now, but later refuses to pay the extra amount, the court will probably not require it to pay. Why not? Because F.M. Sound did not offer new consideration for the modification. Suppose, however, that F.M. Sound offers to provide KOOO a five-year free service contract in addition to the sound board, if KOOO agrees to pay the additional $15,000. This agreement will very likely be enforceable, even though the service contract is probably worth much less than $15,000, since the Court only looks to see whether *some* consideration for the modification is present on both sides, and does not try to measure its amount. Related terms: *consideration*.

This rule requiring consideration for contract modifications may not apply when one party to a contract has encountered serious and unforseen circumstances. In fact, many contracts provide for revision in the event of cost overruns, a fact of which followers of Pentagon procurement policies and the nuclear power industry are acutely and painfully aware.

The rule requiring mutual consideration for contract modifications also does not apply to contracts involving the sale of goods. However, under the *Uniform Commercial Code*, a party must act in good faith when seeking a contract modifiction, and cannot extort a new agreement just because of his or her more powerful position. Contract modification problems can be avoided if each party agrees to a termination or cancellation of the existing contract. In this situation, a

A meeting of the minds

Contract and Warranty

new contract with new terms can be drafted and signed by both parties.

movie rights, assignment of   Authors of popular novels commonly enter into contracts under which they assign to others the exclusive right to make movies based on the novels. This exclusive right is really a part of the exclusive right to prepare *derivative works* 2 that belongs to every author under the copyright laws. These contracts typically include some or all of the following special provisions, in addition to other standard contract language:

- a grant of rights clause under which the assignee is granted the exclusive and entire motion picture rights in the novel

- a grant of recording rights clause under which the assignee is entitled to record and reproduce the soundtrack associated with the movie

- a grant of the exclusive right to produce foreign-language versions of the motion picture

- a grant of the exclusive right to produce trailers (previews)

- a grant of the exclusive television rights of the movie for a period of years

- a grant of the right to use the novel's title or to select another title

- a grant of rights to use portions of the movie in connection with marketing

- a waiver of any *moral rights* 2 that the author might possess in the work

- standard *warranty and indemnity clauses*

- a requirement that the author be given credit

- a reservation in the author of rights over sequels to the movie, and

- the right of the movie owner to use the author ''s likeness and name in marketing efforts

mutual benefit   See *consideration*.

mutuality of obligation   Where each party to a contract assumes a *duty* or obligation to perform some act benefiting the other party. There must usually be mutuality of obligation on both sides of an agreement if it is to be considered an enforceable contract. In some situations, however, a party who has assumed no obligation may nonetheless enforce

another's promise if he justifiably relied on it and suffered some detriment as a result. Related terms: *reliance and the law of contracts* .

naked license   See this heading, section 3.

new laws, effect of on otherwise valid contracts   See *excuses for breach of valid contract*.

nominal consideration   See *consideration* .

non-competition clauses in employment contracts   See *covenants not to compete by employees* 1.

non-disclosure agreement   See this heading, section 1.

non-exclusive license   See *exclusive and non-exclusive licenses*.

novation   When an existing contract between two parties is terminated, and a new contract covering the same subject is entered into between one of the original parties and a third party. The third party normally takes over the rights and duties of the original party, who is then no longer legally involved. Related terms: *assignment of contracts* and *settling disputes without going to court*.

obligors and obligees   The party having a duty or obligation to do something under a valid contract is called the ''obligor''. The party to whom the duty is owed is called the ''obligee''. In *bilateral contracts* (where each party promises to do something in exchange for the other party's promise) each party is both an obligor (i.e., has a duty to perform) and an obligee (is entitled to receive some benefit, usually the other party's performance of his duty). In *unilateral contracts* , the *obligor* is required to perform only when the obligee (the other party) has performed first.

O.E.M. license   A type of business arrangement, commonly encountered in the computer world, under which software developers grant licenses to specific original equipment manufacturers (O.E.M.s) authorizing them to distribute copies of the software to their retail customers. Suppose, for example, that Filial Techtronics makes a computer that runs a popular **operating system** ② developed by General Software Inc., and called Dos 500. In exchange for a fee, General Software could grant Filial an O.E.M. license to distribute copies of Dos 500 along with its computer.

From the marketing standpoint, when software is combined with the machine in one sale, it is typically called "bundling".

offer and acceptance   The foundation of all valid and enforceable contracts is that there has been a valid offer to make a contract and a valid acceptance of this offer. Just when these events do and do not occur has been the subject of much legal activity. Related terms: **formation of contracts**.

offers   See **formation of contracts**.

options   Contracts where one party promises not to revoke an offer, in exchange for the other party's payment of money or other adequate **consideration**. Ordinarily, a person making an offer can revoke it at any time prior to it's being **accepted**, even if he has agreed not to do so. However, if one party's agreement not to revoke an offer is paid for by the other party, the offer is turned into an "option", and as such may be enforced as a binding contractual obligation. Also, if one party has materially changed his position because of the other party's promise not to revoke an offer, even if nothing was paid for the promise, the offer may be enforced under the **promissory estoppel** doctrine. Option contracts frequently occur in connection with 1) the purchase of stock (e.g., instead of salary, an employee receives options to purchase stock in the future at a set price even though the market price is higher, 2) leases of real property with an option to purchase, and 3) professional athlete and entertainer contracts.

Unlike other types of contracts, options can be supported by **nominal consideration** as long as the underlying contract is reasonably balanced. Thus, payments of a dollar or even a penny have been ruled sufficient as consideration for an option to buy real estate worth hundreds of thousands of dollars. Some states even have a rule that if a promise not to revoke an offer is in writing, consideration will be

presumed to exist.

Courts will often enforce options by ordering **specific performance** (i.e., requiring the **promisor** to perform on the option).

option clause   A common publishing contract clause, requiring authors to afford to their publishers the first option to publish the author's next work under the same terms of the first contract. This option must generally be exercised within a short time after the second or succeeding work is submitted. Related terms: **options** and **right of first refusal clause**.

oral contracts   Agreements that are not written down. Except in certain situations, valid and binding contracts may be formed orally. But because of the difficulty in proving and enforcing oral agreements, it is good practice to put them in writing when feasible. For a list of the types of contracts that must be in writing, see **statute of frauds**.

out of print clause   A **publishing contract** clause establishing the conditions under which a book may be considered "out of print". Generally, when a book is out of print, all rights in the book previously granted to the publisher revert to the author, who is then free to publish the book himself or seek another publisher. When this clause is being negotiated, the author generally wants "out of print" status to be established whenever the publisher is not actively marketing the work or refuses to publish a modified edition, or yearly sales fall below a certain number of copies. The publisher, on the other hand, generally wants "out of print" status to attach only when the book is no longer available for distribution anywhere in the world. This is obviously a subject for heated negotiation.

output contract   An agreement by one party to purchase another party's entire output. For example, the Soma Knicknack shop might promise to buy Bruce the Glassblower's entire output of vases. Related terms: **requirements contracts**.

parol evidence   Any written or oral evidence offered to supplement or contradict the terms of a written contract. Once contracting parties have put their understandings in writing, the law usually

Contract and Warranty

treats such documents as the final word on the areas covered. Accordingly, under the "parol evidence rule' ", one party is barred from trying to prove that the contracting parties actually agreed to something else. However, "parol evidence" may be used to explain the terms of a written contract, or to prove additional agreements where the writing is "incomplete", or to establish any oral or written modifications that may have been made. In fact, the "parol evidence rule" is one of those legal devices where the exception is often the rule.

partial breach of contract Another phrase for "minor breach of contract". See *breach of contract*.

parties clause A provision, found in most contracts, that identifies the persons or institutions who are entering into the agreement (the parties), and who will therefore be bound by it. Often, this clause is used to assign labels (e.g. "BetaTest, hereinafter referred to as licensee", or "Mustytech, party of the first part") by which the parties are then known throughout the rest of the contract.

past consideration See *consideration*, and *modifying existing agreements*.

penalty clause See *liquidated damages*.

performance clause A contractual clause often found in *personal services contracts* for star atheletes, under which the athelete's salary will increase in the event a certain performance level is reached (e.g., if Sam Slugger hits 40 home runs, the Blue Sox will pay an him an extra $100,000).

performance of contracts See *breach of contracts* and *excuses for breach of valid contract*.

permissions clause A common *publishing contract* clause in which responsibility for obtaining permission to use material belonging to another is assigned to the author, publisher, or to both.

personal services contract A contract requiring one party to perform personal services for another, for agreed upon renumeration. All employment contracts fit into this category. As a general matter, the courts will not order *specific performance* of this type of contract if it is breached by the person who is to perform the service. Why not? Because the courts have found that they have no adequate way to force a person or business to perform personal services in a manner that would be satisfactory to the party contracting for them. That is, if a party who agrees to perform "personal services" decides to back out of the agreement, the court may prevent him or her from working for others, or require the cost of a replacement to be paid for, but will not order that person to perform the actual service.

In many situations, personal services contracts are regulated by law so that the person performing the services will not be unduly exploited by the person receiving them. This is especially true in the movie and fashion industries, where children are frequently engaged in modelling and performing activities.

post-employment restraints on employees *personal service contracts* often contain provisions preventing the person performing the personal services from either working for a competitor, or establishing his or her own competing business, for a set period of time after leaving the employment of the person for whom the services are to be performed. To the extent that these restraints on post-empoyment activity operate to deprive people from earning a living, most courts refuse to enforce them. In fact, the laws of some states (such as California) bar them almost completely. Where they are enforced, the courts will often require them to be interpreted very narrowly, so that the person performing the personal services will suffer only minimum restrictions. This type of agreement is often used in an attempt by an employer to maintain business *trade secrets* 1. Related terms: *covenants not to compete by employees* 1.

pre-existing duty rule See *consideration* and *modifying existing agreements*.

pre-printed form contracts See *unconscionable contracts and terms* and *adhesion contracts* .

promises to make a gift A promise to make a gift, without more, is not a contract, since no **consideration** is offered in exchange. Therefore, if a "gift promise" is broken, the injured person generally has no recourse in an action for breach of contract. However, in some situations, if the promisee (the person to whom the promise is made) has justifiably relied on the promise to his detriment (e.g., bought a new car in reasonable reliance on the promise of a $10,000 gift), he may obtain relief from the courts under a judicial doctrine known as *promissory estoppel*. Related terms: *reliance and the law of contracts*.

Once a promised gift is given, it belongs to the recipient and cannot usually be reclaimed. The schoolyard principle of "no take backs" is usually recognized and implemented. However, if the gift was induced by fraud, *misrepresentation*, or *duress*, or if the gift did not belong to the giver, courts may require that it be returned. Also, gifts given because the giver anticipates an early death may sometimes be reclaimed in the event that the person survives.

promissory estoppel A legal doctrine under which courts will require performance of an otherwise unenforceable promise when fairness requires it. If a promise is made, but not supported by *adequate consideration* it is not legally enforceable as a contractual obligation. Yet, the person to whom the promise is made may justifiably believe it to be valid and may rely on it in conducting his or her personal or commercial affairs.

Example: Piranah Pictures promises to pay Elaine Guppy's tuition to film school. If Elaine does not assume a duty or obligation in exchange for the promise, it would ordinarily be considered unenforceable because of the lack of **consideration**. However, if, relying on Piranah's word, Elaine travels to Madrid, Spain, enrolls in school, and manages to attend for a semester before receiving the bad news that Piranah changed its mind, can Elaine get a court to enforce the promise despite the lack of consideration?

The answer is yes, if the court finds 1) that Elaine's reliance was reasonable under the circumstances, 2) that Piranah had reason to expect that its promise might cause Elaine to act, and 3) that Elaine's reliance caused her some detri-

ment (here it obviously did). In essence, the court would substitute Elaine's *detrimintal reliance* for the absent consideration, and require Piranah to perform on its promise, at least in part.

Since "promissory estoppel" is a remedy fashioned by principles of **equity**, the court might not require Piranah to pay Elaine's tuition for the whole course of study, but instead might order it to cough up damages for whatever Elaine suffered as a result of her reliance. These might be the cost of moving to Madrid, and the difference between her first year's tuition at film school, and what her tuition would have been at another school she had planned to attend prior to Piranah's rash words.

public contracts, beneficiaries of See *third party beneficiaries of contracts*.

publishing contracts Contracts between authors (of books, software, etc.) and publishers that establish their respective *duties and rights* in respect to a wide variety of subjects. Among the most common types of clauses found in publishing contracts are the *contract date clause*, the *parties clause*, the *delivery of manuscript clause*, the *grant of rights clause*, the *subsidiary rights clause*, the *escalation clause*, the *advance clause*, the *cross-collateralization clause*, the *revision clause*, the *editorial control clause*, the *publicity and promotion clause*, the *author's copies clause*, the *permissions clause*, the *warranties and indemnities clause*, the *accounting and payment clause*, the *audit clause*, the *competing works clause*, the *remainder clause*, the *out of print clause*, the *agency clause*, the *option clause*, the *right of first refusal clause*, the *assignment clause* and the *boilerplate clause*.

publication date clause A common *publishing contract* clause, in which the estimated date of publication is specified so that the author will have a benchmark to judge whether the publisher is fulfilling its obligation to publish.

publicity and promotion clause A common publishing and software contract clause that articulates the responsibilities of both the author and publisher in connection with publicizing and promoting the work. The publisher may agree to 1)

promises to make a gift

Contract and Warranty

5

place ads in certain periodicals, 2) promote the book or software to certain markets (e.g., schools, libraries) or 3) spend a certain sum on promotion. The author, on the other hand, may agree to be available for media appearances and book or software store signings, and to give up a substantial portion of his or her privacy in support of the publisher's marketing efforts.

punitive damages in contract actions A type of remedy under which, in the **contract law** context, a party may recover money damages for the breach of certain **duties** by another party, where the breach could reasonably be anticipated to result in great hardship or emotional distress. Punitive damages may be awarded over and above actual damages, and are intended as punishment for an intentional personal wrong, and as an example for other potential wrongdoers.

Generally, courts are not authorized to award "punitive" or "exemplary" damages as a remedy for breach of regular commercial contracts. This is because of the view, long held by the courts, that remedies for contractual breaches should be limited to compensating the injured party rather than "punishing" the wrongdoer. Punitive damages are thus usually only awarded when the defendant's activity qualifies as an intentional tort (a civil wrong which results from a person's intentional acts, such as battery, fraud, or false imprisonment) rather than from mere carelessness or negligence.

Recently, however, the courts in many states have begun to allow punitive damages in breach of contract lawsuits where 1) the defendant has intentionally acted in bad faith, 2) the contract involves a relationship based on trust, such as those between an agent a performer or author, or between a trustee and beneficiary, and 3) the victim of the breach is particularly vulnerable under the circumstances.

For example, if an insurance company refuses to act in good faith when denying an insurance claim, the results can be catastrophic for the beneficiary. Therefore, the courts have labeled such malfeasance as a **breach of the duty of good faith and fair dealing** and have allowed punitive damages to be awarded. Similarly, if an employer unfairly fires a long-term employee, the consequent suffering can

be great. Labeling such employer actions as "wrongful terminations of employment", some courts have allowed punitive damages in this contractual context as well. Related terms: **breach of duty of good faith and fair dealing**.

In addition to these "common law" situations where a court will award these types of damages, many statutes also provide for a variant of punitive damages, often termed "treble damages", in the event of a willful violation of their provisions. For instance, a willful **infringement of a mark** 3 belonging to someone else may result in the infringer having to pay three times the actual damages suffered by the **owner of the mark** 3. This is also true in **infringement of patent** cases. Under the Copyright laws, the courts may, in some circumstances involving a willful **infringement of copyright** 2, award up to $50,000.00 **statutory damages** 2. Finally, under the laws of many states, regular punitive damages may be awarded for the willful and **wrongful acquisition of trade secrets** 1.

quasi-contract Situations where parties will be treated as if they had agreed to be contractually bound, even though they didn't in fact. Related terms: **express contracts and implied contracts**.

reformation of a contract Where a court changes the express terms of a written contract to reflect more accurately the original intentions of the parties. A contract may appear adequately to reflect an underlying agreement when it is signed, but later events may show that a mistake was made, and that the written words do not reflect the underlying agreement in some particular. In this instance, the court will rewrite the written terms (called "reforming the contract"), to better reflect such agreement. For example, if Corn and Pone Publications and Alice Photographer both mistakenly sign an agreement that calls for Alice to deliver C&P 4,000 photographs instead of the 400 they both intended), a court will reform the contract if the parties cannot agree to do it themselves. Related terms: **equity**.

reliance and the law of contracts
When one party reasonably undertakes some activity in reliance on the words or activities of another, the law of contracts

generally provides that the party inducing the reliance must perform his or her end of the bargain, whether or not a true contractual obligation exists. For example, suppose that Toni Avanti, the publisher of *Avvenire*, a woman's fashion magazine, offers to publish anything that Karen, a prominent fashion writer, produces in the next six months. If Karen relies on this promise and writes a work of fiction, Toni might be forced to publish and pay for it, even though her original promise might not have been contractually binding for one reason or another (say for lack of consideration or lack of specificity). Related terms: *promissory estoppel*, *options*, *unilateral and bilateral contracts*, *detrimental reliance* and *remedies for breach of contract* .

reliance damages   See *remedies for breach of contract*.

remainder clause   A *publishing contract* clause that determines the conditions under which a publisher may "remainder" a book (i.e., attempt to dispose of all remaining books by offering huge price cuts). While a publisher often wants to remainder a book whenever regular sales have dried up and it appears to be the only economically feasible alternative, an author will usually have an interest in his or her books not being remaindered (since royalties customarily decrease for remaindered books and the next step after a book is remaindered is usually to declare it out of print). Accordingly, the remainder clause is often the subject of intense negotiation.

remedies for breach of contract   The specific ways a court is empowered to respond if asked to resolve a dispute arising from a contractual breach. When a *breach of contract* occurs, there are two essential approaches to resolving the problem. One operates outside of court (extra-judicial) and the other involves going to court (judicial). For the extra-judicial techniques, see *settlement of contract disputes without going to court* and *arbitration*. This entry discusses the judicial approaches.

In the U.S., there are three basic types of potential judicial remedies available to the "innocent" party in the event of a contract breach, each designed to deal with a specific type of problem or injury.

The first major type of remedy ("expectation damages"), addresses the failure of a party to realize his or her profit or other gain, that was reasonably expected to result from the contract. In some instances, the court deals with this problem by awarding money. In others, the court may order **specific performance** of the particular obligation specified in the contract.

The second major type of remedy, reliance damages, addresses the loss that results when one party mistakenly relies on fulfillment of the contract.

The third major type of remedy, restitution, addresses situations where one party has conferred a benefit on the other, and seeks to have the benefit restored rather than be awarded expectation damages. Let us examine these remedies in more detail.

- **Expectation damages (money):**   The primary remedy favored by U.S. courts in breach of contract actions, this remedy focuses on the reasonable expectations of the injured party. This involves giving the injured party the **benefit of the bargain** under the contract, or, in other words, putting her in the position she would have been in had the contract been fully performed by the other party. The "formula" for this remedy is to award the plaintiff (injured party) the difference between the value of the broken contract and the cost (presumably higher) of obtaining a suitable substitution for the other party's performance, plus any incidental expenses incurred in obtaining the substitute, and minus any money saved as a result of the breach.

What does this mean in real life? Suppose that Fast Lane Data Corp. contracts to pay Tina $2,000.00 to perform some programming in the computer language Lisp on a **work made for hire** basis. Tina finishes half the job, takes $1,000.00, and quits. Fast Lane hires another Lisp programmer, Andrea, for $1,500.00, to finish the job, and sues Tina for breach of contract. Because Fast Lane expected to get its programming for $2,000.00 but ended up paying $2,500.00, its expectation damages are $500.00 (the difference between the value of the contract, or $2,000.00, and the cost of obtaining a suitable substitution, or $2,500.00). In addition, Fast Lane might be entitled to recover for such incidental damages as the cost of an advertisement to find

remainder clause

Contract and Warranty

5

Andrea.

In contracts for the sale of goods, the buyer's expectation damages are determined by the amount it takes to "cover" for the goods in the marketplace, plus any incidental expenses incurred in obtaining the replacement goods.

Example: BioTime Chemical breaks a contract to supply Benson Pharmaceuticals with a patented enzyme made from kelp. If BioTime spends an extra $300,000 to buy a similar product from the only other source and, must also pay an employee $50.00 an hour for 40 hours to close this deal ($2,000.00), BioTime may be found liable for $302,000 in expectation damages ($300,000 + $2,000).

A seller's expectation damages are measured by the price he or she would have gotten under the contract, minus the price he or she actually got when forced to sell elsewhere.

- **Expectation damages (specific performance):** In some situations, money damages cannot adequately compensate a party for his or her reasonable expectations under a contract, because the item contracted for is "unique" (e.g., an heirloom, a specific house, a manuscript, a patent license). In such cases, the court may order *specific performance* of the contract (i.e., the second party must specifically honor his promise rather than pay damages).

  Example: Biotime Chemical is the only producer of the enzyme mentioned in the previous example. If Bensen Pharmaceuticals can't get it from them, they will have to do without it. Since the patented enzyme is unique, a court would probably order Biotime to perform its obligations under the contract.

  Contracts for the sale of land may similarly be specifically enforced, as all land is considered to be unique. However, specific performance of a *personal services contract* is rarely ordered, due to the "involuntary servitude" nature of such an order. Suppose, for example, that Linda Fineline agreed to make drawings to order, and then reneged on her obligation. A court probably would not force Linda to make the drawings although it might hold her liable in money damages for the extra amount spent to replace them.

- **Damages based on reliance interest:** In some instances, a party has been more damaged by her reliance on a contract or promise than in her expectation interest. Thus, if Broadway Designs contracts with the Jackson Theatre to build sets for a new production of School for Scandal for $50,000, they may have little or no expectation of a profit, but may spend considerable money in obtaining materials. If the Jackson Theatre Board later changes its mind, Broadway Designs would want to be paid back for their expenditures rather than for their expectations.

- **Damages based on restitution interest:** Occasionally, one party to a contract will choose to recover for injury resulting from a contract breach on a theory of *restitution* (restoring property or benefits to their rightful owner). This means that he or she will be awarded the very benefits she conferred on the breaching party prior to the breach.

  Example: Carrie Anne buys her way into a partnership by putting up $50,000 cash. Subsequently, Carrie Anne discovers that the partnership is not complying with its obligations under the partnership agreement, and accordingly, she attempts to recover her money. If the partnership refuses, Carrie Ann can sue and ask the court for restitution of the money.

- **Consequential or special damages:** In some instances, the damages someone suffers as a result of a contract breach are different in nature, or larger, than might have ordinarily been anticipated. These are termed "consequential" or "special" damages. This type of damages often involves lost profits or personal injuries that logically result from the breach.

  Example 1: A contractor installs the wrong floor material in a physics laboratory, and the owner slips and falls, incurring back injuries and large medical bills as a result.

  Example 2: The artificial intelligence division of a robotics company suffers a huge loss of profits because its supplier breaches a contract to provide custom-designed semi-conductor chips. Recovery for this type of damages is usually not permitted in contract actions, unless such damages were easily forseeable to the breaching party at the time the contract was initially formed. Such forseeability is determined on a case-by-case basis.

repudiating contracts in advance See *anticipatory breach or repudiation of contract*.

requirements contract A contract under which one party agrees to purchase all of his material needs of a specified type from the other party. These contracts usually occur when a supplier of materials is willing to give a buyer a substantial break in price in exchange for the buyer's agreement to use the supplier as his exclusive source of the materials in question. For example, Dune Computer Company might contract to buy all of its microprocessor chips from Sylvan Semiconductors, in exchange for Sylvan's promise to knock 15% off its usual wholesale price. This kind of contract is usually made for a set period of time (e.g., one year), typically involves a minimum order by the purchaser, and cannot be broken or cancelled until such period has elapsed. *Continuing offer* contracts, on the other hand, are usually open ended, and can be terminated by either party upon reasonable notice.

rescind See *rescission of contract*.

rescission of contract The mutual termination of a contract, so that the parties will be restored to the positions they occupied before the contract was made.

Example: Floral Age Books and Roger Organic enter into a publishing contract, under which Roger will receive a $5000.00 advance and royalties for writing a book on raising orchids in cold climates. After Roger submits his first couple of chapters, however, Floral Age has second thoughts about the economic wisdom of the project. Roger also is having trouble finding the spare time to write the book. If Floral Age and Roger mutually agree to cancel the publishing contract, and Roger agrees to return all or most of the advance, the contract will have been "rescinded", and the parties will be back in nearly the same positions they were before the contract was made. Related terms: *settling contract disputes without going to court*.

In addition to contracts being rescinded by mutual agreement of the parties, courts have authority to impose rescission on the parties where circumstances dictate. These circumstances tend to be

many of the same ones involved in *defenses to breach of contract based on lack of contract formation*, such as *mental incapacity*, no *meeting of minds*, *undue influence*, *misrepresentation*, *unconscionability*, and *mutual mistake*.

reservation of rights clause A clause commonly contained in a *publishing contract* in which the author (artist, composer, programmer) expressly holds on to (reserves) all copyright rights not expressly granted in the contract. For instance, if an author grants the publisher the exclusive right to prepare copies of, display, and distribute the work, the "reservation of rights" clause will allow the author to retain his or her exclusive right to prepare *derivative works*.

restatement of contracts ..an exhaustive description of the U.S. law of contracts, arrived at by a committee of contract law experts convened by the American Law Institute (a private organization). This compendium was first published in 1932, and then was revised in the 1960''s and 1970's as the "The Restatement 2d of Contracts". The "Restatement" does not constitute the law itself (as do statutes, cases, and regulations, for example), but it is referred to by lawyers and judges when they want legal support for their positions.

Suppose a lawyer wants to convince the judge that his client should be excused from performing a contract because he was mentally ill at the time the contract was made. In addition to any case or statute that may be applicable, the lawyer might also refer to the Restatement's comment on mental illness as an excuse for breach of contract. The Restatement of Contracts can be found in most medium and large law libraries.

restitution The restoring, or giving, of property or money to one who has wrongfully suffered its loss. A court may order restitution made if it determines that one party has been unjustly unriched at the expense of another, or if it finds that economic injury has been caused by one party's wrongful actions.

Example: Apollo Biotechnology Enterprises improperly acquires certain valuable *trade secrets* from a competing firm, Hudson Genetic Engineering, and uses them to produce a new drug through gene splicing techniques. If Hudson were to bring a *trade secret infringement action* against Apollo, the court might well order Apollo to make "restitution" to Hudson of all or some of the profits they earned from the new drug. Related terms: *remedies for breach of contract*.

revision clause A common publishing and software contract clause that establishes 1) who will be responsible for writing any necessary revisions to a published work, 2) whether (and when) the publisher is required to make such revisions, and 3) what happens if the publisher and/or author fail to make revisions as specified in the clause.

Example: Press Davidson agrees to write a legal self-help book for businesses desiring to register and protect their own trade secrets. Because this area of the law is subject to rapid change, Press negotiates a revision clause under which he will assume responsibility for the revisions, and the publisher agrees to publish a revised version within at least three years of each previous version. In addition, the clause states that if Press fails to meet his responsiblity, the publisher may provide the revisions itself, and deduct the cost from Press's royalties. If the publisher fails to meet its responsibilities, Press may opt to declare the book *out of print*, recapture all of his copyright rights, and either re-negotiate a contract with the original publisher, or find a new publisher.

right of first refusal clause A common publishing and software contract clause that affords a publisher the opportunity to match a deal offered to the author by another publisher for a second or succeeding book. This clause does not favor the publisher as strongly as an *option clause*, under which the publisher is given an option to publish the second or succeeding book on the same terms as the first. See *option clause*.

right to adequate assurance of performance Procedures allowing one party to a contract either to obtain some assurance from the other party that the contract will be performed, or, to treat the contract as breached. This sort of assurance is commonly demanded when circumstances convince one party that performance by the other is unlikely.

Example: John Fillmore, who has created and operated a highly successful low-cost family law clinic under the *servicemark* ③ FDC (Fillmore Domestic Center), decides to license other lawyers to use the FDC mark in connection with similar centers in other cities. John's standard license specifies that any licensee using the FDC mark must primarily offer legal services connected with domestic relations disputes; that they must charge no more than $75.00 per actual hour worked on a case; and that they must set out the client's *duties and rights* in a written contract.

John learns that Harry Holoway, one of the licensees, is planning to practice primarily patent and trademark law under the FDC servicemark, in violation of the license. John can request assurance from Harry that in the future he will only offer the types of legal services specified in the license. If Harry fails to give this assurance, John can treat the license as breached, and sue Harry to prevent his further operation under the FDC servicemark. Related terms: *anticipatory repudiation of a contract*.

sale of goods, contracts for See *Uniform Commerical Code*.

satisfaction or approval of contract performance In many instances, a party's right to payment for performance under a contract is expressly made dependent on the other party's approval or satisfaction with the job performed. Computer programming and author/publisher contracts often fit into this category. Courts usually uphold such agreements, but will impose a duty on the person receiving the performance to use "good faith" and reasonableness in determining whether the "satisfactory" condition has been met.

For example, a publisher's assertion, under a *publishing contract* , that the author's manuscript is not *satisfactory in form and content* will not discharge the publisher's duty to pay the author under the contract, if the manuscript is up to or above prevailing industry standards. However, it must be realized that in all areas where *intellectual property* is developed, we are dealing with an incredibly subjective standard when we try to measure whether a particular work is satisfactory. Traditionally, considerable leeway is given to the person receiving the performance to accept or reject the final product.

satisfactory in form and content clause
A standard clause found in publishing and software contracts, under which the publisher reserves the right to reject a manuscript unless it is ' 'satisfactory in form and content''. Related terms: *satisfaction or approval as a condition of contract performance*.

security agreement
Installment contracts for the sale of goods that reserve legal title to the goods in the seller until the buyer has completed paying for the goods. In essence, security agreements use the goods (and often additional property as well) as collateral for the loan that allows the purchaser to pay over time.

sequel rights clause
A clause commonly found in contracts granting exclusive movie rights in books, under which the author either reserves the exclusive right over any sequels to the movie that might be prepared, or assigns this right to the grantee of the basic movie rights.

settling contract disputes out of court
Many disputes arising under contracts are settled short of litigation. The law uses several phrases to describe the ways this can be legally accomplished. If the parties agree to call the deal off and return to the positions they occupied before the contract was made, it is called **rescission**. Related terms: *rescission of a contract*.

If too much of the contract has been performed for the parties just to "call it off", they may settle the contract through a process called **accord and satisfaction**. In this process, one party agrees to perform a part of his or her duty under the contract (by definition, less than the actual obligation) in exchange for a release by the other party from any further obligations under the contract. Contracts may only be settled this way when 1) there is a good-faith dispute regarding a particular contractual duty, 2) an actual agreement (accord) is reached, and 3) actual satisfaction (payment or otherwise) occurs in a correct and timely fashion. Related terms: *accord and satisfaction*.

A third way that contract disputes can be settled without going to court is

termed a **novation**. Here, a third party steps into the shoes of one of the parties and takes over his or her duties, as well as receiving the benefits of the original bargain. For example, if Zoom Lens Repair agrees to service One Shot Videos cameras for one year in exchange for $27,000.00, and then decides to go out of business, they can arrange (with the consent of One Shot) for the original contract to be replaced by a new one under which another company (say, Total Technology) agrees to perform the service under the original terms. Related terms: *novation*.

Contract disputes are also increasingly solved outside of court under contractual **arbitration** clauses which require the parties to submit their dispute to arbitration in the first instance. Related terms: *arbitration* .

severable contracts
Contracts under which a party must perform many of the contract provisions, even if he or she is legally excused or prevented for some reason from performing others. Usually, written contracts that allow unenforceable provisions to be severed from the rest of the contract specifically say so.

Example: International Software Inc., an American computer game developer, enters into a **requirements contract** with Oxford Software Limited, Inc., a United Kingdom firm, under which International will provide Oxford with all of its computer games for re-export to Eastern Europe countries. The contract contains a provision stating that "Should any clause of this contract be declared or found to be unenforceable, the remaining clauses shall be deemed to be in full force and effect and binding on the parties".

Shortly after this contract is made, International discovers that under U.S. Customs regulations several of its games may not be exported under the contract with Oxford, because they involve simulation technology considered to be of strategic value to the U.S. military. In such a case, the overall contract would probably still be valid, even though a portion of it could not be enforced. However, if the games in question constituted the major portion of International's product, the bar on export might result in the entire contract being declared invalid. Related terms: *excuses for breach of valid contract*.

Contract and Warranty

5

shrink-wrapped license An attempt by software manufacturers to impose restrictions on purchasers of retail software by warning them that when they open the external wrapping of the software (most software is "shrink-wrapped") they automatically agree to the terms of a *license* included in the package. Typically, this license (sometimes called a "box-top license") imposes greater restrictions on the purchaser than would generally be true under the *U.S. Copyright Act* . Because there is no *meeting of the minds* or *consideration* that has been bargained for in the context of a retail sale, it is highly doubtful that these "shrink-wrapped licenses" are true contracts that could be enforced in court. Related terms: *adhesion contracts* and *consideration*.

special damages See *remedies for breach of contract*.

specific performance See *remedies for breach of contract*.

specific performance of covenant not to compete See section 1.

statute of frauds An old law, first developed in medieval England, which precludes court enforcement of certain types of *contracts* unless they are evidenced by a writing (sometimes called a "memorialization"). Every state in the U.S. has a statute of frauds in some form. Also, most countries whose legal systems are based on the English common law recognize the need to have certain kinds of contracts evidenced by a writing if they are to be enforced. Typically, the kinds of agreements that the statute of frauds requires to be memorialized by a writing are 1) contracts for the sale of land, 2) contracts that cannot possibly be performed in less than a year (e.g. a two year employment contract), 3) contracts for the sale of goods over a certain value, and 4) promises to pay another person's debts in the event of default (called guarantees and suretyships). There are other instances where specific state and federal laws require certain types of contracts to be in writing. For example, a *work made for hire* 2 contract and a *transfer of a copyright right* must both be in writing under the U.S. Copyright laws.

As the purpose of the statute of frauds is only to require some evidence that the contract in question was actually made, the writing does not have to be the complete final contract. Instead, an exchange of letters, a series of entries in a ledger, or even a sales receipt have all been found to be sufficient "memorialization" of an agreement to satisfy the statute of frauds. In other words, the writing need only refer to the bare-bones "essential terms" of the contract and only need be signed by the person who is being sued for enforcement.

Example: If Krypton Technology Inc. agrees to sell Kent Enterprises a mini-computer for $20,000, and signs a letter to this effect, Kent can sue on the basis of the letter, if Krypton should breach the contract. On the other hand, if Kent sends a letter to Krypton without requiring Krypton's signature on it, the statute of frauds has not been "satisfied", since the party who is being sued for breach — Krypton — is not the one who signed the "writing".

As with other requirements of contract law, there are often ways around this "writing" requirement, especially in situations where fairness so dictates. The most common exception to the requirement of a writing is called the doctrine of "part performance". This means that if one party honors his end of an agreement otherwise covered by the statute of frauds, the courts will often require performance of the other party as well, even though there was no writing. Also, in the event a party changes his or her economic position on the basis of an oral promise made by another, the promise may sometimes be enforced under the doctrine of *promissory estoppel*, even though the statute of frauds otherwise requires the promise to be in writing. Related terms: *promissory estoppel* and *equity*.

statutes of limitation The time period in which a case having to do with a particular legal area must be initiated is termed its "statute of limitations". Almost all cases must be filed in court within certain and definite time limits. Otherwise, they will be barred from adjudication foreever. There are different periods of time for different types of situations. For example, depending on the law of the particular state (or nation) a defamation action (i.e., libel, slander) might have to be filed within one year of the defamatory publication. And in many states, a lawsuit for damage caused by a defect in a building's structure must be filed within ten years after construction. Generally, there are different "limitation" periods for actions brought in respect to written contracts, oral contracts, personal injuries, injuries to property and actions affecting title to real property.

Normally, the statute of limitations time period begins to operate (starts to run) from when the wrongful act was committed. However, in many other types of cases, the statute only begins to run when the harm is discovered or should have been discovered. Thus, if a scalpel is left inside of a patient during surgery, the statute of limitations for a medical malpractice action will begin to run from the time the person becomes aware of it, not from the time it was "misplaced".

Many contracts contain provisions setting limitation periods that are shorter than the statutory ones. Depending on the situation, the respective bargaining positions of the parties, and the reasonableness of the period, courts may or may not enforce these provisions.

In some defined circumstances, the period of time during which the statute of limitations is running may be suspended. This is called "tolling" the statute of limitations.

Assume that Phil wants to file a breach of contract action against Don in a state where the statute of limitations for breach of contract actions is four years. If at any time during the four year period between the contractual breach, and Phil's filing of the lawsuit, something occurs to "toll" the statute, the four year period will simply stop running. Depending on the event, the statute may be tolled for an indefinite period, or, it may be only tolled for a short period. The period of time during which a statute of limitations is tolled is added to the overall period. Put differently, the tolling time extends the statute of limitations. Here are some of the events that typically operate to toll a statute limitations:

- the defendant is out of the state
- the defendant is in prison
- the defendant is in the military services and cannot be served with process

- the defendant is mentally incompetent, and
- the defendant is a minor

stipulated damages See *liquidated damages*.

subsequent events, effect on contract See *excuses for breach of valid contract*.

subsidiary rights clause A common clause found in publishing, recording, and performance contracts that deals with the rights owned by the author (composer, artist, or programmer) that are less important than (subsidiary to) the primary right to publish (record, display, produce) normally granted to a publisher (studio, recording studio, promoter). Examples of subsidiary rights (sometimes called "sub rights") are: control of first and second serialization, newspaper syndication, digests and abridgments, overseas rights, and recording rights. Some or all of these rights are commonly granted to a publisher (studio, recording studio, promoter) along with the primary right to publish. Others are withheld by the author (composer artist, programmer). See *grant of rights clause*.

substantial performance of a contract The performance by a party of his contractual obligations in sufficient degree to trigger the other party's obligation also to perform his end of the contract. For example, suppose Zebra Graphics Associates agrees to paste up Creative Consulting's new catalogue. They finish the entire job on schedule, except for two order pages, whereupon they are forced to quit due to financial difficulties. Creative claims breach of contract and refuses to pay Zebra anything. The court would probably order Creative to pay Zebra all or the bulk of the contract amount, on the ground that Zebra had substantially performed its end of the contract. See *conditions precedent*.

supplementing a writing with terms not contained in that writing See *parol evidence rule*.

suretyship A contractual obligation to pay someone else's debts. In contracting situations involving a large amount of

Contract and Warranty

money or a large potential liabilty, such as building construction contracts and shipping contracts, it is common for the party paying the money or taking the risk to require the other party to obtain a suretyship in the form of a bond or guarantee. Under this arrangement, the "surety" agrees to pay the party at risk in the event the other party fails to perform as required.

technological assistance contract
See section 1.

termination of contract offer See *formation of contracts*.

territorial restrictions and trade secret licenses See section 1.

third party beneficiaries to a contract One or more persons (third parties) who will benefit from an underlying contract between two or more other parties. For example, suppose Dan Bettleheim agrees with Standard Publishing Company to have Dan's royalties paid directly to Dan's aging sister Hillary. The contracting parties would be Dan and Standard, while Hillary would qualify as a third party beneficiary.

time is of the essence clause

Under certain circumstances, a third party beneficiary has rights under such an agreement, and can sue to have it enforced. In other situations, the third party beneficiary has no such right. One circumstance where a third party beneficiary gets a right is when the contracting parties intend to confer the particular benefit involved. Then, the beneficiary is termed an "intended beneficiary". In the example just above, Hillary would be an "intended beneficiary". An intended beneficiary can enforce an agreement benefiting her if her rights have become settled or "vested". The right of a third party beneficiary vests when the beneficiary 1) relies on the contract to his or her detriment, 2) brings suit on the contract, or 3)actually assents to the contract at the request of either party.

The type of contract where no right is created usually involves an "incidental beneficiary " (i.e., the benefit to be conferred is purely incidental). If Bruce contracts with Rackafrax Records to ship him twelve dozen Loosey Goosey albums by

way of Acme Freight Lines, Acme Freight will obviously be a "beneficiary" of the agreement but not the intended beneficiary.

Third party beneficiaries are sometimes divided into two other groups — "donee beneficiaries" and "creditor beneficiaries". A creditor beneficiary is already owed something by the contracting party conferring the benefit. If Ken owes Paul $500.00, and Ken contracts with Ruth for Ruth to pay Paul the money, Paul is a third party beneficiary. If, on the other hand, Ken owes Paul nothing, but still wants him to have the money, Paul is a "donee beneficiary".

time is of the essence clause When the time of a party's performance under a contract is crucial, the contract will usually contain a statement that "time is of the essence". This means that if the offending party's performance is late, the other party can treat this tardiness as a major breach of the contract and not perform his or her end of the agreement (i.e., not counter-perform). For example, if a software retail store orders 1,000 hot new computer games for its Christmas sale, its order contract will probably specify that time is of the essence, since a late delivery would defeat the primary purpose of the order. If delivery is thereafter made on January 8, the store will not have to pay for the goods, unless, of course, it decides to keep the games anyway.

total breach of contract Another phrase for *material breach of contract* or *substantial breach* . A total breach of contract allows an injured party to escape his or her duties under the contract.

transfers of copyright ownership See section 2.

U.C.C. Abbreviation for the *Uniform Commercial Code*. Related terms: *Uniform Commercial Code*.

unconscionable When one or more contractual provisions are considered too unfair under the circumstances to enforce. Related terms: *unconscionable contracts and terms*.

unconscionable contracts and terms

Contracts and contract provisions (terms) that are very unfair, and derived from the favorable or superior bargaining position of one party over another. As a general rule, the law pretends that most contracts are the result of a "meeting of the minds" between two parties with equal bargaining power. On many occasions, however, this is nonsense. Such types of contracts as *licenses*, *assignments*, leases, loans, *installment sales agreements* and *security agreements* are generally contained in standard printed forms, and the average person has little or no bargaining power to get these contracts changed.

In such situations, when a contract is outrageously one-sided and unfair, the courts will either refuse to enforce the contract at all, or strike out the offensive provision, on the ground of unconscionability. See *adhesion contracts*.

undue influence
See *defenses to breach of contract based on lack of contract formation*.

unenforceable contracts
See *defenses to breach of contract based on lack of contract formation* and *void and voidable contracts*.

unfair contracts and terms
See *unconscionable contracts and terms*.

unforeseen circumstances
See *excuses for breach of valid contract* and *modifying existing agreements*.

Uniform Commercial Code (U.C.C.)

A model set of statutes designed by scholars to serve as a uniform basis in the U.S. for rules governing the sale of goods and other types of commercial transactions. Over the years, all states except Louisiana have adopted major portions of the U.C.C. into statutory form, including the portions governing contracts for the sale of goods. In California, for example, substantial portions of the U.C.C. are contained in the "California Commercial Code". See *formation of contracts* and *modifying existing agreements*.

unilateral and bilateral contracts

Bilateral contracts are the classic kind of agreement, where the parties each promise to perform some duty or confer some benefit on the other, sometime in the future. Under bilateral contracts, therefore, each party owes an obligation to the other during a specific period of time. Thus, if Southern Star Software Services agrees to program Wonderword's computer and Wonderword agrees to pay Southern Star $5000.00 for the job, each party owes the other a future reciprocal obligation dependent upon some act happening. These are called bilateral obligations and the overall contract is accordingly called "bilateral".

Suppose, now, that Wonderword offers Southern Star $5000.00 to program its computer, and instead of agreeing to do so (i.e., accepting the offer) Tom from Southern Star just shows up one day and does the job. Has a contract been formed? If so, where is the *consideration* on both sides (i.e., *mutuality of obligation*), the *offer and acceptance*, and the *meeting of minds* which are necessary for a valid contract to be formed? The answer is, they come into existence at the exact moment performance is made. The law refers to this situation as a unilateral contract, meaning that only the offeror has an obligation (unilateral) to perform. Thus, Wonderword does not become obliged to Southern Star until Southern Star accepts the offer by actual performance. Southern Star, on the other hand, was never under a duty at all.

If, however, after Tom has begun the programming, Wonderword changes its mind, Southern Star may force Wonderword to allow Tom a reasonable time to finish the job.

vague and indefinite terms
If the terms of a contractual offer are too vague or indefinite to enable a party reasonably to know what the material terms of the contract consist of, the contract may be unenforceable even if an *acceptance* occurred. Put differently, a court will generally not enforce a contract if it doesn't know what it's enforcing. Related terms: *formation of contracts*.

violation of license restriction, copyright infringement
See *infringement of copyright* 2.

Contract and Warranty

void and voidable contracts A contract is "void" if it imposes no legal obligation on either of the people involved (i.e., no consideration on either side), or is illegal, such as a contract to export embargoed technology), or is against public policy (such as an agreement that would result in a child performer not receiving an education). A void contract cannot be enforced even if the parties agree that it should be.

A voidable contract, on the other hand, is where one party has a choice of either complying with it or getting out. Contracts formed with an individual who is temporarily insane, contracts entered into as the result of *duress*, and contracts made by minors who subsequently reach legal age, are all voidable for a reasonable period of time after the person has regained the capacity to act or has escaped from the duress. Related terms: *defenses to breach of contract based on lack of contract formation* and *remedies for breach of contract*.

voluntary disablement See *anticipatory repudiation*.

warranties Generally, express and implied representations by a seller that the object of a sales transaction (e.g., computer, factory tool, car, whatever) will properly do what it is supposed to do for a specific or reasonable period of time, and that the seller will fix or replace it if it does not. Warranties come in the form of "Express warranties", "Implied warranties", "Full warranties" and "Limited warranties". The various legal concepts and phrases associated with warranties are presented below in alphabetical order.

• **Breach of warranty:** When goods are sold in the course of business, they generally carry either an *express warranty* or certain *implied warranties*, or both. If, later on, the goods prove defective, and the seller of the goods fails to repair or replace them in accordance with the warranty, it is called a "breach of warranty", and the buyer can seek relief in the courts. In many states, the law gets tough with merchants who breach their warranties, and hefty damages can be imposed in the event that the buyer prevails in a lawsuit.

• **Express warranty:** When a seller of goods makes an actual promise about how the goods will work, whether orally or in writing, the goods are said to be covered by or "under" a warranty. Express warranties can last for any period of time (three months, five years or fifty years, it makes no difference), or even for the life of the product. To "warrant" something means that some or all defects in the item will be repaired, or the item will be replaced, during the particular period promised.

• **Goods sold on an "AS IS" basis:** Many retail businesses dealing in used goods or experimental products, such as computers and software, expressly disclaim any warranties, whether express or implied, by offering their wares "AS IS", meaning they may or may not work, or be fit for their intended purpose. In most states, and under the leading consumer protection statute dealing with warranties (Magnuson-Moss Warranty Act), this type of disclaimer is allowed. In some states, however, it is considered to be contrary to the public policy of merchants standing behind their goods, and is therefore given no effect, if and when the matter reaches the courts. While an "AS IS" statement will protect a merchant from many types of claims, it won't protect him from charges of outright fraud (if he lied about the goods in question).

• **Implied warranties, generally:** In every commercial transaction involving the sale of goods, and some services, certain representations by the seller are assumed to be made, even if they never are. When goods are sold, for example, they are assumed to be fit for their commonly intended use, and the seller is assumed to agree to this, even if nothing is said about it. This type of "implied agreement" is called an implied warranty. The primary implied warranties are:

• implied warranty of merchantability (the goods are merchantable or fit for their purpose — see discussion below)

• implied covenant of good faith and fair dealing (which applies to certain types of service businesses, such as insurance companies, banks, and real estate agencies (see discussion below)

• implied warranty of fitness for a particular purpose (see discussion below), and

• implied warranty of Title and against infringement (see discussion below)

As in the case of **express warranties**, the failure of a seller to honor implied warranties can be corrected in court and can result in certain law-imposed liabilities against the seller in favor of the buyer.

- **Implied warranty of fitness for a specific purpose:** In many situations, consumers have a specific use in mind for a particular item being purchased. For example, a person may buy a computer because of a desire to do his or her business accounting on it. If the merchant becomes aware of such specific intention for use of a product, knows that it won't do the job, and doesn't disabuse the customer, the product becomes impliedly guaranteed or warranted for that particular use. Thus, if the customer tells the computer salesman about his or her accounting plans and is sold a computer unable to handle normal accounting software, the merchant has breached his "implied warranty of fitness for a specific purpose". This "implied warranty" is made a part of most commercial contracts by operation of law under the **Uniform Commercial Code**. As with other implied warranties, this one may be disclaimed in most states if the seller expressly does so and uses the term AS IS in the contract.

- **Implied warranty of title and against infringement:** When goods are purchased, the buyer is entitled to believe that the merchant has a right to sell them free and clear from another's claim to ownership, unless a specific and prominent statement to the contrary is provided you in writing.

   Example: If a person unknowingly purchases illegally copied computer software from a software dealer, the dealer has breached his or her "implied warranty of title and against infringement" and the purchaser is entitled to recourse (e.g. he or she can return the software and receive compensation for any damages suffered from the transaction). This would be the case, even if the seller didn't know the software was pirated.

- **Implied warranty of merchantability:** The implied warranty of merchantability provides that goods sold by a merchant are fit for their commonly intended use. Thus, an industrial robot made to turn screws should function like one, a camera should function as a camera, and a computer as a computer. Clearly, the more complex and generalized a product gets, the harder it is to define exactly what its

intended use is. This question must be resolved on a product-by-product basis. If a purchaser buys a dishwasher that doesn't wash the dishes, or breaks under normal usage, the implied warranty of merchantability gives the buyer recourse (i.e., the right to return the product for a refund and compensation for any damages suffered as a result. It is possible for merchants to disclaim this implied warranty by selling the product on an "AS IS" basis.

- **Limited warranty:** A seller of goods can impose a time limit or other limitation on his **express warranties** and turn them into "limited warranties".

   Magnuson-Moss Warranty Act(15 U.S.C. sec. 2301): The Magnuson-Moss Warranty — Federal Trade Commission Improvement Act of 1975 regulates warranties on consumer goods sold in the U.S. (i.e., on goods sold primarily for personal, family or household use). It affects all merchandise costing $5.01 or more. The Act does not require that goods be "warranted" as such, but does regulate the effectiveness and clarity of such warranties as the manufacturer or retailer chooses to give. The Act also prohibits the use of deceptive warranties, i.e., promises, descriptions, or representations that are false, fraudulent, or misleading. The Act provides definitions for "full warranties' " and "limited warranties", and greatly limits the ability of a merchant or manufacturer to restrict the effect of implied warranties.

warranties and indemnities clause A standard publishing contract and software clause containing representations (warranties) by the author that 1) he or she has the full legal right to offer the material in his or her work for publication, and that such material does not violate anyone's copyright or constitute libel, and 2) in the event that these warranties are breached, the author will pay (i.e., indemnify) the publisher for any losses that occur as a result. In essence, these clauses place on the author the full burden to make sure that no successful lawsuits result from the work being published. See **indemnification clause**.

Contract and Warranty

Research Notes

This note assumes that you wish to delve deeper into the topics defined in this part of the dictionary. Instead of just providing you with a bibliography, we want to suggest a general research strategy. First, find some simplified background resources (often published as "self-help" law books) to obtain a general overview of your subject. Some of these are listed in **Step #1** below. Then consult more intensive background materials (listed in **Step #2**). These will go into greater detail and will also usually provide you with references (citations) to the primary law itself (**Step #3**). Finally, use *Legal Research: How to Find and Understand the Law* by Stephen Elias, Nolo Press, or another basic legal research guide, to assist you in using the law library and understanding the law you find there.

Step #1: Simplified Background Resources

There is no one book that provides a good but straightforward overview of the legal principles governing contracts. For the non-lawyer, probably the best best is to consult one of the lawschool outlines, such as *Contracts* by Stephen Emanual, or the Gilbert's contract outline. For more specific questions relating to particular types of intellectual property contracts, the following resources can be used to obtain a basic overview:

Author Law by Brad Bunnin (Nolo Press) (1983) is excellent for author/publisher contracts.

Legal Care for Software (2nd ed. 1984) by Dan Remer (Nolo Press) provides a good overview for different types of software-protection contracts.

Patent it Yourself by David Pressman (Formerly published by McGraw-Hill, 1979, now published by Nolo Press, 1985) discusses the ways in which patent rights may be licensed.

How to Copyright Software by M.J. Salone (Nolo Press) provides an overview of the ways in which copyright rights can be transferred to others.

More generally, *An Intellectual Property Law Primer* by Earl Kintner (C.Boardman Co.) is a good overall source for contract law as applied to the different forms of intellectual property.

Nimmer on Copyrights (Mathew Bender) provides a comprehensive discussion of copyright contracting as well as sample forms.

Step #2: Intensive Background resources

Contract and Warranty

To obtain more detailed information about the contract laws of your state, consult an encyclopedia that is specific to your state, assuming one exists. In California, for example, you can consult *California Jurisprudence, Third Series (Cal.Jur.3d)*, or *Witkin's treatise on California law.*

If there is no encyclopedia written for your state, the discussions under "contracts" in *American Jurisprudence, Second Series (AmJur.2d)* and *Corpus Juris Secundum (C.J.S.)* will be helpful. However, contract law is generally a matter of state law concern, and while the discussions in these national encyclopedias may occasionally refer to state court decisions or statutes, it is often difficult to find out exactly what the law is in your particular state. On the other hand, you will pick up the general vocabulary necessary to research your problem further. Once you have the vocabulary, you should check the card catalog for a book that looks appropriate.

For an understanding of the law applicable to warranties, and many types of retail transactions, the *Uniform Commercial Code (U.C.C.)* can be a good resource. This is because each state, except Louisiana, has adopted all or part of the U.C.C. into its own statutes.

Law review articles: Especially in regard to recent contracting developments in such new fields as computers, software, biotechnology and robotics, the best sources of information are often articles appearing in scholarly journals called "law reviews". By looking under "Contracts" in the *Index to Legal Periodicals* or *Current Law Index*, you will find frequent references to articles on current topics of interest. These references refer you to law reviews. A key to the abbreviations used is located at the front of the index volume you are using. Law libraries always store law review publications alphabetically in one particular location. The reference librarian can help here.

For additional resources regarding intellectual property law contracts, consult the research notes following the other parts of this dictionary.

Index

About the Author

Steve Elias received a law degree from Hastings College of Law in 1969. He prac-
ticed in California, New York and Vermont until 1983, when he decided to make a
full-time career of helping non-lawyers understand the law. Steve is the author of
Legal Research: How to Find and Understand the Law (Nolo Press) and also the legal
editor of several other Nolo Press books, including *How to Copyright Software*. Steve
has written widely on the relationship between computers and law, and is one of
the developers of *WillWriter*, a computer program and accompanying manual
designed to help non-lawyers prepare and update their own will. In addition, Steve
has taught a variety of legal topics in paralegal institutes, and currently teaches
legal research in the Nolo Press Saturday Morning Law School.

SOFTWARE

ESTATE PLANNING & PROBATE

willmaker

Nolo Press/Legisoft
Recent statistics say chances are better than 2 to 1 that you haven't written a will, even though you know you should. WillMaker makes the job easy, leading you step by step in a fill-in-the-blank format. Once you've gone through the program, you print out the will and sign it in front of witnesses. Because writing a will is only one step in the estate planning process, WillMaker comes with a 200-page manual providing an overview of probate avoidance and tax planning techniques.
National 3rd Ed.

Apple, IBM, Macintosh	$59.95
Commodore	$39.95

california incorporator

Attorney Mancuso and Legisoft, Inc.
About half of the small California corporations formed today are done without the services of a lawyer. This easy-to-use software program lets you do the paperwork with minimum effort. Just answer the questions on the screen, and California Incorporator will print out the 35-40 pages of documents you need to make your California corporation legal.

California Edition (IBM)	$129.00

for the record

By attorney Warner & Pladsen. A book/software package that helps to keep track of personal and financial records; create documents to give to family members in case of emergency; leave an accurate record for heirs, and allows easy access to all important records with the ability to print out any section
National Edition

Macintosh	$49.95

nolo's simple will book & nolo's simple willbook with tape

Attorney Denis Clifford
We feel it's important to remind people that if they don't make arrangements before they die, the state will give their property to certain close family members. If there are nieces, nephews, godchildren, friends or stepchildren you want to leave something to, you need a will. If you want a particular person to receive a particular object ,you should have a will. It's easy to write a legally valid will using this book, and once you've done it yourself you'll know how to update it whenever necessary.

National 1st Ed.	$14.95
wi/30-min audio cassette	$19.95

plan your estate: wills, probate avoidance, trusts & taxes

Attorney Denis Clifford
A will is only one part of an estate plan. The first concern is avoiding probate so that your heirs won't receive a greatly diminished inheritance years later. This book shows you how to create a "living trust" and gives you the information you need to make sure whatever you have saved goes to your heirs, not to lawyers and the government.

California 6th Ed.	$15.95

the power of attorney book

Attorney Denis Clifford
The Power of Attorney Book concerns something you've heard about but probably would rather ignore: Who will take care of your affairs, make your financial and medical decisions, if you can't? With this book you can appoint someone you trust to carry out your wishes.

National 2nd Ed.	$17.95

how to probate an estate

Julia Nissley
When a close relative dies, amidst the grieving there are financial and legal details to be dealt with. The natural response is to rely on an attorney, but that response can be costly. With How to Probate an Estate, you can have the satisfaction of doing the work yourself and saving those fees.

California 3rd Ed.	$24.95

the california non-profit corporation handbook

Attorney Anthony Mancuso

Used by arts groups, educators, social service agencies, medical programs, environmentalists and many others, this book explains all the legal formalities involved in forming and operating a non-profit corporation. Included are all the forms for the Articles, Bylaws and Minutes you will need. Also included are complete instructions for obtaining federal 501(c)(3) exemptions and benefits. The tax information in this section applies wherever your corporation is formed.

California 4th Ed. $24.95

how to form your own corporation

Attorney Anthony Mancuso

More and more business people are incorporating to qualify for tax benefits, limited liability status, the benefit of employee status and the financial flexibility. These books contain the forms, instructions and tax information you need to incorporate a small business.

California 7th Ed. $29.95
Texas 4th Ed. $24.95
New York 2nd. Ed. $24.95
Florida 1st Ed. $19.95

1988 calcorp update package

Attorney Anthony Mancuso

This update package contains all the forms and instructions you need to modify your corporation's Articles of Incorporation so you can take advantage of new California laws. $25.00

the california professional corporation handbook

Attorney Anthony Mancuso

Health care professionals, marriage, family and child counsellors, lawyers, accountants and members of certain other professions must fulfill special requirements when forming a corporation in California. This edition contains up-to-date tax information plus all the forms and instructions necessary to form a California professional corporation. An appendix explains the special rules that apply to each profession.

California 3rd Ed. $29.95

marketing without advertising

Michael Phillips & Salli Rasberry

There are good ideas on every page. You'll find here the nitty gritty steps you need to–and can–take to generate sales for your business, no matter what business it is.—Milton Moskowitz, syndicated columnist and author of The 100 Best Companies to Work For in America
Every small business person knows that the best marketing plan encourages customer loyalty and personal recommendation. Phillips and Rasberry outline practical steps for building and expanding a small business without spending a lot of money.

National 1st Ed. $14.00

the partnership book

Attorneys Clifford & Warner

Lots of people dream of going into business with a friend. The best way to keep that dream from turning into a nightmare is to have a solid partnership agreement. This book shows how to write an agreement that covers evaluation of partner assets, disputes, buy-outs and the death of a partner.

National 3rd Ed. $18.95

nolo's small business start-up

Mike McKeever

…outlines the kinds of credit available, describing the requirements and pros and cons of each source, and finally shows how to prepare cashflow forecasts, capital spending plans, and other vital ideas. An attractive guide for would-be entrepreneurs.—ALA Booklist
Should you start a business? Should you raise money to expand your already running business? If the answers are yes, this book will show you how to write an effective business plan and loan package.

National 3rd Ed. $17.95

the independent paralegal's handbook: how to provide legal services without going to jail

Attorney Ralph Warner

Warner's practical guide highlights the historical background of self-help law, and then gives a great deal of nuts-and-bolts advice on establishing and maintaining a paralegal office …Highly recommended…—Library Journal
A large percentage of routine legal work in this country is performed by typists, secretaries, researchers and various other law office helpers generally labeled paralegals. For those who would like to take these services out of the law office and offer them at a reasonable fee in an independent business, attorney Ralph Warner provides both legal and business guidelines.

National 1st Ed. $12.95

getting started as an independent paralegal (two audio tapes)

Attorney Ralph Warner

This set of tapes, approximately three hours in all, is a carefully edited version of Nolo Press founder Ralph Warner's Saturday Morning Law School class. It is designed for people who wish to go into business helping consumers prepare their own paperwork in uncontested actions such as bankruptcy, divorce, small business incorporations, landlord-tenant actions, probate, etc. Also covered are how to set up, run, and market your business, as well as a detailed discussion of Unauthorized Practice of Law. The tapes are designed to be used in conjunction with The Independent Paralegal's Handbook.

National 1st Ed. $24.95

how to do your own divorce

Attorney Charles E. Sherman

This is the book that launched Nolo Press and advanced the self-help law movement. During the past 17 years, over 400,000 copies have been sold, saving consumers at least $50 million in legal fees (assuming 100,000 have each saved $500—certainly a conservative estimate).

California 14th Ed.	$14.95
Texas 2nd Ed.	$12.95

(Texas Ed. by Sherman & Simons)

california marriage & divorce law

Attorneys Warner, Ihara & Elias

Most people marry only with the idea they are in love—that's not enough. This book should be a text in every California high school and college.—Phyllis Eliasberg, Consumer Reporter, CBS News

For a generation, this practical handbook has been the best resource for the Californian who wants to understand marriage and divorce laws. Even if you hire a lawyer to help you with a divorce, it's essential that you learn your basic legal rights and responsibilities.

California 9th Ed. $15.95

practical divorce solutions

Attorney Charles Ed Sherman

Written by the author of *How to Do Your Own Divorce* (with over 500,000 copies in print), this book provides a valuable guide both to the emotional process involved in divorce as well as the legal and financial decisions that have to be made.

Getting the "legal divorce," says Sherman, is "a ceremony you have to go through." The real divorce involves the many emotional and practical aspects of your life that are inevitably altered. To ensure the best possible outcome you must educate yourself. The worst thing you can do, he counsels, is to run directly to a lawyer and get involved in an uncontrolled battle.

California 1st Ed. $12.95

how to adopt your stepchild in california

Frank Zagone & Mary Randolph

For many families that include stepchildren, adoption is a satisfying way to guarantee the family a solid legal footing.This book provides sample forms and complete step-by-step instructions for completing a simple uncontested adoption by a stepparent.

California 3rd Ed. $19.95

how to modify and collect child support in california

Attorneys Matthews, Siegel & Willis

California has established landmark new standards in setting and collecting child support. Payments must now be based on both objective need standards and the parents' combined income.

Using this book, custodial parents can determine if they are entitled to higher child support payments and can implement the procedures to obtain that support.

California 2nd Ed. $17.95

a legal guide for lesbian and gay couples

Attorneys Curry & Clifford

The edge of the law... will be much less fearful for those who have this book. Full of clear language and concern for realistic legal expectations, this guide well serves and supports the spirit of the law.—Los Angeles Times

In addition to its clear presentation of "living together" contracts, A Legal Guide contains crucial information on the special problems facing lesbians and gay men with children, civil rights legislation, and medical/legal issues.

National 4th Ed. $17.95

the living together kit

Attorneys Ihara & Warner

Few unmarried couples understand the laws that may affect them. Here are useful tips on living together agreements, paternity agreements, estate planning, and buying real estate.

National 5th Ed. $17.95

your family records

Carol Pladsen & Attorney Denis Clifford

...a cleverly designed and convenient workbook that provides a repository for legal, financial and tax data as well as family history. —Los Angeles Times

Most American families keep terrible records. Typically, the checkbook is on a shelf in the kitchen, insurance policies are nowhere to be found, and jewelry and cash are hidden in a coffee can in the garage. Your Family Records is a sensible, straightforward guide that will help you organize your records before you face a crisis.

National 2nd Ed. $14.95

collect your court judgment

Scott, Elias & Goldoftas

After you win a judgment in small claims, municipal or superior court, you still have to collect your money. Here are step-by-step instructions on hwo to collect your judgment from the debtor's bank accounts, wages, business receipts, real estate or other assets.

California 1st Ed. $24.95

chapter 13: the federal plan to repay your debts

Attorney Janice Kosel

For those who want to repay their debts and think they can, but are hounded by creditors, Chapter 13 may be the answer. Under the protection of the court you may work out a personal budget and take up to three years to repay a percentage of your debt and have the rest wiped clean.

National 3rd Ed. $17.95

make your own contract

Attorney Stephen Elias

If you've ever sold a car, lent money to a relative or friend, or put money down on a prospective purchase, you should have used a contract. Perhaps everything went without a hitch. If it didn't, though, you probably experienced a lot of grief and frustration.

Here are clearly written legal form contracts to: buy and sell property, borrow and lend money, store and lend personal property, make deposits on goods for later purchase, release others from personal liability, or pay a contractor to do home repairs.

National 1st Ed. $12.95

social security, medicare & pensions: a sourcebook for older americans

Attorney Joseph L. Matthews & Dorothy Matthews Berman

Social security, medicare and medicaid programs follow a host of complicated rules. Those over 55, or those caring for someone over 55, will find this comprehensive guidebook invaluable for understanding and utilizing their rightful benefits. A special chapter deals with age discrimination in employment and what to do about it.

National 4th Ed. $15.95

everybody's guide to small claims court

Attorney Ralph Warner

So, the dry cleaner ruined your good flannel suit. Your roof leaks every time it rains, and the contractor who supposedly fixed it won't call you back. The bicycle shop hasn't paid for the tire pumps you sold it six months ago. This book will help you decide if you have a case, show you how to file and serve papers, tell you what to bring to court, and how to collect a judgment.

California 7th Ed. $14.95
National 3rd Ed. $14.95

billpayers' rights

Attorneys Warner & Elias

Lots of people find themselves overwhelmed by debt. The law, however, offers a number of legal protections for consumers and Billpayers' Rights shows people how to use them.

Areas covered include: how to handle bill collectors, deal with student loans, check your credit rating and decide if you should file for bankruptcy.

California 8th Ed. $14.95

29 reasons not to go to law school

Ralph Warner & Toni Ihara

Lawyers, law students, their spouses and consorts will love this little book with its zingy comments and Thurber-esque cartoons, humorously zapping the life of the law.—Peninsula Times Tribune

Filled with humor and piercing observations, this book can save you three years, $70,000 and your sanity.

3rd Ed. $9.95

murder on the air

Ralph Warner & Toni Ihara

Here is a sure winner for any friend who's spent more than a week in the city of Berkeley...a catchy little mystery situated in the environs and the cultural mores of the People's Republic.—The Bay Guardian

Flat out fun...—San Francisco Chronicle $5.95

poetic justice

Ed. by Jonathan & Andrew Roth

A unique compilation of humorous quotes about lawyers and the legal system, from Socrates to Woody Allen.

       $8.95

for sale by owner
George Devine
In 1986 about 600,000 homes were sold in California at a median price of $130,000. Most sellers worked with a broker and paid the 6% commission. For the median home that meant $7,800. Obviously, that's money that could be saved if you sell your own house. This book provides the background information and legal technicalities you will need to do the job yourself and with confidence.
California 1st Ed. $24.95

homestead your house
Attorneys Warner, Sherman & Ihara
Under California homestead laws, up to $60,000 of the equity in your home may be safe from creditors. But to get the maximum legal protection you should file a Declaration of Homestead before a judgment lien is recorded against you. This book includes complete instructions and tear-out forms.
California 6th Ed. $8.95

the landlord's law book:
vol. 1, rights & responsibilities
Attorneys Brown & Warner
Every landlord should know the basics of landlord-tenant law. Everything from the amount you can charge for a security deposit to terminating a tenancy, to your legal responsibility for the illegal acts of your manager is closely regulated by the law. In short, the era when a landlord could substitute common sense for a detailed knowledge of the law is gone forever. This volume covers: deposits, leases and rental agreements, inspections (tenants' privacy rights), habitability (rent withholding), ending a tenancy, liability, and rent control.
California 2nd Ed. $24.95

the landlord's law book: vol. 2, evictions
Attorney David Brown
Even the most scrupulous landlord may sometimes need to evict a tenant. In the past it has been necessary to hire a lawyer and pay a high fee. Using this book you can handle most evictions yourself safely and economically.
California 1st Ed. $24.95

tenants' rights
Attorneys Moskowitz & Warner
Your "security building" doesn't have a working lock on the front door. Is your landlord liable? How can you get him to fix it? Under what circumstances can you withhold rent? When is an apartment not "habitable?" This book explains the best way to handle your relationship with your landlord and your legal rights when you find yourself in disagreement.
California 9th Ed. $14.95

the deeds book:
how to transfer title to california real estate
Attorney Mary Randolph
If you own real estate, you'll almost surely need to sign a new deed at one time or another. The Deeds Book shows you how to choose the right kind of deed, how to complete the tear-out forms, and how to record them in the county recorder's public records. It also alerts you to real property disclosure requirements and California community property rules, as well as tax and estate planning aspects of your transfer.
California 1st Ed. $15.95

how to copyright software
Attorney M.J. Salone
Copyrighting is the best protection for any software. This book explains how to get a copyright and what a copyright can protect.
National 2nd Ed. $24.95

the inventor's notebook
Fred Grissom & Attorney David Pressman
The best protection for your patent is adequate records. The Inventor's Notebook provides forms, instructions, references to relevant areas of patent law, a bibliography of legal and non-legal aids, and more. It helps you document the activities that are normally part of successful independent inventing.
National 1st Ed. $19.95

legal care for your software
Attorneys Daniel Remer & Stephen Elias
If you write programs you intend to sell, or work for a software house that pays you for programming, you should buy this book. If you are a freelance programmer doing software development, you should buy this book.— Interface
This step-by-step guide for computer software writers covers copyright laws, trade secret protection, contracts, license agreements, trademarks, patents and more.
National 3rd Ed. $29.95

patent it yourself
Attorney David Pressman
You've invented something, or you're working on it, or you're planning to start...Patent It Yourself offers help in evaluating patentability, marketability and the protective documentation you should have. If you file your own patent application using this book, you can save from $1500 to $3500.
National 2nd Ed. $29.95

dog law
Attorney Mary Randolph
There are 50 million dogs in the United States—and, it seems, at least that many rules and regulations for their owners to abide by. *Dog Law* covers topics that everyone who owns a dog, or lives near one, needs to know about dispute about a dog injury or nuisance.
National 1st Ed. $12.95

the criminal records book
Attorney Warren Siegel
We've all done something illegal. If you were one of those who got caught, your juvenile or criminal court record can complicate your life years later. The good news is that in many cases your record can either be completely expunged or lessened in severity.
The Criminal Records Book takes you step by step through the procedures to: seal criminal records, dismiss convictions, destroy marijuana records, reduce felony convictions.
California 2nd Ed. $14.95

draft, registration and the law
Attorney R. Charles Johnson
This clearly written guidebook explains the present draft law and how registration (required of all male citizens within thirty days of their eighteenth birthday) works. Every available option is presented along with a description of how a draft would work if there were a call tomorrow.
National 2nd Ed. $9.95

fight your ticket
Attorney David Brown
At a trade show in San Francisco recently, a traffic court judge (who must remain nameless) told our associate publisher that he keeps this book by his bench for easy reference.
If you think that ticket was unfair, here's the book showing you what to do to fight it.
California 3rd Ed. $16.95

how to become a united states citizen
Sally Abel Schreuder
This bilingual (English/Spanish) book presents the forms, applications and instructions for naturalization. This step-by-step guide will provide information and answers for legally admitted aliens who wish to become citizens.
National 3rd Ed. $12.95

how to change your name
Attorneys Loeb & Brown
Wish that you had gone back to your maiden name after the divorce? Tired of spelling over the phone V-e-n-k-a-t-a-r-a-m-a-n   S-u-b-r-a-m-a-n-i-a-m?
This book explains how to change your name legally and provides all the necessary court forms with detailed instructions on how to fill them out.
California 4th Ed. $14.95

legal research: how to find and understand the law
Attorney Stephen Elias
Legal Research could also be called Volume-Two-for-all-Nolo-Press-Self-Help-Law-Books. A valuable tool for paralegals, law students and legal secretaries, this book provides access to legal information. Using this book, the legal self-helper can find and research a case, read statutes, and make Freedom of Information Act requests.
National 2nd Ed. $14.95

family law dictionary
Attorneys Leonard and Elias
Written in plain English (as opposed to legalese), the Family Law Dictionary has been compiled to help the lay person doing research in the area of family law (i.e., marriage, divorce, adoption, etc.). Using cross referencs and examples as well as definitions, this book is unique as a reference tool.
National 1st Edition $13.95

intellectual property law dictionary
Attorney Stephen Elias
This book uses simple language free of legal jargon to define and explain the intricacies of items associated with trade secrets, copyrights, trademarks and unfair competition, patents and patent procedures, and contracts and warranties.—IEEE Spectrum
If you're dealing with any multi-media product, a new business product or trade secret, you need this book.
National 1st Ed. $17.95

the people's law review:
an access catalog to law without lawyers
Edited by Attorney Ralph Warner
Articles, interviews and a resource list introduce the entire range of do-it-yourself law from estate planning to tenants' rights. The People's Law Review also provides a wealth of background information on the history of law, some considerations on its future, and alternative ways of solving legal problems.
National 1st Ed. $8.95

nolo

SELF-HELP LAW BOOKS & SOFTWARE

ORDER FORM

Quantity	Title	Unit Price	Total

Prices subject to change

Subtotal _____

Tax (CA only): San Mateo, San Diego, LA, & Bart Counties 6 1/2%
Santa Clara & Alameda 7%
All others 6%

Tax _____

Postage & Handling

No. of Books	Charge
1	$2.50
2-3	$3.50
4-5	$4.00

Over 5 add 6% of total before tax

Postage & Handling _____

Total _____

Please allow 1-2 weeks for delivery.
Delivery is by UPS; no P.O. boxes, please.

Name_____

Address _____

_____

☐ VISA   ☐ Mastercard

_____ Exp._____

Signature _____

Phone (   )_____

ORDERS: Credit card information or a check may be sent to:

Nolo Press
950 Parker St.
Berkeley CA 94710

Use your credit card and our **800 lines** for faster service:

ORDERS ONLY
(M-F 9-5 Pacific Time):

US:	**1-800-992-6656**
Outside (415) area **CA:**	**1-800-445-6656**
Inside (415) area **CA:**	**(415) 549-1976**

For general information call: **(415) 549-1976**

☐ Please send me a catalogue

One Year Free!

Nolo Press wants you to have top quality and up-to-date legal information. The ***Nolo News***, our "Access to Law" quarterly newspaper, contains an update section which will keep you abreast of any changes in the law relevant to **Patent, Copyright & Trademark: Intellectual Property Law Dictionary**. You'll find interesting articles on a number of legal topics, book reviews and our ever-popular lawyer joke column.

Send in the registration card below and receive FREE a one-year subscription to the ***Nolo News*** (normally $9.00).

Your subscription will begin with the first quarterly issue published after we receive your card.

- -

NOLO PRESS
Patent, Copyright & Trademark: Intellectual Property Law Dictionary Registration Card

We would like to hear from you. Please let us know if the book met your needs. Fill out and return this card for a FREE one-year subscription to the *Nolo News*. In addition, we'll notify you when we publish a new edition of **Patent, Copyright & Trademark: Intellectual Property Law Dictionary.** (This offer is good in the U.S.only)

Name_____

Address_____

City _____ State _____ Zip_____

Your occupation_____

Briefly, for what purpose did you use this book?

_____

_____

_____

Did you find the information in the book helpful?

 (extremely helpful) 1   2   3   4   5 (not at all)

Where did you hear about the book?

Have you used other Nolo books?____Yes, ____No

Where did you buy the book?_____

Suggestions for improvement: _____

_____

_____

_____

_____

_____

_____

_____

_____

_____

_____

_____

_____

▲

[Nolo books are]..."written in plain language, free of legal mumbo jumbo, and spiced with witty personal observations."

—ASSOCIATED PRESS

▲

"Well-produced and slickly written, the [Nolo] books are designed to take the mystery out of seemingly involved procedures, carefully avoiding legalese and leading the reader step-by-step through such everyday legal problems as filling out forms, making up contracts, and even how to behave in court."

—SAN FRANCISCO EXAMINER

▲

"...Nolo publications...guide people simply through the how, when, where and why of law."

—WASHINGTON POST

▲

"Increasingly, people who are not lawyers are performing tasks usually regarded as legal work... And consumers, using books like Nolo's, do routine legal work themselves."

—NEW YORK TIMES

▲

"...All of [Nolo's] books are easy-to-understand, are updated regularly, provide pull-out forms...and are often quite moving in their sense of compassion for the struggles of the lay reader."

—SAN FRANCISCO CHRONICLE

> Affix
> 25¢
> Stamp

NOLO PRESS
950 Parker St.
Berkeley, CA 94710